GROWING UP IN CENTRAL AUSTRALIA

Growing Up
in Central Australia

New Anthropological Studies of
Aboriginal Childhood and Adolescence

Edited by
Ute Eickelkamp

Berghahn Books
NEW YORK • OXFORD

First published in 2011 by

Berghahn Books

www.berghahnbooks.com

Library of Congress Cataloging-in-Publication Data

Growing up in Central Australia : new anthropological studies of aboriginal
childhood and adolescence / edited by Ute Eickelkamp.
   p. cm.
   Includes bibliographical references and index.
   ISBN 978-0-85745-082-1 (hardback : alk. paper) — ISBN 978-0-85745-083-8
(ebook)
   1. Children, Aboriginal Australian—Australia—Central Australia. 2. Adolescence—
Australia—Central Australia. 3. Central Australia—Social conditions. I. Eickelkamp,
Ute.
   DU124.C45G76 2011
   305.23089′99150942—dc22

2011000950

British Library Cataloguing in Publication Data

A catalogue record for this book is available from the British Library

Printed in the United States on acid-free paper.

ISBN 978-0-85745-082-1 (hardback)
ISBN 978-0-85745-083-8 (ebook)

For Nina and Anton

In Memory of YY

Contents

PART III.
YOUTH, IDENTITY AND SOCIAL TRANSFORMATION

Figures

Tables

Acknowledgements

I would like to acknowledge with thanks the funding received from the Australian Research Council for the study of Central Australian Aboriginal children's lives. The making of this book took substantially longer than anticipated, and I am grateful to all the contributors for their patience. For their enthusiasm about this collection, I thank the families and staff at Ernabella, and John von Sturmer and Jadran Mimica for their continuous and generous intellectual support. I especially and warmly thank Pauline Fietz for her initial editorial input, which had to end when her own children claimed her back.

Place Names on Map

1 Alice Springs
2 Hermannsburg (Ntaria)
3 Lajamanu
4 Yuendumu
5 Tempe Downs
6 Warburton
7 Ernabella
8 Kintore
9 Papunya
10 Kiwirrkura
11 Jigalong
12 Newman

Introduction

Aboriginal Children and Young People in Focus

Ute Eickelkamp

Indigenous people, while still a small minority, represent the youngest and fastest-growing population sector in Australia. Arguably, their culture is also the most profoundly transforming.[1] Yet there is astonishingly little research on how Indigenous children and adolescents experience life, shape their social world and imagine the future. The idea for this collection began with the observation that there exists no concerted effort that describes the lives and self-perceptions of young Indigenous Australians within a broadly defined cultural region. To produce such a record has an intrinsic intellectual value. Potentially, it also has a political value given the persistent view of governments that the shaping of child development is the 'royal road' to the socioeconomic 'adjustment' of the Indigenous citizenry. It is hoped that this collection of essays may encourage further research into young people's social, cultural and lingual competences and, in the non-Indigenous public, more recognition of and openness towards the orientations and life projects of Aboriginal Australians.

International Research Context

The diverse cultures of childhood and adolescence are gaining renewed and intensified attention in sociology, psychology and anthropology, and this book brings Australian material to the international scholarship in that field. Specifically, it shares the focus on the young people themselves with the 'new sociology of childhood and children' (e.g., Corsaro 2004; James, Jenks and Prout 1998), which has established itself in the United States and Europe since the 1980s. The essays assembled herein also invite comparison with recent studies of the changing social significance of generations. It is interesting to observe, for example, that, in contrast to Pacific Island societies where age has come to override

1

gender as an organizing social force, and where the young generation is now a catalyst for sociocultural change (Herdt and Leavitt 1998: 8, 4), young Aboriginal people in Central Australia continue to follow the older pattern of gender-separate activities. A view to recent developments in European countries highlights another aspect of the meaning of generations. In Germany and Finland, multigenerational groupings in particular milieus such as neighbourhoods and clubs now afford feelings of belonging and social integration, more so than the family or the society at large (Zinnecker 2003; Alanen 2005). The Aboriginal communities too are meaningful cultural milieus with which young people identify rather than with the larger Australian society (*see especially* Brooks, this volume). However, here it is kinship networks spanning across the generations sustained by shared experiences – especially of nurturing – that play a significant role as group container in the formation of personal identities (*see* Myers, Brooks, Tonkinson and Moisseeff, this volume).

Moreover, as several chapters illustrate through case material, there are two other sources for a secure sense of self in Central Australia – identification with a place, that is, a home community, and connectedness with the Dreaming. The cultural and social basis for the feeling of belonging has been examined in colonized Indigenous minority groups in other parts of the world, for example by Colin Samson (2004) in his study of the 'ontological insecurity' experienced by the Innu people of Northern Labrador. It would be instructive to compare in some depth this study of psychosocial suffering with Myers's discussion herein of the anchoring of Pintupi selves. Both ethnographers employ Laing's notion of 'ontological security' to describe the relationship between self and world, and the pathways for coping with stressful life events. Briefly, in contrast to the highly disrupted ontology of the Innu people and the related psychological trauma, the life-world of the Pintupi – as well as of some of their desert neighbours – appears relatively integrated. It is worthwhile emphasizing the finding that Aboriginal groups in Central Australia have been able to sustain a continuity of being at cultural and personal levels, seemingly more so than Indigenous minority groups elsewhere.

Furthermore, this collection redresses the fact that Australian Aboriginal childhoods have received little attention in cross-cultural child development studies; Australia does not feature, for instance, in the most recent reader in that field (LeVine and New 2008). Nonetheless, the essays herein underscore one of the major findings of such comparative research, namely, that even small children are not just at the receiving end of traditions or being moulded by their environment (LeVine and New 2008: 3). Children are active learners; they make and remake culture and history – as innovators and as keepers of language, certain modes of knowing and bodies of knowledge, artistic practices, moral codes, patterns of behaviour and social norms. In fact, it could be argued that a theory of culture must be able to account for the agency of the young, as, without it, a society cannot reproduce itself.

Similarly, the interrelated processes of modernization, individualization and urbanization – established fields in the sociology of Western societies and colonization studies – have hardly been canvassed in relation to Australian Aboriginal family life (*but see* Merlan 1998) and from the perspective of the young. In spite of the prominent place of Aboriginal societies in the history of social theory, such paradigms of analysis have found little application to Aboriginal life-worlds in Australia. However, as these developments are having an impact on local Aboriginal polities as well as on those larger communities in which the Aboriginal population sector is growing, this is changing: there are signs of an emerging research field that promises to enhance local, regional and wider comparative perspectives on intercultural phenomena and modernization, and in particular on the effects that such processes have on Indigenous people's personhood. The dynamics of childhood and adolescence are critical in the transformation of culturally specific subjectivities and they therefore present a pivotal field of investigation.

Content and Aims

Assembled herein are new observations on the contemporary life experiences outside the institutional settings of childcare and education, of those growing up as Aboriginal people either in Central Australia or with strong links to the region. The dominant topics relating to young Aboriginal people in the older ethnographic literature are initiation rituals, socialization, family and the life cycle, and games and toys. More recent studies appear to be problem centred and responsive to the growing number of policy-relevant reports on the low social indicator levels of the Aboriginal population – in health, education and housing – and on substance abuse and family and sexual violence involving the young, all of which have become established themes in the public media. With few exceptions, studies of socialization and problems of welfare have not been child centred; rather, their starting point has been the views and behaviours of adults vis-à-vis the young, while childhood and youth have been dealt with as transitional stages towards adulthood (Eickelkamp 2010). The present collection seeks to redress this imbalance to some extent: it too describes intergenerational relations and societal models of child development and adolescence, but its primary concern is the practices and experiences of children and young people. A number of contributors have turned towards the self-perceptions, normative experiences and symbolic expressions of Aboriginal children and youth, to encounters with young people and to memories of childhood. The emphasis is on the present. However, from an experiential point of view, the line between the past and the present is not necessarily fixed, and distinct 'chapters' in the life of a person as well as of a society may only become visible in hindsight. Hence the inclusion of contributions that engage earlier studies, or offer personal reflections on the past, or open up a life-span perspective; these are intended to complement recent works that portray contemporary young people's life.

The focus is on young people in so-called remote communities in Central Australia, of which there are roughly 1,200 across the continent, but also including reflections on life in the racialized milieu of the small town and city. The area here loosely referred to as 'Central Australia' stretches across parts of the Northern Territory and the states of South Australia and Western Australia, covering the bigger part of the 'Desert' area, so called on Horton's (1996) wall map of Aboriginal languages.[2] In order of appearance, the following languages and dialects represented herein are: Arrernte, Pitjantjatjara and Yankunytjatjara, Warlpiri, Pintupi, Light Warlpiri, Luritja, English, Ngaanyatjarra and Mardu. In the sparsely populated area in the interior of the continent, different cultural maps stemming from different times and imaginaries coexist: the Ancestral landscape, pastoral properties, mining zones, a national park, regional and remote communities connected by a few main arteries and townships.[3] However, the linguistic and local cultural diversity notwithstanding, it is important to also consider the life-space of young Aboriginal people at a regional level because of linguistic, social and economic interconnections that seem to have intensified over recent decades.

This collection seeks to convey through the lens of various local contexts how Aboriginal children, teenagers and young adults make and sustain their own social world and identity. It asks: which are the most important social contexts for young Aborigines? What is the nature of interaction among peers? How may this differ from the social life of young people in the past and from engagements between the generations? Are age-based groupings as significant as intergenerational links in terms of their extent and meaning for identity formation? What are the main themes in the lives of young Aboriginal Australians? What are their joys, hopes, worries and concerns? How do both inner life experiences and social dynamics find expression in the practices of children and young people? And what are their images of self and others, including non-

Aborigines? Implicitly, these questions concern the process of how a society imagines and reimagines itself.

The choice of focus is also motivated by the understanding that insights into 'natural' social settings such as self-directed play, peer interaction and family dynamics, and into people's self-perceptions, local forms of being socially productive and of creative action, can make important and specific contributions to population-level research. Arguably, qualitative investigations can act as concept 'drivers' to meaningfully inform research on Aboriginal family issues across the social and psychological sciences, as well as inspire Aboriginal leaders, educationalists, health professionals and policy makers. Building a knowledge base for and about young Aboriginal people and identifying core issues and concerns in their lives from the local cultural point of view seem necessary prerequisites for the development of meaningful support strategies aimed at enhancing existing strengths, reducing risks and preventing harm.[4] In Australia, the current concern of government policy is to close the measurable social indicator gap between Aboriginal people and other Australians and to enhance Indigenous well-being through integration in the urban economy. However, as Taylor (2006) observed:

> [W]ithout a common agreed view of different and shared perceptions of well-being, the danger is that indicators become ethnocentric and the notion that Indigenous people may have their own life projects is obscured by the pressing moral and political objective of achieving statistical equality that comes with the policies of practical reconciliation and mainstreaming.

Importantly, the lives of young Aboriginal people can neither be documented nor conceptualized without the input of the families and communities concerned. Indeed, it would seem that in the field of understanding children and youth, access to which can be denied outsiders, progress will rely crucially on the desire by Aboriginal people to objectify their knowledge in new ways. Efforts by Aboriginal people are underway to establish research and thereby a public voice on family matters in their own terms, and to advance existing knowledge systems as academic collaborators or through initiatives for their own ends and purposes.

The Chapters

The studies in this collection tell us about the lives of children, teenagers and young adults. They describe in the form of self-accounts, through ethnographic case studies and through sociological and linguistic observations what young people do, think and talk about, in their play and in everyday interaction with peers and family. At the same time, the studies can be seen as describing historical processes in various ways: by considering past experiences of childhood and adolescence in relation to the present as well as future prospects, by describing the flow of knowledge and practices between the generations, and by recognizing that child development and adolescence are integral to the constitution of human temporality. Each with its own focus, the chapters deal with the stages of the life cycle and life trajectories, the formation and everyday life of families, the relationships between the generations and the sexes, material culture, the meaning and methods of learning, outlook on life, horizons of understanding, expectations, hopes, desires, fears, and, with this, social categories, self-perceptions, and forms of consciousness. All these have changed enormously over the last hundred years and longer, perhaps for Aboriginal societies more so than for the rest of Australia. Yet, especially when read comparatively, the contributions also demonstrate the existence of substantial continuities of values, attitudes and social norms.

The book is organized into three parts. Part I, 'Childhood across Time: Historical and Life Span Perspectives', consists of four chapters dealing with historical reflections on childhood and society, memories and anticipations, psychosocial well-being, the cultural logic of life stages, cosmology and socialization, and the social basis of personal identity. In chapter 1, anthropologist John Morton analyses children's 'free' sexuality as documented and interpreted by the psychoanalyst Géza Róheim, who conducted ethnographic research in Central Australia in 1929. Róheim, Morton argues, has shown how children's psychosexual development is integral to and indeed instrumental in building the 'social contract' in Central Australia. This is related to current debates of child sexual abuse and social 'dysfunction' in Aboriginal communities, and to questions about the role of the state as an external source of authority and moral order.

In chapter 2, Aboriginal authors Katrina Tjitayi and Sandra Lewis from Ernabella, an Anangu Pitjantjatjara community in northern South Australia, offer reflections on their own childhoods in relation to the current situation. Tjitayi tells us how the future looked in the past, and how children's games and family dynamics prepared the younger generations for a fulfilled life as Anangu. Lewis focuses on the Anangu psychology of well-being with special emphasis on the challenges of young motherhood today.

In chapter 3, anthropologist Yasmine Musharbash examines Warlpiri practices of socialization – of turning infants and young children from a state called *warungka* (deaf, crazy, forgetful, mindless or intoxicated) into persons. She then contrasts these with Warlpiri practices of engaging people suffering old-age dementia. Describing how such practices include inversions of child socialization, the author discusses the involvement of others in shaping the Warlpiri person, ideas of personhood, and the symmetry between becoming and unbecoming a fully socialized being.

Chapter 4 by anthropologist Fred Myers explores the significance of social and emotional attachment during childhood for a secure sense of self and a specific social identity later in life, and conversely, how loss impacts on the 'ontological security' of the person. Sketching the formation of a distinctively desert masculinity, he describes how certain men in Pintupi society have coped, through symbolic working through at later stages in their lives, with the loss of significant others that had occurred in earlier years. Loss through death is an overwhelmingly widespread experience for all Aborigines (*see* Glaskin et al. 2008), and Myers shows how this affects the life trajectory of individuals and families he has known over several decades.

As a whole, Part I aims to open up a perspective on the sense of continuity of being that facilitates human action and secures a sense of self. Taken together, the chapters show how, from the early years on, both good and painful experiences are embedded in symbolic systems that lend coherence and meaning to a person's existence. When social dynamics shift profoundly, cultural forces can also challenge the integrity of a person who may either seek to mobilize her creative energies or withdraw in an effort to find a new inner balance.

Part II, 'Stories, Language and Social Space', explores the social significance of stories and play. It also considers the mental space of storytelling as an important part of growing up in Central Australia.

Extending the portrait of Anangu childhood begun by Tjitayi, I focus in chapter 5 on storytelling in the sand, which is a recognized tradition of girls and women. The practice is explored from various angles: the developmental stages in the acquisition of the technique, types of stories, contexts of performance, historical changes and the social significance of story making in the minds of children and their families. Particular emphasis is placed on the role of the creative imagination and how it relates to tradition and transformations. At times, the girls make stories in a contemplative fashion, but often they create stories spontaneously, by developing a narrative as they are talking that is at the same time illustrated visually with graphic sketches in the sand. Such stories often circulate and become part of the children's stock of knowledge, that is, they can flow into children's traditions, if only for transitory periods. Sand stories present an ongoing engagement with memory, as well as projections of the self into a coherent social frame and into the future. According to Heath, this is significant for the process of language learning, since 'regulatory private speech, dramatic play and visuo-spatial working memory relate to verbal knowledge' (Heath 2008: x). The chapter highlights the importance of social spaces that children inhabit without direct input from adults.

In chapter 6, linguist Carmel O'Shannessy analyses how children create social meaning in and through a new language that emerged among teenagers in the Warlpiri community of Lajamanu about a generation ago. Her findings that the children 'use play to exercise safety and control in a world that is often violent and disruptive', that they enact both culturally specific and universal themes and that they adopt the culturally available space for storytelling in order to perform personalized plots and stories resonate strongly with the functions of a more formalized narrative practice by girls at Ernabella.

In chapter 7, psychologist and Jungian analyst Craig San Roque analyses space from yet another point of view. Rather than writing 'about' Aborigines, he describes the setting and nature of encounters between Aboriginal families and his own family in his home in Alice Springs. Adopting a systemic perspective, the significance of spatiotemporal boundaries between indoor and outdoor, house and yard, and self and other are shown to be established, shifted and dissolved through social practice and interpersonal experiences. Taking up Winnicott's notion of 'transitional space' where play and imagination occur and culture begins, San Roque offers the reader an unusual journey across the borders between inner world and sociality and through a section of the multilayered cultural field of the 'capital' of Central Australia.

As a whole, Part II turns attention toward the world of children as they make and remake it – in their play, stories and in other social spaces temporarily shared. It explores processes of symbolization that are part of the construction of self, of others and of things in childhood. As von Bertalanffy (1967: 32–33) writes: 'By means of symbols and naming, things outside, people around, and the experiencing self – the It, Thou, and I – differentiate from the stream of experience; the *ego barrier* is established.' These processes also involve transformations of the symbolic universe and hence of social knowledge, actively brought about by the children in their own terms either in response to adults or in relationship to their peers.

Part III is dedicated to studies of 'Youth, Identity and Social Transformation'. Aspects of change were already evident in the nature of childhoods described in the previous two parts: sexuality seemed less censored in the past; anticipations about being grown up were more positive than what they appear to be now; experiences of loss have become intensi-fied; children increasingly participate in intercultural milieux; and they have even created a whole new language. However, while such histori-cal transformations have been noted, practically nothing is known about how Aboriginal children perceive the present sociocultural changes – if they do. Children may know that their grandparents' childhood differed from their own, and that, as Anangu children say, people in the past 'had no flour, sugar, money, motorcars, houses, or clothes'. But if and how they experience the ongoing transformation of their life-world and their own role in this process seems to be less clear and a worthwhile research subject for the future.

In adolescence, however, (maturational and social) change is much more foregrounded. By definition, adolescence is a time of change – from childhood to the reproductive stage and the responsibilities of adulthood. It presents a threshold at which implicit assumptions and understandings need to be articulated and forged into choices about personal life, so-cial and political allegiances, work and, if not always explicitly, cultural identity. In modern Western societies where formal rites of passage have ceased to be significant, this transition is often experienced as challeng-ing and confusing. For Indigenous young people who belong to minority groups in settler societies, the challenges of identity during adolescence and young adulthood can be particularly severe – potentially, they need to cope with racism, discrimination, cultural insecurities, intergenera-tional trauma and the socioeconomically marginal status of their families. However, depending on the cultural capacity of their local community, such young people may also benefit from traditions and cultural ideals that will support their personal development, their emplacement in soci-ety and their identity. The chapters in this section offer insights into such tensions between positive and negative conditions that shape young lives in different communities. They also depict young people's perceptions of their crises and problems as well as their strengths.

In chapter 8, anthropologist David Brooks describes the lives of young Ngaanyatjarra men in the Western Desert, where traditional ori-entations are strong. Drawing on case material, Brooks shows how the Dreaming, that is, the anchoring of social relationships in 'country' or the totemic landscape, is integral to their thinking in other domains as well, such as employment. Young people in the Ngaanyatjarra Lands are integrated into a distinctive regional social order, which, Brooks argues, is of greater relevance to their lives and self-perceptions than mainstream parameters and orientations.

The life-world of young Ngaanyatjarra shows many similarities with that of the Mardu described by anthropologist Myrna Tonkinson in chapter 9. This is not surprising as the social, cultural and political histories of the two related groups have much in common. However, in comparison, the overall situation of young Mardu who live in communities to the west of the Ngaanyatjarra Lands seems worse. Tonkinson sketches the views and behaviours of Mardu youth who struggle to find their place both within their own local communities and the wider Australian society. Here the gap between the generations seems to be widening, with negative consequences for young people who increasingly experience difficulties as they become teenage parents, abuse drugs and show high levels of risky behaviours and violence. Like Brooks, the author sees meaningful employment as the key to improving young people's lives in their home communities.

Tension and conflict are further explored in chapter 10, by anthropologist-psychiatrist Marika Moisseeff, but the focus here is on families of Central Australian background who reside in southern towns, that is, in a highly racialized milieu. At the centre of discussion is the inner struggle of young Aborigines to cope with the dual burden of racism on the one hand and cultural demands from their families on the other. Young urban Aborigines are torn between loyalty to their marginalized community and the desire for upward social mobility, often finding themselves confronted with stereotypes on both sides of the racial divide. Racism in the form of patronizing attitudes, Moisseeff argues, has impacted negatively on the reproductive capacities of the Aboriginal society at large: the intergenerational transmission of how to be a parent is impaired because Aboriginal people's treatment as children – first in the form of wardens of the state and later through welfare paternalism – has locked them into a position of dependency on the encompassing White Australian society. Although often not benign, the latter nevertheless also presents a nurturing maternal image. In many families, the transition from maternal to paternal care, that is, to the paternal function of filiation (socialization into a more mature and responsible role), is disrupted, as men in particular have lost their authority and status as able providers. The continuity of a distinctive cultural identity, which is by and large instilled by the male members of a community, is therewith jeopardized.

The chapters within each part and across the three parts of the book invite comparison. The second and the last chapter, by Morton and Moisseeff respectively, explore both the cultural specifics of identity formation and, more specifically, the shift from maternal to paternal nurturance in Aranda families. But where Morton presents a Freudian analysis of children's play in the 1920s, Moisseeff offers a systemic view of intergenerational tensions in families who struggle with racism in southern towns. Both authors consider the role of the state as guardian of children and the effect of paternalism in shaping Aboriginal people's place within Australian society. Morton's discussion of the cultural patterning of psychodynamics during childhood can also be instructively read in relation to particular ethnographic observations from adjacent regions. For example, the egoism and violence of adults that Brooks identifies as long-established behaviours in Ngaanyatjarra society might be pondered as manifestations of a benign superego, just as much as the often-reported generosity. Furthermore, there are links between Moisseeff's contribution and San Roques's (chapter 7) systemic approach to Aboriginal childhood in the intercultural milieu of Alice Springs: in both cases, the setting is an urban racialized milieu and, emphasizing encounter rather than observation, the authors use their own life experiences to shed light on the Aboriginal condition. Myers's reflections on Pintupi life trajectories too could be read in relation to Moisseeff's chapter. Where Myers (chapter 4) writes that a specific social identity derives from experiences in childhood, Moisseeff sees late adolescence and young adulthood, that is, the time of heightened paternal influence, to be the most critical in the formation of a distinctive identity. The difference of views may be interpreted on ethnographic and conceptual grounds: conceivably, the process of identity formation is different in a remote Aboriginal community where the presence of White Australia is less significant – but still a factor, as Myers demonstrates with the case of a young man – than in the racially tense context of the town. The lesser presence of the Black-White juxtaposition also means that identity processes occur largely through social differentiation at a local level in the remote community, while urban youth are faced with the additional significance of being culturally different and judged inferior as a collectivity. Similarly, the three chapters on youth could be seen to indicate that the extent of stressful life experiences among Aboriginal youth is inversely linked to the degree of cultural remoteness from the wider Australian society: the stronger the orientation towards local traditions (as in the Ngaanyatjarra Lands), the better young people fare, if not in terms of mainstream social indicators. A marginalized position as a minority group in urban contexts appears to provoke the most severe forms of psychosocial stress, while the Mardu seem to occupy a position halfway between the two. If this view proves accurate, it would challenge the conviction held by some commentators and policy makers that remoteness equals social degradation.

Childhood and adolescence in Central Australian Aboriginal families show distinctive cultural markers of Aboriginality. At the same time, it is important to recognize as social fact that young Aborigines grow up in particular local milieux that differ from one another. They sustain and create a variety of languages, forms of relatedness, artistic expressions, and social and cultural knowledge. In other words, the culturally distinctive ways of social action that can only be sustained through living engagement contribute to the possibilities of human existence at large. Here, in the life-worlds of young 'remote' Aboriginal people, one could argue, lies some potential to enhance the benefits of cultural and social pluralism for Australia at large.

Notes

1. 'Indigenous' is used to refer to Australians identifying as Aboriginal or Torres Strait Islander. According to the Australian Bureau of Statistics ATSI projections 2001–2009, the demographic profile of the Indigenous population shows an age pyramid heavily weighted at its base towards young people, with nearly 40 per cent aged fifteen or under, and with a median age well below the national level.
2. The groups within this expansive area are represented by landholding bodies with legal (and in some cases statutory) authority that began to be established in the 1970s during the land rights movement: in 1974 the Central Land Council which represents 18,000 Aboriginal people from different language groups across an area of over 770,000 square kilometres; in 1981 the Anangu Pitjantjatjara Yankunytjatjara Land Council representing about 3,000 people across 102,000 square kilometres; in 1988 the Ngaanyatjarra Council which represents 2,000 members across 220,000 sq km; and in 2003 the Western Desert Lands Aboriginal Corporation (*Jamukurnu-Yapalikunu*) representing the Native Title interests of around 1,000 Mardu people over an area of 136,000 square kilometres. Importantly, Aboriginal people are the large majority in the communities across these areas, meaning that the young generation there does not experience directly the minority status of the national Indigenous population.
3. An illustrative example of such a coexistence is the Arrernte map of Apmere Mparntwe, 'Alice Springs,' in Wilkins (2002: 24).
4. For an extensive discussion of the intersections between child well-being and culture, policy and research *see* Robinson et al. 2008.

PART I

Childhood Across Time
Historical and
Life Span Perspectives

CHAPTER 1

'Less was hidden among these children'

Géza Róheim, Anthropology and the Politics of Aboriginal Childhood

John Morton

On 13 January 1929, Sydney's *Sunday Pictorial* carried the following headline: 'WILL ANALYSE PRIMITIVE MAN'. The accompanying text included the following statements:

> Freud's theory on the analogy between civilised neurotics and primitive man will be tested in practice, it is hoped, by an expedition that has left Europe for Australia and New Guinea.

> The party is headed by Dr G. Roheim, Hungarian anthropologist and psycho-analyst. His wife, who is expected to be a valuable aid with women and children among uncivilised tribes, accompanies him.

> The aim of the expedition is to analyse primitive man – to discover the origin and significance of his myths, folk-lore, and dreams, and the thousand other phenomena that constitute his mental life. …

> Dr Roheim chose Australia and New Guinea 'because', he says, 'it is here … that we find the nearest approach to what mankind must have been like in the Stone Age.' (Anon 1929: 7)

In the event, Róheim was to accomplish his fieldwork and write about Central Australian Aborigines, mainly Arrernte and Pitjantjatjara, as 'the children of the desert' on at least three separate occasions. On the first occasion (1932: 23–37) he described actual children's play; on the second (1974) and third (1988) occasions he also described the life-worlds of adults.

Equating Aboriginal people with children (or with the 'childhood' of humanity) is ostensibly off limits in the twenty-first century, which can make Róheim's work, like Freud's (2001[1913]), now look rather quaint and antiquarian, not to mention offensive. Nevertheless, I want to use his equation as a provocation, particularly in light of the fact that Australia has now entered a period in Aboriginal affairs when there is much talk about Aboriginal people being encouraged or forced to 'take responsibility' (Pearson 2000), a matter which is tied to a deep interrogation of the post-1970s self-determination policy and the corresponding failure of Aboriginal people to have 'snuggled comfortably into the warm and welcoming embrace of the nation' (Cowlishaw 2003a: 121). Under modern conditions, all citizens are in a sense children of the state, which is thus charged with a 'duty of care'. In the current cultural climate, there is a strong public desire to move recently fashioned Aboriginal citizens from maternal to paternal care; that is, away from dependence on a 'Nanny State', typified by a regime of passive welfare, to genuine autonomy and full independence created by neopaternalist discipline and what has been called 'coercive reconciliation' (Altman and Hinkson 2007). The psychoanalytically minded will recognize in this shift a transition from 'mother right' to 'father right' – a kind of Oedipal drama in which the father severs the tie between mother and child to create the child's self-regulating existence.

Róheim believed implicitly in the universal truth of this drama in human affairs, both primitive and modern, and it is in this light that I propose to examine his work and assess its relevance for a contemporary understanding of what is happening in and to Aboriginal communities today. In the first place, I want to suggest that Róheim's interpretation of childhood sexuality as a constructive force in the perpetuation of culture is historically significant. Róheim, I want to say, can be said to have uncovered the basic Freudian form of the social contract in Central Australia, shedding particular light on the place of child development in it, and it is this which needs to be compared with the modern imposition of the social contract from a large-scale, centralized, 'civilizing' government at the present time. Related to this, I also want to suggest that Róheim's Central Australian ethnographic project renders insights into the meaning and causes of the current upsurge of paternalism in Aboriginal affairs, particularly insofar as the upsurge centres on a 'project of saving children' (Hart 2006: 6) from violence and sexual abuse. Róheim's ethnography of childhood, I want to say, is a useful, if partial, gauge for measuring both the real and imagined dimensions of child abuse in Aboriginal Australia.

I begin by discussing Róheim's ethnographic account of Central Australian childhood and character development, also explaining his sometimes difficult and, for many anthropologists, alienating Freudian terminology (*cf.* Morton 1988: xi–xvi). I then consider the implications of Róheim's account, together with its relationship to more recent ethnographic reports and analyses, for understanding Aboriginal relations with the state, particularly as these have been refracted through official investigations into child abuse in Central Australia. I conclude with comments on how Róheim's frame of understanding sheds light on the problem of articulation between primitive and modern forms of the social contract.

Róheim on Aboriginal Childhood and Character Development

Róheim's first field report contained a large section on children (1932: 23–37), and this material was partially repeated and supplemented in a number of other places (*see especially* Róheim 1950: 54–74, 1974: 65–121). The overall portrayal is one of liberty; or as Róheim actually stated: 'The children of an Australian tribe enjoy a fair amount of freedom' (1934: 30). As a Freudian drawing attention to this 'freedom', he naturally emphasized its origins in childhood sexuality, which he summarized as follows:

> As far as cleanliness is concerned the requirements of the adults is very moderate. The child is indeed told to defecate out of doors, but this rule is not taken very seriously. Children are never weaned and the mother never refuses them her breasts. Only one thing is forbidden; they must not see their parents in the act of coitus. The married couples only copulate when the children are supposed to be asleep. The children feel naturally that the enjoyment of the primal scene is a forbidden pleasure. Therefore they repress what they have observed. (1934: 30)

The notion of the 'primal scene' here is taken from Freud and references a kind of 'ur-fantasy' in which children begin to disturbingly discover their origins in an act which appears to them as both threatening and sexually exciting (Laplanche and Pontalis 1985: 335–36). The primal scene is also what instigates Oedipal dynamics, inasmuch as it places the parents in an exclusive relationship to which the child cannot be party (and to which it can *never* be party), thus bringing the child towards individuation.

Sex, Aggression and Latency

As is well known, Freud regarded the Oedipal situation 'as the central phenomenon of the sexual period of early childhood' (Freud 2001[1924]: 173). But he also regarded it as a temporary phenomenon that required resolution and dissolution for individuation to occur.

> After … [the sexual period of early childhood], its dissolution takes place; it succumbs to repression, as we say, and is followed by the

latency period. It has not yet become clear, however, what it is that brings about its destruction. Analyses seem to show that it is the result of painful disappointments. The little girl likes to regard herself as what her father loves above all else; but the time comes when she has to endure harsh punishment from him and she is cast out of her fool's paradise. The boy regards the mother as his own property; but he finds one day that she has transferred her love and solicitude to a new arrival. ... In this way the Oedipus complex would go to its destruction from its lack of success, from the effects of its internal impossibility. (Freud 2001[1924]: 173)

But while Freud put forward the Oedipal situation as a human universal, he also qualified it by saying that the latency period, as a time intervening between 'the sexual period of early childhood' and adolescence, was peculiarly open to cultural influence, suggesting that latency, as a surrender of sexual strivings, was subject to variable 'reaction-formations', including those of 'morality, shame, and disgust' surrounding childhood sexuality (Freud 2001[1925]: 37). However, ten years after writing these words, and three years after Róheim's first published field report, he added a footnote saying:

The period of latency is a physiological phenomenon. It can, however, only give rise to a complete interruption of sexual life in cultural organizations which have made the suppression of infantile sexuality a part of their system. This is not the case with the majority of primitive peoples. (Freud 2001[1925]: 37)

In his 1932 field report, Róheim referred to the fact that Central Australian Aborigines had 'a minimum of reaction formations in character-development', something which he believed left people 'happy' (1932: 119). This judgement was implicitly comparative, since he had in mind the absence of the 'tortures ... inflicted on the ego by the super-ego' characteristic of modern subjects, something which he related to Aboriginal disbelief in the face of missionary pronouncements about original sin (Róheim 1932: 120). Hence, he was not saying that Aborigines were 'happy' because they never had problems; rather, he was suggesting that they were far less prone to guilt.

Of particular note in this regard was his writing on child discipline and pedagogy, which he sharply contrasted to the views and practices of the Lutheran missionaries at Hermannsburg Mission. In one recounted incident, an eight-year-old boy had thrown an hour-long tantrum after being locked up by a missionary, who responded by giving the boy a beating. This in turn prompted outrage and anger from adult Aborigines who regarded the missionary's actions as nothing less than child abuse

(Róheim 1974: 73). On another occasion, when an Aboriginal mission school monitor beat some small children with a whip, he was threatened with his life by outraged adults, who stated that such punishments should never be performed by Aboriginal people (1974: 74). Róheim was quick to point out that older Aboriginal people did sometimes punish their children or scold them, usually out of frustration with bad behaviour, which prompted him to ask: 'What is it that the Australians resent so violently in Western methods of corporal punishment, since they themselves are quite capable of slapping or beating a child?' (1974: 75). His answer was that Aboriginal adults were 'scandalized' by mission discipline because they rightly understood it to be 'sadistic pedagogy' (1974: 75) – something which they deemed entirely inappropriate for prepubescent children. He further suggested that the only legitimate fear that could be instilled into children was via warnings about 'bogey man' figures in the bush – warnings which had the effect of keeping children close to camp (1974: 75–76). In conclusion, he stated:

> We may therefore say that if we consider the four main techniques of pedagogy – erection of an ego-ideal, use of a bogey to create fear, corporal punishment, and preaching – the first two predominate, while the third and fourth are nearly absent in the Central Australian nursery. On the whole, it can be said that the parents rule with a lenient hand and, that techniques of intimidation are brought into action only at the threshold of adult life. (1974: 76)

By 'ego-ideal' Róheim was referring to the image of 'good parents' – the very image which was contradicted by 'sadistic pedagogy'.[1] The symbolic potential of 'good parents' was apparent to Róheim in Aboriginal children's games, since these were largely about 'growing up' to be like their elders. Boys would play hunting games and present their pretend game to girls, who would not only pretend to cook it, but also gather their own pretend food and look after pretend babies. The children also combined these activities with an oracular game, sometimes explicitly sexual, which would foretell their futures as adults (Róheim 1974: 76– 79). In the play sessions which Róheim organized with children at Hermannsburg Mission and Tempe Downs Pastoral Station (1974: 80–120), he was to see a great deal of explicit sexual content, although he drew a distinction between the play sessions at the mission and those with the still-nomadic Western Desert people (mainly Pitjantjatjara) camped at Tempe Downs. He was struck by the fact that:

> whereas the Mission children were constantly talking about cohabitation and making the [European] toys [which Róheim provided] perform coitus, the bush [Pitjantjatjara] children acted out the game, either with

their own bodies or with objects held to the proper parts of their own anatomy. The difference between the two groups of children was the result of the influence of the school and the Mission. If we compare these Australian children to European children, there is a striking contrast between the direct libidinal gratification of the first group and the sublimation of the second. (1974: 119)

Hence, the difference between the Aboriginal playgroups and European children was itself writ small in the difference between the Mission and Pitjantjatjara playgroups, since, in the Pitjantjatjara case, it was evident that 'less was hidden among these children' (1974: 120) due to their not having been subjected to the restrictions and 'sadistic pedagogy' of the mission regime (1974: 105). Latency at the mission, Róheim suggested, lay more on the side of what Freud called 'morality, shame and disgust', albeit imperfectly when compared with latency among 'European children'. The contrast was most powerfully illustrated in Róheim's different descriptions of particular play sessions:

Depitarinja, who was generally a very lively [ten-year-old] boy, was very sad. … He had been beaten by a missionary, because he *aruntjima* a little girl, a baby of about four. The missionary gave him a very severe thrashing. After a little pause he began the game by saying that the [toy] snake was sad. Then the snake smells the vagina of the [toy] nanny goat. Then the snake marries the nanny-goat. Now this is just what Depitarinja had been doing, for *aruntjima* means to kiss and he has been kissing the little baby's vagina. That is what he got the thrashing for. The game goes on and all the toy dolls and animals are made to smell the vagina and anus of the monkey, who has kept her role of mother all along. Then a big rubber doll is made to represent the *inkata* (the chief, in Hermannsburg the head of the Mission) and he beats all the others for smelling the monkey. (Róheim 1932: 24; *also see* 1974: 94–95)[2]

On the other hand:

I have seen a Pitchentara [Pitjantjatjara] boy of about three throwing a girl of about two down on the sand and going through the regular coitus movements on top of her. Two big girls came and picked the boy off the baby-girl. They go on doing this whenever they get the chance through their whole life. … When the Pitchentara and Yumu [Jumu] children were beginning to make themselves familiar with the new toys, Wili-kutu, Jankitji and the others began by putting the serpent and the paper trumpet to their penis as a sort of elongation and then they would run to the little girls or to each other and use this toy penis in exactly the same manner as they would have used the real one. The performance was realistic, the laughter and pleasure genuine. … Wili-kutu took the rubber doll and rubbed his penis on it, he not only said that he was *muranyi* [copulating with] the girl, but I could see that his penis was erected and a few drops of semen were ejaculated. (Róheim 1932: 35; *also see* 1974: 116)[3]

Róheim originally suggested in this field report that 'the natives have no latency period' (1932: 35), but he immediately corrected himself by saying:

> It would be more exact to say that only small quanta of libidinal energy are diverted from their original direction in the latency play-period and that the line of demarcation between the desexualized and the unmodified libido is very weak. (1932: 35)

However, from a European perspective, it might appear that the latency period is not 'desexualized' at all, since 'there is nothing that compares quantitatively to the latency period of European children' (Róheim 1974: 244). Hence, recognition of the innocence of childhood sexuality in related cross-cultural contexts, such as schooling, would be 'no mean accomplishment' (Money et al. 1973: 412), something which Róheim clearly believed to be beyond the capabilities of 1920s mission staff at Hermannsburg. It is therefore worth underlining the fact that, while Róheim strongly emphasized the explicitness of childhood sexuality in Central Australia, he did not suggest that this sexuality was in any sense perversely practised as premature sexual connection or as anything other than *play*. Indeed, he emphasized the fear and anxiety which children attached to the mature sexual act – a point I return to in detail below.

Children's play at Hermannsburg was less direct and more projective than the play at Tempe Downs. Generally speaking, the mission children used Róheim's introduced toys to dramatize '*other* boys and girls in the act of coitus' (1932: 36), unlike the Western Desert children. Róheim linked this contrast to the mission's disciplinary regime:

> The mission children go to school and although they are still in many respects real children of the desert they have undoubtedly been modified in certain respects. Out in the bush they run, wrestle, roll about and perform coitus, but I have never seen anything like the sadistic and masochistic games in which Depitarinja indulges. He has frequently been punished for the perfectly natural manifestations of his libido and these functions have thus become associated with the idea of torture and of being tortured. For the native may have an aggressive but he has not got a sadistic character. He will roar at a child or hurl a boomerang at him in a sudden fit of anger, but he will never deliberately punish him. Thus the child in the bush will never introject a sadistic super-ego and never enjoy the game of punishing or being punished. (Róheim 1932: 37)

In an accompanying footnote, Róheim defined 'sadistic' as 'taking pleasure in a systematized "exhibition of power"', which he contrasted with his definition of 'aggressive' as prone to 'a simple outburst of rage' (1932: 37). Hence, Róheim understood Aboriginal pedagogy, as a moral orientation towards preadolescent children, to be free of 'exhibitions of power', but far from free of aggression as a 'natural manifestation of libido'. Although he implied parental tolerance of children's 'self-assertion' (Sutton 2001: 155) and consequent adult 'demanding behaviour' (Sutton 2001: 156), he did not address these matters explicitly, speaking only in general terms about parental lenience (1974: 76) or what has been called typically Aboriginal 'over-indulgent love' (Hernández 1941: 129): 'the Australian baby', he said, 'is treated with the utmost consideration on the part of the mother and can always get what it wants' (1932: 78). Róheim does not appear to have witnessed the practice, documented elsewhere, of 'cruelling' (Sutton 2009: 111–12) – the deliberate, violent and painful provocation of young children, often mere babies, in order to elicit self-assertion. However, he does describe cognate practices rationalized in terms of creating sexual modesty, with infants' genitalia and cheeks being aggressively treated to discourage genital growth, and therefore libidinal excess in adult life (Róheim 1974: 67–68). Moreover, his ethnography also describes maternal and sibling aggression expressed as both infanticide and infant cannibalism (1974: 70–73).[4] He also spoke of 'libidinal propensities' towards children (1974: 73) and witnessed at least one example of persistent genital stimulation of a son by his mother (1932: 55) – something which he clearly regarded as indicative of a more general expression of incestuous desire in the mother-son situation (1932: 54). Following Carl Strehlow (1913: 3), Róheim accepted that infants were sometimes neglected when older siblings deprived them of the mother's breast (1950: 56).[5]

Aggression is not the only 'natural manifestation of libido' relevant to this situation, since there is also the correlative matter of erotic trends. Children, says Róheim, 'are brought up to be generous, and the efforts made in this direction are as successful as possible' (1950: 58). Moreover, 'there is no emphasis on competition. Sharing and giving are the outstanding virtues' (1950: 146). He also states that, far from being inconsistent with the free expression of aggression, compassion and reciprocity are manifestations of the same lack of 'super-ego pressure' (1950: 146) which accounts for overt aggressive trends in situations where demands are not met. In addition, he suggests that one should not 'assume that selfishness is absent' simply because sharing and compassion are 'socially reinforced' (1950: 146), but it is evident that he does not correlate 'selfishness' with 'competition'. Children, Róheim seems to suggest, grow into a strong sense of autonomy and self-interest, but it is this very same sense of integrity which allows for sympathetic identification with others, so that a sense of self and a sense of consociate kinship are in some measure the same thing – as has been more explicitly stated by Myers (1986: 109, 116) for the Pintupi.

For Róheim, however, the matter is specifically one of ego strength tied to what he called 'oral optimism' – gifting (particularly of food) to others being a 'natural expression of good will' (Róheim 1932: 77) based on 'the primitive non-retentive structure of the ego' and an 'expulsive type of character development' (1932: 117). Both are correlated with the absence of 'sadistic pedagogy' and 'anchored in a healthy foundation of narcissism' or 'original and natural self-love' (1932: 106). While Róheim does not speak of 'demand sharing' (Peterson 1993) as such, his description of 'oral optimism' growing from parental indulgence is completely in line with descriptions of this activity as 'mutual taking' or 'tolerated theft' (Peterson 1993: 861) – including in the mother-child situation (Myers 1986: 178–79), since narcissism (love of self) is not only the basis of sympathetic identification with others (Róheim 1932: 106) but also the means by which the right to demand is emotionally articulated. Hence Róheim also speaks of a typically 'oral-aggressive' (1932: 77) attitude:

> Look at the zest with which the children eat each other's lice or dig for witchetties, the love of the chase, the pleasure the young men take in tracking big game, and you cannot doubt that you see a happy people … [who] confidently expect that their food quest will be successful. A boy about seven, Jankitji, was acting as head of the family in Pukuti-wara's absence and he could always manage to get a wallaby or some lizards to feed his mothers and brothers. (Róheim 1932: 78)

In Róheim's scheme of things, hunting, as an expression of oral aggression, is metaphoric of demand itself, but he also gives considerable weight to children's phallic aggression (associated with the use of weapons) in character formation (1932: 91). In addition, he notes that anal aggression (associated with fastidiousness, stubbornness and stinginess) is completely absent (1932: 84–85).

Taming the Appetites: Towards Adolescence

Róheim was of course aware that Central Australian children, particularly boys, were on coming of age subject to tyrannical powers through initiation and related disciplines, but in his first field report he made a remark which linked initiation to children's character formation. 'I have repeatedly been told', he wrote:

that if a boy were not initiated something terrible might happen. He might become an *erintja*, i.e. devil, fly up into the air and kill and eat all the old men of the tribe. This is what the ritual must prevent. (1932: 72)

He later reported that *erintja* are one particular form of a class of demonic beings which, in Arandic and Western Desert dialects, also include *bankalanga, nananana, mamu, manataitai, mingalpintji* and *malpakara*. Their general characteristics were a 'taste for human flesh', bodies 'completely covered with hair', 'exaggeratedly large sexual organs' and 'enormous sexual appetites' (Róheim 1988: 95). In folktales, these demons or monsters were generally ranged against 'good, beautiful, and normal people', known as *indatoa, tneera, kunindjatu* and *aneera* (Róheim 1988: 95). These 'normal people' were regarded by Róheim as personifications of the ego-ideal used in childhood pedagogy – as images of 'good parents' and as models for children's aspirations in growing up. In the stories:

> The normal people or human beings generally triumph in the end, frequently against the most impossible odds. Not only are the normal people unusually heroic, but they are also markedly beautiful, with fair skin and fair hair. … The 'growing up' aspect of the tales is … confirmed by the nature of the happy ending. The monsters are generally killed and burned, the boys are initiated into adulthood, they marry and they all 'live happily ever after'. The Central Australian equivalent of this latter familiar formula is: 'They all sit down (that is, settle or camp) there for ever'. (Róheim 1988: 96)

However, while the 'normal people' were seen as perfected images of 'good parents', Róheim clearly established that the demonic beings were counterimages or 'bad parents' created through the typical splitting of 'good and bad objects' that had originally been described by Klein in her analysis of child development (1997[1932]: 153; *also see* Eickelkamp 2004: 164). As he said:

> It is not necessary to stress the parental quality of the monsters. They are frequently called by parental or grandparental terms, and they obviously represent the child's view (and projection) of the highly aggressive and sexual parents. The symbolism is not especially complex. … The tales abound, in fact, with themes of castration, cannibalism, murder and coitus. (1988: 96)

Róheim collected no less than 129 of these folktales (1988: 98–198) and even a cursory look confirms his opinion about their sado-sexual nature (*cf.* Róheim 1934: 23–41), particularly in relation to cannibalism and oral aggression (*cf.* Eickelkamp 2004). The manner in which the stories unfold, with 'good' invariably triumphing over 'evil', is related to

Róheim's views of Central Australian latency, in which children's sexual play, however explicit, *remains* play. Full sexual connection, as acted out by demonic figures and correlated with various forms of sadism, is avoided and projected into the demonic figures themselves, who are then defeated by 'normal people' – parental images which have been voided of sado-sexual content. Hence, the question is begged: what has this sado-sexual content have to do with initiation? Why would a child become a cannibalistic monster if not initiated in early adolescence?

Róheim does not explicitly answer this question, although he immediately suggests that it has everything to do with the manifest purpose of initiation, which is to separate boys from their mothers and the world of women, and bind them to the exclusive world of men (Róheim 1932: 72). The theoretical context for this remark is conditioned by what Freud called 'the diphasic onset of sexual growth' and the manner in which puberty reanimates 'the impulses and object-relations of a child's early years' (2001[1925]: 37), so that, in the Central Australian context, pubertal sexual awakening reengages with the psychosexual source of the imagined sadistic demons found in folktales. In childhood, the image of the sexualized 'bad parents' is expelled and thus no longer a threat to ego integrity, something which Róheim related to Klein's (1997[1932]) suggestion that the 'bad object' played a crucial role in early superego development (*cf.* Eickelkamp 2004: 172). But, said Róheim:

> Such a concept is only a forerunner of the true super-ego because its character is solely determined by the infant's aggressiveness and is independent of the parent's real attitude. Moreover, as an introjected object it does not affect the structure of the character, since it is immediately disposed of by projection. All children deny that their parents have intercourse; humanity has invented demons for this purpose instead. (Róheim 1934: 41)

On the other hand, puberty is the time when maturing children are to be prepared for marriage and the fuller expression of their sexuality, which implies that the 'bad' aspect of sexuality must be reversed and transformed into a 'good'. For Róheim, this meant the formation of a 'true super-ego' out of its 'forerunner', which implied that a failure in 'true super-ego' development would indeed turn a maturing child into a demon – a frighteningly indiscriminate sexualized being. Unlike Freud, whose writing is unclear on the distinction between the ego-ideal and the superego (Laplanche and Pontalis 1985: 144–45), Róheim drew a line between the two.[6] While the Central Australian ideal ego is, for him, forged out of the image of parental body integrity (the 'normal people') and correlated with 'oral optimism', with 'mirroring' being the means by which the positive injunction of generosity is encouraged, the superego is in some sense the *negation* of these things – hence its organic relation to the demonic figures ranged against the 'normal people' in stories. While the ego-ideal *encourages,* the superego *prohibits.*

Róheim appears to have been the only early ethnographer to systematically relate adult ceremonial life and its grounding in 'The Dreaming' (*Altyerre* or *Tjukurrpa*) to supernatural beliefs in these demonic figures.[7] Exoteric folktales are referred to as 'dreamings' (Róheim 1988: 95) and thus in some sense regarded as equivalent to the esoteric stories of adult ceremonial life. However, according to Róheim, this equivalence is by way of structural inversion. Hence he describes:

> the essential difference between the two forms of Central Australian religion. The belief in devils begins with the anxiety reaction to the primal scene … ; but in the projected version of this memory … , those who copulate are not the parents but non-human devils. … After the initiation the youth again sees the primal scene, but this time in a sublimated super-ego-syntonic form. Humanity first tries to dispose of the disturbing content (primal scene) by projection (devils); but introjection follows the failure of this attempt. … Then they [the devils] are changed from anthropophagous and phallic demons into protecting ancestors who are removed from all contact with women; anxiety gives way to reverence, love, and identification. (1934: 157)

There is no room here to unpack the intricacies of initiation, but it is important to note that the purpose of initiation – for girls as well as for boys – is to instil shame[8] and respect for the Law through disciplines which are explicitly sexual and which literally open up the body. While girls classically underwent introcision and ritual defloration as part of their coming of age and as a prelude to marriage (Róheim 1933: 234–35), boys undergo separate but parallel and more elaborate rites, including circumcision and subincision, in which they must adopt an equally submissive, sometimes explicitly homosexual, role (Róheim 1974: 243–44). In both cases, entry into adult life means participation in ceremonial activities in which sexuality and aggression are as explicit as in childhood play, although the libidinal economy of adult life and ritual remains distinct. While adult ritual may in some sense be 'play', it is also restriction and submission to the Law, with young men in particular being 'given a whole series of "don'ts"' (Róheim 1950: 84–85) – commandments or rules. This is the very 'sadistic pedagogy' or 'intimidation' which Róheim states (*see above*) is absent from childhood and 'brought into action only at the threshold of adult life' to prevent adolescents turning into sado-sexual monsters (*erintja*).

Hence, it is the basic idea of 'commands' or 'rules' which characterize the superego, and rules, as Róheim remarked, are the domain of 'moral inhibitions' (1932: 106), 'prohibitions and rules of conduct given by the parent and accepted by the child' (1932: 108):

> If we say that initiation is the dramatization of the super-ego, or if we call it the dramatization of repression, we are saying nearly the same thing. ... At the initiation ceremony the society of adults behaves like a powerful army which has been hitherto content with occasional threats against the rebellious forces, but now seeing them growing in strength, decides to make a serious effort to quell the rebellion. A systematic effort is made to tell the boy what he may not do, i.e. an effort to reinforce the repressive forces at the time when puberty shows that his sexuality must now be taken seriously. An organized attempt is made to put repression into action. (1932: 109)

The superego is, therefore, a limiting agency and its repressive force is characteristically felt in relation to incest avoidance and the shame relationships accompanying it, typically in relation to affinal authority (Róheim 1974: 11–31). It arises out of what Róheim calls the 'powerful army' of the 'society of adults' – a metaphor which he appears to have taken from Freud, who characterized the internalization of this force as: 'mastery over the individual's desire for aggression by weakening and disarming it and by setting up an agency within him to watch over it, like a garrison in a conquered city' (2001[1930]: 124). Central Australian childhood is free of this 'agency', thanks to its threatening qualities being projected into the world at large, where they appear as sado-sexual monsters. With their bodies 'closed', preadolescents are not 'open to influence'. Consequently, they are regarded as 'deaf' – unable to understand, think and comprehend (Myers 1986: 107–08).

Anthropology, the State and 'the Domestication of the Savage Mind'

Anthropology, Aboriginal Childhood and the Social Contract

W. E. H. Stanner once implied that Róheim was not much better than nineteenth-century commentators who saw Aboriginal people as 'men of Sodom, sinners exceedingly' – this because 'recent Freudians' (Róheim was unnamed) have looked at Aboriginal religion and 'given the sexual symbolisms a grotesquely exaggerated significance' (1979: 140). And yet Stanner also spoke of Aboriginal religion as the 'magnification of life'

(1979: 119), with an overt emphasis on '[v]itality, fertility and growth', and on corresponding symbols, including:

> water, blood, fat, hair, excrements; the sex organs, semen, sexuality in all its phases, the quickening in the womb; child-spirits, mystical impregnation and reincarnation; the development of the body from birth to death; the transitions of the human spirit from before organic assumption until after physical dissolution. (Stanner 1979: 119)

But Róheim did not correlate such overt emphasis with 'sin'. Like Stanner, he maintained that such projection of moral deficit onto Aborigines was an ethnographic error, although he also suggested that it was motivated through the typical structure of the modern psyche. As he said:

> With a super-ego based mainly on deflected phallic strivings, with a phallic and aggressive ego, and a minimum of reaction formations in character development, the Aranda is a happy man. … [Aborigines] certainly have a super-ego, but not too much of it, and there is more real danger in their lives than intrapsychical danger. The tortures which in neurosis are inflicted on the ego by the super-ego are here really carried out by the old men at initiation, but not introjected by the young.[9] They are men who get what they want, or, as this is not possible in human conditions, we should say they get a substitute not too far removed from the original. We know them from the cradle to the grave and can say: they are not wicked because they do not try to be good.
>
> When the Lutheran missionaries began to talk about the doctrine of original sin and to tell these descendants of the eternal dream folk that they were all sinful, wicked beings, they answered with great indignation: *Aranda inkaraka mara*. 'The Aranda are all good.' And in this we heartily agree. (Róheim 1932: 119–20)

Far from 'grotesquely exaggerating' the significance of sexual symbolism in Central Australian life, Róheim actually suggested that it was shallow and less complex than the symbolism arising from the heightened sublimation typical of modern experience. Hence, the symbolism might only appear 'exaggerated' to those who, like Stanner, had habituated avoidance of the sexual content of culture. T. G. H. Strehlow, while a measured critic of Róheim's descriptions of Aboriginal sexuality,[10] agreed that the latter was 'not covered under a spurious cloak of outward virtue' (1971: 462) – a cloak typical of public or official morality in Australian society, if not private or unofficial practice (Strehlow 1971: 462–64). It is not surprising, Strehlow said, that somebody 'perusing the pages of Dr Róheim' might 'be filled with something like disgust or horror' (1971: 465), but this is precisely because the shallow sublimations of primitive life mistakenly appear to cultured readers as incomparable to those of advanced civilization.[11] Aboriginal song-poetry, Strehlow said, makes 'virtually no mention of the spiritual side of love', although it has much to say about 'attractiveness ... on a purely physical level' (1971: 473) – this because:

> the natives in their original state showed little of that particular prurience and morbid preoccupation with matters of sex which is so noticeable a feature of much white European behaviour. From their infancy sex in its normal aspects had been treated amongst them as a fit subject for conversation. No parents had ever prevented them from talking about it in their childish way. Even more important, no parents used to be embarrassed by hearing their children bringing up innocently any matters connected with this topic; and sex consequently never had for the Central Australian boys and girls that morbid interest which springs from a sense that it is something inherently and intrinsically shameful and disgusting. ... Even when they were breaking the tribal laws governing marriage, no great sense of moral guilt or sin was experienced by the transgressors, unless such irregular behaviour had in addition violated the rules against 'incest'. (Strehlow 1971: 473–74)

This statement is in complete agreement with Róheim's description of the absence of original sin in Central Australia and a corresponding absence of sadistic discipline leading to the inoffensive 'acting out' of sexual play.[12] At the same time, however, Róheim explicitly rejected a noble savage view of this permissiveness and lack of morbidity.[13] As he wrote shortly after returning from the field:

> Transference ... is the basis of all anthropological work, although the non-psycho-analytical anthropologist does not call it transference and knows nothing of its infantile origins. He gets the transference instinctively, because he likes his work and therefore also the people he is studying. ... The anthropologist ... works with an unanalysed transference and especially, what is worse still, with an unanalysed countertransference. ... The anthropologist, although theoretically he may believe in the unity of mankind and therefore expect to find that the black or brown man has strivings, yearnings and fears like his own, is still the child of a different race and civilization. As he slowly overcomes the feeling of strangeness in his new environment, the sorcerer and cannibal becoming as commonplace acquaintances as his school friends, the pendulum will naturally swing in the opposite direction. Instead of a group of uncanny beings, he now sees an idyll of the type imagined by Rousseau. Human beings untrammelled by the cares and conventions of civilization, innocent children who lead a happy life where all is love, play and good-fellowship. He does not notice that he is also reacting against the opposite extreme, unmitigated racial hatred,

as manifested in the opinions of the white trader with whom he comes into contact. (Róheim 1932: 16–17)

This passage speaks volumes to the contemporary situation in which the meanings of culture and childhood in Aboriginal communities are subject to intense public debate. Most significantly, it cautions against confusing methodological and ethical relativism and suggests that rigorous reflexivity is needed to avoid their conflation.

It is clear that, while Róheim wants to say that Aboriginal children 'lead a happy life', he does not want to say that this life is free of problems, anxieties and aggression. As a psychoanalytically trained anthropologist, he was aware that to address the first matter without paying attention to the latter would betray an unanalysed positive transference relationship with informants[14] – what he called 'idealizing the native beyond measure' (1932: 17). The opposite situation was implicit in his analysis of the early Lutherans who, in claiming that the 'good Aranda' were all 'sinners', were projecting negative sentiments about themselves as a result of having internalized a typically severe nineteenth-century version of 'sadistic pedagogy'. Such 'demonizing' of Aboriginal people in turn reserved the image of 'good people' for the Lutherans themselves – although not from an Indigenous point of view. It would be true to say that Róheim thought one could not be an adequate anthropologist without also being an adequate psychoanalyst (1932: 7), although he naturally could not foretell the future and anthropology's later postmodern dedication to reflexivity (Marcus 1998: 181–202).

Several anthropologists have recently focussed public debate on Aboriginal children being corrupted by problems partly internal to Aboriginal society. In a much-publicized essay and subsequent book, Sutton (2001, 2009) made a plea for anthropologists and others of liberal persuasion to reconsider their view of classical Aboriginal cultures, particularly in view of the recent descent into dysfunction in remote settlements, where 'culture' is ostensibly most strong. Amongst other things, Sutton highlighted the need for 'more and better ethnography … on how violence is learned by the growing child' (2001: 155), illustrating his case with some examples of child-rearing practices. As indicated earlier, he particularly drew attention to the practice of 'cruelling' infants to make them more assertive (2009: 111–12), but he also mentioned children's witnessing of accepted violent behaviour by men towards women (2009: 113–14)[15] and the way in which children's (especially boys') tantrums are tolerated, leading to 'irrational demanding behaviour of adult men over women' and ensuing 'overt aggression' (Hamilton 1981: 151, cited in Sutton 2001: 156). Sutton suggested that, while such learned aggression may have been 'extremely useful training' under classical sociopolitical conditions, it was likely to be counterproductive in contemporary circumstances (2001: 156–57). He does not suggest that 'post-conquest, historical factors of external impact' are irrelevant to an understanding of dysfunction, but he does suggest that the specific form which dysfunction takes must be analysed as a problem of genuine articulation rather than mere imposition (2001: 127), if only to undermine the romantic undercurrents which have driven ideas about 'culture' and 'self-determination' since the 1970s (Sutton 2009: 63–86).

A cognate case was put much more bluntly and provocatively by Maddock (2001) in a paper on the recognition of customary law. Citing Robert Tonkinson's (1982) work in the Western Desert, he noted how children's behaviour there was seemingly sliding into chaos after the mission era, in part due to the collapse of a missionary regime and in part due to parents' 'reluctance to interfere with children's autonomy' (Tonkinson cited in Maddock 2001: 160). He continued:

> What he [Tonkinson] called children's autonomy looks more like a euphemism for Brat Power. In effect, the little horrors blackmailed their parents who were afraid to take action against promiscuity, vandalism and breaking and entering. … [M]ission paternalism had relieved parents of most of the responsibility for bringing up children. … In fact, much that the missionaries did was appreciated by Aboriginal adults, if only because it relieved them from a range of responsibilities. When government policy imposed 'self-management' the adults found themselves not only free of missionaries but destitute of ideas on how to cope. (Maddock 2001: 160)

Sandall's (2001)[16] take on these and related matters located the problem in social contract theory, his polemical suggestion being that Indigenous community dysfunction in general came about in the era of 'self-management' (or 'self-determination') as result of an academic and political love affair with the Rousseauian idea of the 'noble savage'[17] and the subsequent creation of remote Indigenous communities as 'ethnographic zoos' full of 'vocationally disabled' people dwelling in a 'New Stone Age' (2001: 17). Echoing Róheim's warnings about ethnographic transference, Sandall also diagnosed the way in which the alleged 'goodness' of alterity and 'self-determination' is constantly hitched to a resentful critique of modernity (Sandall 2001: 95–97, 151–52, 176–77). However, he failed to register the extent to which his sweeping generalizations about 'bad primitive culture' and 'good modern civilization' mirrored this very same resentment from a Hobbesian position (Morton 2001). In fact, public debate had for some years previously been engaged with the spectre of Hobbes in relation to the forced removal of Aboriginal children from their families, with suggestions that these children had been 'rescued' rather than 'stolen' (Manne 2001: 47–48) from conditions in which life was, as Hobbes famously put it, 'solitary, poor, nasty, brutish and short' (Manne 2001: 56).[18] It is noteworthy, too, that ex-prime minister John Howard justified the State's recent radical turn towards 'coercive reconciliation' in the Northern Territory by stating: 'In our rich and beautiful country, there are children living out a Hobbesian nightmare of violence, abuse and neglect' (Howard 2007:1).

When, as in Sandall's case, anthropological insight gets wedded to a wholly polemical agenda, it is necessarily compromised or corrupted. Similarly, accounts of Aboriginal dysfunction suffer from the related problem of what Marcia Langton calls 'public spectacle', particularly in relation to the recent 'accelerated and uncensored exposé of the extent of Aboriginal child abuse' (Langton 2008a: 145). In her view, this spectacle is not only 'obscene and pornographic' (Langton 2008a: 145), but is also appropriated by Left and Right alike to function as alibis for the schismatic vanities of the so-called 'culture wars' – vanities which have 'very little to do with Aboriginal people' (Langton 2008a: 161). Between a Rousseauian Left, which according to Langton requires 'perpetual victims for their analysis to work' (2008a: 146), and a Hobbesian Right, which seeks willy-nilly to 'impose punitive measures on entire populations' (Langton 2008a: 156), it can be difficult to find room for a 'radical centre' (Pearson 2007) to emerge.

Róheim's take on the social contract in Central Australia contains an implicit critique of extreme Hobbesian and Rousseauian positions in relation to classical Aboriginal culture, as well as an implicit endorsement of a more dialectical approach to understanding Aboriginal childhood. In her criticism of Sutton's remarks on Aboriginal childhood, Cowlishaw suggests that Aboriginal children's autonomy might be construed as 'the legitimation of desire' forming the 'foundation for a fully realised, *self-disciplined* human personality' (2003b: 9). In fact, this view approaches, but is not identical with, Róheim's position on the Central Australian social contract. Róheim's findings do not support Cowlishaw's suggestion that 'indulged children … allowed a considerable degree of autonomy' might not be irresponsible or 'undisciplined' (2003b: 9), since it is clear that 'techniques of intimidation' occurring at adolescence are designed to *create* responsibility through discipline. On the other hand, Róheim does support the view that childhood autonomy is a *foundation* upon which these techniques build.

It is clear, for example, that Róheim follows an orthodox line in endorsing paternalist regulation and superego development as 'the Freudian counterpart to the social contract of Hobbes' (Roy 1984: 68), for just as Hobbes spoke of the human tendency towards war 'of every man' and 'against every man' (1968[1651]: 185), so did Freud describe the inherent 'hostility of each against all and all against each' which continually opposes the 'programme of civilization' (2001[1930]: 122). On the other hand, a purely Hobbesian take on culture and civilization wrongly assumes, as Rousseau pointed out, that humanity is 'naturally wicked' (1973[1755]: 65) – a claim which founders on extensive evidence for 'the force of natural compassion' (Rousseau 1973[1755]: 67). As I have shown, Róheim fundamentally locates this force in the maternal order of Central Australian childhood. His position is also Rousseauian to the extent that the maternal order involves the education of children in genuine self-interest. While Róheim favoured the Freudian term *narcissism* to describe this situation, particularly in relation to the erection of an ego ideal, Rousseau spoke simply of authentic 'love of self' as 'a natural feeling which leads every animal to look to its own preservation, and which, guided in man by reason and modified by compassion, creates humanity and virtue' (1973[1755]: 66). For Róheim, Aboriginal childhood, far from being a Hobbesian state, is preparation for a necessary ensuing onslaught of Hobbesian forces – but forces which were peculiar to 'primitive' rather than 'modern' conditions.

Les Hiatt has suggested that Aboriginal initiation rituals are not 'programmes in preventive medicine' and that they do not appear to be 'necessary for normal male sexual development' (Hiatt 1987: 97). More significantly, Hiatt says that, while initiation certainly brought about 'abiding submission to collective male authority', there does not appear to be:

> any evidence to suggest that, after European colonisation and the decline of traditional religion, Aboriginal males in increasing numbers began to suffer from unresolved Oedipus complexes and attendant abnormalities in sexual behaviour. (1987: 97)

Yet this seems to flatly contradict the Indigenous idea that uninitiated youths are in danger of turning into 'devils', so, in light of Róheim's analysis, it is worth asking what 'unresolved Oedipus complexes' and 'attendant abnormalities' might consist of.

The explicit purpose of initiation – both male *and* female – is to *set limits*, particularly in matters of sexual propriety, since adult standards in this matter are quite the opposite of those of children. Annette Hamilton, for example, draws attention to the 'extraordinary contrast' between, on the one hand, the overt obscenities characteristically uttered (violent cursing and swearing)[19] or acted out by children (and tolerated by adults) and, on the other hand, mature comportment marked by restraint, the

'greatest modesty' and public silence on 'the question of sexual connection' (1979a: 273).[20] At the same time, however,

> the entire realm of symbolic activity, of myth and story, of dance, de-
> sign and song, of ritual actions and even interpretations of the physi-
> cal landscape, is filled with a discourse which relates to sexuality. This
> interpretation … is explicitly stated by those producing the symbols;
> stated, that is, in reference to Others [Ancestors], not themselves, and
> to another Time [The Dreaming], not their own, when these objects and
> events were not symbolic but real. … They refer … not to the modified
> and modest sexual activities of normal human beings, but to the fanta-
> sised, perhaps hallucinated, images of sexuality such as might exist in
> the earliest mental representations. (Hamilton 1979a: 274)

What Róheim specifically showed, however, was that the 'sexual
activities of normal human beings' were not at all 'modest' in the symbolism of folktales. Rather, they were completely *absent* and ranged
against the utterly *immodest* libidinal strivings of 'devils'. Initiation into
adult life serves to *create* modesty. More specifically, it creates *shame* –
a sentiment which, while initially corresponding to childhood shyness
and fear of strangers (Myers 1986: 120), differs from the latter in being
a sentiment prompted from within and by respect. Shame distinguishes
a proper human being from 'egotism, selfishness, individuality, or "ani-
mality"' (Myers 1986: 121), just as it distinguishes those who pursue appropriate sexual relations from the 'promiscuity of dogs' (Myers 1986:
123) – dogs being one of the favoured reference points for the projection
of the primal scene onto 'demons' (Róheim 1934: 28–29; Eickelkamp
2004: 172, 174–76). The presence of such promiscuity represents a failure of the Law – in Freudian terms, the failure of the superego as 'those
aspects of the psyche which attempt to rule the person through a claim
of higher authority' (Bettelheim 1985: 59). 'Monsters' who escape the
Law are those with 'no shame'; neither do they have 'authority' or 'take
responsibility' for their actions.

Towards Aboriginal Modernity

More modern Hobbesian forces were brought to bear in Central Australia in 2007. In April that year Rex Wild and Pat Anderson submitted to
the Northern Territory Government a report which carried the short title
'Little Children Are Sacred' – its long title being 'Report of the Northern
Territory Board of Inquiry into the Protection of Aboriginal Children from
Sexual Abuse' (Wild and Anderson 2007). The report, like others before
it and like others since (e.g., Mullighan 2008), dramatically captured
the public imagination. In June 2007 the report was used by the federal

government to justify 'national emergency' measures (or what has since come to be known simply as 'the Intervention') ostensibly designed to eradicate child sexual abuse. Having suspended the Racial Discrimination Act, the government implemented the restriction of alcohol consumption in all seventy-three Northern Territory Aboriginal settlements, quarantined welfare payments to families, enforced school attendance, implemented compulsory health checks, altered land lease arrangements, policed law and order, promised to clean up community living spaces, introduced market-driven pricing for housing, banned pornography, increased public media coverage of community life and sought to improve local governance (M. Hinkson 2007: 1–2). Such radical measures, to be backed by a Foucauldian force of army, police and medical staff, were unprecedented in Aboriginal affairs. While the Intervention was justified by the federal government and its supporters as a matter of duty of care to vulnerable citizens, it was also widely interpreted as nothing more than 'punitive action' and 'top-down, paternalistic imposition' (Behrendt 2007: 15–16) disguising 'a sinister destination for Australian nation building' through a new form of 'cultural genocide' (Behrendt 2007: 23). Hence, much of the ensuing debate was concentrated as a battle for sacred ground under two totemic flags – 'the rights of the child' (as part of a suite of universal human rights) and the right 'to preserve the integrity of Indigenous cultural assumptions' (J. Hinkson 2007: 293).

The 'Little Children Are Sacred' report (Wild and Anderson 2007: 57–59) set out to dispel a number of 'myths' about the involvement of Aboriginal men, law and culture in violence and child abuse. It also drew attention to the historical circumstances of Northern Territory Aboriginal communities which have led to a serious disruption of law and culture, particularly mentioning problems with alcohol consumption, drug use and petrol sniffing related to boredom, poverty, unemployment and poor education and housing – all said to be implicated in 'excessive violence', with 'the worst case scenario' being the 'sexual abuse of children' (Wild and Anderson 2007: 12). The report went on to recount a stark example of this 'worst case scenario' involving four closely interrelated cases of anal rape occurring between 1972 and 2004, adding that all 'Australians should know of the problems' (2007: 12). 'The problems' are, however, subject to definition, and the report admitted that its notions of child sexual abuse were built on ideas abroad in 'the white Western world' (2007: 42), noting in particular the disjunction between definitions of coming of age in Aboriginal culture and definitions informing the Northern Territory Criminal Code (2007: 43). While it may be true that it is 'too easy' for naïve commentators (Kimm 2004, Kearney and Wilson 2006 and Nowra 2007 are mentioned in the report) to create or reinforce the

'myth' of Aboriginal law and culture being 'the real problem' in high levels of Aboriginal child abuse (Wild and Anderson 2007: 57), disjunctions
such as the one mentioned above do highlight the difficulties attached
to attempts to mutually accommodate 'two laws' and formally calibrate
two styles of conscience[21] and sexual propriety, one 'primitive' and easily perceived as either 'natural' or 'vulgar', the other 'modern' and easily
perceived as either 'morbid' or 'refined'.

A child in purely Hobbesian clothing is a danger to society, so I find
it unsurprising to see pronouncements about Aboriginal children's 'Brat
Power' in contemporary discourses aligned with policies of strong and
coercive intervention in Aboriginal communities. The same Hobbesian
attire often cloaks images of Aboriginal communities as being either in-
trinsically violent or dilapidated in the face of European colonization.
It has been argued that the unleashing of Leviathan under the guise of
humanitarian concern for child welfare tends to cast Indigenous populations as abusive because, in some measure, Indigenous children fail
to live up to some standardized image of civilized childhood (Pupavac
2001). On the other hand, such Rousseauian vision fails to register how
Indigenous children might actually be judged to be in need of protection
within some schematic notion of (universal) 'human rights'. The matter is
profoundly contradictory, so that questions about the ethical dimensions
of Aboriginal parenting and childhood are fraught with the dangers of
what Róheim described as transferential moral certitude. Langton's 'public spectacle' of Aboriginality in its 'obscene and pornographic' guise is
one manifestation of this certitude, but 'play[ing] with the warm, cuddly
cultural Aborigine' (Langton 2008a: 161) is another. There can be no
doubt that Aborigines are at their 'warmest and cuddliest', their most
Rousseauian, when they are children – hence the latter's constant appearance on postcards and in other media.[22] Equally, Aborigines are at
their most 'obscene and pornographic' when they are these very same
children sexually abused and subject to neglect. It is clear from Róheim's
descriptions, as well as other ethnographic accounts, that under classical
conditions, Aborigines did not sentimentalize children in the way that
each of these attitudes entails.[23] The emotional economy was different
and indeed coarser by comparison.

However, in Róheim's Central Australia, as well as elsewhere in the
Northern Territory up until the 1960s, there appears to have been little
to no evidence of explicit child sexual abuse or related paraphilias. An
early investigation into 'sex training and traditions' in Arnhem Land concluded that there were very few 'ascertainable examples of male sexual
behaviour that might be classed as disorder or misdemeanour', but that
the few cases in question were more or less exclusive to a minority of

'youths who had the monopoly of delinquency, stealing and petrol sniff-ing' (Money et al. 1973: 412; cf. Pearson 2000: 37–38; Sutton 2001: 128–30). This supports the 'Little Children Are Sacred' report's suggestion that it is not 'Aboriginal culture' in the round, but rather the decline of proper local authority, which is critical in the understanding of increased sexual abuse:

> A constant theme during the Inquiry's consultations was that Aboriginal children had become unruly, disrespectful and lawless. The Inquiry was told that in many communities, the younger generations are living in anarchy and associated with this is rampant promiscuity and violence.[24] This is seen as a major contributing factor to children being vulnerable to sexual abuse and also perpetrating abuse. (Wild and Anderson 2007: 72)

As indicated above, the 'Little Children Are Sacred' report gave a number of reasons why Central Australian children might now experience increasing failure of 'the facilitating environment' (Winnicott 1965a). There are many others, including the poor ecological balance between classical parenting practices, service delivery, poverty and semiurban dwelling (Hamilton 1982) and an expanding, increasingly youthful pop-ulation (Boulden and Morton 2007: 168; Caldwell 2002). One would reasonably expect increasing failure to be felt systematically in both ma-ternal and paternal registers, in relation to both ego and superego devel-opment. Naturally, the failure will appear as 'part of the culture', since there is no 'not part of the culture' where it could realistically be located. For the same reason it is equally true that remedial measures, success-ful or otherwise, must also appear as 'part of the culture'. If Aboriginal culture is not overobjectified, but rather seen as an 'interplay between "unreflexive daily practice" … and our partial awareness of what we are doing and thinking' (Sutton 2001: 135), then it is tantamount to what Róheim would have called a dialogue with the unconscious. With cul-ture thus defined, arriving at 'culturally appropriate' solutions to failures of the facilitating environment can only be a kind of therapeutic exercise for all concerned. But there is no therapy which does not encounter re-sistance to the truth of its problematic situation.

Although the 'Little Children Are Sacred' report was keen to not blame 'Aboriginal culture' for child abuse, it did state:

> It would be helpful if dialogue began with Aboriginal people with a view to determining the strengths and weaknesses of traditional child-rearing practices in a modern context. Measures could then be put in place to build on the strengths and deal with the weaknesses. (Wild and Anderson 2007: 72)

How can it be that such seemingly contradictory attitudes exist within the framework of the report? The short answer is that its authors are negotiating the contradiction between what Kowal calls 'the two pillars of post-colonial logic: remedialism and Orientalism' (2008: 343) – the desire to bring about change by way of 'practical reconciliation' and the desire to maintain difference by way of 'symbolic reconciliation'. While remedialism is about reducing a *quantitative difference* between Aborigines and other Australian citizens measured by a battery of statistics indicating Aboriginal disadvantage, Orientalism – or positive 'primitivism' (Kowal 2008: 342) – is about the magnification of incommensurable *qualitative difference*. For Róheim, following Freud, the difference between primitives and moderns is explicitly quantitative, measured in terms of less and more repression. But the difference also has qualitative dimensions, since modern children are said to be introduced more systematically to shame and conscience at a much earlier age, leading to the desexualization of childhood, greater sublimation and a more intense sense of refinement in adult life.[25] In relation to remedialism, this appears to have everything to do with 'the critical and central role of the socialisation of children' in bringing about 'deep and dramatic cultural change' (Sutton 2001: 136). But it is surely just as relevant to the 'Orientalist' push of the civilizing process which seeks to fashion Aborigines into a 'deeply spiritual people' (*cf.* Sandall 2001: 179–81).

Kowal makes the point that the attempt to close the gap between Aborigines and other Australians in the register of practical reconciliation is in fact an attempt to raise them to the standards of 'White, middle class, educated people' (2008: 343). But the attempt to maintain qualitative difference is merely the other side to the coin in this assimilationist project, since such difference is modelled on an idea of Aboriginality which contains 'all that is congruent with liberal morality: songs, dances, art and stories' (Kowal 2008: 344). When the coin is flipped back again this same 'good Aborigine' becomes the 'bad Aborigine', the bearer of 'all that is dissonant with liberal morality: fighting, drinking, eating fast food, and … the sexual abuse of children' (Kowal 2008: 344). Either way, the desired image is quite the opposite of the Aboriginal culture of 'the children of the desert' witnessed by Róheim in 1929.

Conclusion

I have shown how Róheim found the elementary form of the social contract in Central Australia. Unlike Freud (2001 [1913]), whose 'primal horde' account of the original social contract was heavily skewed towards the

Hobbesian paternal order, Róheim was equally emphatic about the maternal order, childhood and the contract's Rousseauian dimensions – a synthetic mix of narcissism, personal autonomy, aggressive self-assertion, vigorous demanding behaviour, spontaneous generosity and sympathetic identification with others. This, while organically limited by the rigours of adolescent initiation, was the basic building block of the mature moral universe. However, Róheim and Freud were as one in their understanding of the paternal order being the source of the limiting effect. They were also as one in emphasizing the widening and deepening of the range of superegoic effects in the transition from primitive to modern social conditions: 'The main difference between Central Australians and Europeans', said Róheim, 'lies not in the id, but in the range, depth, and function of the superego' (Róheim 1974: 255).[26]

Freud's idea of the superego as a 'garrison inside a conquered city' (*see above*) calls to mind the Foucauldian idea of governmentality (Foucault 1991) and the way in which modern government has diffused power through the strategies of discipline, punishment, correction and 'normalization' (Foucault 1979: 308) – what Róheim called, without irony, 'the advantages of education' (1974: 255). One result of this education was that sexually 'knowing children' seemingly disappeared among the 'Victorian bourgeoisie' (Foucault 1981: 3), in whose mores children's sexuality was systematically occluded (Foucault 1981: 4), so that the ideal child was both 'innocent and natural', as well as 'inherently dependent and helpless' (Hart 2006: 6). But, while this ideal child came to inform the Victorian philanthropic movement (Hart 2006: 6), the same repression and articulation of taboo served to 'invent' sex as a central aspect of modern human identity, most particularly in relation to the distinction between 'normality' and 'perversity', with the latter being discursively and actively generated as a polymorphous phenomenon in its own right (Foucault 1981: 36–49). Morbid fascination and moral panic inspired by actual and imagined cases of paedophilia, which rapidly mobilize 'child savers' against 'folk devils' (de Young 2004),[27] suggest that child sexual abuse is now regarded as the very epitome of all that is perverse and 'unnatural'. As Freud 2001[1919] himself illustrated in detail, children subject to what Róheim called sadistic 'exhibitions of power' exercise a powerful, convoluted and nontransparent influence on the human imagination.

Róheim's Freudian emphasis on the timing of superego development in Central Australia is of critical importance in this regard. I have shown how Róheim connected this with what he called 'sadistic pedagogy' associated with 'corporal punishment' and 'preaching'. However, superego development is associated with a much larger range of phenomena than this might imply, since limitations on ego expansion are also inaugurated by emotional discipline and the anxiety which stems from a more general 'fear of loss of love' (Freud 2001[1930]: 124). As practising analysts dealing systematically with patients' neuroses, both Freud and Róheim emphasized the manner in which the superego 'tortures' (Róheim, *see above*) or 'torments' (Freud 2001[1930]: 125) modern subjects. Freud especially noted that those 'who have carried saintliness furthest' tend to be the very same people who 'reproach themselves with the worst sinfulness' (2001[1930]: 126), so that the highest moralism is tightly bound to the strongest feelings of temptation to sin. This not only matches Foucault's claim that sexual normality and sexual perversity are two sides of the same coin, but also has implications for how we interpret the economy of love and aggression in the discursive and practical interventions in the lives of Aboriginal citizens, particularly in relation to matters of child abuse and neglect.

The superego is the voice of conscience, and I have used Róheim's investigations to show how this voice was constructed under classical conditions. It is important to understand that this construction, particularly in its connection with initiation, is ideally and practically constructed as a form of care. It is what Róheim called 'mitigated' aggression – that is, aggression tempered by fellow feeling and sympathy derived from the maternal order (Róheim 1945a: 75, 1945b: 135). It has been more recently documented as the 'looking after' or 'holding' of initiates as a specific conflation of 'authority' and 'nurturance' (Myers 1986: 236). Hence, if it is to *result* in good conscience, initiation must be *performed* in good conscience – which is to say that 'sadistic pedagogy' must not signal an excessive 'loss of love'.[28] It is, however, certainly the case that, within this frame, coercion can – indeed *should* – be performed under the rubric of 'duty of care'.

It has been suggested that Róheim's writings betray a degree of 'hostility to [modern] culture', but that he shared neither 'the tortured acquiescence of Freud' in the face of modern forms of repression nor 'the unqualified opposition of [writers such as] Herbert Marcuse' (Robinson 1972: 64; *cf.* Freud 2001[1930]; Marcuse 1955). I do not think, therefore, that it is quite right to say that Róheim 'was heir to a long tradition of primitivism in European thought' (Robinson 1972: 111), because, while Róheim himself actually stated that psychoanalysis was marked by 'its hostility to culture', even speaking of advanced civilization's 'insane methods' of education, he nevertheless agreed that analysis also 'tries to make us capable of sublimation' (Róheim 1934: 244) – that is, of moving on successfully to 'higher things'. In this context, he quotes Otto Fenichel's observation:

The child who learns to write well and with special inner participation has transferred anal erotic impulses to his writing just as much as the child who smudges his page and displays inhibitions of the writing function. But in the first child we find a sublimation; he does not want to smudge, he wants to write. In the second child, this canalization of the impulse has not succeeded. (cited in Róheim 1934: 245)

At no stage did Róheim speculate about the potential for Aborigines to enjoy such sublimation over the long term, but it is evident that this is *exactly* what the contradiction between 'remedialism' and 'Orientalism' is about. Listen, for example, to Louis Nowra:

Indigenous communities have to recognise that they are part of Australian society and integrate into their cultural sensibility the idea of personal and individual responsibility for their actions. Furthermore, they need to accept that certain aspects of their traditional culture … are best forgotten. … If [abusive] men refuse to do anything then they are responsible for the slow death of the many wonderful aspects of their culture, traditions and customs. (Nowra 2007: 92–93)

In this frame, the remedialist death ('forgetting') of 'certain aspects of … traditional culture' would actually be the Orientalist birth ('re-membering') of those 'wonderful aspects of … culture, traditions and customs' – a substitution of 'the normal' for 'the perverse'. Nowhere would the complex processes of such sublimation be more apparent than in the recent 'making of an Aboriginal high art' (Myers 2002).

In that light, we could legitimately ask what a Róheimian approach to the Northern Territory Intervention might look like. In my view, it would begin by emphasizing that in myth, if not so simply in history, the Australian nation conceived its Indigenous citizens through the idea of assimilation, eventually giving birth to them as 'the First Australians' through the 1967 referendum (Attwood 2007). It would continue by saying that conception, birth and recognition were followed by a growing sense of aggressively asserted Aboriginal autonomy (Coombs 1994), nurtured by an obliging parental regime of 'passive welfare' and 'service delivery' (Pearson 2000: 43). And it would finish by saying that the contemporary passage from 'rights' to 'responsibility' (Pearson 2000) is the necessary paternal imposition of a limit, and thus a kind of initiation or turning point apparently signalling 'the death knell of the self-determination era' (Kowal 2008: 345). I say 'apparently' because Róheim knew well enough that initiation, as a drama of death and rebirth, substituted one kind of autonomy ('self-determination') for another, thus realizing what Myers calls an 'increase in value' (1986: 236).

It would follow from this that modern Australia engages with its own maternal and paternal orders, which devolve broadly into a kind of moiety system where the (Rousseauian) left opposes the (Hobbesian) right and vice versa. We know from another study that the strategic deployment of child abuse in Western democratic public life emerges partly because it 'functions as a generative metaphor, serving to displace other collective unconscious anxieties and contradictions' concerning the fate of children, so that abuse is not only an actual behaviour, but also a 'cultural fantasy' implicated in 'blaming, scapegoating, and stereotyping' certain sectors of the population (Scheper-Hughes and Stein 1987: 341). We also know that the Northern Territory Intervention was the culmination of a long process in which the legitimacy of related interference had been fiercely debated in relation to the 'Stolen Generations' (Manne 2001) and therefore the rights and wrongs of the policies of 'assimilation' (in the mid-twentieth century) and 'self-determination' (in the late twentieth century). Each of these policies has been simultaneously accused of being responsible for the abuse of Aboriginal children *and* praised for the saving of those very same children (e.g., Wilson 1997; Bolt 2006).

As I write, a highly crafted national mythology, simply called *Australia,* is being screened in Australian cinemas. Although up against the likes of Nicole Kidman and Hugh Jackman, not to mention seasoned Aboriginal actor David Gulpilil, a young and previously unknown Aboriginal child actor, Brandon Walters, remains the undisputed star of the film. At once sentimentalized as 'cute', 'gorgeous looking', 'captivating', 'natural' and 'the heart and soul' of the film,[29] the half-caste character he plays, Nullah, is central to the film's redemptive structure, as he becomes the object of the childless White heroine's love and affection (after the script has his Aboriginal mother drown). Set at the beginning of the assimilation era, and against the backdrop of a cattle station called Faraway Downs, this contemporary love affair with an Aboriginal child is, for some, a 'fabulous … myth of national origin' carrying 'a credible rendition' of the severe anxieties experienced by half-caste children during the assimilation era (Langton 2008b); for others, it is a 'fraudulent and misleading' fairy tale whitewashing the deprivations inherent in those very same experiences and in their legacy (Greer 2008). Perhaps, however, like all myths and fairy tales, *Australia* is a compromise formation dealing with profound contradictions in the present, since

> the relationship of one historical formation to another, like that of one type of man to another, will never be simply the relationship of true to false. The 'healthy' man is not so much the one who has eliminated his contradictions as the one who makes use of them and drags them into his vital labours. (Merleau-Ponty 1964: 131)

In light of Róheim's comments about sublimation, we might equally well say that a 'healthy' country is the one which similarly negotiates its paradoxes. For in post-Apology Australia, one cannot bring the past into the present – that is, *make history* – without also assigning it to a land long ago and far away.

Notes

I am grateful to a number of people for assistance in the writing of this paper, particularly Ute Eickelkamp, who proffered a number of very useful editorial suggestions and helped me impose some structure on the argument, and Peter Sutton, who subjected an earlier draft to some vigorous constructive criticism. I also thank Jenny Green and David Wilkins for assistance with the interpretation of Arandic languages. All errors in the paper are, of course, my own, not theirs.

1. While Róheim discusses the Central Australian 'ego-ideal', he does not differentiate it from the 'ideal ego' – and in this he followed Freud, who used the concepts without distinction (Laplanche and Pontalis 1985: 201). While I cannot discuss the matter in detail here, there are a number of reasons why a distinction between the 'ego-ideal' and the 'ideal ego' is important (Laplanche and Pontalis 1985: 201–02), and I have elsewhere briefly discussed the significance of the distinction for understanding the passage from early infancy to latency in Central Australian childhood (Morton 1989: 282–83). Róheim's ethnography of children is quantitatively biased towards an understanding of the latency period and therefore the Central Australian ego-ideal, as well as secondary narcissism. His discussion of earlier childhood and the formation of the ideal ego in primary narcissism, while not insignificant, is less rich and informative by comparison. On the distinction between primary and secondary narcissism, see Laplanche and Pontalis (1985: 255–57).

2. Depitarinja was the most prominent child in the Hermannsburg playgroup and, while Róheim confessed to know not nearly enough about him, he stated that 'Depitarinja was in 1932 the best-known primitive child in the world' (due to Róheim's 1932 publication of *Psycho-Analysis of Primitive Cultural Types*). Róheim gives a personal profile for Depitarinja in the first volume of *Children of the Desert* (1974: 102–05; also see 1932: 26–27), interestingly commenting on the 'strong transference relationship' which existed between Depitarinja and both Róheim himself and his wife (1974: 103). T. G. H. Strehlow has stated that Depitarinja 'was *not* regarded by his own relatives or playmates as a "normal" Aranda boy, but as a difficult problem child' (1971: xlii), although Róheim himself describes Depitarinja as a habitual thief living in the mission 'boys' house, where homosexual practices and sadomasochistic perversions were rife' (1974: 105). Nevertheless, Róheim thought Depitarinja to be 'a bright, intelligent boy, full of life and fun' (1974: 103), sociable and of 'good temper' (1974: 105).

3. Róheim thought Wili-kutu (or Wilikutuku) to be 'about nine years old' (1974: 107). He also stated that he was sexually active as 'a passive homosexual, the "boy wife" of his future father-in-law, with whom he camped' (1974: 117). Ritual homosexuality in Central Australia is connected to initiation, in which a young

man's father-in-law typically acts as circumciser. Róheim states that, although Wili-kutu was in a 'passive homosexual' relationship, this 'had not deprived him of his virile temperament. He missed no opportunity to give the [play]group and myself evidence of his virility' (1974: 117). Wili-kutu's aggressive leadership of the Western Desert children's playgroup is evident from Róheim's fullest description of the play sessions held at Tempe Downs (1974: 106–17).

4. Strehlow states that Róheim's findings in relation to such matters should be 'treated with care' on account of Róheim never having actually witnessed concrete evidence of cannibalism (1971: xlii). However, in an accompanying footnote Strehlow goes further and says, 'These allegations of cannibalism must be regarded as untrue, since no positive evidence has ever been advanced in their support' (1971: xlii). Strehlow does not comment on infanticide, but the basis of his judgement on child cannibalism as being 'untrue' rather than 'unproven' is obscure. In my view, Róheim would have regarded mere *reports* of cannibalism as sufficient evidence of parental aggression towards children, even if such aggression was infrequently inflicted. In fact, Róheim argued that, in the main, parents were 'protective' of their children, tending more to project 'their cannibalistic and libidinal propensities onto … demons' (1974: 73). I discuss these 'demons' in more detail below.

5. One commentator has accused Róheim of duplicity in this regard, suggesting that the material on childhood in Róheim deals in euphemisms calculated to disguise a world of endemic parental neglect (Hippler 1978: 228–29). However, there seems to be no real substance to Hippler's criticism, which appears in a paper that has been convincingly demonstrated to be so academically deficient as to be highly unreliable (Hamilton 1979b; Pastner 1982; Reser 1981, 1982; *also see* Hippler 1981). I note that Hippler's 1978 criticism of Róheim refers to a 1932 paper titled 'Children of the Desert' which Róheim allegedly published in the *International Journal of Psychiatry* (Hippler 1978: 244). No such paper exists; the correct reference is to pages 23–37 of Róheim's 1932 field report in the *International Journal of Psycho-Analysis.* I note, too, that Lloyd deMause (2002: 229–84) consistently duplicates the content, tenor and associations of Hippler's criticisms of Róheim and often (seven times) cites Hippler approvingly, almost entirely ignoring the convincing negative criticisms which Hippler's paper has received. In chapter 7 of *The Origins of War in Child Abuse,* in a section provocatively titled 'Murder, Rape and Torture of Australian Aboriginal Children', deMause (n.d.) has written: 'Roheim calls the constant rape of Aboriginal children "far more 'normal' than the sexuality of the European male" since "their repression of sexuality need not be as deep as it is among Europeans."' In fact, Róheim said absolutely nothing about 'the constant rape of Aboriginal children'. The relevant quote, extended in full, reads: 'The sexual life and potency of the Australian male is far more "normal" than the sexuality of the European male. This is undoubtedly due to the fact that he has received fewer of the advantages of education. While he still must repress his incestuous desires, the repression need not be as deep as it is among Europeans, and therefore the sexual impulses are not as fatefully distorted' (1974: 255). It is true to say that Róheim was often an incautious writer (Morton 1988: xii), but nowhere have I found evidence of him deliberately distorting his material in the manner shown by deMause.

6. Although not a consistent one. For example, at one point Róheim follows Freud and writes as if the ego-ideal and superego are the same thing (Róheim 1945b: 136–37).

7. However, Nancy Munn (1973) was to later come to related findings in relation to Warlpiri iconography when she discussed the early learning of basic graphic forms and the extension and elaboration of these designs in adult life. There are also related findings in Fred Myers's Pintupi ethnography, particularly in relation to the origins of the idea of *kanyininpa* ('holding', 'looking after') in the mother/child dyad and its extension across broader fields of responsibility (Myers 1986: 212).

8. *See* Myers (1986: 120–24) on the idea of shame in Central Australia. It is clear from Myers's account that shame has to be understood in a number of senses ranging from shyness and embarrassment to respect and avoidance. At this juncture I am particularly emphasizing the more severe forms of respect typified by affinal avoidance relationships (Myers 1986: 123; *also see* Róheim 1974: 28–30).

9. This remark perhaps needs clarifying, since it appears that Róheim is saying two completely contradictory things – that Aboriginal people 'certainly have a superego' and that the 'tortures … carried out by the old men at initiation' are 'not introjected by the young'. I think this is a typical case of Róheimian overstatement. I believe the intended meaning is that the introjected superego in Central Australia is shallow when compared with its scope under modern conditions. I return to this matter in more detail below.

10. Strehlow repeats a not uncommon charge against Róheim: 'I was assured that some of his native informants had gone to a great deal of trouble in thinking out fresh matter in order to please the Freudian tastes of their erudite investigator' (1971: 464). Of course, while this may well be true, it is also true that one would expect Aborigines to go to 'a great deal of trouble' to present more 'decently' to other investigators – including Strehlow himself, who was the son of Lutheran missionary Carl Strehlow. This is simply an aspect of the fieldwork transference relationships which Róheim regarded as 'the basis of all anthropological work' (*see above*).

11. Compare this with what is stated in footnote 5. It seems to me that such unreflexive 'disgust and horror' is readily apparent in Hippler's account of Yolngu parenting and childhood. *Also see* footnote 14 for further discussion of this.

12. *Also see* Berndt and Berndt (1951: 87) for a parallel assessment of the situation in Arnhem Land: 'There is no morbidity expressed in this [childhood] preoccupation with sex. … Their whole attitude towards sex is of natural growth, and their behaviour, within conventional limits, requires no external censure nor repression'. The Berndts reported a similar situation at Ooldea: 'At an early age the child is aware of the functions of the male and female bodies and the manifestations of sex. He has a natural attitude towards it. … Sex … is centred round the direct reference to the functions of the genital organs, to the formulae of love magic, pre-coitus love-play and the sexual act. … These Ooldea people have a great interest, perhaps a predominant interest, in the erotic' (Berndt and Berndt 1945: 16). Contrasting 'natural growth' and 'a natural attitude' with Western 'morbidity' and (what Strehlow calls) 'prurience' perhaps betrays something of

a romantic outlook on Aboriginal sexuality. On Strehlow's struggles to come to terms with Aboriginal sexuality, *see* Barry Hill's (2002: 462–68) pertinent and revealing discussion, particularly where he describes Strehlow's 'shy defence of matter-of-fact carnalities' (2002: 468).

13. Nevertheless, Paul Robinson finds a certain positive primitivism in Róheim's work and regards Rousseau as Róheim's 'great forebear' (1972: 111). I do not deny that Róheim's uses something like positive primitivism by way of a 'cultural critique' of modernity (Marcus and Fischer 1986), but I make it clear below why I think this is only part of the story.

14. Contrast this with Hippler (1978), who makes a great deal of such 'problems, anxieties and aggression' in Arnhem Land, but says absolutely nothing about Yolngu 'happiness'. Although I cannot pursue the matter in detail here, the contrast is of particular interest in view of the fact that much of Hippler's modelling of Yolngu psychodynamics is consistent with Róheim's own. Hamilton (1979b: 164) convincingly identifies Hippler's unreflexive negative transference onto the Yolngu, while Reser (1981: 388) lists some of the projective terminology symptomatic of this transference.

15. Róheim's writing about Central Australian gender relations is generally in line with this observation. He labels men's attitude towards women as 'sadistic aggressive, or phallic' (1974: 223) and claims that this attitude 'is best exemplified by the custom of *mbanja*' (1974: 223) – a forceful dramatization of 'marriage by capture' (Róheim 1974: 228–30). Elsewhere he describes men's 'cave-man style', but also says that this is something of an ethno-stereotype which fails to register the degree to which courtship can be based on 'persuasion and patience', as well as women's own 'initiative' (1933: 241).

16. Sandall is best known as an ethnographic filmmaker rather than an anthropologist per se. He did, however, take a degree in anthropology and was a member of the University of Sydney's Anthropology Department for some twenty years – this in spite of anthropology being for him an 'alarming subject' (Sandall n.d.).

17. Although it is well known among Rousseau scholars, it bears repeating here that Rousseau did not coin, nor did he use, the phrase 'noble savage'. Also, his related idea of precultural 'natural man' was never intended to be anything other than 'a deliberate work of fiction' (Ellingson 2001: 80) not to be confused with the people or culture of any ethnographic report (Ellingson 2001: 84). The notion of a 'noble savage' first entered European discourse through the early seventeenth-century ethnographic reports of Marc Lescarbot (Ellingson 2001: 21–34).

18. Also see Bolt (2006) and Hughes (2007: 31–33) for more recent Hobbesian takes on the treatment of Aboriginal children.

19. Róheim (1974: 238–40) gives an extensive list of Arandic and Western Desert 'curses'. He gives polite, euphemistic translations, but most of them evidently contain references to either 'cunt' or 'prick'.

20. Berndt and Berndt (1951: 21) also draw attention to the explicit contrast between childhood license and adult propriety in sexual matters.

21. Peter Sutton (personal communication 20/1/08) has suggested that the word *conscience* is perhaps inappropriate in this context. I do not disagree with Stanner when he says that, in classical Aboriginal life-worlds, there is a 'concept of

goodness, but it lacks true scruple'; or that there is 'a moral law but … men are both good and bad, and no one is racked by the knowledge'; or that 'Aborigines are not shamed or inspired by a religious thesis of what men might become by faith or grace' (1979: 31–32); or that Aborigines 'lack what we recognise as moral zeal' (1979: 57); or that 'a strong, explicit religious ethic was absent', serving to make 'the moral aspect of the religion rather amorphous' (1979: 120). All this is consistent with Róheim's account: however, I do not think that any of it implies an *absence* of conscience – which is why I speak of a 'style of conscience'. In my view, Róheim's material illustrates why this 'style' is not particularly agonistic ('racking') when compared with typically Western forms of high-minded 'moral zeal'. Of course, the social distribution of styles of conscience is a matter for empirical investigation in *any* social or cultural context, even where we make assumptions about there being a 'modal personality'.

22. For striking examples, *see* the Oz Outback web site at http://www.ozoutback .com.au/postcards/postcards_forms/abor_children_1/index.htm. Accessed 28 January 2009.

23. Although one could be forgiven for thinking otherwise given the title of the *'Little Children Are Sacred'* report, which I think contains a number of interesting discursive manoeuvres. In the first place, I note the use of the phrase '*little* children', which tends to foster an across-the-board infantilizing of the children suffering abuse. While there are graphic examples of the abuse of infants in the report (e.g., Wild and Anderson 2007: 62), it deals with abuse across a much greater range of ages up to sixteen years (Wild and Anderson 2007: 59–72). Secondly, I note the report's appropriation of the Arandic title *Ampe Akelyernemane Meke Mekarle,* from which the translation 'Little Children Are Sacred' is derived. In fact, after consulting two linguists (Jenny Green and David Wilkins) and entries in two dictionaries (Green 1992; Henderson and Dobson 1994), I believe the translation is a kind of intercultural adjustment involving something of a semantic shift. The word *meke-meke* (from which '*Meke Mekarle*' is derived) has a variety of meanings associated with the idea of restriction and can be translated as something like 'blocked', 'avoided', 'off limits' or 'out of bounds'. However, the word is often used to describe restricted men's business, including sacred sites which are off limits to the uninitiated (women and children). In my experience, Central Australian men will commonly gloss *meke-meke* as 'secret' or 'sacred' in the context of site documentation, so that *meke-meke* has come to be widely understood as synonymous with 'sacred'. So, while 'little children are off-limits' appears to makes good sense as a translation, 'little children are sacred' does not – that is, unless the sense of 'sacred' reflects common English phrasing rather than common Arandic usage. As an English speaker, it seems to me that the translation 'sacred' is received from the report to mean 'special' or 'precious' (perhaps as a gift from God) rather than sexually 'off-limits' or 'out of bounds'. This is intuitively in line with the sentimental, infantilizing phrase 'little children'.

24. I take this quote to be indicative rather than conclusive. The extent to which Indigenous local judgements of moral decline are relative to falling standards of behaviour as opposed to changing standards of moral judgement remains an open question. Interrogating the particularities and extensions of this problem

is beyond the scope of this paper, but I note the complaint, canvassed in the recent Report of the Northern Territory Review Board, that rates of child abuse in remote Aboriginal communities in the Northern Territory, as opposed to rates of child abuse in Australia at large, may have been exaggerated by media over-exposure (Yu et al. 2008: 34). I have avoided engaging with statistics in this paper, as it is widely acknowledged that they are unreliable. I accept, however, that rates of abuse in Central Australia and in other Indigenous communities are much higher than the national average (Richardson 2005) and therefore high enough to warrant urgent attention.

25. I note in this regard Eickelkamp's (2004: 173–74) report from Ernabella – as far as I know, the first of its kind – of 'protective' *mamu* ranged against 'evil' *mamu*. This shift is interpreted by Eickelkamp in terms of perceptual adjustment to modernity (2004: 174), although the idea of a 'good *mamu*' also seems to be a novel concept. My suspicion is that the distinction between 'bad *mamu*' and 'good *mamu*' is, in Róheim's terms, correlated with the distinction between a projected and introjected superego.

26. It is possible to interpret Róheim's statement about the id – that it is not the main axis of differentiation separating primitives from moderns – as a 'constructionist' stance; that is, as the rejection of a race-based explanation of difference. While the id is a psychic agency, it is partly organized by the 'genetic layering of the instincts' (Laplanche and Pontalis 1985: 199). Róheim incorporated a large section on the Central Australian id in his first field report, concentrating on what he called 'the oral zone' (1932: 74–82) and 'the anal and urethral zones' (1932: 82–94). At the end of this section he stated that 'the id manifests itself properly speaking only in its relation to the ego and super-ego' (1932: 94) – that is, via the 'reality principle' and the subject's 'reality-testing' of the life-world (Laplanche and Pontalis 1985: 379–85).

27. Freud himself became one such 'folk devil' thanks to Jeffrey Masson's (1984) much-publicized accusation that he suppressed evidence of child abuse. In saying this, I do not entirely discount Masson's claims. Rather, I am simply suggesting that they need to be contextualized in terms of the way they were elevated to the level of scandal and even legal action (Malcolm 1997).

28. This is dramatically portrayed in an Arrernte myth about the echidna who '"spoilt" himself and all his totem kindred' by exercising excessive violence over young men in his charge. The 'spoiling' refers to how the echidna 'castrated some of the youths who ought [rather] to have been subincised' (Róheim 1925: 152).

29. The quotes are from a blog at http://www.bigpondmovies.com/libraries/article_library/news/australia/cast_and_crew_biographies/brandon_walters_nullah/. Accessed 30/01/09.

CHAPTER 2

Envisioning Lives at Ernabella

Katrina Tjitayi and Sandra Lewis

This chapter is an edited translation prepared by Margaret Dagg and Ute Eickelkamp, of spoken reflections by two women from Ernabella (Pukatja) on the Anangu Pitjantjatjara Yankunytjatjara (APY) Lands in South Australia. With a highly fluctuating population of between 350 and 670, Ernabella is the largest and oldest of seventeen communities and ninety so-called homelands dotted across the 103,000 square kilometres of the APY Lands. The Aboriginal population in the area has grown fourfold over the last five decades to an estimated 2,500 in 2004. The APY Lands have been held under inalienable freehold title since 1981, when Anangu gained – at least on paper – administrative control over government reserves and pastoral leases in the area. This followed upon the decentralization movement of the 1970s, when communities were incorporated, a Land Council was formed, and families set up small satellite settlements called homelands. As heirs to these developments, the authors are actively engaged in stemming current pressures by the state and federal governments to diminish the political power of Anangu communities. They see the future of their cultural integrity to depend on 'being bosses' for their lives, and this is what they seek to instil in the upcoming generation. As members of the Western Desert cultural group, Tjitayi and Lewis offer insider perspectives on how Anangu see the psychology of children and personhood in relation to a changing and difficult life-world. The contributions by each author are kept separate in two sections. In the first section, former director of the Pitjantjatjara Yankunytjatjara Education Committee, Katrina Tjitayi, considers the nature of childhood and child development from an Anangu cultural and historical perspective. Her discussion is motivated by a lifelong intellectual and practical commitment to fostering a secure cultural identity that allows Anangu to respond proactively to the whims of changing government policies and administrative regimes. Additional comments by two Ernabella women, Margaret Dagg (MD) and Nami Kulyuru (NK), are included in square brackets; they indicate the conversational style in which ideas are customarily conveyed.

U. E.

49

Memories for the Future (Katrina Tjitayi)

Infancy and Early Childhood

Newborns have no understanding at first. This develops as they grow and at about five months of age, babies begin to comprehend – they look at things, smile, respond and make sounds. [MD: They also cry when they are hungry.]

Ngurkantankupai: Recognizing the Origins of Character Development

People who are not close family members and hence have an outsider's view of the child can recognize what a particular baby or young child will be like in the future. They can see that a child will have problems as he or she matures and become a bad person. [MD: Early signs of a poor future as a person include a toddler biting his arm or pushing others away, in other words, he is socially unresponsive.] People might say about this child, 'When he grows up he will be a bad boy – *tjitji kura.*' They perceive this child's future and see that he will be swearing at others, and they also look back and see the origin of this behaviour in older family members. They might say, 'This child is following in his father's footsteps, *mamanguru,* and he will be just as bad,' or 'This boy will be like his mother, *ngunytjunguru,* who is *rama-rama,* a mindless crazy person.' That is the way of this family, and the child continues the personality traits that are already there in the father or the mother. [MD: They share one blood, meaning that the kind of person you are is to a great extent a matter of predisposition.]

Tjitji Kura Tjitji Wiṟu: Becoming a Person in Social Context

However, these early 'diagnoses' influence how others will treat the child. A child considered a bad person would be teased; he will be pushed around, mocked, and provoked to fight. [MD: It is common for children to tease a marginalized child by saying something like, 'He's *rama* ['crazy'], go and tease him!' In this way, the peers actually make the child become *rama;* they reinforce what is beginning to manifest in this young person.] Then that child learns; he begins to talk and absorb what is being said about him. He hears people say, 'Look, that boy will act like his father, he will be making trouble for other people in the future.' And similarly with a child who is perceived to be a good person, *tjitji wiṟu.* Such a girl would be talked about like this: 'Oh, she's just like her mother, she will be doing good work and grow into a respectable woman.' The very young child is not aware of his own character yet, but for other people, his temperament is visibly manifest. These are the ways in which children are seen – either as destined to experience and cause problems, or as socially positive. Those are the future paths that people can perceive by closely observing the very young child.

Childhood and the Family

Following the earlier comments by distant relations, close family members, that is, the grandparents and parents of the child, bring out further the character of the young person. Through comments about and to the child they assess what he is like.

Mirawaninyi: The Good Child

Here is a typical example. Grandfather and grandmother are watching their granddaughter. They see that she is helpful, showing all the signs of becoming a good and supportive person. The grandparents spread the good news, *mirawaninyi*, about this girl, making it known to her and to others that she has a good character and listens, and that she is obedient and mindful. They say that her social responsiveness means that she is learning from her mother from early on, beginning with small things, towards becoming a good woman. They are proud of her and praise the child. This has a strongly positive impact on the girl who in turn feels pride in herself, *kanany-kananypa.* Her soul grows happy; she will keep these good words in her heart as a source of strength and they become part of who she is.

Emotional participation and praise in support of the child's development are also important for physical and motor skills. As older sisters, we used to pay close attention to our younger siblings as they began learning to walk. The first signs of the newly acquired skill would make us very happy and we would help in this way: over and again, we would place the baby on the ground at some distance away and she would walk towards us. Soon, other people would take notice and say: 'Have you perhaps seen it? This child is starting to walk!' The whole family would comment and praise the child, as they watched him grow.

Kuranmananyi: The Bad Child

The same pattern is at work with a child who is perceived as bad. For instance, the mother might ask the child to do something for her, but the girl does not respond. She is lazy. Soon, adults in the family will say to her, 'You are useless,' and the girl begins to believe that she is unwanted, that she is talked about in negative terms, and she will feel sad. Her mother's words are hurting her and the girl's reaction is to turn away; she stays at other people's homes without telling her mother. The negative cycle is reinforced when the mother scolds her upon her return the next morning. She might say something like: 'You are always staying out and with other people. *Tjitji kura nyuntu*!' – you are a bad child. If the child is growled at in this way in front of other people, the humiliation is even greater. The mother is hurting the child's feelings and he or she is likely to respond by withdrawing even further. [MD: This form of consolidating a negative image of a child by spreading the bad news is called *kuran-mananyi*.] [NK: It may be that today, people do not assess the character of children anymore in the way they used to.]

Memories of Play

As young children, we used to play in the dry creekbed. We played at being a woman, *minyma-minyma,* and Nami and I used to climb up the rocky hills to play together, climbing up high without fear. And in the scrub, we played being in the choir.[1] We also climbed trees. Then, under the bloodwood trees in the creekbed, we used to dig around for witchetty grubs. We would reprimand other children making noise, 'Be quiet, the grubs will move away!' Then, in wet weather, we played in the saltbush scrub, making damper from mud, and building beautiful little shelters called *wiltja,* just like our mothers, who built firm and strong shelters for us to live in. [NK: Sometimes the boys would approach our playground in the bush, and we used to send them away, saying, 'You are boys and should be playing a long way away from us!') [MD: I too remember making play *wiltja*. The boys sometimes set them on fire and a fight would begin.]

We picked up old metal tins that we used as water containers. We would make real tea in them, go and fetch tealeaves from the camp and make cups of tea for our playmates. We were able to detect dangerous objects on the ground that could pierce the bare foot, and we never fell when we climbed the hills. So we played happily and safely on our own, without the presence of adults.

The older sisters would send the young children away; they want to play with their age-mates. The girls would leave on donkeys, but of course, the little ones tried to run after them. Then the older sisters shooed them away by calling, 'Stay where you are!' It was important for the older girls to play among themselves outside the community, perhaps at Itjinpiri, a place that is now a homeland. However, the older sisters also used to look after their younger siblings. They took care of them as they all played together out bush. For example, they would carry them on their back so that the little ones would not have to walk through prickles, or they would clear the path with their feet for the young children. These days, it seems, the older sisters do not look after the small children in the same way.

We also spent some afternoons on the playground at the school – on the swing, or playing ball, much enjoying the play facilities that the White people had set up. Then, at the end of the day, we would go home to listen to 'bedtime stories.'

Al-piri: Evening Rant

Once at home after a day's play, we used to hear the old men talk. This customary public talk in the evenings (and mornings) that is not directed at anyone in particular was part of camp life. It is called *al-piri*. Someone would ask, 'Are you people listening?' 'Yes, we hear you,' some would reply. And perhaps again, 'Yes, yes,' with their voices becoming quieter as they grew tired. So the man would repeat his question, 'Hey, are you listening to what I have to say?' And other people respond, 'No, they are all falling asleep.'

Al-piri and children's bedtime stories have similar functions, if on a different scale. The children's stories told in the intimacy of the family around the evening campfire would make the children fall asleep. In addition the stories are educational on many levels. They were a form of learning in the family setting that strengthened its unity and the children's sense of belonging. Similarly, the men's evening rant supported the flow of information. Yet the calls from one fireplace to another also connected people and embraced the camp as a whole.

Bedtime

There are several customary ways of comforting children into sleep. For instance, grandmothers would gently stroke the head of a girl or boy, or she might pretend to pick lice from the child's scalp while telling a story. If none of these techniques helped and the child were still restless, the mother or grandmother would resort to scaring her. She would evoke an ogre figure called *mamu*, with a mock question like this: 'What's that? Did you hear this?' Then from somewhere would come a 'miao,' and the growling of a bushcat. As children, we were very scared, which exhausted us so that finally we became tired and found sleep.

Inculcated from infancy onwards, the fear of child-attacking creatures remains a powerful reality for years to come. An older child might hear some unidentifiable noise and think, 'Oh, this growling is what my mother told me about, just this sound of a cat miaowing.' Another sign of approaching danger is a movement in the branches of a tree, together with a scratching rustling sound that our parents had also warned us about. So when we children stayed out playing in the dark and heard something in a tree, we would think, 'This is it, the rustling noise!' We would be so frightened that we cried. Father and mother then came with a burning bunch of spinifex grass to light up the path and we would quickly run home.

Sand Stories

In the late afternoons, we girls often went to a secluded playground, perhaps the creekbed or the scrub. Having explored all other play opportunities and with our minds filled with the events of the day, this is the time for telling sand stories, a practice that is called *milpatjunanyi*.

Imaginary Stories

First we collected gum leaves to be the play characters. Those with a chip or a bent represented sick or crippled people, and a yellow leaf was a part-Aboriginal person. A very small leaf would be a baby. We learnt a lot by watching and creating our imaginary play stories. [MD: We even anticipated events. Before we knew part-Aboriginal children existed, we played about them in our stories, which later became a reality.]

Enactments

Another type of stories is the enactment of an event that actually took place. Piercing a leaf with a small stick, for example, would perform the punishment of a troublemaker. This depicts the spearing in the thigh, the customary way to deal with male wrongdoers. In this way, even if we had not seen the incident ourselves and only heard about it, we learnt family history.

Cautionary Tales

An important function of sand stories is to teach children social rules. We older girls would create a story such as this for the young children: two leaves are arranged on the ground, the play characters of a mother and a father. The parents are about to punish their daughter by beating her with a stick. The daughter had sneaked out her family camp at night to go and sleep with one of the boys in seclusion who are called *nyiinka*. This represented the breach of a very important rule, namely to keep the adolescent girls and boys or young unmarried men apart. The leaf representing the disobedient daughter is hit and beaten, and we would pretend to cry our eyes out. The young children, by listening to and watching this lively performance, took part emotionally. In this way they understood its meaning and internalized the dynamics.

Bird Characters

Folktales about birds present a distinctive genre of sand stories. The different birds are associated with certain character traits, such as cranky

Kanka, the Crow Woman whom everyone tries to avoid. She is a trouble-maker. Then there are the Kakalya, the Cockatoo Woman and Walawuru, the Wedgetail Eagle Man. Other characters in traditional stories are yellow butterflies associated with women, and the fox. These figures were enacted with gum leaves. The bird characters remain an important medium through which girls recreate actual family life and tell a story about what happened at home.

Walytjarara-walytjarara: A Family Guessing Game

The significance of social knowledge and in particular family dynamics in the shaping of children's worlds is also evident in the guessing game *walytjarara-walytjarara*. It can be played as sand stories where a short line represents a person that is then placed in social context by spatially relating him or her to other persons, or as a finger game. In the latter version, each finger would be identified in kin terms, 'This is the older brother, this the younger one, this is the older sister, and this a little baby.' The other children try to make out which family is meant. They make a guess, and if it is wrong, the player offers further clues, 'This baby is learning to walk.' The guessing team might ask, 'And what is the colour of the baby's hair?' And they might be given another clue, 'The child in question has big eyes.' This continues until the family or person is finally identified.

Changing Perspectives

Children's Anticipations

We used to imagine our future – *kuranyukutu nyakunytjaku*. I remember as a child looking forward with excitement to what was lying ahead, thinking that I would live like my mother. My generation felt confident about the future; we were on the right path, doing good things. The inspiration came from our parents, who helped us young people envision life clearly. The old way of learning was focused and required moments of withdrawal when the children would assimilate and think about what they had heard. They would go into the bush, for example, and spend some time contemplating. It seems that many children now are unable to develop a long-term vision for their lives. They are stuck in the community, constantly exposed to the activities, noises, demands, and events of everyday life. This leaves little scope for focused reflection so that they are rather short sighted, just thinking about the next moment. [MD: For me, God is the interpreter of life. He reveals my path and its meaning.]

Children today need to develop a positive perspective for their lives. Their outlook straddles two worlds, the White world and the world of Anangu. At present, the two are severely out of balance; one is up and one is down. Whitefella culture is up; it has come to dominate young lives.

[NK: And Anangu culture is down. Children are not growing up anymore in ways that allow them to become a fully integrated Anangu person; their views are strongly influenced by the culture of White Australia.]

Time, School and Money

We used to go out hunting and on camping trips. Our evenings were filled with stories and we would hear the old people's rant before falling asleep. We have lost these customs. Now, Whitefella ways have taken over, with television, video, a whole battery of games, and other entertaining things that keep the children awake until late and tiring them out. Their minds are exhausted and instead of going to school, they sleep during the day. Looking back, I can see that my generation, in contrast, grew up much more healthily; we were full of energy. Our daily routine was good. We used to get up early and run about, after an early night. People would call us 'early birds,' because we would rise with the sun like the birds. Even on rainy days we would happily play outside in the mornings, racing each other and being full of life. We felt trust in our future.

Education was an important part of this vision. We loved going to school and would always be there before the teacher arrived. In winter we lit a small fire nearby the school building to keep warm, as we were waiting for the lessons to begin. It was always us children waiting for the teacher, and there was only one teacher. Today, it is all upside down. There are many teachers and they usually spend half the morning waiting for the children to arrive. [NK: Families today are trying to make their children want to go to school. They buy things and give money to their children. But it seems never enough. Each day, the children demand: 'Give me more money! Buy me this, buy me that! Or else I will not go to school.']

The Good Future of the Past

Not too long ago, when I started my working life, we were comfortably well off. Everyone looked for work and made a living. Now, we have become impoverished. People are unemployed, they have no money, not even blankets to keep warm, or diesel for their vehicles; the most basic things are missing. However, the good and focused way of life of the past has not disappeared. It is still there, but it is buried under the weight of our present problems. It is most important that we make it visible again for the young generation. Children need to be able to envision a positive future for themselves if they are to live well. They need to be able to see how the children of the past, that is, my generation, imagined a future for themselves, so that today's children can comprehend an alternative to what they perceive is the natural way to live.

Finding a New Path

Our way of life used to be good. I have happy childhood memories of beautiful family homes in the bush that were kept clean. The children used to listen well and knew how to be quiet. Unlike today, they did not yell and shout all at once as if they had to compete for attention. We children took part in adult life. For example, when the men came back from a day's hunt, we used to watch how they cook the kangaroo in an earth oven. So this is how I became strong, mentally and physically.

But what is the situation now? Where is our society going? Our children are not frightened anymore when we tell stories about spooky creatures in the dark. They watch movies and television until late into the night, and have become used to seeing horrible images on the screen. The night is not associated with fear anymore. This is very different to the old days when children would listen to stories before falling asleep. To imagine what an ogre looks like, that is, to create your own image of it, has a much more profound effect on the mind. It becomes more real in a sense, because it is infused with the reality of your inner life, maybe dreams. So we were very scared. Children today say that it is just a picture, made by people like they make movies today, and that can be switched off. [MD: It is as if the children have become deaf.] They tell us this is all make-believe and claim to possess new forms of knowledge. As a consequence parents cannot make the old techniques of influencing the mind work anymore. There is no more dreading of the dark, children have stopped to fear the old stories, and one could say that the young people have broken the laws of the mind. [MD: Young people and even children now drink, sniff petrol, gamble and some girls become prematurely pregnant.]

Today, our society is like a jigsaw puzzle whose pieces have gone missing, one by one. We are like a thousand pieces scattered across the ground, and we cannot fix the picture. We cannot piece the puzzle together anymore, because we have lost sight of the bigger picture, the vision of who we are as a society. The pieces do not add up.

Different stories are being told today and I wonder how children process the events in their lives in their play. They still go out to play among themselves, and I ask myself: 'Are they perhaps playing in the same way we used to? Are they telling sand stories, or maybe play at being grown up? Do they still go and play in the rocks?' I never see these kinds of play when I look around close by. But the children still make many beautiful things in their play, even if it is different to what I remember. And that is good. Nevertheless, I keep asking myself: 'How do children feel today? What are their lives really like? How are they growing up, and where are they going? The world they live in is much larger than ours of the past, and it is tough. But we have to go through it. We parents need to look after our children as best as we can; feed them well, make sure they get enough sleep, and keep them safe. This is about securing a better future for Anangu. It is not easy to find the right path. Which way of action is open to us? Where are our children travelling? What is their vision? Are they looking at all beyond these troubled times, or is the present situation all that they can see? As I explained, our grandparents, thirty and forty years ago, helped us children develop a long-term vision for our lives. This might be our most urgent task now: to assist each child in creating a perspective of the future. Talking will not be enough. We need to show by example what can be done. We adults should be role models and work in the community. The children need to see that not only Whitefellas work, but that Anangu too can be professionals. [MD: Do the White people who work in our community put our children to bed? Do they feed them? No, but the missionaries did. They truly had our welfare in mind. Now welfare is a service to be delivered, and White people deliver it to make money.]

We need to be strong indeed to accomplish this task of creating a viable path for our children. I have in mind the image of a rabbit warren. The present generation is all over the place; there are too many holes everywhere and a unified vision is lacking. We should close the many holes of the burrow that we have become and leave only one path open, through which the young people can go together. Otherwise, they will continue to harbour wrong ideas about the future. Looking back I realize that mine might be called a happy generation, because our future was looking bright.

On Children's Soul and Young Mothers Who Sniff Petrol
(Sandra Lewis)

This section presents the Anangu notions of soul and mind in relation to, on the one hand, psychological strengths in children and, on the other, weaknesses in young mothers who sniff petrol. Links between body, soul and social experience are made transparent in accounts of sickness and health. The speaker substantiates generally held views with accounts of concrete incidents.

U. E.

Children's Soul

Children and infants have special abilities of the soul, *kurunpa*, and some more so than others. Children can see things that are invisible to adults, both good and bad things. They can see *mamu*, evil spirits that live in the bush and try to bite the soul of small children. In the past, when families were living in the bush, walking from place to place and resting in traditional shelters, in the open behind a windbreak or sometimes in caves, babies in particular were vulnerable to attacks by *mamu*. When an infant was bitten, his soul would fall ill and the baby got unwell. Today, such attacks occur rarely. The three factors that have changed this are the church, the motorcar and the house. When church services began to be held at Ernabella in the late 1930s, and more and more people accepted the message of Jesus, the *mamu* became frightened and moved further into the bush. Since we now travel in vehicles instead of walking long distances even in the dark, children are protected from the danger of the evil spirits. To live in modern houses that can be locked up rather than in camps has made it difficult for *mamu* to enter when we are asleep at night.

Children are able to see Jesus and angels, and those with a special gift can see relatives who have passed away. My nephew is such a child. He saw Jesus who asked him who he wanted to see, and the boy replied, 'My grandfather.' The old man, that is, my father, had suffered a terrible illness before he died and his body had wasted away. In his visitation to the boy, my father looked rejuvenated and his health was completely restored. Our family thinks that, when he grows up, this child might become a minister of the church.

Boys go and play in amongst the rocks and in the bush because they follow a child from the Dreaming. On rainy days the children become excited; the rain makes them happy and they want to play outside because they think that the rain will make them grow tall and strong.

Young children especially are perceptive through their soul. They can sense approaching visitors who are coming for some social occasion. As the visitors travel towards the community where the child lives, they might be talking about this particular girl or boy, thinking about the child with anticipation. At home, the young child will touch his or her genitals, which signals to the parents that visitors are on their way.

We take care of our children's soul and try not to lay infants on their back to put them to sleep. Instead, they should lie on the side because if the baby gets a fright, by a sudden loud noise, for instance, his soul will jump out of place. If this happens, the baby starts vomiting, and someone with the know-how will have to push the soul back into its proper place at the sternum for the baby to recover. But if a baby's soul becomes so frightened – by a looming illness for example – that it jumps out of the body and tries to hide away from whatever danger it may perceive, a healer (*ngangkari*) will be able to find it straight away. However, if the same happens to an older person, whose soul is much stronger than those of infants, it can be difficult to retrieve it. For instance, after a car accident or during a sickness, the soul of a person will try to protect itself from being harmed by running away from the body. It can hide a long way away and for a long time. In cold weather, this older soul will grow a fur, *inyutjararinganyi*, which makes it even harder for the healer to locate it. The person without a soul will become progressively weak and sick.

We say about hiccups in adults that they signal the looming demise of the person affected. In some cases, however, it can mean that the soul of the person is trying to reveal something, as if to 'speak up.'

Volatile Substances: Emotions and the Problem of Petrol Sniffing

I coordinate a special project for young mothers who sniff petrol. From my work, it seems to me that often the soul of young women who misuse substances is lonely and sad. The world is changing and their families are going separate ways, with the effect that these women do not receive the recognition they need.

Another psychological problem is that young people are not familiar with the traditional way of seeking forgiveness, nor do they behave like Whitefellas who would go to the person they have offended and simply demand forgiveness by saying 'sorry.' That is not our way. It used to be the custom that, when someone was left out and not given a share of meat, he or she would complain and hit the relative whose duty it was to provide the meat. And after this, the two would make peace and share camp behind a windbreak. That was our way of forgiving, *kalparinganyi*. We used to slowly approach the person offended and, without raising the subject, sit down and share a meal together or money, talking and being in each other's company. Young men and women have not learnt this technique and instead 'bottle up' their feelings of guilt, shame or hurt. As a result these negative feelings about the self grow bigger and, at some point, the person might start sniffing petrol. In order to fill the gap in reconciling behaviours and forge new ways of coping that fit into con-temporary living conditions and perceptions, we are encouraging young people and children to speak about their feelings in a safe situation.

For Anangu, shame is a strong feeling that has an effect not just on the individual but also on relationships between people. Sniffers are deeply ashamed, *kuntaringkupairingu*, in front of the community about their behaviour, but not in front of close family members. They only perceive shame when they have a break from sniffing, and in order to get rid of this unpleasant feeling they take to the petrol can again. It makes them feel strong and lose their shame while they are intoxicated. Drug mis-users, sniffers or those who smoke marijuana, withdraw and hide from others when they feel shame. They can quickly become isolated, espe-cially young men. Our effort – not just in my project but also throughout the community – is to reintegrate these young people by inviting them to participate in football matches. We cheer them on, provide food and camp together, and this recognition can make all the difference, because it is a way of making a link with their soul.

Substance misusers are not the only ones suffering from social isolation and loneliness. Anyone who is poverty stricken, and this includes young women with whom I work, might be too ashamed and weak to ask for food or money. It is humiliating to be forced to beg. Our approach in the project is to emphasize that the community as a whole is one family, despite the fact that there are tensions and arguments. In other words, we are telling the person that there is a communal right to request help. Those who are strong still have culture inside them. Our goal is to support those in need to get their culture back, by which I mean to reintegrate socially in ways that Anangu consider to be healthy. We encourage participation in socially positive things, such as sharing meals, and spending time together talking and travelling. When we go on a trip and make camp, it is important that the camp layout does not exclude anyone. One way of camping in a larger group is to sleep in a long row, with small fires in between swags.

Young Mothers

At present [July 2006] in Ernabella we know of four or five young mostly single mothers who are in their late teens and early twenties and who sniff petrol. Other members in their family, their own mothers, sisters and/or their spouses, also sniff petrol, some of them severely, others only occasionally. Parenting is a big problem for these women, especially if the family cannot offer the right support. Even the so-called occasional sniffers can have a chronic problem, namely, to take on responsibility. They try and give their children into the care of another family member, often a grandmother or grandfather. They want to be 'free,' or skinny, and some feel that they just cannot cope, that it is too hard to bring up a child. However, the mother has the primary responsibility for her children when they are young, and in the past, she would have been punished severely if something bad happened to them. They are not to deflect responsibility, because the soul of mother and child are linked together. It is not the soul that petrol sniffing destroys, but the mind, and the link or bond between the baby and the mother must be looked after. Fathers develop a close relationship with their children gradually, and this is just as important as the early bond to the mother. Only when children enter adolescence are the grandparents expected to take on some educational and other tasks of care, and later also other family members.

Individual families deal with the problem in different ways. One old man who is strong, *kunpu pulka,* has consistently refused taking over the care of the child of his daughter who used to sniff petrol very heavily. He kept telling her that this would be wrong, and that she must look after her child. He was, in fact, fulfilling his customary role as a father who is expected to keep an eye on how his children look after his grandchildren. The woman was thus able to learn and that is also what I mean by culture. At present, she is trying hard to stop sniffing petrol and spends much time with her son. Another old man is not so strong. He sometimes looks after his young grandson who is between two and three years of age. The mother of the boy sniffs petrol and has 'passed around' this baby to several people. The poor child has no home. It is understandable that the grandfather wants to help, but he is only aggravating the situation; in the long run, that child will suffer from having lost the bond to his mother. In another case, the young mother gives her two children into the occasional care of a woman who is also a sniffer. But this woman is stable and stops misusing when, in her role as spouse, she stays with the father of the two children's mother. The children's grandmother died some time ago and this second partner of the children's grandfather is their classificatory grandmother. She is especially good at caring for the younger child, a boy, because her husband, the boy's grandfather, loves him. We consider this arrangement to be *tjaka,* that is, customary, because it has been good common practice that the new spouse looks after the children and grandchildren from the first marriage. Today, people are often too selfish to do this.

I conclude by saying that it is important to understand and respect each person as an individual. Support programs that offer group-based activities make sense to us as long as they provide a safe space for each individual. The mothers who come into the project and do cooking, listen to music, clean up and participate in workshop-based learning about health and parenting each have their own personal style and preferences also called *tjaka.* The aim of our work is not to change a person's character, but to offer a place in this group, at least for a while, that acknowledges exactly the special ways of each person.

Notes

1. The internationally known Ernabella choir was formed at the beginning of the mission era in around 1940. Associated with the performing arts curriculum of the school, the choir is significant as a socially meaningful context in which children learn through shared activity from and with senior family members.

CHAPTER 3

Warungka

Becoming and Unbecoming a Warlpiri Person

Yasmine Musharbash

In this chapter, I discuss the socialization of Warlpiri children in relation to the treatment of old, socially incapacitated people, focusing in both contexts on the key concept, *warungka*. This Warlpiri term encompasses a range of meanings, including deaf, crazy, forgetful, mindless, unconscious, intoxicated and irate. In addition to these situationally ascribed meanings, it is also used to label the state of being of (a) children from their conception until they become social persons, and (b) old persons when they begin to lose their social capacities. I explore this perceived resemblance between the two phases at the beginning and the end of the life cycle through the anthropological literature on Warlpiri (and neighbouring) understandings of personhood. As I will show, these two phases are viewed as thresholds between corporeal and noncorporeal life, and *warungka* – with its connotations of mindlessness, craziness and not-knowing – brackets and is contrasted with full social personhood. Drawing on data from participant observation-based research with Warlpiri speakers at the remote community of Yuendumu in the Alice Springs region, I describe how the processes of becoming and unbecoming a Warlpiri person are shaped, guided and engendered by others. Contrasting certain practices of child socialization with certain forms of interaction with old people who are becoming senile, I suggest that the former can aptly be described as 'pulling' children out of the *warungka* state and the latter as 'pushing' senile people into it. Furthermore, such 'pulling out of' and 'pushing into' the *warungka* state can be related to Warlpiri notions of being in the world, ideas about the person and conceptualizations of the life cycle.

Warlpiri Personhood in the Anthropological Literature

In Warlpiri thought, much as elsewhere, ideas of and about the person are intricately linked to beliefs about body and spirit and their relationships to the physical and 'metaphysical' world. I here appropriate and draw together a number of views that originally did not necessarily speak to each other, including Meggitt's (1962, 1987) postulations about Warlpiri spirit composition; Munn's (1970) elaborations on spirit forces contained in Ancestors, country and people; Morton's (1987a, 1989) relating of the life cycle to country and spirit forces; and Dussart's (1988a) description of the Warlpiri categorization of life stages.[1]

An initial step towards understanding Warlpiri ideas about the person can be taken by examining considerations of 'spirit composition', as detailed by Meggitt (1962, 1987). He maintains that spirit composition is used to explain individuality as well as gender differences, as it takes different shapes for men and women, and from person to person. According to his elaborations, a person's spirit is composed of three elements: (1) conception spirit (*kuruwarri*), (2) matrispirit and (3) lodge spirit (*pirrlipa*).[2] These are 'acquired' in the following ways:

(1) Warlpiri people recognize the necessity of sexual intercourse in creating children, but this in itself is not considered sufficient. For life to be engendered, it is believed that spirit forces, *kuruwarri,* emanating from Dreaming sites, must animate the foetus. As soon as a pregnant woman feels the first flutter of movement, these spirit forces are said to have entered the womb and animated the foetus – presenting the child to-be-born with a localized conception spirit.

(2) The members of each matriline (male as well as female) share a common unnamed spirit (which Meggitt terms 'matri-spirit'). He writes:

> [E]ach child, while in foetal form, automatically receives a portion of the spirit which the mother carries in her uterus. … The spirit lodges in the uterus of a girl, whence part of it later enters her children, or in the kidney fat of a boy. At death the maternal spirit leaves the corpse in the form of a ghost and, after men from the matriline avenge the death, dissipates. (1987: 126)

(3) Boys acquire a lodge or patrispirit at initiation: 'When a boy is circumcised and initiated into his father's lodge, he is ritually killed and then reborn as dreamtime power in the form of the lodge totem [that] becomes part of his psyche or spirit' (Meggitt 1987: 123). He goes on to explain that, 'At death this man's portion of the lodge's spiritual essence (bilirba [*pirrlipa*]) returns to the dreaming sites to merge again with the eternally existing pool of dreaming power and to await reincarnation in a future member of the lodge or in members of that totemic species' (123).

Since girls are not initiated into a lodge, according to Meggitt, their lodge spirit is notional only. Summarizing the Warlpiri ideas about the origins of personality, Meggitt writes:

Hence, whereas the assumed possession of conception dreamings helps to account for the fact that all Walbiri are human and one people, albeit intimately related to other species, their random acquisition explains why all Walbiri differ as individual personalities. It is true, say Walbiri, that some people are more alike physically and in personality than are others because they share a common matrispirit or, apparently less effective in this respect, a common patrilodge spirit. The personalities of men who share both are, of course, decidedly alike. (1987: 127)

In short, Meggitt outlines Warlpiri understandings of gender differences as explained through males possessing a tripartite spirit and females a bipartite one; and individuality through idiosyncratic combinations of conception spirit, matrispirit, and lodge spirit (*see* Figure 3.1).

Rather than dwelling on the intricacies of spirit composition, I highlight below the significance of something relatively implicit in Meggitt's postulations, namely, the fact that both an individual's physical features and their personality traits are thought to be determined by spirit forces. First, though, I further outline the relationship between spirit forces and people.

Nancy Munn's work with Warlpiri and Pitjantjatjara people provides an excellent exegesis of this relationship, most explicit perhaps in her 1970 article on the transformation of subjects into objects into subjects (and so on). Beginning with the creative acts of Ancestral beings and their ensuing transmutation into features of the landscape, she delineates three such types of transformation: (1) metamorphosis, where the body of the Ancestral being is changed into some material object; (2) imprinting, where the Ancestral being leaves behind the impression of his or her body; and (3) externalization, where the Ancestral being takes some object out of her or his body. Thus, Ancestral bodies, parts thereof, or traces

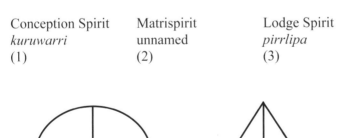

Conception Spirit	Matrispirit	Lodge Spirit
kuruwarri	unnamed	*pirrlipa*
(1)	(2)	(3)

Figure 3.1. ▼ Warlpiri Spirit Composition according to Meggitt

of Ancestral action such as tracks turn into creekbeds, rocky outcrops, trees, soakages, and so forth. Only rarely is an Ancestral being embodied by a single transformation only, and it is more usual that these beings left an indefinite variety of such transformations behind, thus creating the Warlpiri cosmos and, importantly, while creating it, imbuing it with lasting Ancestral power. The underlying linkage between such subjects (Ancestral beings) and objects (features in the landscape) is semantically rendered in the Warlpiri term *kuruwarri,* which among other things means Ancestral mark, track, design as well as spirit force. As spirit forces emanating out of features in the Warlpiri landscape, *kuruwarri* in turn are the life-creating forces in the procreation of plants, animals and people. This circular transformation from Ancestral beings (subjects) to features in the landscape (objects, but containing within them the essence of the Ancestral subjects) to subjects (animals, plants and human beings), whose life force at death returns to where it came from, underlies Munn's argument, namely, that 'the country is the fundamental object system external to the conscious subject within which … consciousness and identity are anchored' (Munn 1970: 143). Another set of relations these transformations bring about is located in the temporal realm. Warlpiri people use the same term for the period of Ancestral creation, Ancestral beings, the act of dreaming and dreams: *jukurrpa.* Acts of transformation thus establish both a contrast and a link between actual people (*yapa*), Ancestral beings (*jukurrpa*) and the temporal orders of the here and now (*yijardu*) and Ancestral time (*jukurrpa*).

In his discussions of Arrernte cosmology, John Morton (1987a, 1989) transferred Munn's ideas onto the life cycle and anchored his analysis around the Arrernte term *rramarrama.* This term, as far as I can tell, seems identical to the Warlpiri term *warungka,* both in its depth and width of meaning and in its applications.[3] Of particular relevance for the present discussion is Morton's postulation that conception is considered as an act of embodiment of *kuruwarri,* with the foetus more spirit than person and closer to *jukurrpa* than to the here and now. Accordingly, infancy is a state of not knowing, or *warungka* (*rramarrama* in Arrernte), where the person is not a full social being yet, in need to be taught, and closer to 'the earth' (meaning 'country' or Ancestral land). The ensuing states of the life cycle are characterized by an increase first in social, then in ritual knowledge: childhood is the process of slowly becoming a (knowing) person, followed by initiation and the gaining of names that make one a fully responsible social person and culminating in the acquisition of ritual powers. Therefore maturity is the height of and control over social and ritual powers, a state that Morton conceptualizes as furthest from the earth (ground, country).[4] Accordingly, he sees senility as a tipping towards the earth through gradual loss of social and ritual powers, a sliding back into a state of *rramarrama* (*warungka*), concluded by death and the reentering into the realm of *jukurrpa*. Morton depicts the life cycle as a circular motion out of, away from, and back towards the earth (ground, country). This motion, as I show, is propelled by others at the points of transition out of and back into 'the ground': children need to be pulled out of the *warungka* state through socialization, and old people are 'pushed' towards it through desocialization.

A similar, albeit implicit, argument about the involvement of others in the progression through the life cycle has been proposed by Françoise Dussart (1988a) in her description of the Warlpiri categorization of life cycle stages. Most pertinent here are the age-graded and gendered classifications of life cycle stages, and the fact that progression from one to the other is dependent on age as much as on the involvement of others in the ceremonies marking the transition from one phase to the next. Crucially, the life cycle trajectory begins and ends the same for males and females: the Warlpiri term for children is *kurdu-kurdu* (singular: *kurdu*), and, according to Dussart, gendered distinction into girls (*kamina*) and boys (*wirriya*) begins only once children are given their personal Warlpiri name,[5] around roughly the age of five. From then onwards they embark on a gendered trajectory of differently named stages according to age, physical and ritual maturity, and marital status, culminating in respectfully being called *muturna* or *wurlkumanu* (older woman) and *ngarrka* or *purlka* (grey-haired man) before entering the *warungka* state, where once again, gender is not distinguished. In short, in opposition to all other life stages, only those of early childhood and senility are not gender specific, and the same terms of address (*warungka* or skinnames[6]) are used for either stage – and I point out that both are structural terms in the sense that they describe a person's place within a system of categories.

The notions outlined above are taken from considerations spanning several decades and postulated by different anthropologists. According to my experience, they (more or less) realistically reflect contemporary perceptions.[7] And while these authors pursued different aims than I do here, I find that together they provide an excellent groundwork from which to further explore Warlpiri personhood and being in the world. What I take from them is an understanding that Warlpiri personhood is immutable in some regards and acquiescent and malleable in others. There are certain characteristics of the individual that are determined by what Meggitt calls *spirit composition:* gender, personality traits and physical appearance are considered to be what they are because they are shaped by spirit forces and hence immutable and not 'socializable'.[8] Awareness of and knowledge about the social world, on the other hand, is to be imparted by others – *this* is what Warlpiri childhood socialization is about.

Warlpiri Socialization

Babies and young children are *warungka* – coming from the realm of *jukurrpa*; animated by and imbued with *kuruwarri*, they do not know the human world 'above the ground' and therefore need to be familiarized with it. Myers describes the same Indigenous perceptions for Pintupi children:

> A young child continues to sleep in camp with its parents because, as the Pintupi say, the child is 'unaware', 'oblivious' or 'deaf' (*patjarru* or *ramarama*). Children do not *know;* they understand neither events nor when to be ashamed (*kunta*). Small children are said to be 'unheeding' (*ramarama*) in that they literally do not comprehend the importance of social events; rather, they throw tantrums, do not listen or respond to parents, sit close to an affine, play with fire, and so on. (Myers 1979: 349)

Responsibility for familiarizing young children with the human world lies with those others they are in contact with; close and classificatory relatives who guide them into the universe of kin and of rules and regulations they need to understand and follow while 'here' and 'with others'. It is the obligation of those others, those who 'know', to turn babies and young children into the opposite of *warungka:* from unconscious to conscious, from deaf/uncomprehending to hearing/understanding, from mindless to sensible, from uncaring to caring, from unknowing to knowing, from 'natural' to socialized. Socialization could then be understood as another form of transformation, in accord with the cosmological project of turning objects into subjects – and, as I describe below, back into objects. Such socialization is achieved by imparting the ground rules of engaging in social life within the cornerstones of autonomy and relatedness, 'being boss' for oneself and looking after others (*see* Myers 1986, 1988a for in-depth analyses of these complexities).[9] Below, I present three examples of such teaching: familiarization with kin, engagement upon eye contact, and ideas about sharing and fighting. These (as well as the many other practices that make up childhood socialization, as outlined in Hamilton 1981) are imparted to every child and by everybody the child is in contact with – meaning all children learn the same lessons; such teaching is not tailored to specific needs of specific persons. Imparting these ground rules is a responsibility that not only lies with a child's parents but with the wider network of people in which the child is placed. Obligations of care and nurture are formally instituted in the rituals of infant care and often openly called upon. For example, a young girl calls her husband's mother's sister on her mobile phone immediately after birth asking for an 'English' name for her child; a young mother yells abuse at her own mother for being lazy and not changing her grandson's diapers often enough; grandmothers 'cook' babies in the smoke of aromatic leaves to make them strong; various people 'sing' a child's legs as it approaches walking age so that they may become strong; cosleepers other than mother engage a baby when it wakes up at night, and so forth.

Childhood socialization entails and is aimed at creating a solid understanding of relationships between people and of the ground rules (of autonomy and relatedness, demand sharing and looking after others) that govern social life and that all (should) adhere to. In fact, lapses or nonadherence to these rules after childhood and before senility are labelled *warungka* as well, as becomes evident from this example about anger taken from Myers's research with Pintupi people (who use the term *ramarama*). Exactly the same would be true in the Warlpiri context:

> The relative significance of 'anger' (in relation to compassion) is further clarified by the phenomenological image of turbulence it has for Pintupi. When one is 'angry', they maintain, one 'loses one's idea'. Following this understanding, 'angry' people are characterized as *ramarama,* which means 'crazy', 'unheeding' or 'deaf' – a state they may share with unsocialized children. A person who is *ramarama* is unable to recognize his or her shared identity with others, unable to take notice of warnings, and might harm his or her own kin. (Myers 1988a: 598)

Warlpiri childhood socialization is thus not about creating or shaping a particular kind of person but rather about familiarizing each 'new arrival' into the universe of the living and the rules that order relations among them. Who children turn into, what they will be like as persons, including their physical appearance and their particular personality traits, is considered 'predetermined' (by *kuruwarri*) and hence immutable. There is no coaching to curb, say, arrogance or a propensity to sulk, there is no promoting of, say, intelligence or a sunny temperament – unless it is there already. What Tjitayi (this volume) observes for Anangu families is true here as well: once the temperament of a child is recognized, adult family members reinforce it verbally, regardless of its positive or negative nature. This rather particular way of understanding certain aspects of the person as acquiescent (able to take on board the rules) and others as immutable (one is the person who one is, physically, psychologically, emotionally) comes into stark relief when comparing Warlpiri (*Yapa*) and non-Indigenous (*Kardiya*) ways of gossiping about others. I am certainly generalizing here, but I believe it holds true to say that the key difference between *Yapa* and *Kardiya* gossip is that the latter tend to 'condemn' the person gossiped about, as in 'He is stupid', 'What would you expect of her', 'He is a compulsive liar' and so forth. *Yapa* gossip, on the other hand, tends to focus on the things done wrong by someone rather than on the person, e.g., 'She shouldn't have done that', 'He should have listened', 'She talked [when she shouldn't have done so]', 'He was starter [of an argument, without provocation]' and so forth. Focusing one's criticism on people's action rather than on their personality traits implies an understanding that in order to be 'a good person' one should *do* the right thing (in any situation), rather than *be* in a particular way. Since traits and physical appearance are considered pregiven, they are not grounds for change and hence they are not open for criticism or laudable, nor are they considered 'teachable' (*see also* Burbank 2006).[10] The values underlying this particular constellation of certain ways of doing and certain states of being become apparent when contrasting the socialization of children with the desocialization of old people. I approach this by first introducing Nora, an old Warlpiri woman, and the changes she has undergone over the last decade or so, as well as the changes in the ways in which others relate to her.

Nora

I met Nora on my first visit to Yuendumu in 1994 when she was in her late sixties or early seventies. Some years later, in 1998, I moved into the camp[11] she was living in; this was when I came to know her well. Previously, I have described her like this:

> Nora had 'won' a 'medal from the Queen' for organising Yuendumu Night Patrol, she had been a big business woman [ritual leader], a very experienced singer, dancer, and painter. She was cranky a lot when I lived with her, often because she was ageing too quickly. While very much alive and full of ideas, her bones hurt and walking became more and more difficult. To be limited by one's own body is a most frustrating experience and Nora did not give in to that easily. To have been powerful and now becoming 'just another old lady' was very, very hard for her. In turn, I often found her demands on me a challenge mainly because they were made with an almost royal air. There was no way to refuse a request of Nora's. Thus, I would drive her to the shop, to the clinic, to look for her grandson, to go hunting, and I would bring her

meat, tea, fruit and soft drinks from the shop whenever she asked. And it must be said that she always reciprocated, she would sing songs or perform love magic for me in the evenings, and sometimes she would slip me a twenty dollar note on pension days. (Musharbash 2003: 115–16)

Over the next few years her physical decline continued, and senility set in as well; she forgot people's names, and started accusing others of hiding money and food from her. As I drove into Yuendumu in 2003, she was the first person I saw: I stopped the car, got out and walked over to greet her. To my surprise she recognized me straight away. 'Napurrurla' [the subsection term which is used as my name at Yuendumu], she said, 'I'm so glad you're here. Did you bring your car? Please, please, take me back to Yuendumu!'[12] In 2005, we were again living in the same camp. One day I found her sitting on the floor, four or five meters away from the bathroom, where she said to me, 'Missus, please, show me the way to the bathroom!'

As these examples illustrate, Nora's decline accelerated with the onset of senility: she failed to recognize place (asking me to take her back to Yuendumu when we were in Yuendumu, not recognizing the layout of her own home) and people (here: first addressing me by my name, later calling me 'Missus', a generic term for White woman). Ultimately, her decline involved behaviour contradicting the simplest rules of social relations. Nora began to develop great skill at stealing people's food, tablets and money, and at hiding the stolen as well as her own things, forgetting that she had hidden them and constantly accusing everybody else of theft. She also forgot that she had eaten, continually complaining about being hungry, not being fed and not being looked after, 'Poor bugger me, no breakfast, no tea, no bread, no meat, hungry one!' She would talk loudly about and name deceased people (a severe taboo at Yuendumu; *see* Musharbash 2008a; Nash and Simpson 1981) and often confused the identities of the living.

Young children make similar 'mistakes': they do not always correctly know their relationships to others, or the relationship between others, they occasionally break name taboos and they are considered greedy. Children, as long as they 'don't know', sometimes steal food or small amounts of money rather than ask (or steal if their requests are refused). The similarities in some of the conduct of old people and very young children contrast with the ways in which people relate to children and old people respectively. These ways of others to relate to the very young and the very old, in some instances at least, can be seen as reversals of each other.

Socialization and Desocialization

I introduced Nora by outlining who she *had* been: a ritual leader, a key organizer of night patrol, an important woman in Yuendumu life because of the things she did. This was never taken into account when relating to Nora on a day-to-day basis once she became senile. What she had done in the past had no bearing on what she was doing in the here and now. As I have written elsewhere (Musharbash 2007), Warlpiri seem to privilege the 'immediate present' over other temporalities. In fact, when old people considered *warungka* 'revert' back in their imagination to earlier times, they generally are laughed at. Consider, for example, the comments made in the morning to another old lady I once shared camp with after she had whimpered all night long because of ear pain. She was calling out for her mother who had passed away several decades earlier. At night, she was ignored by all, but as people sat around the breakfast fire they mocked her, 'No Mummy left, only dogs' – reminding her, not so gently, that she lived in the present.

To tease out further how people relate to old people considered *warungka* by placing them and their action firmly in the here and now and divorcing them from anything that they might have done in the past, I contrast examples of three socialization practices with their opposites of relating to senile people:[13] (1) familiarization with kin and kinship, (2) eye contact and (3) issues of sharing and fighting.

Familiarization with Kin

From the moment a child is born, his or her kin relations to the persons around are explained to him or her.[14] 'Mama, I'm your Mama', 'Look, your granny', 'That's your big sister, your cousin, your auntie', are pointers she will hear every day, from morning till night for the next few years; in fact, they make up the bulk of verbal communication with babies and little children (*cf.* O'Shannessy, this volume). And not only verbal; most verbalized kin relationships are accompanied by the according hand sign (*see* Kendon 1988), and before children begin to speak, they are praised for making the right hand signs on recognizing (or on being thought to recognize) the right relationship, e.g., slapping their wrist when a prospective husband or wife enters the camp. An advanced version of this is the delighted laughter children elicit if they start crying when told, in a sad voice, that their granny (or auntie, sister, etc.) is leaving the camp, '*Jaja ka yanirra*' [Granny is leaving]. In short, their earliest social interaction consists of introductions into their universe of kin, and the first praise they receive is for recognizing kin correctly.

While children receive praise when recognizing kin relations rightly, the opposite happens with Nora and old people considered *warungka* generally. They are as incessantly *asked* about people and their relationships to them as children are being *told*. Pointing to different people present, for example, Nora is asked: 'What's that person's skin?' and 'Whose baby is that?' and 'What is her name?' If she gets it right, people continue to ask questions until she makes an error, and only then does she receive a response: everyone laughs and the story of how Nora thought Polly was Penny is retold to later arrivals to the camp with great hilarity. While children are told and taught kin relations, and praised if they recognize them, senile people are asked about kin relations in order to provoke wrong answers as this triggers valued emotional responses, first in the listeners and then in the old person. In fact, the more wrongly they identify a particular relationship, e.g., mixing up generational levels or messing with avoidance relationships, the bigger is the amusement of others. When people laugh at a wrong response of Nora's, her face lights up, happy she has satisfied them, happy to have done something right. 'Too much *warungka*', everybody else says: 'She doesn't know anymore'; 'She doesn't recognize'; 'She doesn't remember'. This somewhat cruel play sanctions senile people's status as not being responsible for their actions. Such mockery is also commonly linked to ambivalent expressions of compassion and pity: '*Wiyarrpa*' [poor thing].

Eye Contact

Eye contact is thought of as an indicator of the child's will to engage in social interaction, an attempt requiring instant affirmation: a baby or young child who makes eye contact with a person is immediately engaged with through talk and physical contact. Warlpiri people are very good at picking up on this; I am not. Statements such as 'Napurrurla, Micky is looking at you', are often levelled at me – containing implicit criticism that I did not spot it myself, and a summons to engage with the child immediately. This regularly takes seemingly absurd proportions such as being told that a child held by a woman on the backseat of my Toyota is looking at me while I am driving, to which the only correct response is to look over my shoulder, no matter what lies ahead on the road, and to engage with the child. What this instils in children, I am sure, is a deep-seated knowledge that their social surroundings are there for her or him, that they are mirrored, cared for, looked after and enfolded into manifold and always available social relationships.

Unlike babies and young children who are immediately responded to when making eye contact and thus included and affirmed into the social universe, old people who are considered *warungka* have difficul-ties making themselves seen. Often, for example, people's gaze seems to jump over Nora, and for her to receive attention through visible means is almost impossible. Instead, she has to call out and ask for help, food, blankets, clothes or money. In direct reversal of the immediate response to children's demands for social engagement or things, senile people's demands are often ignored for as long as possible.

Sharing and Fighting

Children seem to cry very seldom, mostly when they want something, when something they want to keep is taken from them or when they do not get what they want – in which case it is normally immediately given to them by an interlocutor. As O'Shannessy (this volume) also describes, children are taught giving and taking, or the rudiments of demand shar-ing (*see* Peterson 1993), from a very young age: if other children (or adults) have something that the child may want, it is given to the child and then someone else will ask for their share of what the child received (for more details *see* Hamilton 1981). Just as often, things are demanded from the child. If another child, or for that matter adult, takes from her something she wants to keep, or teases her, the child is taught to hit that person: '*Pakaka! Yungkarni-manta!*' [Hit her! Get it!]. Hitting is 'prac-tised' with people in particular kin relations, ensuring that children grad-ually learn which actions to retaliate for with force and which ones to ignore, whom they can fight with and who fights with them and so forth (*see* Burbank 1994 for more on fighting). For example, one afternoon, Kaylene (two years old), her mother Beatrice (seventeen years old), and Beatrice's grandmother Polly (in her seventies) were lying on a blanket in the shade under a tree. Polly was teasing Kaylene, poking her and say-ing, '*Jinti, jinti, jinti*' [vagina, vagina, vagina], whereupon Beatrice told Kaylene to hit Polly, giving her a spoon to do it with. This went on for over an hour and when Polly left, Beatrice instructed Kaylene to hit some puppies next. Equally, when a child just learning to walk stumbles, he is instructed to hit whatever it was that made him stumble (a chair, the ground, a person's leg, and so forth). On the other hand, the same child will be told off or receive a 'fake hit' for hitting another child or adult without provocation.

Where children are taught to share and demand, and to fight if curtailed in their desires or in their autonomy, Nora reverts to stealing. Nothing is safe from her; food, money, towels, clothes, blankets, keys – anything she can get her hands on, she takes. And then hides. And then forgets where she has hidden it or indeed that she has taken it – proof, if proof was needed, that she is indeed *warungka,* having forgotten all rules for social interaction. If Nora tries to fight for what she thinks is hers or her due, her attempts either cause others to laugh at her, not taking her fighting (and implicitly, her autonomy) seriously, or, more usually, she is told off: '*Kulu-wangu nyinaka, warungka nyuntuju*' [Sit down/be without anger, you are *warungka*].

By slightly reformulating Morton's insights, we can define childhood and senility as prolonged thresholds between corporeal and noncorporeal existence, or, as stages of arrival into and departure from the social world. I want to examine further some qualities of being in this social world by comparing details in the lives of Janama, Kieran and Nora.

Janama

Janama is a little boy who has just mastered walking and is beginning to speak. As is common for Warlpiri children of this age, there is something he is 'renowned' for, something only he does, something that people often mention when they talk to or about him. In Janama's case this is the particular way in which, for the last few months, he has been crying. Rather than producing the common sounds of children's crying (wailing and unformed words), his crying is a litany of kinship terms and names. If he is upset, tears start rolling down his little cheeks, and his wail takes the shape of 'Jajaaaaaaa, Mamaaaaaaa, Papaaaaaaa, Alaluuuu, Jajaaaaaaa, Ankuuuuuuu, Mamaaaaaaa, Uwaiaiaiai' and so forth. When he cries, no matter whether he is upset, hungry, scared or angry, he literally cries for his grandmother, mother, father, uncles, sister and favourite dog – an idiosyncratic expression we can interpret as encapsulating the desire to be surrounded by familiar sociality to combat distress.

Kieran

There are a dozen or so of us sitting in the shade, dozing, gossiping, watching the dogs play, when we see seven-year-old Kieran bouncing up to us, followed by his mother.[15] Their entry into the camp is aided by a number of the women calling out to a young girl present: 'Look, Kieran coming', thus giving Kieran and his mother oral clues that they have been seen and are welcome to enter. Kieran's mother settles down with some of the ladies to tell them the latest gossip, and Kieran comes over to me and sits on my lap. 'Napu Napu', he says to me and pinches my arm. 'Kiwi Kiwi', I reply and pinch his toe. 'Napu Napu', he says in a whisper, while pinching my leg. 'Kiwi Kiwi', I growl and pinch his cheek. We both laugh and continue 'Kiwi Kiwi', 'Napu Napu', in all sorts of tones, spoken softly, loudly, quickly, slowly; and pinching here, there and everywhere. This is our game; we play it every time we see each other, often many times a day. When I drive past Kieran on the way to somewhere he yells 'Napu Napu' at the car driving past and I yell 'Kiwi Kiwi' in return. Nobody else calls Kieran Kiwi Kiwi – unless they talk to me about him, or when they tell a story about Kieran and me. Nobody else calls me Napu Napu (a diminutive of my skinname 'Napurrurla', that Kieran coined), unless they are referring to Kieran and me, or, are talking to Kieran about me.[16]

While this is Kieran's and my special way of relating to each other, similar games are played between other children and adults, and Kieran also has other special games he plays with other people. What they entail is an – always answered – desire of reciprocal engagement by the child with the adult. The kind of personhood and understanding of social relationships and practices that are shaped through these efforts (and the many other efforts of socialization) may be gleaned from the photographs that Kieran once took with a disposable camera he had 'nicked' from his grandmother. He took the camera and went off to take photographs, the largest number of which, and first on the roll of film, were of people, followed by pictures of dogs and then of his own shadow and of graffiti containing his name or initials. The photographs of people show certain of his relatives, but not others.[17] They include his real and close classificatory mothers, brothers, grandmothers and some more distant relatives. The youngest is less than a year old, the oldest over eighty. There is only one photograph of a child close to his own age, which seems to substantiate Fietz's (2005) point that orientation towards family is more important than the 'peer group', at least for young children. Once Kieran had taken all the photos he wanted to take of people, he turned to the dogs, his great passion. Lastly, he took photos of his own shadow and graffiti containing his name, an adroit way of self-portraiture for a seven-year old. We can look at these photos as an unwitting and ingenuous portrayal of Kieran's world: a social universe filled with the people most important to him, the dogs he loves playing with and himself.

Nora

To exemplify the nature of the social world Nora finds herself in today, I want to contrast what I said about Nora in an earlier account, namely, that 'there was no way to refuse a request of Nora's' (Musharbash 2003: 115–16), with an incident that took place when Georgia Curran, a PhD student, first came to Yuendumu in late 2005 in order to begin her research. When she arrived in the settlement, I picked her up and took her to my camp to introduce her to the women I lived with, many of whom Georgia was going to work with. A year later, Georgia told me how puzzled she had been when we entered the camp and purposefully strode past a woman she now knows as Nora, to a group of women to whom I did introduce her. As confused as Georgia was for not being introduced to the first Warlpiri person she walked past, as little did it occur to me to introduce her to Nora *before* introducing her to everybody else. This little (and a little uncomfortable) episode illustrates a number of issues I have outlined in this chapter: while, I am sure, Nora would have looked at us entering the camp with curiosity, my gaze must have jumped over her – avoiding eye contact with Nora, interaction with whom seemed futile at that juncture. As it was my responsibility to introduce Georgia to people in Yuendumu, that is, help her enter the social universe, Nora would have been the last person to introduce Georgia to – not only because Nora could not be expected to greatly contribute to Georgia's work, but also because of Nora's status as *warungka.* Introducing new people to someone who is 'departing' the social universe just did not seem like a priority.[18]

We can take this vignette and compare it to Kieran's photos: while the photos show a seven-year-old's positioning within a world focused on him, Nora appears on the margins of and drifting away from social relationships – through the ways in which others, including myself, behave towards her. Janama draws all around him in with his particular way of crying; Kieran (in the same vein as other children) designs games to connect himself to others. Nora, on the other hand, actively – if unwittingly – herself contributes to her own drifting away from others. I described Nora in the 1990s by saying that 'it must be said that she always reciprocated' (Musharbash 2003: 115–16) – as she did not anymore in 2006. In fact, she confirmed her *warungka* status by 'forgetting' how to adhere to the cornerstones of Warlpiri sociality (autonomy and relatedness, being boss for oneself and looking after others). She became 'child-like' and 'un-knowing' through not being able any more to reciprocate, to assert her autonomy, to look after others, in short, through not recognizing and not realizing the relations with those around her. Entering the *warungka* phase at the end of one's life is not only a loss of social (and physical) capabilities, but it is also a culturally salient natural transition, which is the inversion of childhood, away from the social realm of the living and towards *jukurrpa.* This goes some way towards understanding how and why the practices of relating to children and senile people respectively are inversions of each other. While children, who are 'not knowing yet' are cared for with patience and compassion (*see* Myers 1979 and 1988a for more details on this sentiment), senile people considered *warungka* are 'not knowing anymore', and do not require compassion of the same kind. Their basic physical needs continue to be looked after, their social needs, on the other hand, are understood within a framework of 'departure' from the social.

Conclusion

As I have outlined in detail elsewhere (Musharbash 2007), the Warlpiri way of being in time is to live in the immediate present. We gleaned through the case of Nora how this affects Warlpiri people's interaction. Nora *used* to be important, within her personal networks, in terms of the wider well-being of Yuendumu residents and as a ritual leader. She is *not* anymore – and people do not treat her any different to any other senile person. Who she used to be is insignificant in regards to tailoring behaviour towards her. In the same vein, at Yuendumu, who a baby may turn into is insignificant in the here and now; what counts is that she is a baby. Not only children's and senile people's actions, but the nature of specific social interactions of others with them marks their *warungka* status. One way of characterizing these practices would be to say that others have an obligation to 'pull' children out of, and, if you like, 'push' senile people into the *warungka* state through practices of (de)socialization. In short, what is important is the triad of where people are at, currently, in terms of the life cycle, how this is manifest in their own behaviours and how this tailors that of others towards them.

This brings me to the significance of life stages within the life cycle. In the Warlpiri context, I have found the idea of the life cycle more fitting than a lifespan terminology (for detailed accounts of life cycle events in other regions of Aboriginal Australia *see* e.g., Peile 1997; Goodale 1971).[19] There is a larger argument to be made here. The behaviours of Warlpiri people towards individuals indicate that we should look at a Warlpiri person's life as a cyclical journey, from *jukurrpa* into and through the social world, and back to *jukurrpa*. The particular life experiences of a person are certainly important in maintaining links to country and are remembered as such. However, structurally, this journey is the same or similar for any Warlpiri person: for a collective self-perception of Warlpiri people highlights that, at any one time, there are many people 'present on the ground' at different points within this journey. As Klapproth (2004) has shown in her analysis of stories in the Western Desert, such a 'lateral' and nonhierarchical view of life histories is also reflected in the aesthetic of the traditional oral literature; stories typically pay equal attention to different characters and lack a single climax. This view strikes me as significantly different from one that sees life as a personal journey through the lifespan of the individual. This latter view, I would argue, is, among other things, what contributes to the current research emphasis on Indigenous children or youth as a *group*. Academic research, policy, as well as on-the-ground programmes such as substance misuse prevention, youth initiatives and so forth (as a rule) focus on and perceive the current young generation of children and youth as 'the future'. If nothing else, I hope to have shown that the Warlpiri perspective centres on the place of children within a multigenerational setting. From this perspective, what counts is that, in the future, children will be older – while other children will be born and other young, older and old people will be around. When researching children and youth, we need to keep in mind those who shape them and those they will shape in turn as well as the Indigenous framing of temporality and the life cycle that guides people's behaviour.

Notes

Many thanks to Ute Eickelkamp and the earlier coeditor Pauline Fietz for inviting me to contribute this chapter and for their stimulating and insightful comments on earlier versions. Thank you also to the organizers (Andy Kipnis and Martin Forsey) and participants of the Childhood panel at the 2006 annual Australian Anthropological Society conference, where I presented an early version of this paper; and to my colleagues, especially Victoria Burbank, for stimulating debates and exchange of ideas. As always, thank you to *Yurntumu-wardingki-patu warlalja ngajuku* for teaching and looking after me proper.

1. Others have written about Aboriginal notions of the person and how this ties in with cosmological and ontological beliefs. Here, I limit myself to detailing the relevant sources about Warlpiri people (and some of their immediate neighbours).

2. I here outline Meggitt's use of this terminology. Others have discussed *pirrlipa* and *kuruwarri* and their respective meanings in more detail (*see* e.g., Munn 1973; Dussart 2000). Personally, I am more familiar with the term *kuruwarri* being used in Munn's sense (from ancestral spirit force to design in paintings and so forth) and the term *pirrlipa* to refer to one's spirit or soul. During my research, I have not come across postulations about *pirrlipa* as bi- or tripartite, perhaps due to my research interests, which lie elsewhere, or, the lengthy period of missionization between Meggitt's fieldwork and my own. Note that unless citing I use the current spelling, e.g., *pirrlipa* rather than *bilirba* and so forth.

3. Indeed, the Warlpiri dictionary (which currently exists in the form of unpublished and unpaginated electronic files) gives the Warlpiri version, *ramarama,* as a synonym of *warungka.*

4. This distance should not be understood literally, but rather as a structural opposition between *jukurrpa* as 'being there', that is, ontologically given, and ritual power as social achievement.

5. This refers to the personal Warlpiri name (for more detail *see* Dussart 1988b). These days, babies are also given an 'English' name at or shortly after birth, often suggested shortly after birth by the non-Indigenous nurse and increasingly also following input from non-senior female relatives.

6. 'Skin' is the vernacular term for subsection (*see* Wafer 1982 for a succinct introduction to Warlpiri subsections and kinship; *see also* O'Shannessy, this volume). At Yuendumu, skins or skinnames are frequently used as terms of address and terms of reference, and their use in many cases is preferred over that of personal names or nicknames.

7. This seems not to have been altered significantly by mission activity at the settlement since the late 1940s. Despite the fact that many Warlpiri people today identify as Christians (Baptist, Catholic and Pentecostal in the main), in my personal experience, people do not in fact perceive contradictions or an unbridgeable gulf between the above outlined notions and those imparted by Christianity, partly perhaps because vernacular terms such as *pirrlipa* are utilized to characterize Christian notions such as 'soul'.

8. However, the identification with certain spirit forces creates social and even group identity, belonging and cohesion, as Meggitt also showed.

9. Childhood socialization as a teaching of the ground rules of the social world makes an interesting (and somewhat paradoxical) contrast to the achievement of social and ritual status through learning about *jukurrpa*. Unfortunately, it is impossible to discuss this further here.

10. Hiatt's (2007) analysis of the Warlpiri moral lexicon, however, seems to suggest that both a person's character and behaviour may be subjected to critical judgement.

11. In the contemporary settlement context, 'camp' often includes an actual house, the space surrounding it, and continually changing groupings of people using this space (for more detail *see* Musharbash 2008b).

12. Most conversations recounted here originally took place in Warlpiri or in a mixture of Warlpiri and English; and the English translations are my own. Note that pseudonyms are used throughout the paper, with the exception of Kieran, whose real name is used (*see below*).

13. These three are examples of a wide range of practices, not inherently different in regards to practice or intent from the much more detailed description of socialization of Anbarra children by Hamilton (1981). *See also* Burbank's (2006) study about children at Numbulwar and the normative experience of the self as little inclined to submit to nonpersonal restrictions on what is seen to be the autonomy of the person.

14. Note that Warlpiri kinship is classificatory, meaning that every person the child is in contact with (the exception being non-Indigenous nurses) is a 'relative'.

15. I thank Kieran Sims and his mother for allowing me to use this data and his name.

16. This changed over the years; for example, a friend of mine, a classificatory mother of Kieran's, saved my phone number in her mobile phone under 'Napu Napu' and she and her children began to call me thus (and Kieran 'Kiwi Kiwi').

17. Of those people present, he excluded his grandmother, and it is likely that he was afraid that she would take the camera off him. Of close relatives not

present when he had the camera, he 'included' his father by taking a picture of his car.

18. During further discussion about this, Georgia said: 'It is also interesting given Nora's once extensive knowledge of songs etc. and the nature of my research [on Warlpiri songs] that you didn't even point this out to me: "Nora – she used to know heaps of songs but she has forgotten them", or something along those lines – proof in fact that your eyes really did gaze over her as otherwise I'm sure this would have been an interesting snippet of conversation'.

19. I thank Victoria Burbank (personal communication) for directing my attention to this matter.

Fathers and Sons, Trajectories of Self

Reflections on Pintupi Lives and Futures

Fred R. Myers

> Totemism 'as a social institution is a defense organized
> against separation anxiety' (Róheim 1945a: 249).

Questions about childhood in Indigenous Australian communities have
become very significant politically, but – with some exceptions – anthropologists have not developed the ethnography of childhood as one
might have imagined. What this would involve, I have often thought, is a
much greater attention to the interactions and communicative practices
(linguistic and otherwise) between children and caregivers as well as
among children themselves (*see* Ochs and Schieffelin 1984; Schieffelin
1990). I always wished I had been able to do this with the attention it de-
served, because the general models of childhood and socialization that
have been developed (of nurturance, autonomy, and so on) – however
appropriately drawn from Indigenous theories of personhood – do not
engage with the range of practices and subtleties of variations that must
exist and which inform actual histories of socialization.[1] As significantly,
I believe, the questions we sought to ask were not as theoretically elaborated as they needed to be in order to generate the empirical materials
for understanding how children become adult persons. I believe that the
recent work of the editor of this volume makes important contributions
to reestablishing the questions that should be asked about childhood.
With these caveats, my own contribution is surely more speculative than
I would like, but my interest lies in the development of 'sociality' in
Western Desert Indigenous subjects and the relationship of this sociality
to what I would call, with the existential psychiatrists, 'ontological security'. Laing (1965: 39) describes a person who feels secure in his being
as someone who has 'a sense of his presence in the world as real, alive,
whole, and, in a temporal sense, a continuous person'. My hope is that

some perspective from the past may be worthwhile in drawing attention to important questions around the continuity of being here posited as a social phenomenon. How is ontological security established in these communities? Indeed, what does it mean to establish this kind of trust or security?

In the past two years, I have had the opportunity to revisit some of the men I had known originally as boys in 1973 – some of whom I have seen only very briefly and intermittently since 1988. Since the early 1970s, as is known well by most who will read this, the lives of Indigenous people in remote communities have been marked by trauma and loss, with what has seemed to me to be a dramatic increase in the deaths of young men and the passing on of the elder generation. All along the road to communities like Kintore are plastic crosses and flowers marking the location and identities of deadly motorcar accidents, commonly fuelled by heavy drinking. Deaths by violence are certainly not a novel phenomenon, as I have discussed elsewhere (Myers 1986), and the problems of 'loss', 'grief' and 'attachment' are enduring cultural dilemmas in Central Desert Australian communities (*see also* Morton 1987b). But the scale has changed, and these changes presumably are working themselves out against the existing cultural forms. The centrality of 'separation anxiety', as Róheim (1945a) articulated it, suggests a vulnerability of attachment in the processes of life's trajectories towards a healthy self-regard. Indeed, in the face of these losses and with an economy of little prospect, one wonders how young people and children in these communities might envisage a future – a topic that some of my colleagues, such as those represented in this collection, are addressing. Lacking data specific to intrapsychic processes, I would prefer to bracket the psychoanalytic implications of Róheim's insight in favour of a broader notion of attachment or, perhaps better, of *belonging* as necessary to maturation and development. I intend this paper to reflect back on the lives of my young friends with the knowledge of present and past. Insofar as my knowledge is primarily of boys and young men, it should be seen as reflecting on the processes of socialization and identity formation of males towards what appears to be a particular desert Aboriginal masculinity.

Childhood and Social Production

I am particularly struck by the continuing close relationships between the men I once knew as boys, sustaining their intimate knowledge of each other from childhood over thirty years ago. This sustained intersubjective continuity seems a very steadying influence on people's self-regard. I was also very struck, in my original field study, by the affective ways in which one young man, who had lost both his original mother and father, articulated his situation as an 'orphan' (*yapunta*). Later, I wrote about the ways in which the painter Linda Syddick constructed through her art her first father's loss and his replacement by her attachment to her second father (Myers 2002, 2004). Seeing how the Pintupi communities – like many others – have suffered much significant trauma and loss, I would like to look at some details of the families and cohorts of the young people I first knew in 1973, to consider how they have fared in these situations.

When I arrived as a young American anthropologist at the Pintupi outstation community of Yayayi, there were nearly three hundred people living in army tents, with the tents principally providing shelter for 'families' and 'single women' (or widows) and the older boys and young men living with more informal shelters of galvanized iron. I have striking memories of the older boys: Tjampu Tjakamarra – then a young adolescent and recently in from the 'bush' – wearing a denim jacket with 'Make Love not War' on the back and the sleeves cut off, and Bobby West's interest in me as an 'American' like a previous visitor, an American Vietnam veteran, and Paul Bruno's desire to engage with me in English. Even in such a recent community, older boys were living in a world intersected by many fields of attraction. They knew a great deal about their own culture, spoke Pintupi as a first language, but were already adopting the Papunya Luritja style of speech developed at the larger community nearby, and most professed little interest in their own culture or country. Whether the boys were simply circumspect or uninterested, discussion or reference to *tjukurrpa* (Dreaming) either as stories or as sites was not frequent, although after initiation and deeper ritual exposure, they all demonstrated more pride in gaining knowledge about it. It was not clear that these young men were aspiring with the same vigour to becoming knowledgeable in the Law as their fathers did, and they certainly resisted prolonged withdrawal from secular social life for ritual matters. This speaks, I think, to some vulnerabilities of the transition to Aboriginal adulthood. These young men, or late adolescents, considered their elders and realized that the cultural frames had changed; they had other ways in which to imagine themselves.

Hanging around the camps at Yayayi – especially of my friends Freddy West, Shorty Lungkarta and Pinny Tjapaltjarri – I had considerable opportunity to spend time with and learn about family life, no matter how untutored I was in developmental psychology. Four themes particularly express my strongest memories of 'childhood' – of the situation of childhood – there. First, the close contact of small children with their caretakers and the constant attention they received, some of it rather invasive and aggressive – attempting to get a response. Second, the frequent tantrums of small children, whose desires for some object or attention were inconsolable and ultimately to be satisfied by older children giving way to the needs of the younger.[2] Third, what I found to be a 'strange' affective distance of adolescent boys towards their fathers (and mothers), so much so that I was sometimes surprised that a person we were discussing was their father! Fourth, the noticeable and explicit discussion of some young people as orphans (those who had lost close 'parents' who were raising them) and the compassion expressed for them. This was matched by the very noticeable demonstrations of loneliness and grief expressed particularly by young men who were 'orphans' when they were drunk – when their loss (that is, their not having anyone to 'look after' them) was commonly highlighted.[3]

All of these dimensions of children's lives entered into my accounts of the qualities of personhood among the Pintupi and into my understanding of the ways in which persons managed their relationships to others – and particularly into the salience of 'nurturance' (drawing on the metaphors invested in the concept of *kanyininpa*, 'having', 'holding', 'looking after') in the organization of sociality (Myers 1979, 1982, 1986, 1988b, 1993). These analyses from my first periods of fieldwork were based on a life-history and developmental-cycle methodology and a theoretical framework focused on social reproduction. In that work, the principal orientation was to what I described as 'the production of the social person' and in this sense, I approached the 'child' as an intersection or site of value production, a cultural subject in formation. The life cycle of a person comprised, at least for classical Pintupi society, the elementary cycle of social production. While none of my study was what could be called an *ethnography* of childhood, it did depend on the recognition of certain key themes in the lives of children I knew. The key Pintupi concept that, as I have argued, organized this cycle of production was expressed in the word *kanyininpa*, which means 'having', 'holding', 'looking after', or perhaps more figuratively 'nurturing'. Perhaps the most powerful image of this relationship is that of a child being 'held at the breast' (*kanyinu yampungka*). In the first instance, the metaphor would seem to draw on the mother's relationship to the child, of nursing, a theme which Róheim (1945a) took to be central to a subsequent anxiety about separation from the mother – an unwholeness or rupture which he understood to be resolved by or replaced through male initiation and identification with male objects and fantasized permanent union (or what I would regard, following Munn 1970, as ontological anchoring). This suggests the existence of cultural practices to deal with loss. To look after someone, I have maintained, involves a combination of restraint or control in the interests of that person's well-being, and it expresses as well a basis for intergenerational legitimate authority. Finally, and perhaps crucially, in my later considerations of this process, I came to understand that the relationship of looking after also involves an investment of identity in the nurtured person, a contribution. Thus, I wrote (Myers 1993: 38): 'Such "holding" – which connotes a kind of nurturance, protection, or management – confers a significant transmission … of identity to those who are held'.

More closely, in taking some issue with Francesca Merlan's (1986) characterization of nurturance as only a *general* contribution to identity, I argued that 'nurturing' establishes a *specific* individual identity, as part of the kinship system that mediates between two often-contradictory sociopolitical relations – between, on the one hand, relationships a person has with temporary coresidents and, on the other hand, long-term relationships with those who are spatially distant but potential coresidents. Only some seniors actually – in the end – 'look after' a person, and this active relationship establishes a particular component of the younger person's identity – whether expressed somewhat formally in taking on particular rights to place and knowledge (and thus, the senior person's subject position) or more informally in providing an easy nexus of social relations of sharing and exchange. *These are quite literally points of attachment both to a social order and through a sharing of identity.* An implication of these arguments was that being looked after – as materialized in receiving nurturance in the form of food, care, and later esoteric knowledge and rights – was a critical component in one's establishment of, or attachment to, a meaningful social (and psychological) identity. This analysis suggests that lack of 'holding' (of nurturance) could impede the development of adult identity. Insofar as it was a critical component, then, an interruption or loss of this care was potentially very costly – even a trauma. In an admirable recent paper discussing the nearby community of Docker River, Pauline Fietz (2008) describes a thirteen-year-old girl for whom the lack of proper care giving by senior female kin had left her 'significantly socially impaired'. While the girl was able to draw on a broad kinship network for basic support, she lacked the vital provision of 'the moral and ethical support' which proper 'nurturance' requires. The observation of orphans – and neglected children – was fundamental to my development of a similar, if less carefully articulated, understanding. And, as other recent observers have suggested (Dussart, personal communication summer 2007), there may now be a lack of sufficient attention from older men for their younger charges,[4] a decline in ceremonial transmission occasioned both by a demographic decline in numbers of middle-aged men and by their pursuit of interests (in town or elsewhere) that draw their energies away from the activities I described as 'social production'. (Without more systematic observational data, I should acknowledge that I cannot say whether support from kin other than parents – such as brothers, sisters and so on – can substitute or make up for losses, or in what conditions this might be so.)

Vulnerabilities of Attachment

My attention here, however, is more with what one might discern of the vulnerabilities of the local socialization process, of attachment and reattachment. I am not able to characterize confidently why some losses affect individuals differently, which would involve closer study than I was able to do. However, the child's age or level of maturity seems to be important, a guarantee of successful attachment perhaps. There are families in which the older children seem to have adjusted fairly successfully to the loss of a parent – especially through a violent death or accident – but younger children in the same family have done poorly. I can think of two such families, in particular. The younger siblings of one successful friend – who shared a mother with him – mostly died early deaths, from accidents or petrol sniffing, following their mother's tragic and untimely death in an accidental killing by their father. The children of others who died, for example, during the great loss of life in the early Papunya settlement period, were not as marked by that loss. My friends Titjiwin Tjampitjinpa and his half-sister Marlene Ross, for example, both suffered the loss of their father from heat in the Gibson Desert just before the Papunya era, but they have become successful adults. Others I can recall crying mournfully in moments of drunken despair that 'I got no mommy, no daddy. I can die, no worries'. Linda Syddick, the Pintupi woman about whom I have written before (Myers 2002, 2004), has cogently presented in her paintings the sense of loss occasioned by the death of her biological father in her infancy, along with the healing effect of her attachment to her adoptive father – expressed through his giving to her the right to paint his stories. Significantly, the kinship loss (her father) is articulated with the displacement from country occasioned by the early Pintupi relocation and settlement in themes of *E.T.* (Spielberg 1982) and return to country, suggesting that for some in the Pintupi communities, the trauma of loss is compounded culturally by changes in the capacity to maintain the attachments to place in which self-regard is also organized and managed. Indeed, relationships to place constitute an endpoint of the developmental process in which, in a sense, death is transcended, in that the relationships to the senior generation who nurtured one are converted to a more enduring identification with them through place.[5] If Róheim explains the resolution (or mediation) of a fundamental separation anxiety with the male individual's identification with a hard (stone, wood) sacred object, this is not the end point. The developmental process ends, as it were, in establishing a subject's relationship to place – a material form characterized by its enduringness, permanence and resistance to change (*see* Myers 1986, 1988b, 1993). It comprises the existential security that Nancy Munn once called an enduring 'anchor' (1970) and resonates with Craig San Roque's (this volume) emphasis on the necessity of having 'a place to go to' or to be.

Attachment and Reattachment: Changing the Ratio of Autonomy and Relatedness

If such successful processes would be the desirable outcome of the Indigenous socialization process, the point of young people's leaving their natal families must be a very vulnerable point. Indeed, as I think of the dynamic of young men's reserve towards their fathers mentioned above, it seems to me now a rather precarious moment of autonomy – freer of direct control and nurturance and not yet transferred into the nurturance of ceremonial sequestering and discipline by older men. Further, the embeddedness of Indigenous communities such as Yayayi in a larger field of racial and cultural difference adds significantly, I believe, to the vulnerability of this transition. When, as Marika Moisseeff points out (this volume), these young people see the greater value attributed to Euro-Australian culture (marked by the greater material wealth, respect and authority of Euro-Australians in these communities), their identifications and options for identification become more complex.

On the very day I drove out to Yayayi for the first time, to seek permission for research in 1973, thirteen-year-old P. B. Tjampitjinpa jumped into my car at Papunya. When, later, I arrived at Yayayi, it was P. – with a serviceable English – who informed me that 'the old men' were ready to see me. P. spoke to me often in the first few months, teaching me Pintupi words, facilitated by the English he had learned while he lived at the nearby Warlpiri community of Yuendumu. I always felt that I failed him, in some ways, by not reciprocating the attention he desired. His father S. B. Tjangala was, in 1973, the head of the Yayayi Village Council and a strong supporter of my presence, but P., I came to learn, had largely been raised by others at Yuendumu, where he had become a successful student (as marked by his very good English) and acquired a veneer of comfort with Euro-Australian ways. As far as I could determine, P. saw himself as a little different from some of the 'new Pintupi',[6] speaking better English and having resided at Yuendumu – which regarded itself as superior in 'Whitefella ways' to Papunya people. He was, in some ways, also 'between' the two worlds of identification with Euro-Australian models and recourse to the newly emerging discourses of Black Power. An age-mate and friend of Bobby and the others, P. seemed also to hold himself somewhat apart from them. Was it because his mother, S. B.'s first wife, had become 'mad' (*ramarama*) and wandered the camp, had been cast out and replaced by subsequent wives? P., I was told by an older classificatory 'brother', had been raised more by other Pintupi 'fathers' at Yuendumu, men whose nurturance of him gave them a special place in his initiation. But in this sense, he might not have been very securely any of their 'sons', and he sought attachment elsewhere, as with me.

As I have written elsewhere, the situation at Yayayi was tense. I remember that it was P. who told me that the radical Aboriginal activist Neville Perkins had visited Yayayi and that the White Department of Aboriginal Affairs (DAA) community adviser 'doesn't help the Pintupi but that Neville does'.[7] (Perkins had arrived with a truck being delivered from a government grant, which local people saw as his doing, but in fact he was delivering one supplied by the DAA.) Neville and Laurie Owens (the DAA adviser) had an argument, P. told me. He reiterated that Laurie 'doesn't do anything for the Pintupi but Neville does'. The old men, according to P., were thinking of kicking Laurie out and putting Neville in as community adviser. I realized something political was going on, and I thought I could hear Neville's words echoed in P.'s. I certainly felt very ill at ease, myself, as a possible target of activist anger as a White interloper and also someone who had received some help from the actual target of Perkins's accusations, but I now also see that this discussion shows a great deal of P.'s struggles with identification. He admired Whites, I believe, with whom he found some success as a schoolboy and whom he sought to emulate (in hygiene, styles of living), but – as was typically the case – he could not really be White. Thus, he had contradictory options, once the straightforward option of becoming adult had become complicated by intercultural options, troubled by his parental dislocation and embarrassed by his mother's demise. With whom could he reliably identify?

It is some indication of the mixing of cultural worlds that my notes record the conversation with P. swinging abruptly to talk about a classical anthropological topic – *kurtatjas* (magical revenge killers, the 'featherfeet' killers made famous in Spencer and Gillen [1899]) – intended, I believe, to warn me of the dangers of living alone in an Aboriginal community:

> They sneak up in the dark and you can't see their footsteps. If you kill a
> *kurtatja* you must pick up a stone and break it in your teeth; your head
> opens and you won't die. Otherwise that man still might kill you. Old
> men can see a *kurtatja* approaching – they can see inside and they sing
> and he can't harm them. [P., author's journal, Saturday, July 28, 1973]

But who was I to P.? I was a newly arriving White person from Amer-
ica. Perhaps he sought common ground or some assurance from a presumed Christian, another option for identification, like the missionaries
he knew? Shortly after this, P. began to talk about God 'who is coming
very soon. He will say to the dead: "You aren't dead, only sleeping.
Wake up now!" God gives people a chance, and if they don't take it, he
might punish them'. 'God made everything', P. said, 'me, you, the earth,
the trees. He sees everything, even in the dark. Some of the old men tell
me not to believe ... but I do'. I think this is part of the story of our interaction, but more important is P.'s active construction of a relationship
between us and his hope for sharing and sorting out these complexes
of information. A few years later, when P. was a teacher's aide in Papunya, he formed a very close friendship with the schoolteacher-poet Billy
Marshall-Stoneking – an affiliation with many of these qualities. By this
time, P. had more anger towards Whites, less innocence about his acceptance by them and resentment about his situation. Marshall-Stoneking
was identified with a more literary group of Euro-Australians working in
Papunya, and differentiated himself politically from many others. In affili-
ating with Marshall-Stoneking, P. may have been able to manage some of
his concerns, of being both Indigenous and different. This, too, probably
ended in disappointment, when the teacher returned down south. I do
know that P. died an untimely death, and I believe it to be a consequence
of failing to find an adequate place, a secure belonging – as it were, an
enduring anchor.

Apart from P., efforts to create attachments were something I found
happening repeatedly with older boys in the age range of twelve to fifteen years. For example, despite my close relationships with their fathers,
I hardly knew that P. was S. B.'s son, or that Bobby was Freddy West's son.
Indeed, these older boys seemed to seek out new people from whom
to gain recognition, attention, goods and friendship beyond their immediate families. At this age, my impression was that their fathers reciprocated and perhaps affirmed the boys' growing aloofness from them
by treating them in turn with a degree of diffidence and distance, more
comfortable in expressing their intimate affection with the younger children. The theme of their 'growing up', I argued, was in establishing such
relationships beyond the family of orientation as a means of gaining autonomy through increased social connections. Following the longstand-

ing, prescribed habitus of reattachment, these older boys, then, did not hang around their families or their families' camps – except for visiting their mothers for food. And, in 'classical' times – that is, 'in the bush' – their activities must have been even more independent, travelling with young men and getting food. They are and were regarded as somewhat wild, as difficult to control and unlike mature men who have seriousness of purpose and direction (see Myers 1986). They lack understanding and before becoming men they must submit themselves to discipline and control by older men. But clearly, as well, this is a vulnerable point in the cycle of personal development, a point at which secure prior attachments – as marked by expressions of 'nurturance' – are significant. Such cultural psychodynamics are part and parcel of 'man-making' – the work that men (and women) do for society – which had also been perceived by Stanner. He observed that 'older Aborigines had much insight into the elements of human psychology', and they would seize on natural stages of growth for the purpose of fitting boys into the adult scheme of life, often beginning 'when a boy had given up playing in mixed groups of boys and girls, and is starting to run around with a gang of boys of about his own age' (1979: 346). From then on, in the long course of male initiation,

> [t]hey worked on the boys' imaginations. They built up the sense of being prepared for an unknown and mysterious climax. Discipline and kindness, fear and reassurance, gravity and jollity, danger and protection, mystery and mundane things were blended within a wider plan to make the boys feel all the time they were in good hands. (Stanner 1979: 349)

Identity in an Interracial Field

What I did not recognize effectively, it seems clear now, was the complexity of becoming an Aboriginal adult in this intercultural or interracial field, where being 'Aboriginal' – in the history of its derogation – can produce ambivalent feelings. I am not saying the young are simply ashamed of their parents, but to become like them is surely more complex. That the feelings are not simple is evident in people's discussions of themselves. For example, once when I went out hunting in an old Land Rover with a group of Aboriginal men, we broke down and had to sleep out for the night. When the young men from Yayayi came out looking for us, one told me in laughter, 'I told you never to go out in any *Wonggai*'s [Aboriginal person's] motorcar!' But this kind of travel was all right for them, I learned. They could travel '*Yarnangu* way [Aboriginal way]. Any way!'

For most of the boys, the movement to adulthood consolidates their Aboriginal identity as men. With initiation, almost all the boys I knew became far more confident of their identities, more interested in their traditions and confirmed in their course – if, perhaps, resentful of or competitive with what they took to be Euro-Australian models. They could be mildly contemptuous of White men like me who were not really 'men' (*wati*). Yet, the frame has changed; they have more information and fantasies of options than was typically the case in the past, for their predecessors.

Perhaps it is of significance that a number of the older girls, especially those who had gone to school and were friendly with the women schoolteachers, seemed to want to be married to White men. They had learned how to keep a house, how to cook and other modes of comportment transmitted in the school, and the future in which these modes of comportment were possible involved the imagination of being married to a White man. If, in fact, this was not a very likely or productive option, it was fantasized as one, a way to take on the hygienic and stylistic way of life to which they were introduced. It struck me, if I might put it this way, that the boys wanted to be like or liked by White men and the girls wanted to marry White men. It has sometimes been suggested, indeed, that the Papunya painting movement's start, with old men painting Ancestral designs onto the school wall, represented a claiming back or competing with this new setting of socialization and young people's novel aspirations, as it did more explicitly at Yuendumu (*see* Warlukurlangu Artists 1987).

Cohorts and Produced Familiarity

I camped at Yayayi in the company of young men and older boys, and – indeed – more with some groups of them than with others. For much of my time during 1973–1975 at Yayayi, I lived in a small caravan very close to what was known as a 'single men's camp' (*tawarra*), which included unmarried males ranging from the ages of nine or ten to twenty-five years.

These were my closest personal relationships – with young men like Jeffrey James Tjangala (now a leader of the community at Well 33), George Yapa Yapa Tjangala (now at Kiwirrkura), Kanya Tjapangarti (a well-known painter at Kiwirrkura, recently deceased), Joseph Tjaru Tjapaltjarri (another well-known painter, at Kiwirrkura), Bobby West Tjupurrula (at Kiwirrkura), Tjampu Tjakamarra, Titjiwinpa Tjampitjinpa, Ray Tjangala and Morris Gibson Tjapaltjarri. There were others, but this was the 'single men's camp' (*tawarra*) that was often my home. Some have passed away – too many before their time – victims of the traumatic his-

Figure 4.1. ▼ Members of the Single Men's Camp at Yayayi, 1973
Note: Boys and a young man who were members of the single men's camp at Yayayi in 1973, including Ray James Tjangala (far left), Jeffrey James Tjangala, Bobby West Tjupurrula (far back) and Titjiwinpa Tjampitjinpa (far right) (Fred Myers).

tory that has accompanied the incorporation of Indigenous Australians into more settled life. I spent a good deal of informal time in this camp, sitting and chatting, and these young men and boys frequented my caravan for food, cigarettes and entertainment in a small remote community. Indeed, these were the first of the Pintupi people I knew. This was rather a large group, an artefact of settlement, surely larger than was common in precontact times, when people lived in small bands for most of the time. Yet, as Fietz's (2008) article suggests for young people at Docker River in the recent period, it was not just the entire 'peer group' of young men.

Inter- and Intragenerational Ties

There was a logic to the inclusion of these people in this *tawarra*. They were largely the children of the western, 'new Pintupi' mob, those who arrived in Papunya in the early to mid-1960s from areas out near the Pollack Hills (Walawala) and Jupiter Well (Puntutjarpa), and they were closely related in kinship terms – through marriages of their parents and siblings. For example, Joseph Tjaru's sisters Payungu and Parara were married to Bobby West's father, as was Tjampu Tjapaltjarri's sister. Kanya

Tjapangarti's father had been Bobby West's father's mother's brother. Ray Tjangala's sister was promised to Morris Tjapaltjarri's father. Indeed, they had grown up together in the 'bush' – by which I mean that their families had often camped together during periods of the year. This made them, by Pintupi reckoning of the time, *ngurrakutjungurrara* or 'one country-men'. While Fietz's critique of the youth culture 'peer group' model is certainly well taken, showing that young Pitjantjatjara are most actively influenced by those of their 'family groups' rather than 'the peer group', in fact, it is rather difficult to separate inter- and intragenerational rela-tions. As the brief discussion of genealogy suggests, the *relationships of the past were also projected into the future as enduring ties* among these boys and men, perhaps transformed into affinal connections and – ulti-mately – ritual sharing of ties to country. At the time, however, the boys of this group showed no interest in such futures, and were tied together as much by everyday histories of juvenile disturbance (stealing cars for joy rides) and exuberance as by anything as portentous as kinship and marriage in the formal sense.

It is not easy to figure out how to think about the tensions between the forms of solidarity developed between the nurturing generations and among the closely resident peer group. I think it likely that in the precon-tact past, when the age demographic was far less weighted towards the young, there were not always large enough numbers of children to con-stitute the intragenerational groups for long. These presumably intensi-fied with sedentary life and larger and increasingly younger groups, even though other forces might have led to greater emphasis on individual families. Children may have travelled for periods of time with other fami-lies, with their uncles/aunts and with other relatives, which would have increased their contact with people in their own generation. This is how the relationships of nurturance, the shared identity with senior kin who 'looked after' one, are reproduced in the relationships within the peer group that is established through shared residence. Indeed, I remember that in Shorty Lungkarta's life story, I often came to realize a good deal about current political relationships by learning with whom he had lived in the past. The connection between inter- and intragenerational ties is important: if your mother or father's 'close relatives' are people with whom they regularly aggregate, then the children of those people would also be likely part of your intragenerational group. I think this is a natural extension of past ties into the present, and it is engaged by the notion of 'countrymen' – which, for example, would collapse more distant kin categories into closer ones. For men, too, the intragenerational ties are certainly reified and marked in initiation. In this group, I do not see that school cohort ties or Christian identifications have reorganized affiliation, but that may be a factor for others. As for the present, I am inclined to see the intragenerational ties as extensions of ties from the past generation. They are both intra- and intergenerational at once – more like descending kindreds. When people are asked to list relatives, they show all the siblings of a generation (in birth order from left to right) and then below them all the children of all those siblings (*see also* Hamilton 1971; Dousset 2003). That has to mean something about how they experience this. So, I am inclined to see the parental home as aggregating more than immediate biological kin, but as regularly including the children of siblings who, as a group, are replacing the older set of siblings.

Undoubtedly, other dimensions of childhood escaped my immediate understanding, but more than a trace of them surfaced in the life- and travel-histories that I recorded – most in 1973–1975 and a few others in 1981. Listening to those histories – of life in the bush mostly – were what allowed me to understand what Pintupi people meant by 'one country-man' – which, I came to realize, included anyone with whom one frequently camped (*see* Myers 1976). Something very like this is what Basil Sansom described in his monograph, *The Camp at Wallaby Cross* (1980), as 'people running together'. I believe this is a very significant structure of Indigenous sociality more widely. However, it may be even most important as a formative structure of childhood extended into the future. Shorty Lungkarta's travel history first brought this home to me (published under the pseudonym of Maantja [Myers 1986]). In following his life, and particularly his accounts of those of his contemporaries he knew as a boy, I heard about what I took to be the equivalent of the 'single men's camp' I frequented: Shorty recounted his visits with the family of Mick Namarari (another well-known Papunya Tula painter) in the north and east of Shorty's home country, and his visits with Tapa Tapa Tjangala, who preceded him in leaving the bush for the Lutheran Mission at Hermannsburg in the 1930s, and with Ratji Tjapangarti, the father of Willy Tjapanangka and one of the important senior Pintupi at Papunya in the 1960s. These men, in turn, formed a core of the 'old Pintupi mob' at Papunya – a cohort who had known each other since childhood, men whose familiarity with each other was not simply the assumed familiarity of people in a small-scale society, but a *produced* familiarity, the outcome of family and visiting relationships projected onto a new generation.

Thirty Years On – Return to Kiwirrkura

After many years away, in May 2006, I was able to return to Kiwirrkura for a few days and this visit brought me back to the voices of 1973 – the voices of my friends that I had first heard then were coming back to me when I saw them in 2006. Here is what happened. I had planned to visit Kiwirrkura – the remote community of Pintupi and Kukatja people in Western Australia established in the early 1980s. This community included mainly people who had previously lived in Papunya and Balgo Hills Mission when they first left the desert. While they had entered the Euro-Australian administrative domain in different places, they had a prior association from living together in the bush. These were mostly people from the regions of Pollock Hills and Jupiter Well, and they had reaggregated after these many years close to their home countries at Kiwirrkura.

In 2006, I was bringing to Kiwirrkura ten hours of very lightly edited film from 1974, shot by my friend, the filmmaker Ian Dunlop and a Film Australia crew at the then Pintupi community of Yayayi. The footage, now stored in the National Archive of Australia, had never been made into a film and had never been seen by the people from the community (although I had translated the film in Sydney with two men from Yayayi). Because we did not know whether seeing the film was desirable, I wrote to my friend Bobby West Tjupurrula – now one of the leaders of Kiwirrkura. He wanted to have it shown and offered to oversee its screening. We set a date for my travel.

Bobby was – along with P. (who I discuss above) – one of the first people I knew at Yayayi in 1973, and he had sought me out as a friend. Very comfortable with White people, as was his father Freddy, Bobby had been to Darwin shortly before I knew him. He had been a resident of Essington House, he told me, a juvenile home, for stealing a teacher's car with his friend David Yupupu Tjampitjinpa. Bobby had really enjoyed Essington House, where he was taught to drive a tractor and had three square meals a day. Bobby has always been popular with White people – having a great interest in new opportunities and new phenomena – and he is very able to accommodate and negotiate with people. In 2000, when I went to Sydney as part of the retrospective celebration of the painting movement, Papunya Tula: Genesis and Genius, I saw Bobby for the first time in some years, but he greeted me with the warmth of our old relationship – built out of my closeness with his father, his mother and his brothers. Indeed, he asked me to speak in translating his words when he opened the celebration at the art exhibition and he told me that he hoped when they got their land back in the Native Title case that I would be there with them on that day. I say this because it indicates something about the relationships we had as part of the same tawarra with the implications this has for attachment to country, and because it explains why it made sense for us to collaborate on showing the film.

I drove out to Kiwirrkura with two friends to help screen the footage. After stopping at Kintore, the first Pintupi community on the route, we made our way to Kiwirrkura for what was to be the initial screening. When we got there, however, Bobby was gone. He had gone up to Balgo in pursuit of some ends of his own, and he seemed to have forgotten our arrangement. Because of the limitations in my travel time, we had a preliminary viewing of the footage in private with another senior Pintupi man (Jimmy Brown) who told us he thought it would be okay for people to view it. That night, at the meeting hall, we showed the first few hours of the footage. Still uncertain how people would respond to seeing their deceased relatives, talking and acting, I sat with Joseph Tjaru (another resident of the original *tawarra*) – who rolled with laughter and pleasure at the sight of his relatives, enjoying the sounds of their voices and what he identified as their personal antics. It was not until the second night of screening, however, that Bobby was able to return from Balgo – arriving just as we turned the lights off. He had not returned alone. He had brought back with him Titjiwinpa Tjampitjinpa – his close friend from their boyhood. Titji was always a lively and voluble person, and I was very happy to see him along with Bobby.

Now I began to see a shape of social relations. I had talked with Kanya Tjapangarti the day before, but he had remained distant. On the following day, yet one more visitor arrived, Jeffrey James Tjangala, asking to see any pictures I had of his father, who had died in 1977. Another *tawarra* person, and he came to visit with Kanya, who was now openly

Figure 4.2. ▼ Bobby West Tjupurrula, Fred Myers and Titjiwinpa Tjampitjinpa
Note: Bobby West Tjupurrula (left of author), and Titjiwinpa Tjampitjinpa (to the right), Kiwirrkura 2006 (Fred Myers).

friendly, the distance and diffidence overcome. My position and identity was coming into focus. Tjangala asked me to come back to where he was camped, to show the pictures to his son, and the pictures ignited recollections of the events we had shared. I sat with Kanya, Jeffrey and his son, as he pulled out the blanket next to the fire in front of a house. Then Bobby and Titjiwinpa joined in, and if I closed my eyes, the voices sounded no different than they had some thirty years before, the natural continuation of conversations and events shared.

Conclusion

I have argued that 'produced familiarity'[8] that is a projection from the past is the template of cohort relationships. In this formation of sociality, intergenerational histories are constantly 'updated' on each generational level. This fits with the general model of knowledge transmission and ideology organized around the conception of *tjukurrpa* and also with a ritual model in which relationships within one's generation are necessary to become like – or take the social place of – one's adult parent. Since my knowledge of this process is based primarily on my experiences of young men, I have entitled the essay 'Fathers and Sons'.

It has always seemed to me that there was something vital in Róheim's delineation of what he called 'totemism' – really the whole complex of objects and ritual involved in male initiation and the ideology of *tjukurrpa* – in his view that such totemism 'as a social institution is a defense organized against separation anxiety' (Róheim 1945a: 249). To me, the vitality of his argument does not lie in the specifics of psychoanalytic theory. Róheim saw male initiation as substituting for the separation of sons from their mothers, the rupture of a fundamental identification, and its replacement by relationships with men and the return of one's autonomous self in the form of a sacred object (the newly integrated self) that combined male and female. Any reader of this essay will recognize that I do not have as much information as I might like to clarify the attachments I describe in such a way. But surely the crying of men with compassion when they visit their country testifies to the significance of this identification. Nonetheless, I see 'attachment' less as a particular theory of psychology but more in its original ethological formation, more sociologically. Thus, I am referring to the detachment and reattachment of subjects as points in a social trajectory. These points, I believe, represent possible loci of identification and articulation but they are also points of vulnerability – especially insofar as the means of establishing trust and security – what I am referring to as 'ontological security' – may not be available in ways they previously have been. Moreover, I believe it is possible that some of the traumas of the present have echoes in the experiences of orphaned young people in the past, so that the circumstances of the present are not utterly distinctive. These are communities in flux, and we should be concerned to identify the sources of security and challenge. Róheim's brilliance was to recognize a trajectory in the formation of Aboriginal selfhood in Central Australia, to draw attention to its dynamic as one of attachment and identification and also to the profound insecurity addressed in the social production of a self. Ultimately, the significance of the 'unchanging landscape' as the fundamental anchor of identity is meaningful within the terms of this dynamic, as a particular resolution. But surely, these matters are more unsettled than they once were, and identities may be constructed out of other materials – with unknown effects. There is much to be done to understand the responses of individuals and to clarify the gendered dimension of selfhood. After all, not every orphan is or was traumatized, and we do not know how much the contribution and nurturance from nonparental kin may distinguish one person from another.

I left my visit at Kiwirrkura with a sense of what joy there can be in the recognition of oneself in familiarity with one's long-time countrymen. When, more recently, I viewed David Betz's (2007) film about Paddy Sims Tjapaltjarri, I also recognized the sadness he expressed that none of his countrymen were left to help him with his ceremonies. 'Only one fella living now', he said. 'Me'. The sorrow in that expression is central to the dynamic of selfhood in Central Australia.

Notes

My thanks to Ute Eickelkamp for urging me to write this and for spectacular editorial comment, and to Bambi Schieffelin for her careful reading and comments on this paper and long-term contribution to my understanding of the issues of studying childhood and culture.

1. Bambi Schieffelin and Elinor Ochs (see 1986; Schieffelin 1990) have made me profoundly conscious of these lacunae in the existing work.
2. Unfortunately, I cannot tell whether there is a gendered dimension to this pattern.
3. My impression is that loss of this magnitude was most typically related to loss of a parent or parents, although people clearly felt sorrow in other losses.
4. In a different way, Nicolas Peterson has also frequently made a similar observation to me about the demographic profile of Central Australian communities.
5. An analyst might say that human ancestors 'accumulate' at a place and become *tjukurrpa* – which, in this way, comes from people.

6. The 'new Pintupi' were those who came in from the bush to Papunya in the 1960s, and who differed from the 'old Pintupi' who had left the bush for the mission station/government depot of Haasts Bluff before most of the population shifted to Papunya.
7. A nephew of the very well-known Aboriginal activist and leader Charles Perkins, Neville Perkins had family origins in the Alice Springs area, but had grown up down South and was a student at the University of Sydney.
8. I thank Ute Eickelkamp for this coinage and for helping me clarify what the main points of my argument should be.

PART II

Stories, Language and Social Space

Sand Storytelling
Its Social Meaning in Anangu Children's Lives

Ute Eickelkamp

At Ernabella on Anangu Pitjantjatjara Yankunytjatjara (APY) Lands in north-west South Australia, the creation of stories drawn in the sand is a favourite medium for girls to present their thoughts. Since I first began research in this remote Western Desert community of around five hundred people in 1995, I cannot recall a day there passing without seeing sand stories being performed. The telling of sand stories, like the activity of dreaming (Poirier 2003), is part and parcel of the daily 'flow of events'. Girls begin to practice the bodily posture and movements of the distinctive technique at about two years of age before their narrative skills begin to emerge. Sand storytelling is a life-long practice, but most prolific during childhood and adolescence. It is a multidimensional form of expression and communication that, through its rhythmic and even musical quality, engages all senses and layers of experience, including those beginning in early infancy (Eickelkamp 2008b).

My starting point for the discussion of the social meaning of sand stories is that children create meaning through play talk.[1] Such a perspective emphasizes the well-established observation that, similar to ritual, playing constitutes a particular dimension of reality – it occupies a designated social and psychological space. Storytelling has much in common with playing, especially pretence play (play talk, narrative play).[2] Through storytelling children foster reasoning, imagination and memory as they work through difficult issues, relive and interpret particular events, invent personas that reflect their inner world or project themselves imaginatively into the future. Furthermore, an understanding of stories by children as a vehicle of meaning making can contribute to understanding the nature and status of stories in Anangu society (Klapproth 2004), and perhaps in Aboriginal societies at large.[3] As I seek to show, telling stories is a social activity; a form of record keeping, a narrativization of the experience of the self in relation to others, a communicative act that involves recognition of the role of listeners and withdrawal from others in the case of solitary story sessions, which too is socially sanctioned and significant (Sansom 2009). In sharp contrast to the short, plain and seemingly nonjudgemental utterance with which Aboriginal children I know impart painful facts – 'My Dad is in gaol', 'My little brother, he's dead' – stories are what John von Sturmer (2005) calls 'socially productive', and valued as such. A story allows narrator and listener to leave things open to interpretation, to conceal and reveal, to contest and then arrive at a shared version, to include others both in the plot and the telling (by allowing side comments), and to take turns as narrators. In short, storytelling creates social spaces.

This chapter considers some types of stories, themes, contexts for performing, links to other areas of children's lives and historical changes – all with a view to understand how Anangu children at different ages produce social meaning through sand stories. Although many elements are comparable to children's story performances elsewhere (e.g., story knifing by Yup'ik Eskimo girls in Alaska, and the widespread sidewalk drawings, picture books or any play talk), as a social practice, *milpatjunanyi* epitomizes a culturally specific fact. This is the emphasis on having a mind of one's own in the company of others. I consider this dual principle, first made explicit by Fred Myers (1986) in predominantly sociological terms as autonomy and relatedness, as a psychological reality in child development. Furthermore, for Anangu (meaning 'person' and 'body', but used to collectively refer to Aboriginal people with recognized ties to the APY Lands), the social and cultural significance of sand storytelling derives from its origin in the Dreaming, and I will discuss some aspects of the relationship between children and the Dreaming as it manifests in the medium of sand storytelling. The present focus on the social meaning of stories forms only one dimension of a larger, three-year-long study of how the children's inner world relates to the social field. The study examines – mostly outside the institutional settings of school and childcare – the symbolic and social development of three girls whose activities I have documented through participant observation and note taking, photographs and film, and children's drawings on paper. Fieldwork at Ernabella stretched over seven months and was distributed over several trips across the three years.[4] The girls were three, five and eight years old when I began focused observations with them at the end of 2004. It is their play and their sand stories in particular that I captured on film. I estimate that, on average, the two older girls, advanced to ages seven and ten, told sand stories for two hours per day, in sessions ranging between one minute and one hour. Occasionally, a girl took over the filming and offered a 'guided tour' through the community. At the end of each day, I transcribed and translated the play dialogues from Pitjantjatjara into English with the child's mother (in case of the youngest), a professional Anangu interpreter or a teenage girl. Good rapport with families prior to working with their children provided the basis of trust that has allowed for the relatively free movement through the community with the observing 'eye' of the camera. The focused observation of and engagement with three girls was supported by cross-sectional observations of children in peer groups and in the context of family life.

Milpatjunanyi: Technique, Contexts and Language

In sand storytelling, the girl at play sits on the ground alone or with others. She is speaking towards a small cleared patch in front of her where she illustrates her account by drawing lines in the sand, often tapping a bent piece of wire into the story field as she is speaking or silently thinking. At the end of the session, the marks are wiped out, leaving a smooth fan-shaped patch of sand. The local Pitjantjatjara term for this is *milpatjunanyi,* which literally means 'putting (*tjunanyi*) the story-stick (*milpa*)', or *walkatjunanyi,* ('making marks'). Sometimes, the practice is simply called 'storytelling' (*tjukurpa wangkanyi*).

The word *milpa* refers to a twig, now a piece of bent wire about fifty centimetres long, 'story-wire' as the children call it, that is used to beat a rhythm, draw lines, poke and swipe clear the ground or, less frequently, to point to something outside the representational story field. Unless the storyteller is left-handed, the wire at play is held in the right hand and often employed in alternation with one or several fingers and other parts of the left hand to draw graphs (*see below*). Before metal wire became available and until about forty years ago, women used flexible sticks as their story-stick, as well as eucalypt leaves (*nyalpi*) to represent play characters. The wire is a personal possession that, borrowed for too long or stolen by another girl, may quickly become a source for serious argument. Carried slung around the neck throughout the day, it signals being 'street smart', that is, readiness at any moment to demonstrate local knowledge, current relations to peers and state of mind. 'Putting the story-stick' in a variety of ways is a prosodic device that helps expressing emotions: the wire can be tapped gently on the ground, hammered restlessly, beaten steadily or held in suspension; it is flexed affectionately by stroking it with the hand, or bent and stretched vigorously.

By 'graphs' I mean simple shapes – circle or semicircle, square, straight or meandering line, or dots – that are drawn, scratched or poked into the sand. Individual shapes have a range of meanings that are not preestablished, yet personal and group conventions play a role. Moreover, the objects referred to are morphologically related (*see also* Munn 1966). For instance, whether in a single story or in separate accounts, a circle usually refers to round things such as the wheel of a car, a waterhole or a bucket. A single line most frequently represents a person. Placed in relation to other graphs and drawn longer or shorter, variations of the simple line illustrate posture (e.g., sitting when strongly bent), location, activity and perhaps relatedness to other people.[5] To illustrate: remembering her own childhood sand stories, a young woman, mother of the youngest girl I worked with, depicted (Figure 5.1) how she and other girls used to play '*wiltja-wiltjangka*' ('in the playhouse').

In this case there is a double reference to *milpatjunanyi:* she pictured a 'cubbyhouse' by way of illustration in a sand story and then showed how the girls would play sand storytelling inside the cubbyhouse. The scene traced in Figure 5.1 depicts a number of girls (the small semicircles whose equal size may indicate that all are children) sitting around a fire (central circle) inside a playhouse in the shape of a traditional shelter called *wiltja* (large outer circle with opening). A blanket is spread out on the ground (larger rectangle) and there are a lunchbox with hot chips and soft drinks (small squares) from the store that the girls have brought along.

Figure 5.1. ▼ Sand Storytelling in a Cubbyhouse

Note: Illustration in the sand by a young woman of how she used to play sand storytelling with other girls in a cubbyhouse, Ernabella 2005 (Author's sketch).

The drawing illustrates a generic yet highly realistic situation: the young woman did not say what stories were being shared or who was present, yet other women would readily verify the account as a correct 'template' for their own specific memories of playing 'cubbyhouse'.

Combined with one another and verbally linked to objects, places, people and events in time, the graphs obtain specific meanings. They cannot be read like an alphabetical script – but note that the girls occasionally include this into a sand drawing, especially initials of personal names – as they are an integral part of live conversations. In other words, the graphic depictions can only be understood through participation in context-specific communications.[6] Importantly, it is mostly the children themselves who create the contexts for such communications, by finding the time and a reason to play sand stories, by choosing a location, and by identifying what is to be told.

Contexts for engaging in sand stories vary within and across ages. A little toddler girl might be scratching lines into the sand at her grandmother's encouragement; a group of three, five and even up to fifteen girls between ages five and twelve may be immersed in cheerful and rather noisy exchanges of stories by the side of the road, during breaks at school or while attending community meetings (Figure 5.2). A lonely teenager might be absorbed in what looks like the performance of an internal dialogue, as she sits by herself in the yard of her home. Senior women often extended our conversation into visual comments in the sand, thereby transforming the ground on which we sit, and indeed the entire sphere of the group, into a demarcated communicative space. In preparation of a genealogy recording session, a woman might sketch silently her family tree with tallying lines in the sand (*see also* Dousset 2003) only to wipe it out and clear the ground when the interview begins.

From around the age of five, the most frequently drawn motif is the house. Rather than round bush shelters as in Figure 5.1, girls today depict the floor plan of rectangular houses, as they exist in the community (Figure 5.3). Such floor plans often set the scene in which a family story

Figure 5.2. ▼ Schoolgirls Illustrating their Conversations in the Sand

Note: Schoolgirls illustrating their conversations in the sand during a community meeting about school issues. Five separate story spaces have been marked, by wiping clear the ground with the story wire or hand, as does the girl in the front. Note that the boys are in a separate group by the fence, Ernabella 2006 (Ute Eickelkamp, with permission).

Figure 5.3. ▼ Floor Plan of a House
Note: Floor plan of a house with two people (U-shapes) sitting outside to the right, drawn by a c. twenty-year-old woman at Ernabella, 2005 (Ute Eickelkamp, with permission).

is reenacted, and there is also a guessing game about whose house has been drawn in the sand. Stories by children that relate concrete events from everyday life seem to outnumber children's performances of folk and fairy tales, and, when they do enact such canonical stories, girls tend to transform the fictional characters into real family members (discussed below).

Milpatjunanyi is nearly always performed in the children's first language, Pitjantjatjara or Yankunytjatjara. Lesser-known dialects and languages spoken by only a few children are sometimes mocked. For example, girls mimicked the sand stories performed by a young Luritja speaker, by producing an unintelligible staccato that was meant to mimic the sound of that language. Young girls in the process of language acquisition are able to sound like an older storyteller on account of their prosodic skill, and they are also adept at strong facial expressions.

Tjukurpa: The Place of Story in Anangu Children's Life

O'Shannessy (this volume) has offered pertinent observations about the social functions of stories in the life of Warlpiri children in northern Central Australia. These also hold true for Ernabella: storytelling in the family context is a highly valued practice and an important vehicle of knowledge transmission. Children recognize that 'talking story' is a designated social technique. Furthermore, adults may encourage children to 'talk story', or they engage in children's play talk in order to manipulate the child's behaviour; for example, to prevent a fight between children.

In the mind of Anangu, sand storytelling is especially important at another level: it is one of many practices of everyday life that adults say originates in the Dreaming. The term for Dreaming, *tjukurpa,* which refers to the world-shaping Ancestors of the deep past and their abiding manifestations – in sites, songs, designs, birthmarks, names, oral accounts, sacred objects, customary law and social practices – can be glossed as 'story' or 'law'. *Tjukurpa* is also used for stories of any kind, including sand stories. Another term for 'story', but less used by the children, is *ara*. According to Goddard (1992), *ara* can refer to 'story, yarn, history'; 'thing said'; 'occasion, time'; 'way, custom'. The particular meaning range of the two terms is an indication that the sanctioning of action and knowledge through narrativization presents an important link between Dreaming Ancestors and people, across time and generations. Children not only sanction certain versions of events in their lives through repeated storytelling, they are also regarded to be especially close to the Ancestral realm. Having just come out of the Dreaming, the soul or spirit (*kurunpa*) of infants in particular is still closely linked up and in communication with the Ancestors. However, with their 'ears not yet opened' (*pina pati*) to the teachings of song and ritual and to customary law at large, children are considered to know the Dreaming unconsciously, that is, in socially unmediated ways and in this sense directly.[7] Although unaware of the link between their play stories and Ancestral practice, it is precisely the performance of Ancestral activities unbeknownst to the children which demonstrates the link: children's play is one form through which the Dreaming reveals itself. And, as I elaborate further below, for the Anangu this intrinsic link is the foundation for other, more marked forms of knowing the Dreaming later in life. It is proper Ancestral Law and custom for children to play in general, and although young women and girls do not tell Dreaming stories in *milpatjunanyi,* it is nevertheless the sanctioned playful practice for girls. Like the typical childhood occupations of boys, such as killing birds for eating by throwing rocks at them in the context of make-believe play at being grown up, the gender restriction of *milpatjunanyi* as a female activity is *tjukuritja,* meaning something they do in continuity with Ancestral women's practice.[8] In this sense, children are thought of as following the 'Law' of the Dreaming. But if *milpatjunanyi* is part of the Dreaming, as Anangu say, it is a 'small' Law, not a 'big' one like the man-making ceremonies or determination of marriage partners (Peter Nyaningu; personal communication 2007). Nevertheless, the status of sand storytelling as a lawful and ordering activity is important; not as a ritual performance in the strict sense, but as a ritualized expression in everyday life. In the modus operandi of 'law as story', social efficacy is achieved by 'witnessing' (Sansom 1980; von Sturmer 2002), and in *milpatjunanyi* too the presence of onlookers and listeners is important. Establishing relatedness by sharing news and memories is complemented by the personal autonomy and authorship of the owner of the story-wire who rarely allows her audience to make a mark in the patch of ground cleared in front of her. Girls often sit together but simultaneously each performs a different story (*see* Figure 5.2).

Stories convey a socially significant message, yet not necessarily in narrative form. It is not unusual for a story to be only alluded to by personalized signs – marks on canvas, or initials of a person's name scratched into the bark of a tree or written on the wall. These instances make clear that the message may not be 'in' the story or hidden 'behind' the sign, but in the fact of the appearance of that sign: already 'telling' is that somebody has made it, at a certain time and place. As von Sturmer (2002) poignantly observed, making marks is more than linking people, places and time – somebody has created a moment and a place in the first instance by making a mark then and there. After all, this is how 'story places', that is, Ancestral sites, came into being and therefore may be regarded as embodying Ancestral activity. Here then may lie the primary social meaning of making marks and of 'talking story' in the realm of Ancestors and living humans alike: to mark the presence of people, that is, to assert the 'pure and utter beingness of the person' (von Sturmer 2002), which is the point of departure for any forms of engagement and communication.[9] Moreover, the 'now' of the mark, and especially the repeated instantiations in sand stories, presents an ongoing engagement with memory. Like those senior artists whose paintings flow from a reverie in Ancestral country, sand storytelling by girls produces a 'stratification of the memory of events in places' (Dolk 2006: 40). Dolk's view of the visual poetry of Gija painter Paddy Bedford is true for *milpatjunanyi* – an 'imaginary space' is filled between place, story and gesture made tangible in images.

The filling of an imaginary space with symbols is a complex process in which thought, image, speech and mark-making gesture are closely intertwined. This intertwining is also embodied in the story-wire, which is both symbol and symbol-making tool. As such the story-wire shares with ritual objects their dual meaning-structure (Moisseeff 2002). Indeed, *milpa* is not just any twig (called '*punu*'), but that which 'got story' acquired through use.[10] *Milpa* is the storytelling instrument but also the idea of story and it can be referred to as *tjukurpa*.[11]

Types of Children's Sand Stories

For children, sand stories are a sign of mental strength and highly realistic, including those that an adult would regard as fantasy. They most commonly depict events – remembered, as they are being observed, and sometimes in anticipation – that preoccupy the child at the time, consciously or unconsciously, and hence reflect how children perceive the structure of their everyday life. To relate an experience in the form of a story as well as remembering and telling a story, is called '*kulira wangkanyi*' ('recount'), whereas to make up a story in one's mind that does not relate an experience or shared knowledge is referred to as '*katangku kulira wangkanyi*' (literally 'the head is thinking a story', meaning 'fantasy'). However, unlike O'Shannessy (this volume) who reports that Warlpiri children at Lajamanu only rarely produce fantasy stories, I have observed that young girls in particular are adept at mixing the two types of narrative. Interlacing perceptions with personal associations (and hence subjective experiencing), their story sessions can be fragmentary and replete with transitions from one topic to another, and from observation to fantasy, similar to free-play activities in general. Some common early-childhood fantasies become collectively instituted (mostly as a kind of monster) and are reported as 'real' even among teenagers.[12] A further distinction is made between 'talking story' in the company of peers or in solitude, and it seems that *kulira wangkanyi* is the most common type in talking in front of others, while the spontaneous expression of thought and fantasy, *katangku kulira wangkanyi,* is reserved for solitary sessions.

A distinctive form of narrative is a name-guessing game (*see also* Tjitayi, this volume) that encourages inferential thinking. The player begins by describing a distinctive feature of the person in mind, for example, 'long curly hair'. She will add further information about family status, place of residence, etc. until another child has identified who is meant. A variation of this game is to write the initials of a person's name in the sand, which may also be used to silently name a particular person in a conversation. The primary function of this form of playful encoding is to test social knowledge and to thereby identify the insider status of the children present.

To be able to identify people on the basis of concealed or 'encoded' messages is indeed of critical importance. A secret language used by Pitjantjatjara teenage girls has been described by Langlois (2006) and one could similarly interpret as in-group markers the prolific graffiti on the indoor and outdoor walls of houses (Nicholls 2000) and children's cutting of letters into the bark of trees. I was taken on a graffiti sightseeing tour by two seven-year-old girls who unravelled the layers of family histories in each room of a residential house, where individuals had left their initials and other 'tags' in an effort to leave their mark – meaning presence – for those who can decipher it.

From middle childhood onwards, a reportage style of sand stories is prolific that, moreover, shows commonalities with the narrative traits of traditional Pitjantjatjara folklore.[13] Klapproth (2004: 282ff.) identified aspects of text-building conventions and story schemata that appear to also characterize at least some contemporary stories by children. These include a 'shifting character focus', the motif of a journey that structures stories into a rhythmic cycle, the 'retracing' of the same event by different characters in a process of slow discovery by way of reconstruction, and an overall nonhierarchical structure. There is an important difference between our approaches: Klapproth aims to identify Pitjantjatjara narrative aesthetics, where I seek to understand the inner life of individual children. There is also a difference between the emotional significance that self-created stories have for children on the one hand, and collectively held stories transmitted by adults on the other. The child who recounts what happened last night at home, imagines with anticipation the next trip to town or enacts fantasies of being a mother instantiates the self. Moreover, I think that children's stories told by adults are hierarchical in the sense that they have dramatic peaks that are prosodically emphasized. For example, when Whirlwind takes a girl away, the storyteller launches into a high pitch and then pauses looking up into the sky; the killing of Black Crow Woman in a story about marital dispute is recounted with a tone that evokes heavy blows and sadness.[14]

'Proper Stories', Different Truths: Continuities and Changes

As mentioned earlier, storytelling is important for the immersion of children into the reality of the Dreaming. Do children think of the Dreaming as story? Nancy Munn's observations on Warlpiri sand storytelling from the 1950s at Yuendumu are instructive here. There, the main narrators were women and, like at Ernabella until a few decades ago, the typical sand story at the time was an account of the daily activities of Ancestral people and of events that took place in the Dreaming. Such stories, told in the casual context of the family camp, would describe ordinary things done by anonymous human beings of the distant past who lived like the present generation of people. Children would learn to follow such accounts of the Dreaming by watching from an early age older female kin perform sand stories, telling them that these stories were *tjukurpa* (*djugurba* in Munn's spelling). Occasionally, the graphic system of sand stories was used for other narratives, such as invented tales or accounts of personal experiences. The women referred to such stories also as *tjukurpa*, but distinguishing these clearly from the Dreaming, which would then be labelled 'proper *djugurba*' (Munn 1963: 41). Unlike the more guarded recitations of Dreaming activities that identify particular sites, these 'open' accounts of how people lived a long time ago do not specify place. About the children Munn reports further: 'By the time a child is 5 or 6 he can repeat a few fundamental graphic signs and fragments of typical sand story incidents. These he calls *djugurba*'. A few years later, at age eight or nine, children 'can tell continuous narratives which are usually made-up stories or weavings around personal experiences; but which the children refer to as *djugurba*' (38). For the children, it can be inferred, the Dreaming Ancestors appeared as ordinary human beings with whom they could easily identify; thus *tjukurpa* is psychologically close, familiar and therefore real – it is just like their own stories. I think that, as did the children at Yuendumu, the children at Ernabella take the term *tjukurpa* to mean 'story' in a general sense because, until recently, they were exposed to versions of Dreaming accounts that mirror their own social world, knowledge of which is not restricted. Children are aware of Dreaming knowledge where it is restricted – they avoid 'sacred' areas in the bush, for example. And they anticipate their induction into the esoteric Dreaming knowledge later in life. But during childhood, telling sand stories is part of the everyday. The relationship between stories and the Dreaming is then both continuous and discontinuous, which allows for the meaningful adjustment of the one to the other in accord with the age and knowledge of the person, and in response to historical changes. Munn explained the continuity between ordinary and Dreaming stories to rest on standardization that keeps the Dreaming contemporary:

> On the one hand, the content of the 'proper *djugurba*' is composed largely of everyday events; on the other hand, the same or similar nar-

rative technique may be used to recount everyday incidents or personal experiences. In effect, daily activities are by this means filtered through a culturally standardized formula for storytelling. One can see from this how current events and local gossip might readily be assimilated into 'proper *djugurba*' thus helping to maintain the contemporaneous character of these tales. (Munn 1963: 41)

If this characterization suggests a certain rigidity and repetitiveness, it should be emphasized that the same technique also allows for endless variations – condensations, elaborations, segmentations. One might also note that people look for how the Dreaming reveals itself in the here and now and that the continuity of narrative form is psychologically both reassuring and exciting. However, this continuity, which helps safeguard the children's immersion into the reality and heritage of the Dreaming, appears less pronounced today. Older women at Ernabella say that in the past, *milpatjunanyi* was a more formal affair and that the personalized accounts so common in today's stories by children were rare. They remember the cherished custom of boys and girls to sit around an adult narrator before going to sleep, in order to listen to 'bedtime stories', meaning folktales and family stories that have been transmitted for generations and could be labelled 'canonical'. The girls would then enact such narratives that they refer to with the English 'proper stories' in solitude (*see* Tjitayi, this volume). This is the same specification that women at Yuendumu used to identify stories from the Dreaming. However, the Ernabella children do not say that these old 'proper stories' are Dreaming – even though many of them are. Rather, to their mind, 'proper' means the 'right way' or 'correct' – what a story should be like. As they hear these stories being told by old people – the most important bearers of Anangu social and cultural memory – over and again, they recognize that these are part of a tradition, *ara.* Characteristically, the canonical stories feature birds (*tjulpu*), butterflies (*pinta-pinta*) and other 'natural' phenomena that represent people and human experience.[15] Undoubtedly, these play stories are anchored in and reflect the transformative power of the Dreaming, and some stories are 'public' or 'open' (*ala*) versions of mythic episodes. However, as Munn also reported for sand stories at Yuendumu, other stories are not seen to have originated in the Dreaming and instead are said to have been made up by a particular person for the purpose of entertaining the children in the family, or to have existed as 'anyway' stories for a long time.

Although an analysis of the links and transitions between Dreaming, folktale, memory and fantasy across time and the life cycle exceeds the scope of this chapter, it is worthwhile to sidestep the discussion and point out that children, despite the fact that their storytelling now has little to do with 'proper stories', are regarded as especially sensitive to manifestations of Ancestral presence. They can see the Rainbow Serpent Wanampi and, unlike adults who may encounter Dreaming beings or find songs and designs in their nocturnal dreams,[16] children as young as five have been reported to see the visiting spirits of deceased family members while awake during the night (Lewis, this volume). From the perspective of psychological development, one could say that moments of relative nondifferentiation between conscious and unconscious mental states and between perceptual and projective images that typically occur during early childhood are socially valued; they are regarded as a gift rather than as lacking 'reason'. Children's nocturnal visions obtain concrete social significance when reported to and interpreted by members of the family who may even see it as a sign that this child has the talent to become a *ngangkari* (traditional healer) or a pastor of the church. Interestingly, women insist that they never depict their nocturnal dreams in sand stories and instead relate these only verbally. Until now, I have only once seen children report a dream in the sand, which seems unusual because when asked, older girls say that they would not do it. And while it may well be that young children in particular do not identify dreams as such, it is not clear why they refrain from depicting these in the sand.[17] Perhaps this has to do with the fact that, in *milpatjunanyi,* the sense of agency lies clearly with the player, which is not the case with most dreams. To the contrary, dreams are often felt to have come by force of the volition of another subject – with good or bad intentions.[18] In such instances they are identified as a message from other people or extrahuman powers. The several boys and girls whom I asked individually where their night-time dreams come from, all pointed to the sky and said 'Jesus'. For adults, a dream may be considered 'true' (*tjukurpa mulapa*) – as opposed to originating in one's own mind and in this sense being 'made-up' (*ngunti*) – because it contains a message from Jesus. As one prolific dreamer told me: 'Dream visions come from Jesus'. In contrast, sand stories, especially those by children, are the product of their own mind, and personal authorship is carefully guarded. Here too, truthfulness – in the sense of gaining recognition of ownership and of veracity – is paramount if the story is to afford the teller a social gain.

Munn (1965) noted some forty years ago that Pitjantjatjara children's sand stories introduced iconographic innovations in accord with the changes of the life space. She reported from Areyonga that windmills, trucks and riders on camels, that is, items that came into use with life in settlements, only occur in children's sand stories, where they are constructed in the 'traditional building-block style', that is, individual elements are combined into more complex graphic structures (22). Interestingly, she had found a different situation in the Warlpiri community Yuendumu a decade earlier. There, nothing in the women's sand stories betrayed the changes from a full hunter-gatherer existence to settlement living and all the novelties that contact with Europeans had brought. This nonassimilation of novel elements could mean that a gap between the Dreaming and contemporary living – and therewith a gap between the generations – was beginning to emerge. As Munn (1963: 44) wrote, 'The sand story thus seemed to be in the process of becoming more specifically a story about a past way of life, rather than a story allegedly about the past in which the way of life exemplified is much like that of the present'.

At Ernabella, some girls recognize that their contemporary stories differ from the canonical 'bedtime stories' of their grandmothers, and it is quite possible that they have heard older women comment on this. Asked if she liked to tell such kinds of old stories in *milpatjunanyi*, a very intelligent twelve-year-old girl replied, 'I don't talk story like that – only what's in my head'. She meant that, instead of reproducing established narratives, she is used to telling stories about concrete events that she remembers and might want to share with other children by creating a story about her experiences. Most new stories that I have recorded contain the self-referential pronoun 'I' and the storyteller appears as one of the protagonists. In contrast, older women prefer tacit or oblique references to the self in canonical accounts and tell me that this self-referential personalization is not something they used to do much in their childhood. One woman in fact strongly disapproved of the prolific employment of 'I'. Shaking her head, she said it was not right and improper. She felt uncomfortable to see – by watching most of the footage from my research – the children singling themselves out in this fashion, as if it was immoral to do so.

Traditionally, Anangu, like other Aboriginal peoples, tend to avoid using personal names and are cautious about where they leave traces of their own presence. Such restraint, which is fuelled by fear, namely, of suffering harm from evil attacks on those exposed aspects of the self, fosters social equality in the sense that nobody is to put herself 'in front of' others. Anonymous accounts lend themselves to illustrate the typical, and perhaps my friend's objection to the children's use of personalized stories can also be understood as a concern to uphold the tradition of filtering personal experiences through 'a culturally standardized formula' that, as Munn suggested, in turn facilitates the assimilation of the past into the present, and the present into the past. Today children still avoid naming innovators, which, in light of this woman's reaction, appears as a remnant of the earlier stronger tendency to avoid the proliferation of any personalized account. This condemnation also invites a certain interpretation of the girl's self-assessment in negative terms that subsequently emerged. A few weeks later, the same girl revealed another layer of meaning to her statement, 'I don't talk story like that – only what's in my head'. Asked if there was anything at all that she would like to say about being a child at Ernabella, she explained, '*Wiya* [no], I can't think. My head's *kura* [bad]. That's what they've told me. I can't do it anymore like before'. She said this as she was busily piling up charcoaled and white rocks collected from a burnt-out house, in concert with several other girls who were also getting ready to make floor drawings. Indeed, as one of the oldest, she seemed to be guiding the younger girls and her actions appeared entirely coordinated. As she had identified it herself, the problem for her was to create a story òut of experiences, even if these are about storytelling and drawing. In this sense, one could say she had difficulty translating action into narrative thinking, rather than thoughts into action.

Importantly, the girl's account of her own shortcoming tells us something about the status of 'story' as a designated social category among children. It is a category of reenactment or representational performance, and as such different from an event or circumstance per se. The girl had come to think of herself as unable to talk in a representative, that is, socially sanctioned, manner (she used to depict with confidence her large family tree only three years earlier) because she cannot tell 'proper stories' anymore. The fact that she explained her condition by saying 'they've told me' (she is referring to a psychiatric assessment) indicates how strongly self-perceptions are shaped by what others say. This orientation is inculcated in positive and negative terms from early childhood onwards through socialization techniques and peer behaviour, possibly more so in the past than now (*cf.* Tjitayi, this volume). There still exists a strong concern that others want to manipulate one's mind by weakening the will; for example through dream visitations instigated by 'love magic', bone pointing or modern 'magic' watched on TV.

Not being able to talk 'proper stories' is distinguished from telling stories in a new way – the latter can quickly become the 'proper way'. As is well established, oral traditions are continuously transforming, and the sense of continuity derives from the collectively instituted pathways for change. Children play a key role as innovators but without presenting themselves as such. They also change their play habits – what is played where with whom – from one day to the next, without announcing the change. Rather, in accord with the cultural privileging of collectively sanctioned expressions and practices, they try to make a novelty into a tradition, and a change into the 'proper way' of doing things, by having others adopt the innovation, thus collectively instituting it. This can happen very quickly. 'It's finished', one girl explained to me when I asked why nobody was playing in the shrub on that day after, over several weeks, I had spent every afternoon until then with them there. Although the children might acknowledge an individual child as the originator of a new game, story, song or graphic item for sand drawings or on paper, the 'invention' becomes more respectable at the point of transmission into anonymity, when those who have taken up the novelty do not know its source so that, when asked, they can 'safely' shrug shoulders. The children were generally reluctant to identify individuals as originators other than as perpetrators of a transgression. They would, however, name the place where something originated, which, I think, authenticates the item and the 'rules' for handling it: 'Girls can sing new songs, but only boys can make them. That song, them boys from Amata started it', three girls at Ernabella told me. My impression is that those children in particular who come from other communities or even have different cultural experiences and who are trying to assert their place in the child society at Ernabella introduce novel elements. To achieve assimilation of an idea or way of doing something into the local child society appears to be a measure of their acceptance. A child who fails in this and instead has her ways identified as odd or different (*kutjupa*) runs the risk of attracting ridicule and teasing. Perhaps on account of the increased size of the child population, teasing among children has become a serious problem that often results in severe arguments between their parents. As a social technique confined to specific contexts, teasing safeguards accuracy of performances, as in the mocking by senior women of younger women's ritual dancing.

In the girls' sand storytelling, personal style is valued, but expectations of 'talking straight' or to tell 'proper story' always play a role. These expectations may apply to the content of stories and, as a rule, to the manner of enactment. At Ernabella, it seems that the status of tradition is ascribed to the technique rather than to subject matter and shape of graphs, including such unspoken rules that the wire is held in the right hand by right-handed persons and the last scene is erased at the end of the play session, whereas the content of children's play stories is more a matter of personal choice. The 'rules' of the technique provide a sense of being held safe that is necessary for free play to emerge. However, in addition to feeling secure in drawing on a well-established tradition, the children may also experience restraint in sand storytelling. In a way, the symbolization of their thoughts and feelings in an illustrated story contains the impulse to act things out directly (as in hitting another child in anger). And containment, even if it serves the expression of emotions, has to be learned. Indeed, sand storytelling can be used as a form of disciplining children, as I have often seen women insist that girls who are 'cranky' and quarrelsome sit down and tell a sand story. Furthermore, control of content is a strong element during middle and late childhood when peers check the stories. The child audience does not seem to censor the choice of stories, but safeguards the accuracy of accounts that in turn serve to validate, challenge or build social relationships among the children.

Developmental Thresholds

Sand stories are an important medium of transmitting oral traditions and family knowledge across and among the generations, including between males (who listen) and females. As in other desert areas, the technique is part of the socialization process that varies in locally specific ways. Munn described for Warlpiri families at Yuendumu that very young girls do not perform sand stories. Only at the end of late childhood from around age nine, when the ability to tell stories is consolidated, may girls use the sand story technique to convey personal experiences or invented narratives (Munn 1973: 63–64). Christine Watson, in her account of Kukatja women's sand drawing at Balgo, explains that children and teenagers are instructed in hunting and gathering, social protocol and behavioural expectations (Watson 2003: 82–83) through stories performed by women; she does not report storytelling by children. David Wilkins (1997), who has described Arrernte children's sand drawing patterns, produced a tentative developmental timetable that shows the emergent and differentiating skills between ages eighteen months, when children begin to scribble and mimic shapes, and young adulthood, when women have mastered the full range of verbal, gestural and graphic devices used in sand storytelling.

At Ernabella, sand storytelling begins at a very young age. Children first imbibe the overall movement of *milpatjunanyi* in infancy, by watching and listening and by feeling the moving body, while being held in mother's lap. Sometimes other older female relatives may guide the hand of the baby through the sand. From about two-and-a-half years of age, girls create their own story space and adopt the bodily posture and movements of *milpatjunanyi*–wiping clear the ground, leaning over the story field, hammering it with the wire, drawing lines – in an exaggerated way as if to show that they have mastered the technique. They try out a variety of speech styles, intonations and levels of pretence to enact a baby, for example, or a monster, or a caring mother. They even look like they are pretending to play sand storytelling as they mimic the speech of older girls. If I consider this experimentation with speech styles to be an indication of the emergence of the 'narrated self' (Stern 1989) in Anangu childhood, then it accords with the developmental stage of symbolic play that psychologists, notably Jean Piaget (1962), have conceptualized for Western children.[19] Make-believe play at being grown up flourishes during the third and fourth years of life, when girls literally create for themselves elaborate love stories and encounters with malignant ogre figures.[20] As mentioned above, in sand stories by young children, fantasy and memory are closely related and often fuse into a single account. At this stage, graphic depiction and verbalization appear equally prominent and a story often evolves with the naming of drawn shapes. Typically, young girls create sand stories in immediate response to what they see and hear; they may produce a running commentary or incorporate situational elements into another plot. In either case, watching their narratives come into being reveals something of the young players' social understanding, interests and lingual-graphic capacities in live action. To illustrate:

> On this Good Friday, many families have come to the open-air church meeting at the central meeting place in the community, and there are about twenty children of different ages. The dominant theme of the sermon is the end of the world and Judgement Day, which seems passively inculcated into the children who play through the better part of the event. Lila, aged three years eight months, calls me to come and sit next to her in the dirt. She is playing *milpatjunanyi,* her naked body and face covered in dust. She seems to be working hard in this play session and a bit agitated. Her social and lingual learning is rapid and she enjoys her own development and increased social participation, as her loud self-assertions indicate. Her concern is with familiar adults only, with the children close by, with individual words she picks up from the sermon, like the number of a psalm that she recognizes and transposes to a preschool context, with her imaginary world, which she depicts in the sand. Her play story has nothing to do with what is being said in the service – about sin as a problem that separates people from one another. Lila does not comprehend the message but she does know that the event as a whole is called 'church *inma'.* Her sand story, played with a long wire and hand graphs, appears fragmentary. She depicts herself, a little dog and a few other people, my name is also mentioned. She uses the space in front of and next to her. As I sit down, the first thing she shows me is a heart: she draws it symmetrically using both hands, and then admires her creation. Her graphic repertoire is stabilizing. She often draws the frame of a house (although this may stand for something

other than a house), circles for a face, eyes and mouth. She beats dots with the tip of the wire for emphasis – of an object, location or person. Straight vertical lines are drawn with two or three fingers pulled towards her body to represent a person, often starting by naming herself. Another girl of roughly the same age is sitting nearby. She too beats a stick and draws long parallels towards her body, with a playfully serious, almost seductive expression on her face. And even a young boy taps the ground with a wire; it looks like something halfway between drumming and *milpatjunanyi*. A few older boys sit down next to us, and they write words and draw images in the sand, including a motor vehicle. The children do not show any direct response to the church service, yet taken together, their stories and drawings appear like a subtext to the greater narrative. The children see their play to be unrelated to the sermon which is for grown ups. At the end as we walk away, a ten-year-old girl tells me spontaneously: 'They are talking to God. They want to go to heaven. That's why they're praying. When you go to heaven, you grow wings. See? Coming out here [points to her back], like angels'. I ask if the children at church also talk to God: 'They're just playing'.

From roughly the age of five, the sand stories begin to cover overtly social events in which the child has participated, like a church service, or going on a shopping trip, or a school excursion, or what happened at home. These reportage style accounts are mostly told to other girls and show a marked attention to select details. For example, what an adult would describe as a shopping trip to another community might be pinpointed in the girls' story as 'the trip when the chocolate milk fell off the spare tyre'. These stories are performed with considerable speed, and a high level of action both in the plot and the performance is characteristic and valued in the context of storytelling among peers.

'Talking story' is a sign of maturity and, rather than a diversion from 'real' social life, an indispensable aspect of it. A child who shows that she can tell stories has reached a cultural milestone. She has acquired a capacity that Wilkins (1997), in his discussion of Arrernte children's sand stories, calls 'thinking-for-narrating'. For example, Lila, who possesses notably advanced skills as a performer and imitator of other people's idiosyncrasies of talking, movement of eyes and mouth and gait, has been called 'Little Woman' (*Minyma Kulunypa*) ever since she was about two years old. The term *minyma* is usually reserved for mature women with two children, whereas the term for 'girl' and 'young woman' is *kungka*. This playing with life-stage terms acknowledges this young girl's capacity to mirror others (through imitation) and 'talk like a woman', which in turn is appreciated as a sign that she is on the best way of becoming a socially productive person. Her mother is proud of her and, in the presence of an outsider like myself, more distant kin suggest that her social skill makes her a proud representative of Anangu culture. Furthermore, the discrepancy between the girl's young age and mature demeanour is amusing, and she is often encouraged to perform stories for the entertainment of adults. She willingly does so with pleasure and relishes being watched.

However, it is also possible to unlearn (*ngurparingu*) the art of storytelling and this seems to have happened to this most prolific player. At age five, 'Little Woman' had moved to Alice Springs with her mother. After seven months away from her home community, I asked her to play *milpatjunanyi*. This was on a visit to the Aboriginal community of Santa Teresa not far from town:

> She is delighted at my suggestion and we set out to find a piece of wire in the yard of a relative. I set up the video camera, ready to shoot the latest story by my young friend, who smiles at me with anticipation as she sits down on the ground that she wipes clear. She begins to tap the wire, saying, '*Ngayulu, ngayulu* [I, I] … *ngayulu* [I] … *nyaa* [what]?' Again she wipes clear the ground to start all over, yet she is unable to launch into a story. She seems 'stuck' like a broken record. And indeed, after yet another unsuccessful attempt, she becomes distressed and runs to her mother, asking if she could help her tell a story.

At first, I was surprised. I had thought that *milpatjunanyi* was a skill that would not be forgotten once learnt. However, there is a difference between technique and story, or form and content, and it is precisely the latter that requires a meaningful social context in order to function. Lila was perfectly able to engage in play dialogues with another toddler and me. What was missing, I realized, is the continuous prompting and encouragement by older children and adults, who, like taking a child by the hand, thus guide the unfolding of the story. Indeed, very young children are frequently prompted and prodded to repeat what has been said to them, and warmly rewarded when they do, while creative variations on the part of the child (indicating his or her personal will) are loudly cheered. This and a high level of repetition are part and parcel of the socialization into discursive forms of expression (including through frequent church services, such as described above), and it seems that sand storytelling requires a particularly strong mirroring by others.

Strengthening the Mind

Although the official view is that boys do not play *milpatjunanyi*, several young mothers are allowing and even encourage their toddler sons to take up the story wire. Possibly reflecting formal educational input and new ideas about child rearing, young mothers tell me that it is important for children to play as they like and to thereby develop their imagination.

Géza Róheim (1974: 77ff.) had made a similar point on the basis of his psychoanalytic research with Pitjantjatjara and Arrernte people in 1929, when he interpreted the game as a form of daydreaming and fantasy about the future, especially the girls' future motherhood.[21] I agree that daydreaming and the therapeutic effect it affords are important, as Róheim seems to suggest; this may even have intensified since people began to live permanently in communities where boredom and family conflict pose considerable stress, especially for young adults. In fact, one mother told me that her daughters play *milpatjunanyi* in order to 'give their mind a rest'. In addition to resting the mind, the self-absorbed play has another function. Green (personal communication) pointed out that playing sand stories signals 'minding one's own business', as opposed to being nosy and prying. One can readily see why it is important to have recognized means of distancing oneself from others and especially from trouble in a small community such as Ernabella, where everyone knows everyone else and intersubjective dynamics are intense. Mindfulness and composed, thoughtful behaviour are highly valued attributes.

Adults expressing their views on socialization also make clear the importance of strengthening the mind through storytelling. Director of the Anangu Education Service, Katrina Tjitayi (this volume), gave an insightful account of her childhood memories of anticipations and the experience of learning: how it felt for her to 'be strong within her mind' and why children's capacity to project themselves imaginatively into the future might have deteriorated. She remembers how children used to be confident about their future and that storytelling was an integral part of imagining the self with joy as a grown up. Reflective and absorbed play over extensive periods of time appears compromised today because children who spend much time in the communities are distracted by noise and demands and things within their sight, such as commercial toys and entertainment.

At this point, however, children still manage to carve out time for solitary reflection. A nine-year-old girl explained that sand stories are 'for thinking', upon which she made a drawing of just this idea. Spontaneously and in accord with the basic pattern of contiguity that I have found to be typical of Anangu children's play, she took a piece of white rock and drew the floor plan of a house onto the concrete slab that used to be the veranda of the burnt-out ruin of a home where she was playing with several other girls. Her sketch shows a person in a furnished room, sitting on a sofa, busy thinking. As in the Ancestral songs about *milpatjunanyi,* she did not say what the player was thinking about, because that was not her point. Withdrawal and reflection are especially important in the morning, and children seek to compose body and mind before engaging others.[22] Boys too appreciate the importance of reflection. One early morning, I observed the eight-year-old grandson of a friend sitting on his own in the sun. Still unkempt and before breakfast, he nevertheless looked calm and self-contained. I asked him what he was playing. He replied with a very serious look on his little face: '*Inkantja wiya, kulira*' – 'I'm not playing, I'm thinking'. A ten-year-old girl played *milpatjunanyi* in total silence for about twenty minutes. She had just got out of bed and went straight outside, to sit down on the ground with her back leaning against the brick wall of the house. Looking very sleepy and relaxed, her legs pulled up, she began to draw a silent story into the sand, marking the ground with the wire in between yawns. She would not tell me what it was about, only that she did not depict a dream.

A Final Illustration

To conclude with a brief example, I describe the narrative production of a six-year-old girl, who performed the European folktale Goldilocks and the Three Bears (*see* e.g., Opie and Opie 1974) in a twenty-five-minute session in front of three other girls who were listening and waiting for their turn. Most notable in this creation is that all characters are named members of her extended family, including one of the girls in the audience who, at one point, began to protest. A version of the story had been read to the children at school, and the storyteller seemed to use it as a frame to rework family dynamics and at the same time entertain and thus impress her friends. It is at once 'cheeky' and affectionate. It is 'cheeky' because authority to talk about others and assign roles to them derives in part from the canonical status of the fairytale, which she insists must be told to the end; she dishes out roles to real people like Mother Bear dishes out the porridge. It is also affectionate because her father's sister, who actually cooks porridge for many of the children in the family, is acknowledged and her three male cousins make for very friendly bears. 'Goldilocks' is the blonde daughter of another aunt and her closest friend and age-mate. It is she who tried to intervene when the plot depicts her as eating the porridge – an attempt to insert herself as a real person that made her protest look even funnier, and the narrator had all sympathies on her side. An intervention on a different level occurred when another girl claimed that she would be the first to see the as-yet-unborn baby of the pregnant aunt who is cooking the porridge in the story. This reference erupted when the narrator impersonated the youngest boy (Little Bear) and spoke in high-pitched Baby Talk. The intervention provoked the anger of the storyteller. The ending of the story is very conciliatory. Instead of having Goldilocks run away, she changed the plot and makes the youngest boy ask the aunt if the newcomer could please stay and play with them.

This story illustrates that children move with ease between different social and cultural domains and assimilate material from the classroom into their personal life. It is also a masterful demonstration of how stories can be used to enact, play with and comment on other people without impinging on their personal autonomy; the young narrator has skilfully integrated playing and reality by having inserted real people into a make-believe setting. Her story is in this sense outward oriented and intended to evoke an existing social field. It remains, however, within the family, even though she leaves herself and closest relatives out of the plot – perhaps in an attempt to conceal herself. She does, however, claim her presence in another way, namely, by the act of telling a story, which she recounts in full length and great detail, to the point of putting to the test the patience of her friends who are waiting for their turn. Embodied in this example is then what I had earlier referred to as 'social productivity'. Things are left open to interpretation, concealed and revealed, tested and contested, while including others both in the plot and the telling.

Notes

The material presented here is from field trips in 2004, 2005, 2006 and 2007 that are part of research on children's play and social imagination at Ernabella (Australian Research Council Discovery Project grant DP0556111). Previous fieldwork in the same community was funded by the Australian Institute of Aboriginal and Torres Strait Islander Studies and Macquarie University. I thank Jenny Green for her critical queries and insightful comparative information on an earlier, shorter version of this chapter (Eickelkamp 2008c). My greatest debt is to the children and families who continue to share their life and knowledge with me, and especially to Margaret Dagg for her excellent transcriptions and translations.

1. Much of the literature on the subject of meaning making in children's play narratives is in the fields of developmental psychology and play therapy studies (e.g., Bretherton 1984; Emde et al. 2003; Slade and Wolf 1994), and often inspired by psychoanalytic work with children. In an earlier paper I discussed the nature of symbolization and its therapeutic effect comparatively – in the 'natural' social context of sand storytelling at Ernabella and in the 'artificial' context of psychotherapeutic intervention using the Sandplay technique (Eickelkamp 2008a). Other work includes folklorists (Factor 1988), anthropologists (Goldman 1998) and linguists considering meaning making by children in the context of their

play talk (O'Shannessy, this volume). The present discussion does not analyse the content of play stories, which is reserved for another work.

2. However, as elsewhere, children at Ernabella and their families define story-telling (*tjukurpa wangkanyi*) – if 'properly' done – as different from playing (*ingkanyi*). The former is seen to be a more formalized, technique-bound per-formance that makes the teller socially accountable. Storytelling, and especially sand storytelling, is often used to share information, and reportage-style stories seem furthest from play. A child who offends somebody through her story is likely to attract her mother's admonition, even though she will defend the child in front of the other family should the matter become a cause for grievance. In a more subtle way, accountability also ensues from the fact that the storyteller is using an established tradition – she is expected to stay true to form. By contrast, playing is thought of as providing fun and a certain freedom from the social rules and the world of adults. It is described as 'made-up' in the sense of not having to first learn how things are done, even though children learn tacitly how to play, what, where and with whom. When a child feels the need to ask for impunity – for example, after teasing another child too much – she might say apologeti-cally, 'I'm just playing', meaning that she is not being serious. Adults would say about play in general that it is 'not serious', something that children do and hence it should be left without reprimand unless a young child is crying over the poor treatment by an older child. And as Musharbash (this volume) describes for Warlpiri families, at Ernabella too the offended child is made to hit back the perpetrator. In relation to the freedom of play, I might mention that, unlike past ethnographers (*see* Morton, this volume), I have never seen children engage in sexual play in front of adult members of their family, although it is still common for children to use sexual language for swearing – in English and Pitjantjatjara. Adults talk about the 'sexualized' behaviour of children and teenagers in ways that reflect a history of sexual repression that began in the mission era. Adults also interfere in other ways that may reflect an influence of school pedagogy: as if feeling the need to show the external observer the learning capacities of their child, young mothers in particular would often interrupt their young child's free play and try and make the child perform a song or do a jump or throw a ball.

3. Hiatt's (1975) discussion of the challenge to classify Aboriginal narratives is still the most succinct. For engrossing demonstrations of what stories 'do' *see* San-som (1980, 2001) and Duelke (2005). None of the authors, however, consider the status of stories in the world of children.

4. This totals 369 hours of focused observation with extensive field notes, and c. 30 hours of video footage of various play activities, including 159 play talks of various length.

5. Detailed descriptions and illustrations of Central and Western Desert graphic systems used in the sand and in canvas painting – but not specifically the chil-dren's – have been provided by Munn (1965, 1973) and Watson (2003).

6. For an anthropological discussion of the nature of literacy in Central Austral-ian iconography *see* Biddle 1996 and 2007. The ethnographic exploration of literacy in a Western Desert community by Kral and Ellis (2008) provides several points of comparison with the material presented in this chapter, notably their

observations on the educational role of storytelling, narrative competence and writing in the sand.

7. The explanation of unconscious knowledge was offered by Anangu minister of the church, Peter Nyaningu. Reflecting on the origins of *tjukurpa* knowledge and specifically how the first Anangu came to know how to initiate boys into manhood, he suggested that they intuited it: 'Unconscious', he said in English. The subject of the cross-cultural meaning of the term – especially the self-reflective stance that Anangu have adopted in response to biblical knowledge and encounters with therapeutic interventions – merits further investigations. However, according to the Berndts, Aboriginal people traditionally recognized a stream of 'pre-knowledge': Emerging from the Dreaming at birth, persons 'brought with them, so it was believed, a basic core of knowledge that usually related to their position in the ultimate scheme of things. ... It was this pre-knowledge which was transmuted into constructive or positive knowledge ... through religious experience' (Berndt and Berndt 1981: 217; *see also* Musharbash, this volume).

8. Sand storytelling as Ancestral activity has been described in the ethnographic literature. In the 1930s and 1940s, Mountford (1976) recorded myths linked to a site in the Mann Ranges that feature Ancestral women who play sand stories. Like Róheim in 1929, Mountford also saw sand stories being used to share camp gossip, and he provides beautiful photographs of the use of leaves in what he calls 'playing house' (520ff.) There is a site where Ancestral women used to play sand stories in the Petermann Ranges, which is Pitjantjatjara country, and women performing *milpatjunanyi* appear in Dreaming songs and narratives about sites near Mt Liebig and Lake Wilson (Munn 1965). In the 1990s, Margo Smith (personal communication) documented a Yankunytjatjara site near Kulgera where Ancestral women used to play sand stories. Senior women at Ernabella explained that men and women have a song part about *milpatjunanyi* in the *Kungkarankalpa* (Seven Sisters or Pleiades) story, and I furthermore recorded song verses from the *Minyma Kutjara* (Two Women) travelling myth that begins at Wingellina, where the Ancestral women play *milpatjunanyi,* and again near Kings Canyon. Not only are there songs about *milpatjunanyi,* but affinity also exists at the level of technique: as the women were singing the Two Women cycle, they cleared a space in front of them, beat a rhythm, using any instrument at hand – a twig, rocks, walking stick or water bottle and at the end of each verse wiped away the marks. The only song reference I have learnt of to the content of Ancestral sand stories is in *ilpinji,* a song genre about sexual longing that is said to attract a 'husband'. The phallic significance of *milpatjunanyi* is profound and forms a direct link to the Dreaming. But note here that children are said not to be aware of the sexual behaviour of Dreaming beings, even if, like the Ancestral women, they play 'boyfriend stories' in the sand. Although women might make occasional marks on the ground when they practise traditional songs at Ernabella today, I have not seen older women tell myth segments in sand stories that reference particular Dreamings about the narrator's birthplace and related sites. Munn (1965) had described this as typical for Pitjantjatjara women at Areyonga in the mid-1960s. However, continuity or parallels exist nevertheless: Since about 2000, the most senior women at Ernabella have employed the iconography and content of 'open' versions of such stories in canvas painting. They also

remember the joy of listening to the stories their grandmothers used to tell, as well as their own childhood play stories, and some older women are renowned for their skill as raconteurs in the sand.

9. Von Sturmer (personal communication) pointed out that the notion of law as *tjukurpa* – or 'big story' – indicates that much emphasis is placed on the social use of language. Indeed, knowledge of how to use speech – what to say, how and when, and what to leave unspoken – is part and parcel of safeguarding propriety. In this sense relationships and the social process can be said to rely on the dual capacity to communicate and to withhold. This in turn relates to the valued skill of announcing the presence of the self without denying others the right to do the same, and to refrain from seeking too much attention.

10. Green (personal communication) observes that, in the Arandic region, 'narrators of sand stories are careful with the disposal of the story-telling apparatus, such as leaves. They will say of them that they are '*ayeye-akerte*', literally 'having story'. I assume care is taken because the imbued narrative power represents a kind of agency of the object.

11. There exist symbolic associations between the 'talking' stick and other paraphernalia that forge further links to the Dreaming and other 'mundane' practices. Among the objects that I understand relate symbolically to *milpa* are: the hitting stick of the men (*tjutinypa*) that they use as a clapping instrument in song (which is further related to the boys' passion for drumming that is as developed as the girls' sand storytelling); the ordinary walking stick of old people who are the guardians of *tjukurpa;* the digging stick (*wana*) of women in their reproductive age; their fighting stick (*wana*); the poison stick (bone) of the sorcerer and the women's ceremonial pole (*kuturu*) which, as Ancestral body and penis, emphasizes the interlinking of body and soul as a necessary condition for the perpetuation of life. Watson (2003) describes similar symbolic linkages in women's sand drawings at Balgo. Highlighting the equivalence between ground and human body, she observes that some kind of agency and consciousness are ascribed to the ground, which thereby becomes a witness to human mark making on its surface. The local Kukatja terms *walkala* for public sand drawing and *milpa-pungin* for sand drawings that are accompanied by the rhythmic beating of the wire have special potency. For example, the latter is associated with the sound of cracking joints that in turn relates to the practice of massaging children and hence to ideas about growth, maturation and sexuality (Watson 2003: 76–79). Some icons ('graphs') are gendered; the U-shape commonly represents a shelter (*wuungku*), which is linguistically associated with women, birthing, uterus and placenta, while 'the line is related to concepts of flowing and of water, and is associated with masculinity' (103–4). The 'poking and penetration aspects of walkala are associated with spears and spear-throwers which are symbols of men' (107).

John von Sturmer (1978: 299–303, 501) made the important observation that humans frighten and swear at the Ancestors in order to manipulate them into performing favourable acts, such as 'increasing' the growth of animals and plants. Among the Wik, people say that they are frightening the Ancestors or spirits by stirring the site up (*cf.* Benedict 1970: 332). I am inclined to think that the human manipulation of a story-making (i.e., law-making) instrument is akin to the handling of objects (including places and ritual paraphernalia) with the intention of eliciting Ancestral activity. This has another empirical component: provoking a response and prodding someone into compliance are social techniques that apply to Ancestors and people alike, and especially to young children who are often pinched and poked by others. One could say then that children, when poking the ground in *milpatjunanyi*, are stirring a symbolic place, sometimes with aggression, as if prodding another person.

12. My fieldwork observation on this subject differs from Tjitayi's impression described in chapter 2, that today Anangu children do not feel that these monster figures are real. It is also worth noting that, like O'Shannessy (this volume), I have not heard stories that explicitly create a wished-for situation, although a child may signal in rather concealed ways her desire. Depictions of ideal situations were found in children's drawings on paper of family, with strong resistances to verbalize the scene and name the persons shown and not shown.

13. Children are also exposed to a variety of oral texts, including prayers, songs and sermons in frequently held church services; reporting of community issues, naming of problems and planning in the prolific number of community meetings; acted dialogues in movies on television, video and DVD; news and debates on television and the pedagogical presentations at school. It remains to be examined if and how these differ from the children's stories told in the sand.

14. It is problematic to describe the aesthetic character of stories, when, as Green (personal communication) pointed out, we do not fully understand what constitutes a story in the mind of their creators. Moreover, stories do not exist in a fixed and in this sense objective form. The nonhierarchical organization of content described by Klapproth could be a surface phenomenon, namely, in relation to the performance of stories, especially in the ritual context, which takes into account that some participants know more than others. Furthermore, my impression is that stories for children, such as folktales, are uniquely 'plotted', unusually complete and emotionally engaging.

15. Beautiful performances of such folktales are documented in the video *Pitjantjatjara Sand Stories,* 1999, produced by Ernabella Arts and Lucienne Fontannaz.

16. Françoise Dussart (2000) has provided a detailed discussion of Ancestral dreams in her ethnography of Warlpiri women's ritual.

17. Furthermore, nocturnal dreaming and the inscription of the surface with meaningful marks both present activities in a zone of interaction with Ancestral power (Biddle 2003; Dussart 2000; Munn 1973; Watson 2003), even if, as Munn (1965) noted, this link is less pronounced in the mind of Anangu than in neighbouring regions.

18. Although the dreamer's spirit (*kurunpa*) travels, acts and encounters those of others, there is a passive aspect to it that may be accounted for by the view that originating acts are the privilege of Dreaming beings.

19. Anthropologists have long challenged Piaget's allegedly 'uncontextualized' model of developmental stages of play (*see* Schwartzman 1978: 41–59), which I, however, still find useful.

20. For an extensive psychoanalytical discussion of an ogre figure that features in Central Australian stories for and by children, dreams, play and drawings, *see* Eickelkamp 2004.

21. A missionary at Hermannsburg, Carl Strehlow (1913; cited by Hersey 2004: 27–28) described an oracle sand story game played by grown-up Arrernte girls at the turn of the twentieth century. The game is called *ilbamara,* which he translated as 'the fertile one'.
22. It is regarded as particularly harmful to wake children from their sleep when their soul might still be travelling during nocturnal dreaming.

Young Children's Social Meaning Making in a New Mixed Language

Carmel O'Shannessy

The play and peer interactions of children in many places in the world have been well documented, but there is little documentation of the interactions and activities of young Aboriginal children in remote communities in Australia. In this chapter I present a snapshot of the kinds of spoken interactions young children engage in with each other in one remote Aboriginal community, the Warlpiri community of Lajamanu in the northern part of Central Australia. The data, drawn from approximately eighty hours of videotaped interactions between children aged two years to five years, with other children and with their carers, shows that the children use talk to explore themes and perform functions that are common to other cultures as well as some themes that are specific to their own, as do children from many parts of the world (Bornstein et al. 1999: 318). Further, through play and talk they initiate and control scenes that they might be fearful of in other life contexts (Corsaro and Eder 1990).

A striking property of children's talk in the community reported on here is that rapid and dramatic language change has led to the children speaking in a language that has only emerged in the last thirty years (O'Shannessy 2005: 235, 2008). It is only spoken by young adults and children in this community and is called Light Warlpiri. In the new language elements from Warlpiri, English and Kriol (an English-based creole) are combined systematically. Briefly, verbs and word endings on verbs are from English and Kriol, while most nouns and word endings on nouns are from Warlpiri. The new language is the primary way of speaking for young children and is the first language they produce when they begin to speak. They also learn Warlpiri and produce it from when they are four to six years of age. More detail on Light Warlpiri and the interaction of both languages is given in a later part of the chapter.

Socialization in childhood is seen in an interpretive approach to child development as a collective process that takes place in a public realm (Corsaro and Eder 1990: 199). In this view, children are not acting as isolated individuals who imitate their parents, or for whom the only function of play and peer interactions is to prepare for adulthood. Rather, children actively participate in play routines and talk with their peers to create unique and dynamic peer cultures. Through their participation in everyday sociocultural practices, children learn about the world and simultaneously have an effect on their own developmental experiences (Corsaro and Rizzo 1988: 364; Schieffelin and Ochs 1986: 365). They reproduce elements from their experience of the world in ways that develop their understandings. Children also use games and routines as a way of dealing with fears and confusions from the adult world, by incorporating them into play routines which they initiate and over which they have control (Corsaro and Eder 1990: 361).

Children's play is common to most cultures but may show interests and concerns specific to the culture in which the child is growing up (Bornstein et al. 1999: 362). The types of communicative strategies used by children in play may also differ according to cultural communicative norms (Farver and Lee Shin 1997: 357). For example, children may use language in ways that promote interdependence versus those that promote autonomy, depending on the adult communicative styles valued in their culture. But there is not necessarily a clear divide between play and other types of interaction for children (Thorne 1987: 100). Play involves 'work' in two basic forms: conceptual, by way of developing understandings about the world, and practical, often invisible work – children care for others, construct culture and participate in social organization and might perform household and other tasks. In some cultures children often undertake a considerable amount of adult work (Thorne 1987: 367).

Language and Socialization in Remote Australian Aboriginal Communities

Aboriginal children in remote communities in Central Australia have a great deal of autonomy in making decisions about their everyday activities within family sociocultural constraints (see, for example, Myers 1986: 107 about the Pintupi; Meggitt 1962: 124 about the Warlpiri). Meggitt (1962: 124) writes about Warlpiri at Lajamanu community where my study is set, forty-five years ago, and explains that children were indulged and rarely chastised by their parents. From when they were about five to six years old, children spent most of their time playing with other children and only returned home for meals and to sleep. Young children were nursed and fondled by both mothers and fathers. Both the freedom of behaviour extended by the parents and the physical signs of affection continue in the community today. Similar playful parental techniques are reported with children in a community further north in the Northern Territory, and also that parents distract children away from inappropriate behaviour rather than chastise them for it (Hamilton 1981).

Warlpiri children are socialized into a complex kinship system from an early age, and adults speak to them in a special communicative register, called Baby Talk (Laughren 1984: 73). Meggitt (1962: 116) reports the use of 'baby-talk' in Lajamanu, and a similar phenomenon is reported for Ngaanyatjarra, spoken in a Western Australian community (Kral and Ellis 2008). In the Warlpiri Baby Talk register, adults use fewer consonant sounds in words when they talk to young children or say something about which they intend young children to take notice. Two sets of consonant sounds, those made with the tip of the tongue against the soft palate or palate of the mouth, are not used. Other existing sounds in Warlpiri, made with the blade of the tongue against the palate, are substituted for them. In addition, some consonants are omitted from beginnings of words. Table 6.1 shows the set of Warlpiri sounds that occur in classic Warlpiri, with the subset that occurs in Baby Talk bolded.

Warlpiri Sounds in Classic Warlpiri

Baby Talk also differs from standard adult Warlpiri in terms of words used and their meanings. Generic rather than specific terms are used in Baby Talk, whereas specific terms are typical in adult-to-adult speech. Some particular vocabulary, such as *nyanya* 'food', is used for all foods, whereas adult-to-adult speech would normally show a distinction at least between meats and vegetable foods, then often further distinctions. A simplification of the complex Warlpiri kinship structure is used in Baby

Table 6.1. ▼ Set of Warlpiri sounds that occur in classic Warlpiri, with the subset that occurs in Baby Talk bolded (Adapted from Laughren 1984: 74)

	bilabial	apico-alveolar	apico-dominal	lamino-palatal	velar
stops	**p**	t	rt	**j**	**k**
nasals	**m**	n	rn	**ny**	**ng**
laterals		l	rl	**ly**	
flaps		rr	rd		
glides	**w**		r	**y**	

Talk, such that the main distinction is between maternal and paternal relations (e.g., mother's siblings versus father's siblings) regardless of the gender of the individual being referred to. In the Baby Talk system, a father's sister would initially be referred to by the same name as the father and father's brother. As the child grows older, she learns the finer distinctions.

Dramatic changes in adult speech have taken place in Lajamanu, such that a new language has arisen and is now the primary language of young adults and children. The dramatic change raises two questions in relation to Baby Talk: (1) is Baby Talk still used when adults speak Warlpiri to young children? And (2) is there a Baby Talk register in the new way of speaking, Light Warlpiri? In the section "Children's Interactions" below, I show that despite the changes, Baby Talk is still used when adults speak Warlpiri to children, and similar phonological restrictions have been carried into the new language, Light Warlpiri.

Bavin (1993: 87) explains that Warlpiri children in Central Australia are expected to learn by watching and listening to adults, rather than by being explicitly taught. However, as I will show with examples, in Lajamanu community today, this view requires qualification. Adults do engage in behaviours with young children that teach them about sociocultural relationships and behaviours.

The Sociolinguistic Setting

Lajamanu community is situated in northern Central Australia, approximately 570 kilometres from the nearest town of Katherine, and has a population of approximately six hundred. There is some paid work in the community (in the school, health clinic, shop, police station, homeland resource centre and council office and workshop), but most residents receive welfare payments. Primary school–aged children attend the local government school which until 2009 had a bilingual education program in Warlpiri and English. Now most of the teaching and learning is in English, with only some teaching in Warlpiri. Until recently children had to move to a larger commercial centre (600–900 kilometres away) to receive secondary schooling. Houses have electricity and modern plumbing, and families have televisions, DVD and CD players and telephones. Many families still follow traditional hunting and gathering practices to some extent, but foods obtained from these are a supplement to those bought at the local shop, on which people rely. Families buy toys for their children to play with, but children also spend a lot of time playing with whatever is at hand around the community.

Children in the community grow up in a complex linguistic situation. They learn two languages from birth – the heritage language, Lajamanu Warlpiri (the variety of Warlpiri which is spoken in Lajamanu community), and the newly emerged bilingual mixed language, Light Warlpiri. A bilingual mixed language is one for which there is no single parent language – the language consists of elements from two source languages, in this instance Warlpiri and English or Kriol. The children in Lajamanu target the new mixed language, Light Warlpiri, as the language of their everyday interactions and rarely produce the heritage language until they are four to six years old. Light Warlpiri takes its name from the term older people in the community use to talk about how the children speak. Using terminology such as 'light/weak' and 'heavy/strong' to talk about variants of traditional languages is common among the Warlpiri. The Warlpiri word *rampaku* can be glossed as both 'light' and 'weak' in English, and the word *pirrjirdi* as both 'heavy' and 'strong'. In Lajamanu older people use the term *Warlpiri pirrjirdi* ('heavy or strong Warlpiri') to mean speaking Warlpiri with no borrowing or code switching. They also use it to mean speaking Warlpiri using complex grammatical structures and complex vocabulary that are now used more by very old speakers and less by younger speakers. They use the term *Warlpiri rampaku* ('light or weak Warlpiri') to mean speaking Warlpiri with borrowing from and code switching between English and Kriol, for omitting some morphological elements, and using vocabulary which is produced more by younger speakers than by very old speakers. When I asked older speakers about the children's speech, they would say that the children speak *Warlpiri rampaku*. For this reason I have called the younger adults' and children's way of speaking 'Light Warlpiri'.

Light Warlpiri should not be confused with the Lajamanu variety of Warlpiri (here called 'Lajamanu Warlpiri'), which varies only a little from classic Warlpiri (*see* for example Hale et al. 1995; Laughren et al. 1996; Hale 1973, 1992; Nash 1986; Simpson 2005; Granites and Laughren 2001), mainly in the types of word endings that are used. Lajamanu Warlpiri and Light Warlpiri are two very different ways of speaking. The latter consists of a systematic combination of elements from Lajamanu Warlpiri and Aboriginal English or Kriol (AE/Kriol).[1] The following three examples show how elements from Lajamanu Warlpiri and AE/Kriol are combined in Light Warlpiri. In the examples, elements from Lajamanu Warlpiri are in italics, and those from AE/Kriol are in plain font.

(1)a. *karnta-jarra-rlu*   *ka-pala-ø*   *wajilipi-nyi*   *kuuku*
     girl-DUAL-ERG   IMPF-3DL-3SG chase-NPST   monster
     'The two girls are chasing the monster.'   (Lajamanu Warlpiri)

b. det   tu   gel   jeis-im   monsta
   that two   girl chase-TRANS   monster
   'Those two girls are chasing the monster.'   (AE/Kriol)

c. de-m   jeis-im   *kuuku*   det   tu   *karnta-jarra-(ng)*
   3PL-NFUT   chase-TRANS   monster   that two   girl-DUAL-(ERG)
   'Those two girls are chasing the monster.'   (Light Warlpiri)

Example (1c) shows that nouns (*karnta-jarra* 'girl-dual', *kuuku* 'monster')
and word endings on nouns (-*ng* 'ergative marker') are from Warlpiri,
while verbs (*jeis* 'chase') and word endings on verbs (-*im* 'transitive
marker') are from AE/Kriol. Nouns can also be from English. Ergative
marking (ERG) is part of a grammatical system in which nouns that refer
to an agent performing an action directly on another entity have a case
suffix attached to them. Both Warlpiri and Light Warlpiri use the ergative
system of showing who the agent is (although Light Warlpiri uses it to a
lesser extent), and in both languages the words within a sentence need
not be in a set order. Warlpiri also has a rich system of hand signs for
communication (Kendon 1988), and these are still used in the community, mostly by older women. They are also actively taught to children.

Children in Lajamanu live with their extended families. They are in
constant contact with family members of all ages, from young babies
to adults over seventy years old. So, young children, before the age at
which they attend school, hear Warlpiri and Light Warlpiri from members of their extended family. Their young parents mainly speak Light
Warlpiri but also code switch into Warlpiri, both when addressing the
children and addressing others in the presence of children. In example
(2), a child is sitting with her mother and grandmother. Her grandmother
speaks to her in Warlpiri and her mother speaks to her in Light Warlpiri.

(2)a. Grandm: *nya-ngka jarntu*   (Warlpiri)
                look-IMP   dog
                'Look at the dog!'

   b. Child: a?

   c. Mot: *jarntu* yu   luk   *jarntu*   (Light Warlpiri)
             dog   you   look   dog
             'The dog, look at the dog!'

   d. Mot: i   mait   bait-im   *apuju-k*   ged-im   (Light Warlpiri)
            3sg   might   bite-TRAN   father's.mother-DAT   get-TRANS
            'It might bite your grandmother, get it!'

e. Grandm: *ma-nta!*   *ma-nta!*   (Warlpiri)
              get-IMP   get-IMP
              'Get it!   Get it!'

In example (2), the child's grandmother ('Grandm'), who is in her fifties, uses Warlpiri verbs and nouns: *nyangka* ('look!'), *manta* ('get it!') and *jarntu* ('dog'). In contrast, the child's mother ('Mot'), who is in her twenties, also uses some Warlpiri nouns: *jarntu* ('dog'), and *apuju* ('grandmother'), which is a Baby Talk pronunciation of *ngapuju*. But she uses verbs from AE/Kriol: *luk* ('look'), *baitim* ('bite') and other words from English: *mait* ('might') and *yu* ('you'). The child appears to understand both ways of speaking, Warlpiri and Light Warlpiri.

Children speak Light Warlpiri almost exclusively, with little code switching into Warlpiri, until they reach the ages of four to six years. From then on they continue to speak Light Warlpiri almost exclusively, but children aged six to nine can speak Warlpiri (O'Shannessy 2008, 2009: 431–36) and do so in certain contexts – for example, when speaking to older people – and they increase the amount of Warlpiri they speak as they grow older. They are also spoken to in Warlpiri more often as they grow older, including the use of Warlpiri kin terms that denote complex relationships. Since the first generation of Light Warlpiri speakers are still under thirty years old, it remains to be seen whether they will speak it as their primary language throughout their lives or shift to Warlpiri as they grow older. Older family members speak Warlpiri with considerable code switching between Warlpiri and AE/Kriol, and at times with code switching between Warlpiri and other traditional languages.

When interacting with each other, the children speak Light Warlpiri. They are learning both Light Warlpiri and Lajamanu Warlpiri and could choose to produce both languages from when they begin to speak, but they do not. I suggest that the children have adjusted their speech production to those of other children because they spend a lot of time in each other's company. This circumstance, in turn, appears to have inspired the children to make Light Warlpiri their primary language. From the age of about three years, when they are able to walk independently and confidently, children spend large amounts of time in the company of other children. It is typical for a three- or four-year-old child to spend most of the day playing with other children. This means that from this age other children provide a large part of the children's language input and are the group with whom young children interact most. To be part of the peer group, children need to speak the way peers do, that is, in Light Warlpiri. Additionally, the children with young parents receive mostly Light Warlpiri input from them.

But although young adults and children mostly speak the new mixed language, many traditional cultural practices are still integral to their lives. As Laughren (1984: 81) explains, the Warlpiri have a complex system of kinship structure and vocabulary. Laughren further reports that adults use English terms in the Baby Talk register but combine the English term with Warlpiri meanings: for example, the term *papa* is used with very young children to indicate paternal relations – father, father's brother and father's sister, which is unlike the meaning of the English term *father,* which only includes the child's male parent. Rather, it takes on the meaning of the Warlpiri term for father, *kirda-nyanu,* which includes paternal relations. In Light Warlpiri, the same system exists, except that English terms are used alongside Warlpiri terms among adults and older children as well as with younger children. In fact older Warlpiri speakers, who do not speak Light Warlpiri, also use both English and Warlpiri kin terms to the children. In addition to kin terms, the Warlpiri have a system of naming according to moieties and subsections (commonly called 'skinnames', *see* Appendix B), which indicate each person's relationship to any other. In the system, eight female and eight male names recur through the generations, so that people in different generations might have a classificatory relationship of sibling, or people from the same generation might have a classificatory relationship of grandmother or mother. The subsection classifications determine certain behaviours between people. For example, one should marry someone from the appropriate subsection or skin group; classificatory sons-in-law and mothers-in-law must avoid direct contact with each other and in some relationships, playful teasing and joking is expected. Children are taught the classificatory names of everyone they are in contact with and what the relationships entail. They are not taught avoidance behaviours when they are very young, but are taught the correct marriage choice subsection name from very early on, and behaviours such as who should look after them and who they should joke with. When the children are taught about their relationships and subsection terms, they are also taught the hand signs for many of them. Children use the kin terms when talking among themselves.

Data Collection and Methodology

The data are video recordings of children aged two years and ten months to five years in natural and naturalistic contexts in their homes or in the community, plus observations that I have made over a period of approximately seven years in the community. Since children have a lot of autonomy, they are free to go to almost any part of the community when they want to, which made video recording difficult. To encourage them to stay in one area, I often provided simple props for play stimulus, for example, a plastic bowl and mugs, dolls, a cotton cloth and toy cars and animals. It is common for adults to put a blanket on the ground for children to play on, and the play sessions often took place on a blanket. Children do have access to toys so providing toys was ecologically sound. Adult carers do often enter into play scenarios with children, but may have done so for more extended periods than usual in the initial video sessions to encourage the children to talk for the camera. To avoid contrived contexts as far as possible, I often left the video camera with the adult carers and then went away, having shown the adults how to move the camera if the children moved to another area. I explained that it did not matter if the children did not talk, that whatever they did was acceptable to me, and that neither the carers nor the children had to do anything special. I returned after about an hour to retrieve the camera. The carers and children became comfortable with this pattern fairly quickly, and I am confident that the recordings represent naturally occurring activities and interactions. The data mostly contains speech from girls. I have not examined the data for gender differences in the children's speech. The children represented in the examples are friends of each other and often play together. The video recordings were transcribed in CHAT format (MacWhinney 1987; MacWhinney and Bates 1978) by me with adult speakers of Light Warlpiri, some of whom are the parents of the children recorded.

Children's Interactions

Adult Interactions with Young Children

When young adults (aged approximately fifteen to twenty-six) speak to their young children in Light Warlpiri, the language they usually use with them, they often engage a Baby Talk register. In this register, the sounds in Light Warlpiri that come from classic Warlpiri are reduced in the same way as described by Laughren (1984) for classic Warlpiri Baby Talk, and sounds in Light Warlpiri that come from AE/Kriol are also pronounced using a reduced phonemic inventory. In Light Warlpiri Baby Talk, many English sounds are substituted with the sound 'j' (as in English 'juice") which exists in Warlpiri,[2] English and Kriol. The set of English fricatives (for example, 's' as in 'sand', 'sh' as in 'shop', 'ch' as in 'chair', the middle consonant sound in measure, 'z' as in 'zoo', 'th' as in 'this' and 'th' as in 'theatre') can occur in Light Warlpiri, and they are often substituted by the sound 'j'. The substitution is also common in Kriol and Aboriginal English. In Light Warlpiri Baby Talk, the 'j' sound is used in place of a large range of sounds, and it is possible for every word in a sentence to begin with 'j', regardless of the sound it begins with in Warlpiri, English or Kriol.

English Sounds in Light Warlpiri

Older children often take care of younger children and engage the Baby Talk register when speaking to them. In the Baby Talk register, the sound patterns are not fixed. That is, not all of the sounds in the table (Table 6.2) are always replaced by the 'j' sound. Rather, adults replace some or all of the sounds with 'j' at different times.

Although Warlpiri children are expected to learn from watching and listening to others and are expected to learn a lot of skills and knowledge that they are not explicitly taught (Bavin 1993: 87), children in this community are also often involved in interactions with adults and older children from an early age in which sociocultural knowledge is taught. They are entertained and played with by adults, especially females, and other children, from when they are babies. When the children are a few months old, adults initiate interactions in which they teach the children elements of sociocultural knowledge. Adults use hand signs for the children showing the kinship classification from which the child's future spouse should belong to. For example, when a person in the potential spouse subsection comes along, the adults often make the hand sign for 'spouse' by tapping the top of one hand with the fingers of the other, in a position where the baby can see it, and say the subsection term for that person at the same time. Adults often refer to members of the potential spouse classification group as 'your husband' or 'your wife' when talking to the child. They also often refer to a child who is the classificatory husband or wife of an adult using the terms 'husband' or 'wife' when they may or

Table 6.2. ▼ Set of English sounds that occur in Light Warlpiri, with the subset that occurs in Baby Talk bolded

	bilabial	labio-dental	inter-dental	apico-alveolar	lamino palatal	velar
stops	p, **b**			t, **d**		k, **g**
nasals	**m**			**n**		**ng**
laterals				**l**		
fricatives		f, v	th 'theatre' th 'this'	s, z, sh		
affricates					ch, **j**	
approximants				**r**		
glides	**w**					**y**

may not be in the child's hearing. For example, a woman was looking for her three-year-old son and went to a house where she thought he was playing with other children. She called out to a forty-year-old woman who lived in the house: '*Yu hasbin deya?*' ('Is your husband there?') Both women knew that the speaker was referring to her own three-year-old son, who is in a classificatory husband relationship to the woman. Adults repeatedly name family members when sitting with them or when the family members approach a group with whom the child is sitting. These interactions and namings take place in both Warlpiri and English. An interesting aspect is that although teaching is taking place, the children are generally not expected to demonstrate their learning – it is assumed that they are learning what is said to them and from watching and listening to what goes on around them. It is assumed that they will be able to demonstrate their knowledge at an appropriate contextual time. They are not expected to demonstrate it for demonstration's sake. Young children are taught the reciprocal responsibilities of certain kinship relations and are expected to actively exercise the relationships. For example, when a child sees a person in a relationship such as that of mother's mother or older sibling, the child should ask for money or food from that person either verbally or through hand signs. By doing this, the children demonstrate that they understand the relationship and actively fulfil a behavioural expectation of the role. Mothers and carers actively teach this knowledge and behaviour to the children when they are toddlers. Example (3) shows a mother teaching a two-year-old girl how to behave towards someone in a classificatory older sister relationship.

In the examples 'Chi' represents a child (Chi1 = child 1, Chi2 = child 2, etc.), 'Mot' represents the child's mother and 'Adu' represents an adult other than the mother. Each example begins with Chi1 for ease of reading. Chi1 is not the same child in each example. Names have been changed so that none of the participants can be recognized.

Context: some young children are sitting with their mother on the veranda of their house. The mother sees a woman walk past who is in a classificatory older sister relationship to her two-year-old daughter.

(3)a. Mot: *kapuk wumara*
              sister   money
              'Sister, money!' *(to woman walking past)*

   b. Mot: yu   shaut   *kapuku, kapan kapan* yu   tok
              you   shout   sister   hurry hurry   you   talk
              'You shout, "sister," hurry, hurry, you talk.'

c. Mot: drink i-l   bai-im
         drink 3sg-fut buy-tr
         'She'll buy you a drink.' *(to child)*

d. Chi: *kapuk   umaya*
         sister   money
         'Sister, money.'

e. Mot: ye *Apulu-k   purdanya-ngka.*
         yes name-dat listen-imp (lit: hear-see)
         'Yes, listen to Apulu.' *(to woman walking past)*

f. Adu: e?

g. Mot: *kapuk   umaya*   *(mother is laughing)*
         sister   money
         'Sister, money!'

An adult in a classificatory older sister relationship to a child can be expected to give money or food to a child if she has any. In (3), a mother shouts out to a woman who is in a classificatory 'older sister' relationship to her child as if she, the mother, were the child ('sister, money!'). She then explicitly instructs the two-year-old child to shout out to the 'older sister' also, explaining that the adult might respond by buying her a drink. The child duly imitates her mother, but speaks too softly for the adult to hear, so the mother repeats the call loudly. In (3g) the mother uses the Baby Talk register, omitting the initial sound of the word *wumara* 'money' and substituting a 'y' sound for an 'r' sound, resulting in *umaya* for *wumara*. Perhaps she does this to make the example more salient for the child, or to show that she is speaking 'for' the child.

As mentioned earlier, adults use Warlpiri, English and some Kriol kin terms when speaking to children. In example (4), a mother is telling her daughter to be careful when she swings a stick in the air, so as not to hit a young man. The mother appeals to the child's close relationship with the young man, who is the child's mother's brother. The mother uses both the English and Warlpiri words for 'uncle'.

(Light Warlpiri)

(4) Mot: e *Bima waapa*   *Bima* angkul det   *ngamirni*
          eh name dear.one name   uncle   that mother's.brother
          'Eh! Bima, dear one, Bima, uncle, that's your mother's brother!'

In (4) the mother uses the Baby Talk register, simplifying the word *wi-yarrpa* 'dear one' to *waapa*. By invoking the relationship of the young man as a reason for the child to be careful, the mother is simultaneously teaching the child that the young man is her mother's brother, the Warlpiri and English/Kriol terms for the relationship, and that the relationship demands some care and respect. In Warlpiri culture, the mother's brother relationship is special, as the mother's brother is one of the few adults who is responsible for the child's moral development and may chastise the child if necessary.

In (5) an older speaker of Warlpiri also uses both English and Warlpiri kin terms to a two-year-old child. A child and her grandmother are sitting outside when another child walks over to them. The grandmother names the relationship between the two children, and then says that another child in a classificatory sister relationship is walking past.

(5)a. Grandm: ye   yu   dota   *nyampu-ju, nyuntu-ku,*
             Yes you daughter this-TOP   2SG-DAT

                   yurntalpa nyuntu-nyangu nyuntu-ku yurntalpa Dibi.
                   daughter   2SG-POSS   2SG-DAT   daughter   name
                   'Yeh this one's your daughter, yours, your daughter, yours, Dibi.'

   b. Grandm: an   *inya kapuk, Napanangka.*
             and   there sister   SUBSECT
             'And there is your sister, Napanangka.'

The child who approached the grandmother and her granddaughter was about four years old yet was referred to as the two-year-old's 'daughter', because she is in a classificatory daughter relationship to the two-year-old child, through the subsection system.

Children's mothers and mother's sisters (who are in a classificatory mother relationship with the child) often initiate playful interactions with babies and toddlers, and also follow the children into play scenarios, as in (6).

Context: a group of adult women and young children is sitting on a blanket and on makeshift seats in the shade of a tree. There are some toys on the blanket.

(6)a. Chi1: e   beibi   (playing with a baby doll)
            DIS baby
            'Eh, baby.'

b. Adu1:   a   beibi   *waapa*
DIS   baby   dear.one
'Ah, baby, dear one.'

c. Adu2:   *ngana-kang*   beibi?   *Nampit Nampit*   beibi
who-POSS   baby   SUBSECT   SUBSECT   baby
'Whose baby is it? Nampit's, Nampit's baby.'

d. Chi1:   lalalalalalalalalala

e. Adu1:   beibi   e
baby   DIS
'Baby, eh.'

f. Adu3:   der   beibi   *Jangala-kang*   beibi   si   *(sees Jangala with the doll)*
there   baby   SUBSECT-POSS   baby   see
'There, Jangala's baby, see.'

g. Adu3:   beibi   *Jangala-kang*   beibi   *Jangala-kurlang*
baby   SUBSECT-POSS   baby   SUBSECT-POSS
'Jangala's baby, Jangala's baby.'

In (6), a two-year-old child picks up a baby doll and says 'baby' in English. Three adults follow the child into the baby play scenario by asking whose baby it is and suggesting who the parents of the baby might be, using the names of the children who are holding it. By talking about whom the baby belongs to they are encouraging the children to think about relationships between babies and carers. Each of the adults uses Baby Talk to the child. In (6b) Adult1 says *waapa,* a simplified form of *wiyarrpa* ('dear one') mentioned above. In (6f) and (6g) the adults say *–kang* and *–kurlang* ('belongs to') instead of the classic Warlpiri word *–kurlangu.* Older adults who do not speak Light Warlpiri use these forms to very young children as Baby Talk. In addition the forms are now part of Light Warlpiri and are used by children and adults in contexts beyond those when they would use Baby Talk.

Adults often lead children into a play activity in order to manage their behaviour, for instance to distract children from straying too far from where they are expected to be, or to stop them fighting. In (7), two young children sitting with a group of adults start to fight with each other. The mother of one child at first asks them to stop fighting, and then starts to play with a doll, pretending to feed the doll, to distract them.

(7)a. Mot: No *kuli* no *kuli* yu-rra   bi *ngurrju, warungka.*
           No fight no fight 2SG-NFUT be good crazy (*affectionate*)
           'No fighting! No fighting! You have to be good, crazy one.'

  b. Chi1: *kardiya-ng* i   don like *kuli.*
           White.person 3SG NEG like fight
           'The White woman doesn't like fighting.'

  c. Chi2: a! a!

           (Mother pretends to feed doll)
  d. Mot: ye beibi mm mm hab-um   *nyanya   nyanya.*
           yes baby mm mm have-TRANS food   food
           'Yes, baby, mm mm, it's eating food.'

In (7d) the mother acts as though she were genuinely playing with the doll.

Adults initiate many interactions with children when the children are toddlers – for instance, male and female adults driving past in a car will call out and wave to toddlers who are close family when they are standing in the front yard of their home, or walking along the edge of the road. Adults do not always greet each other when they see each other around the community, for instance at the shop, but they very often call out to or wave to two- to three-year-old children who are in close relationships, often playfully asking the child for food or money, if they are in a relationship in which that is appropriate. This initiating behaviour reinforces that the adults are in close relationships with the children and that there is a reciprocal behavioural expectation. The adults call to the children by their kin terms or their skinnames. Diminutive forms of kin terms are often used, for example *pimi* for *pimirdi* ('father's sister').

At the same time that children are learning their place within the local society, their autonomy is highly valued (Bavin 1993: 87; Meggitt 1962: 124). As mentioned earlier, children spend large amounts of time playing with peers as soon as they are independently mobile. They decide for themselves when to return to the family house for meals. It is not uncommon for five- and six-year-old children to only return home for meals and in time to sleep. Parents and carers consider the community to be a safe environment. They assume that other family and community members will look out for the children, and that the children can mostly look after themselves. Children can ask for food from people in certain relationships and are expected to do so. But parents also show concern for the safety of their daughters – parents and carers are aware that there are reports of sexual abuse in some remote communities.[3] They take no-tice of with whom their children are playing and where they are, and talk to their children about with whom, and where, it is safe to play. Some-times children are told not to play away from the main populated area of the community, for fear of harm. Only parents and adults in specific re-lationships may reprimand children. A dispute between adults may break out if an adult without relevant authority reprimands a child.

The children and their carers have a way of modifying each other's behaviour, which is in keeping with valuing each other's autonomy. The person wanting the behaviour change speaks about the other person's actions within the person's hearing, but does not address the person di-rectly. Example (8) shows this.

(8) Chi1: rong   said   i-m   du-ing   it   Lama-*ng*
          wrong   side   3SG-NFUT do-PROG   3SG   name-ERG
          'Lama is doing it on the wrong side.'

In (8), Lama and Tima are playing with toys. Tima thinks that Lama is putting a toy down the wrong way. Rather than tell Lama directly, Tima speaks about Lama's action in the third person, as if to someone else. This reflects the value of individuals acting of their own volition, but lets the individual know that his/her behaviour is in question. Adult carers also follow this pattern of behaviour management. Children and adults do also speak directly to each other as chastisement, as in example (7) above, but the pattern described here, of speaking about someone rather than to them, is also very common. Although children have a great deal of autonomy and make many of the decisions about their daily activities, adults are still viewed as being in authority over children. The children's autonomy is situated within adult boundaries of permission. Adult au-thority can provide children with an additional resource for modifying each other's behaviour, as in (9).

(9)a. Chi1: Minyi-*ng*   i-rra   luk   yu
            name-ERG   3sg-NFUT   look   see
            'Minyi will see you!'

  b. Chi1: Minyi   luk   *Japayi*   *(pretends she's calling out to Minyi)*
            Minyi   look   SUBSECT
            'Minyi! Look at Japayi!'

In (9) Child 1, a four-year-old, is playing with two other children and one of them, Japayi, is behaving in a way that Child 1 thinks is inappropriate. She tries to get him to alter his behaviour by telling him that his mother,

Minyi, will see him. Then, in (9b), she pretends to call out to Minyi to come and see what Japayi is doing. This shows that Child 1 thinks that Minyi has some authority over her young son and she appeals to this authority.

Young Children's Activities which Reflect Local Community Practices

Some of the children's play activities reflect local community practices. Community members participate in annual traditional ceremonies. For a month or so after the ceremonies are held, children can be seen role-playing the parts of the ceremonies in which they participate. At several points during the ceremonies, women and children sit with their heads bowed and their eyes closed for a few seconds, so that they do not witness certain events. This part is fun for the children as they enjoy bowing their heads and there is an air of excitement and anticipation about what comes next. During their play the children sometimes reenact sitting with their heads bowed. In example (10), three children, about four years old, are playing together. Suddenly one of the children calls to the others to be quiet, because it is ceremony time. She bends her head and holds a small cotton cloth up above her, over her head. The other two children quickly dive in under the cloth, hiding themselves and saying *waja-waja taim* ('ceremony time'). Child 1 adds a sense of urgency by telling another to hurry, replicating the urgency to hide one's face that is part of the adult ceremony. In the real ceremony there are no cloths involved, people simply bow their heads. In their play scenario the children have appropriated the use of the cloth for their own purposes.

(10)a. Chi1: e kwaiyit *waja-waja* taim *waja-waja* taim
             e quiet ceremony time ceremony time
             'Eh, quiet, ceremony time, ceremony time.'

    b. Chi2: *waja-waja* taim
             ceremony time
             'Ceremony time.'

    c. Chi2: haid dem *nyampu-rla*
             hide them here-LOC
             'Hide them in here.'

    d. Chi1: *Marta* *waja-waja* taim *yaruj* *waja-waja* taim
             name ceremony time hurry ceremony time
             'Marta, ceremony time, hurry, ceremony time.'

When children role-play everyday activities, they often pretend to cook damper (flat bread made from flour and water) and tea on an open fire. Damper and tea are staple foods for people in the community and are usually cooked outside over a fire. Adults often encourage children to 'cook damper' by way of playing as a behaviour-modification strategy.

The practice of sitting and talking in a group is highly valued and has been given the English term 'talking story'. Especially in the evenings, groups consisting of adults and children often 'talk story' for several hours, usually sitting outside their houses, around a fire if the weather is cold. The content of the talk covers a range of topics, and is often about historical events, recounts of recent events, or anecdotes about family and community members. Recounts of humorous events are typical and are told repeatedly. Knowledge of kinship, sociocultural practices and family and community history is transmitted through this storytelling. Children are included as listeners and sometimes take a turn to recount an event or add a comment. Children also 'talk story' among themselves, as in (11).

(11)a. Chi1: wi-m   wok   dan   na   Turkey Nest   *kuja*   *kuja*
              1 PL   walk   down   DIS name   thus   thus
              'We walked down to Turkey Nest like this, like this.'

b. Chi2: wi   plai   ospitl   geim   *angka*
         1PL play   hospital game   DIS
         'We played a hospital game, didn't we?'

c. Chi2: an   de-m   al   folo-im   *nana*
         and   3PL-NFUT   all   follow-TRANS DIS
         'And they all followed, you know.'

d. Chi2: an *ngaju-ng* a-m   meik-im fo i-m   Kitni   beibi-*k*
         and 1SG-ERG   1SG-NFUT   make-TRANS for 3SG-NFUT   name   baby-DAT
         'And I made it for Kitni's baby.'

e. Chi1: a i-m   stil   folo   mi   *nana angka*
         a 3SG-NFUT   still follow   1SG   DIS DIS
         'Ah, he/she still followed me you know, didn't he/she?'

f. Chi1: *inya*   luk   dis   *Tima-kang*   hous-*rla*
         there   look   this   name-POSS   house-LOC
         'There, look, this is at Tima's house.'

g. Chi3: yu-du   tok-ing   stori   not   *ngaju*   *angka*
             2SG-DUAL   talk-PROG   story   not   1SG   DIS
             'Ah, you two are talking story, not me, aren't you?'

In (11), two children recount a recent event in which they walked to a nearby water bore. The event is noteworthy because the water bore is several kilometres away from the community and so is an unusually long walk for four- and five-year-old children without any adults. Child 3 did not go on the walk so is not involved in the storytelling. In (11g) she comments that the other two children are 'talking story' but she is not. The comment is interesting in the light of other studies of children's talk and play. A similar kind of reflective analysis by children of the type of talk in which they are engaging, or 'doing', is found in children's talk in diverse cultural settings (Goldman 1998; Sawyer 1997).

Card playing is a common adult activity in the community, both to pass time and to redistribute financial resources. Adults take playing cards seriously as a revenue raiser. Children aged two can hold a hand of cards and pretend to sort them. Children frequently play pretend cards, often with pretend money.

Major Themes in Young Children's Play

I use four main themes to categorize the children's talk and play, following Farver and Lee Shin (1997: 549): everyday activities, family, danger and fantasy. Children often enact everyday activities in their play, and within this theme there is often talk about sleeping arrangements, as in (12).

(12)a. Chi1: luk   i-m   nait   taim   nau   *ngana*
            look   3SG-NFUT   night   time   now   DIS
            'Look, it's night time now, you know.'

b. Chi2: wel   a-rra   slip   *nyampu*   said
           well   1SG-FUT   sleep   this   side
           'Well, I'm going to sleep this side.'

c. Chi1: an   wi-m   bi   *wurnturu*   iij   *nana*   *mayi*
           and   1PL-NFUT   be   far   each   DIS   QN
           'And we're far from each other, you know, aren't we?'

In (12) two girls, aged four and five years, are playing with dolls. They move the dolls around as they talk in the first person. In (12c) one child mentions that they can sleep far from each other, that is, without being in

a crowded sleeping area. This is presumably a reflection of both a preference for not sleeping alone, and of crowded housing in the community.[4]
Typically several family members sleep in one room and mattresses are
arranged on the floor to fit into the room.

There were two danger themes enacted during the children's play.
One was about looking after young children so that they were not taken
by a mythical monster and the other was adult violence.[5] Warning very
young children not to stray far from the populated area for fear of being
taken by a mythical monster is a common strategy for controlling the
children's behaviour.

(13)a. Chi1: wel   wi-rra   go   slip   na   nana
          well   1PL-FUT   go   sleep   now   DIS
          'Well, we're going to sleep now, you know.'

   b. Chi2: *kuuku-kujak*
          monster-EVIT
          'In case the monster gets us.'

In (13), one child tells the other they should go to sleep for fear of a monster, reflecting what the children's carers would say to them.

Australian Indigenous communities have a higher incidence of violence than many non-Indigenous communities. In 2005, twice as many
Indigenous Australians were victims of physical or threatened violence
as non-Indigenous Australians (Australian Bureau of Statistics 2006).
Children in the community sometimes witness violence, and hear adults
talking about it. We might expect, then, to see children incorporating
violence into their play routines and their talk, both to gain control of
the fears and confusions arising from it (Corsaro and Eder 1990), and to
prepare to enter the adult world in which violence is a part. Several times
the children initiated a fight or argument between the dolls they were
playing with. The initiation was usually explicit, the children directed
the action within the fight and it was then quickly over. In the following
example the two girls are playing with dolls and dolls' clothing.

(14)a. Chi1: Tima   de-rra   fait   *ngana   mayi   ngula-jarra?*
          name   3PL-FUT   fight   DIS   QN   these-DUAL
          'Tima, will these two fight?'

   b. Chi1: Tima   yu   wand-im   sket   *ngula?*
          name   you   want-TR   skirt   this
          'Tima, do you want this skirt?'

. . . they talk about clothing for a while. . . .

c. Chi2: Lama dei hab-ing *Mapa-pinki* agumen
         name they have-PROG name-ASSOC argument
         'Lama, they're having Mapa's family's argument.'

d. Chi1: na de-rra jus hab agumen an
         no 3PL-FUT just have argument and

         jinta-ng i-rra hit dem an *nganayi*
         one-ERG 3SG-FUT hit them and something

         'No, they'll just have an argument and one of them will hit the others and something.'

e. Chi1: An de-rra hab bugi *ngana nganayi.*
         and 3PL-FUT have swim DIS something
         'And they'll have a swim, you know, something.'

In (14) Child 1 initiated the idea of a fight between the dolls. The other child didn't take up the suggestion immediately, but did after a short time of talking about another topic, clothing. She suggested in (14c) that the dolls participate in a disagreement that was occurring within one family in the community at that time. Child 1 rejected that particular context for the argument in (14d), and directed that one doll hit the others. She then immediately directed that the dolls go for a swim in (14e), signalling that the fight was over. The fight was not mentioned again in the hour-long play session.

Sometimes the children reported on adult violence or marked behaviour that had taken place, for instance during the previous night. As in (14), the topics involving violence or marked behaviours are usually brought up suddenly with no apparent contextual prompting. Usually the child listening to the report gives a sign accepting the experience or story, or sometimes asks a question, or adds information. There is usually no evaluative judgement given by either speaker. The topic is left as quickly as it was taken up.

Often the children discussed alliances within their peer group that could be called upon when needed, as in example (15).

(15)a. Chi1: Nangala wi-rra go Ketherain an Dawin. Ketherain.
          SUBSECT 1PL-FUT go name and name. name.

          Ngajul an *nyuntulu* an MJ.
          me and you and name
          'Nangala, we'll go to Katherine and Darwin. Katherine. Me and you and MJ.'

b. Chi2: an   Jeni.
        and   name
        'And Jenny.'

c. Chi1: *nana* only *nyampu-rra* *puka.*
        DIS   only   this-PL   only
        'You know, only these.'

In (15) two children are chatting while eating an ice cream. Child 1 suddenly announces that three of them should go on a trip, naming the children who should go. Child 2 adds another child's name to the list. Child 1 accepts the addition but limits the group membership by saying that only those children who were named should go. Through this conversation the children are reinforcing the knowledge of who is in their immediate peer group, even though the make-up of the groups changes at different times and with different children present.

Caring for a baby was a common theme, but may be overrepresented in the data because one of the props provided by me was a baby doll. The children enacted breastfeeding and dressing the doll, and holding it as adults do by laying it along the mother's lap when she is sitting on the ground with her legs crossed. A common scenario when playing with babies was that the baby would be ill, the carer would recognize a symptom of illness and rush the baby to the health clinic.

(16)a. Chi1: *Japalyi* beibi de   sik   wan   autsaid wi teik-im
            SUBSECT   baby   there   sick   one   outside   3PL take-TRANS
            'Japalyi, baby there, sick one, we'll take it outside.'

b. Chi1: beibi i-m   weit-ing autsaid sik   wan
        baby   3SG-NFUT wait-PROG outside   sick   one
        'The baby's waiting outside, it's sick.'

c. Chi2: autsaid jik   wan
        outside   sick   one
        'Outside, sick one.'

d. Chi1: a-l   *pantirn*-im wan   taim
        1SG-FUT pierce-TRANS one   time
        'I'll give it one injection.'

In (16) Child 1 takes on the responsibility of recognizing that the baby is ill, then changes roles and pretends to give the baby an injection. One of the props I provided was a hospital kit, containing a play syringe, so the prop would have encouraged the children to play within the theme of illness. But the children could have given each other injections or pretended that adults were ill. I suggest that frequently choosing the baby as the person who was ill reflects the children's knowledge that babies often receive treatment at the health clinic.

The theme of family occurred when children used names, subsection terms (skinnames) or kin terms of people in their families with dolls or characters in a storybook. Sometimes a child would list the names of people in her family while playing an apparently unrelated game. The fantasy theme rarely occurred, but this may again be partly because of the nature of the props provided, although the props themselves would not mean the children could not create fantasy scenarios with them.

Summary

As in other cultures, young children in the community of Lajamanu use talk and play to reproduce and explore cultural practices. They enact both culture-specific and universal themes (everyday activities, family, danger) and are able to use play to exercise safety and control in a world that can be disruptive. Through their talk with each other they explore peer alliances that assist them with dealing with their wider social group.

They learn two languages in the home, the traditional language, Warlpiri, and a newly arisen language, Light Warlpiri, which is only spoken by them and their parents' age cohort. Parents and carers often speak to young children in Light Warlpiri using a Baby Talk register, which is derived from a similar register used in traditional Warlpiri. Children speak the new language, Light Warlpiri, as their primary means of everyday communication and later add Warlpiri to their repertoire. They add English also once they start attending school.

The children are actively taught specific sociocultural and linguistic practices by their parents and other adults from when they are very young. Parents initiate and follow the children into playful scenarios and exploit these as strategies for controlling behaviour and teaching about relationships and cultural behaviours. Children are viewed as social beings from an early age and inducted into the social behaviours they need to learn. They share and listen to reports about marked adult behaviour nonjudgementally. They engage in community-wide sociolinguistic practices such as 'talking story', and use indirect statements to modify each other's behaviour. The children have a great deal of autonomy in how they spend their time, yet they are expected to conform to sociocultural expectations as deemed appropriate by the community.

Appendix

A – Abbreviations Used in Glosses

erg	ergative case marker
impf	imperfective aspect
npst	nonpast
trans	transitive marker
imp	imperative case
loc	locative case
evit	evitative case
abl	ablative case
sg	singular
dl	dual
pl	plural
fut	future
nfut	nonfuture
dat	dative case
top	topic marker
poss	possessive case
subsect	subsection term
dis	discourse marker
neg	negative
prog	progressive marker
qn	interrogative
tag	sentence tag

B – Warlpiri Subsection Terms

males	females
Jungarrayi	Nungarrayi
Jangala	Nangala
Japaljarri	Napaljarri
Jakamarra	Nakamarra
Jupurrurla	Napurrurla
Japangardi	Napangardi
Japanangka	Napanangka
Jampijinpa	Nampijinpa

Notes

Data collection was supported by the Max Planck Institute for Psycholinguistics, Nijmegen, The Netherlands; and the University of Sydney, Australia.

1. When speaking to non-Warlpiri people from other communities, people from Lajamanu speak a code which could be categorized as either Aboriginal English or acrolectal Kriol (Kriol with relatively more properties from English, as opposed to basilectal Kriol, which has relatively more properties from heritage languages). Kriol and Aboriginal English have some words, sounds and grammatical elements in common, which means that when some elements are inserted into a Warlpiri clause, one cannot state whether the source language of the elements is Kriol or Aboriginal English. For this reason I label the source of elements which could be from either of these languages AE/Kriol, although I am aware that Aboriginal English and Kriol are considered separate languages, with distinct origins (Malcolm and Kaldor 1991).

2. The Warlpiri sound /j/ includes a greater range of pronunciations than does the similar English sound, and all of the Warlpiri pronunciations can be heard in Warlpiri and Light Warlpiri Baby Talk.

3. Across Australia in 2005–06, Indigenous children were reportedly more likely to be involved in child abuse and neglect cases than non-Indigenous children (AIHW 2006: 26), but details of types of communities reported on is not provided. The Bringing Them Home report (National Inquiry into the Separation of Aboriginal and Torres Strait Islander Children from their Families 1997) about the so-called Stolen Generations, and the Little Children are Sacred report (Wild and Anderson 2007) provide details about the causes of child abuse in Indigenous contexts and make recommendations.

4. 'Indigenous households had a higher proportion of two- or three-family households (6.2%) than Other households (1.1%), and a lower proportion (13.4%) of lone-person households than were found in Other households (24.0%)' (Australian Bureau of Statistics 2006).

5. It might be noted in this context of discussing the themes of danger and overcrowded houses that, at the time of writing, child abuse in remote Indigenous communities was an issue of concern in Australia. But there is no talk or behaviour in my data that suggests or alludes to any kind of sexual abuse or sexual activity involving children.

CHAPTER 7

The Yard

Craig San Roque

Living Spaces

I have in mind the image of a rabbit warren. The present generation is all over the place, there are too many holes everywhere and a unified vision is lacking. We should close the many holes of the burrow that we have become and leave only one path open through which the young people can go together.
– Katrina Tjitayi, this volume

I guess rabbits have an innate sense of design. A rabbit warren gives a bunny plenty of chances to get in and out of home in a hurry. Plenty of holes and somewhere deep down there is a place where the rabbit babies are safe. Containment and surveillance, entrances and exits, are significant and some animal, insect and flora 'dwellings' are intricately constructed around safeguarding their offspring's welfare and development.

In *Tristes Tropiques*, Claude Lévi-Strauss (1997: 248–76) describes the circular layout and social activities of a native village in Brazilian Matto Grosso. Especially instructive is his observation that the Bororo were unable to continue their traditions once missionaries had intentionally destroyed the architectural structure of their village. The Indians, he writes, 'soon lost any feeling for tradition; it was as if their social and religious systems ... were too complex to exist without the pattern which was embodied in the plan of the village and of which their awareness was constantly being refreshed by their everyday activities' (249). I suggest that the layout of family dwellings and yards in Central Australia is equally instructive, as some anthropologists have also noted with regard to Aboriginal camps (e.g., Stanner 1979: 345; Musharbash 2003: 28–47). Having spent much time in Aboriginal settings – in fringe camps, remote communities and towns – I have had opportunities to see how Aboriginal people arrange their living spaces, and Aboriginal associates have observed how my family organizes ours. Together we have noticed variations in design in such places and have come to appreciate the pragmatic uses of space in desert dwellings and family arrangements. We

156

have noted also the problems arising when nomadic camp practices and European-designed settlement systems clash or overlap uneasily as they overrule each other's practical and other evolved advantages. How children use such spaces and how they negotiate dogs, drunks, vehicles and rubbish is of concern to many parents who raise children in contemporary Aboriginal environments. When Ute Eickelkamp invited me to write on children in Central Australia, my response was to start 'at home', and so my contribution considers the family living space developed mainly by Jude Prichard (my wife) and our friends over a ten-year period. This domestic yard in Alice Springs was also, on occasion, shared with Aboriginal people. The descriptive mapping of this space gives 'snapshots' of the life-world of Aboriginal children. Their future and the foundations of their now paradoxical life environment is an underlying concern.

At the core of this chapter is the attempt to form ideas about the development of emotional and psychological 'space' between child and parent as manifested in our yard in Alice Springs. Following some orientation to the context of the town, the setting and layout of the house and yard are described with some typical incidents involving children, young people and families, and intercultural relationships in action. This is not an architectural or sociological study of other peoples' domestic organization; it is a simple reflection on the place where we live.[1] It seems problematic to single out (Aboriginal) children for study or broad brush 'intervention' without considering the entire Australian family dynamic and the detailed tensions of life in specific settlements. What is happening to children in Central Australia is a direct consequence of what is happening between Aboriginal and non-Aboriginal people and institutions – it is an interactive relational matter that is complex, confused, ideologically riven and emotional. I share Katrina Tjitayi's hope of helping Indigenous children 'go through the one path together' in the spirit of unified development. Hope is good, but radical change is grown in neighbourhoods and backyards. So we begin at home.

Orientation to Alice Springs, Central Australia

The town grew up dancing.
– Wenten Rubuntja and Jenny Green 2002

In the space of a remembered lifetime, Central Australia has been completely altered. A little more than one hundred years ago, the region was culturally organized according to the principles and practices of Aboriginal life. The receptive area now occupied by the town of Alice Springs was well protected and rich in native foods and water sources. It was recognized as firmly Arrernte country, bordered by and interconnected with Anmatyerre, Kaytetye, Warlpiri, Luritja and Pitjantjatjara speakers and related groupings.[2] There were intricate, explicitly understood boundaries and territories. By all accounts, desert politics were a hard but negotiable reality, including raids, incursions and territorial fighting. Fluctuations in power and territory demarcation occurred within an ecosystem of trade, ceremonial and kinship relations, which probably extended right across the entire Australian and Islander regions (McCarthy 1939). Into this cautious but mostly generous network, British, German, European, Chinese, Afghan and other later 'visitors' were (at first) accommodated with certain expectations of how the protocol of trade, ceremonial activity and relations might be continued with good will and to mutual benefit (Hamilton 1972). Before long there were children of mingled parentage (Briscoe 2008).

The Arrernte region with its sheltering ranges, water sources and protected centralizing environment made it a desirable base for the root-like expansion of Anglo-Australian settlement. The developing needs of cattlemen, churchmen, gold seekers, the camel trains, railways and later the aeroplane, converted Alice Springs into a service township. The Aboriginal groups found that they had nothing much to trade. Perhaps sexual relations, local knowledge and souls to be saved were useful trade for some but, with the exception of a few remarkable locals (for instance, Olive Pink), the White visitors seemed to have no appreciation of or need for any mutual relationships and dependencies. The boundaries of mutual accommodation were rapidly shifting. Every major water source in the desert region became a location of contention. The needs of travelling Aboriginal families, native animals and their sources of food were simply passed over. The incisive movement of trucks, trains and road graders across the Ancestral Dreaming tracks or 'songlines' ruptured the cosmological order and lives of the resilient, secluded desert people, exposing them to new stories, lives and forms of death. Jam, sugar, tea, flour, alcohol, Jesus, guns, wheels, houses, God the Father, surnames, clothing, influenza, smallpox, radioactive poison – these were the new and numinous items delivered in the space of a generation and assimilated and accommodated by descendents with remarkable creativity and subversive wit. Expectations by Aboriginal people that the visitors to their country might follow local, long-established cultural protocols soon gave way to the reality of how the White people negotiate possessions, relationships and the law. Perhaps what was most bewildering about the Whites was (and still is) their total lack of good manners, their absence of consistent civility, their breathtaking sense of entitlement.

All this is known in principle, recorded by anthropologists and historians (e.g., Stanner 1979; Rubuntja and Green 2002) and spoken of by many old people who still recall events and personal experiences of being collected from the bush and 'brought in' to settlements by helicopter and truck. However, the psychological fact of this transition – leaving home and country – and the consequences for family relationships seem difficult to appreciate by the many non-Aboriginal professionals who circulate through Central Australia. What Stanner (1979: 341) said a generation ago still holds true to a significant extent, namely, that 'Aborigines are administered, controlled, educated and so on by people who know almost nothing about them and give a good appearance of believing that there is nothing significant to learn'. Experts external to Aboriginal society are called upon to pick up the pieces or serve the diverse needs, while at the same time witnessing Central Australian children inhabit an environment which appears to be the rag and bone shop of the heart.

Nowadays Alice Springs is the unofficial capital of a unique country internal to Australia. With a total population of around twenty-seven thousand of which roughly 25 per cent or nearly five thousand are Aboriginal, this gathering place, generally referred to in Arrernte language as Mparntwe or Mbantua, is a terrain of converging *Altjerre* (Dreaming) stories. There are many significant locations within this area, among them the publicly acknowledged sites of the story of the Black and White Dogs, the Caterpillar convergence site and lesser-known places that figure in the subliminal map of the town. Many children growing up in this narrative matrix inherit a sense of the presence of those stories. Some absorb 'ownership' and custodial responsibilities and, consequently, participate in conflicts among or on behalf of Aboriginal groupings. Children are awake to danger and some are awake to the poetry. This is a place endowed with living stories from the time of the foundation of the human mind. Mbantua/Alice Springs is now a country town where multiple Aboriginal languages are spoken aloud in the streets, intersecting with English and the languages of European, Asian and African residents and travellers. It makes for an environment of distinctive character, which is multilingual, multicultural and pluralistic. It may be difficult for many persons, even those representing enlightened views of government, to recognize the reality and creative potential of this plurality. 'Alice', like perhaps Darwin and Broome, is a place where it is still possible to experience the vigour, the tragedy and the depressingly desperate drama of a polyphonous life. Diversity, brutality and contradictions help make it into a location that sustains and disseminates original culture and at the same time is generating new creativity. The region attracts people of all kinds, some of them compassionate, others ruthless, vigorous, intelligent or entrepreneurial. There is a visible interplay of creativity, preservation and destructiveness. Destruction almost always has the upper hand. There are many moods in the town, among them a pervading sense of loss, bewilderment, anarchy and perhaps a repetitive grief.

The central desert region and the town attract trouble. So much trouble in fact that the federal government, in June 2007, took the unprecedented step of configuring the Aboriginal situation in the Northern Territory as a humanitarian emergency. Bypassing the local Northern Territory government, it dramatically engineered a substantial intervention into the conduct of Indigenous social and financial affairs – with the stated aim of saving children from repetitive grievous bodily, mental and moral harm or neglect. This harm was/is configured as emanating from within the family systems. The causes, conduct and consequences of the Northern Territory Interventions are yet to be appreciated. Nevertheless, even with such troubles acknowledged, Central Australian local history demonstrates again and again that a creative relationship between Black and White people is possible and productive. It is this factor of relationship which deserves attention.

A Place To Go To

In using the word culture I am thinking of the inherited tradition as something that is in the common pool of humanity, into which individuals and groups of people may contribute, and from which we may draw if we have somewhere to put what we find.
– Donald Winnicott 1971: 116

My understanding of how cultural experience is located and made within early childhood relationships owes much to D. W. Winnicott.[3] This influential English paediatric psychoanalyst developed a way of talking psychologically about *spaces between persons,* and between a person and his or her environment. Most especially he was concerned with the psychological space that is created and held between baby and parent, for which he coined the term 'potential space'. We can think of this as a kind of emotional, mental and psychological receptacle, a cradle or a *coolamon* (traditional Central Australian carrying dish made of wood), that gets made between the bodies of the two people – mother and child. It comes into being and is held in place by listening and looking attentively, by stroking, feeding, holding and playing together. Winnicott noted that when things between baby and mother are going well then the baby goes well, the baby feels, develops and plays. Creative imagination has somewhere to begin. When the mother (or kin mother) is there, the baby has somewhere to put what they together find and make. Winnicott, as a doctor, was also attentive to what happens when the body of the mother is lost, gone, broken up, depressed, psychotic or so confusing to the child that the baby cannot make any sense out of the world into which he/she is born. Winnicott's approach was influenced by the effect of the Second World War on children, especially those children whose families and habitat were destroyed by warfare. Winnicott shaped useful ideas from his observations of subtle, invisible, emotionally charged activities that go on in the space between parents and their children. He described this area as *potential* because there is a lot of 'potential energy' for things to happen, and he thought of it as a *space* because it is a kind of area both physical and psychological at the same time, sort of 'inside' ourselves, in mind and heart and memory, and sort of 'outside' in the world of eyes, faces, hands, bodies and activity. The 'potential space' is a psychological reality, a place where we put things, offer things, exchange things when we are in love, when we are in concentrated communion with another person, and when we are a child playing. It is a geo-physical-mental-emotional space, kinaesthetically felt as containment within an environment, rather like an invisible nest. A well-designed building can be felt as a space with potential wherein imaginative events might happen. The quality of 'potential space' can be seen or felt when children play with absorbed concentration. It is as if a playing child makes a special defined area around herself and playmates. You can see this territory of concentrated imagination when Aboriginal people are sitting 'talking story', drawing illustrations with stick or wire on sand smoothed out on the ground with deft hands (*see* e.g., Eickelkamp 2008b). Here, between people and the ground, a location of intimate human scale is set up and a story can commence.

Winnicott describes this area or space as being *found* by a child when a parent or carer is attentive and willing to play and communicate. The baby *creates* the space instinctively when she demands attention from her parental beings. Her eyes help to make and hold the space, so too does the caressing of warm body to warm body. I speak about something that is simple and natural. The child brings out from the parent the attention and containment she needs and the parent responds or limits the quantity and quality. A baby's ability to make this 'space between' is probably a matter of survival within a felt protected containment between intimate people – which gives a child a chance for maturation. It is a natural activity, let us say, about making territory between close-up bodies. The normal child does instinctive work to make a space for herself in the minds and heart of parental beings, so that the child's mind and heart (attentiveness and capacity for connectivity) can in turn develop and flourish. It is a simple thing and does not have to be overstated. Mostly, we recognize when love is there, when the maternal impulse is working more or less normally among kin whose task it is to pair up with the developing child.

There is the other side of the story. Acts of neglect or hostile attack which break the link between adult and child make one realize sharply what is lost when the 'power of two' is destroyed. Maintaining care between people usually involves some kind of practical respect, which keeps destructive activity limited. Winnicott was, as others are, particularly interested in the psychological effects upon people of having their places destroyed, their place in relationships and their placement in their body. He used the term 'impingement' to indicate coercive interventions and unwanted penetration into the developing structures of the child's self and was alert to how prolonged psychological invasion during childhood makes for a disorder. Extreme anxiety, fear, hatred, aggression and despair can be managed by most children for a while, but without reliable containment, without the felt presence of a protective 'mothering' body, forms of chaos take over a child's self – and as I may here extend – forms of chaos take over the child's country. When country/place/locale is lost, the normal child has no reliable place to go to, to settle the mind in. I speak of 'disorders of self' and also of 'disorders of place' that may occur when maternal spaces are invaded and ruined. (We might consider how ruination has come about in Central Australia.) Of course, resilience and self-preserving adaptation can kick in around the urge to defend home, land and hope.

Why, you might be asking, am I taking the trouble to labour the point about the 'space' between people? It is because if there are problems with child development, education and imaginative growth; if children and young people living in Aboriginal territories are in fact losing their way, losing their spirit (*kurunpa*) or are in troubles of various kinds; if the integrity of Aboriginal cultural progress is in doubt, as some people suggest – then where does one look to fix the situation? Winnicott's extensive experience and well-developed theory suggest that we look directly into what is going on between people in a family set up and then take the next step and look directly into what goes on in the holding culture. That is to say, we should analyse what is passing *between* the people who are forming the culture of Australia. In particular we might look at the little things passing daily in detail between the people who are holding the culture and destroying the culture of Black and White *relationships*. Winnicott (1965b: 39n1) famously said there is 'no such thing as a baby'. What he meant by this ironic little phrase is that one cannot think of a child or baby in isolation – there is only a baby-in-relationship with a mother. This forces us to think about people in relationships, including intercultural ones. Also it is common sense that a child-and-mother are always within an environment. The environment of the Aboriginal desert child-mother relationship has very specific factors. Some of these factors have to do with the links made and broken between Black and White persons. Now and then we might have to say, like Winnicott, that 'there is no such thing as an Aboriginal child', there is only an Aboriginal child-in-relationship with the Aboriginal-and-non-Aboriginal environment. These children live, thrive or die in environments and amid persons who are in conflict, in confusion and in transition. The factors of the conflict, confusion and transition are serious, simple and ordinary, and that is where the trouble is found and the enigmas and the solutions are discovered, I suggest.

Bringing It Home

The present generation is all over the place; there are too many holes.
– Katrina Tjitayi

The notion of finding and creating 'potential space' between persons has underpinned my approach to therapeutic work as a community psychologist, mostly with troubled young people in Central Australia. Containment, care of relationship and adaptation to the actual environment also underlie the approach of Jude Prichard in her work in Aboriginal land care and environmental management and design for health. Since 2007, there has been talk in government about 'Practical Reconciliation', and an apology to Aboriginal Australians was made by the new prime minister in 2008 for failures in childcare and protection, for lack of insight and wrong action during previous generations of Black-White relations. It is necessary to address these historical and ethical matters at a political and institutional level of action; such work is assumed to take place in offices and formal communication systems but, taking a leaf from Winnicott's book, what also counts are the microlevel ideas, feelings and actions which arise between people in and around ordinary domestic spaces.

The container as exemplified in European architectural structures has influence on the urban professional practitioner's mind. Containment and boundaries are important for people of many cultures, and the way their cities, houses, yards, offices and rural enclosures are built supports this idea. Most of the psychological work among people in remote areas of Australia takes place outside walls, outside cityscapes. The metaphor of containment symbolized by a private professional office does not apply. It is not real. Instead, there are bush boundaries, which are often determined by kinship differentiations; they are relational and in that sense obtain a social spatiality. Boundaries are indeed there, but they may not be visible or clear to persons who are not brought up in this Indigenous relational environment or have not cultivated an understanding for the implicit order of Aboriginal social management and time framing. Europeans invented for themselves a form of therapeutic interventions. It suits our systems and moment in history. The European boundary and containment systems are useful and also entirely idiosyncratic. Why is it necessary for the European to destroy the Indigenous systems of containment and psychological order? I hear this question voiced in the zones of the Aboriginal discourse. In such places some of us have indeed listened and invented forms of containment, discovered adaptive intercultural attentiveness, achieved concentrated interpersonal empathy, and found ways for reciprocal firm wise counsel. My story about the yard suggests, like a parable, that it is possible for Black and White people to create a boundary and a space between themselves wherein play, imagination, care, attention, conversation and life can go on in satisfying ways. When I read Tjitayi's lines on the image of a rabbit warren, I think of the many children growing up in the perplexed zone *between* the Black and the White environments. Tjitayi's idea also confirms that it is important to develop a better grasp of what is needed to grow up *together in a shared territory.* My yard parable might present a little idea in that direction.

The Set Up

In our place in Alice Springs, it seemed natural to make an environment which could accommodate Aboriginal and European needs and habits, and where children and adults could be in a place that was interesting, safe enough, contained and interactive when required. It was a space where intercultural imagination could thrive, protected. Jude Prichard had the idea and the designer's skill to make an ordinary place into an unobtrusively potent cultural space. Her vision as a mother of young children was intuitively akin to Winnicott's idea that the feel of the play between mothers and children gradually becomes a foundation for cultural experience. Play, imagination, cultural experience, respect and interpersonal adjustment follow each other. The yard and house in Mueller Street in Alice Springs was such a space where room could be made.

Our yard shown in Figure 7.1 evolved over time. Home locations make childhood memory and adult mentality, so thoughtful design and care of the spaces in which children grow up is a good investment. Special care and thought might be given to the locations wherein children

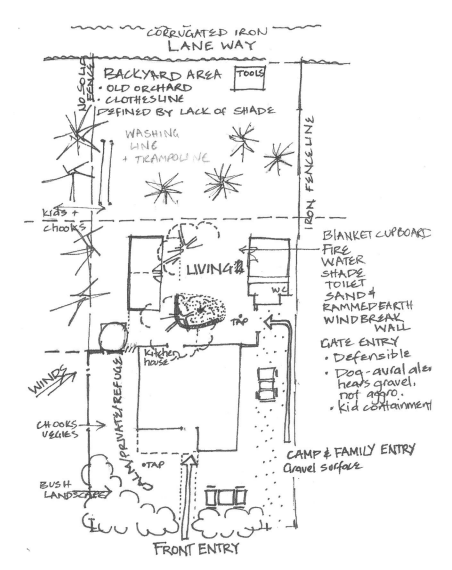

Figure 7.1. ▼ The House and Yard Space

Note: Diagram of our house and yard in Mueller Street, Alice Springs, representative of the period of this account, c. 1993–2003 (Jude Prichard).

of Indigenous affiliation are now developing. Central Australian children live in bush camps, settlements, outstations, town camps and suburban settings and cities. They circulate, often moving between such different locations. Some of these locations are exceptionally neglected, bleak and dangerous; some are interactive, expansive and imbued with cultural vivacity.

The Street

The land where this house is sited was originally a sand and claypan edge of the Todd River. The Coolibah Swamp, as it is known now, is part of a network of sacred story sites. During the Second World War the flat floodplain river edge was cleared for rows of military tents and equipment. After the army left, much of the detritus of war was bulldozed and buried there. The East Side suburb began to be laid out. Our house was built around 1952 to house single men – cattle station workers on town visits. It was minimalist, functional, composed with thick concrete blocks, concrete floors and cement render, high ceilings, white painted corrugated iron roofing, water tanks, bore pump, shed and orchard, all typical of an arid land style and probably built by Italian transient migrants who had memories of simple, cooling rectangular village houses and courtyards. What distinguished this house was that it had the feeling of a courtyard compound. This set the tone. The main house faces east toward the saltbush shrub called Coolibah Swamp and morning sun. Out to the back are a two-room single men's quarters on the south side and a garage shed on the north side. It is set on what was originally a double block including a big shed and citrus orchard. At some point the block was divided. The neighbouring section became a collection of spacious ramshackle dwellings inhabited, when we were there, by an anthropologist whose wife, being Aboriginal, attracted a flow of Western Desert bush visitors. The activities in the neighbours' living area to the south influenced the activity in ours.

In the street there are many yards, reflective of inclusion or exclusion of Aboriginal activities. One or two are built right on old walking tracks or right up against very old sites that have been gathering places for Arrernte people for generations. As local people follow what were once familiar tracks, they encounter fences that cut across or obstruct free passage. Nowadays the paths used by Aboriginal people run from Hidden Valley town camp through the housing of the eastern side of the Todd River, branching off to shops and a liquor store or into the transient camp sites of the river bed – and from there in and out of the town business district. There are lanes too, lanes behind houses originally made for the sewerage collection cart to access the outside toilet systems. Basically it is the conventional street grid system superimposed over meandering original Arrernte walking tracks and story site locations.

There is nothing much to distinguish this house from the front, and in any case it is mostly obscured in foliage. Across the road a row of houses back onto Coolibah Swamp wherein Aboriginal visitors and drinkers camp in the cover of the low bushes. Sometimes the saltbush is quiet, sometimes violence erupts. On occasion an injured, bleeding woman would appear at the door asking for help, a man hovering watchfully, perhaps, in the background. There is a water tap in the front yard. The convention along the street is that Aboriginal campers may come into certain yards to fill a water container. These are the only access points to water. Not all front yards are accessible. Some have high fences and dogs. We had a dog but somehow or other our dog allowed bush people (those who live in remote Aboriginal settlements or outstations) to enter for the water tap. The water tap access was figured as shared neutral territory, and people who, on occasion, came for water understood this convention; they would fill up a can and politely leave. The usual entrance is through the vehicle driveway on the north side, beneath a vine shade with a gravel surface. This, not the front door, was the real entrance for most (Aboriginal) visitors. The gravel noise was a signal. It is thickly spread and crunches underfoot. We hear footsteps on the gravel. At night, there is no need for alarms; the quiet is subtly broken, enough alarm for the finely attuned ear. Our doors were rarely locked. There were no barbed high fences.[4] The gravel crunch, the arousal of the dog, the fiddling with the metal gate, all gave the signal that someone is approaching. This signal was gratefully read by the bush women who would sometimes camp secluded in the back yard. Bush women like to see who is approaching. Camps are often sited at vantage points and define negotiable distances from other families. For this reason, an enclosed European-style building is not always desired. The sightlines and space are broken up in complicated ways; though a room might give a hiding place, it may also be a trap. The house on the northern neighbour's boundary had high metal fences, which gave some protection, but generally our place was characterized by permeable boundaries, which could, however, be observed and defended well enough. The boundary issue is noted as a necessary concern in managing safely the mingling of uses by Aboriginal visitors and our family. It is a big subject. Boundaries and observable space issues in Aboriginal housing deserves more discussion than is possible here.

A Social Space Evolves

The preferred 'living room' for Aboriginal visitors was the courtyard compound. Its original structure allowed this to evolve adaptively and pragmatically over the years.

Women in particular sought seclusion, safety and comfort. These were mostly sober, competent, vivacious women like Jilly Nakamarra Spencer, Marlene Ross or Janie Whistle who took (rivalrous) charge of the yard's cleanliness (Figure 7.2). They brought their kin, children and occasionally their men. Our visitors were from families who we knew, and with whom our family and friends group had reciprocal 'country' rights, meaning that when travelling in Aboriginal regions for work, our family might camp with them. The courtyard play area was used consistently by a neighbourhood playgroup that came together two days a week, and which could, on occasion, absorb children visiting from the bush. The fact of this playgroup and the priority of childcare needs set certain limits on the behaviour of visitors. This fact influenced social behaviours and gave clear reasons for the priority 'rules' (*cf.* Sansom and Baines 1988).

In the Mueller Street compound there were, in fact, few rules. The main rule was 'No Drunks', established by the women and us conjointly. The other 'rule', or rather, understanding, was that senior women were responsible for supervising their own family affairs. The question of who cooked and who supplied food was negotiable and depended upon a mixture of generosity and restraint. With some visitors one had to be alert to overdependence and passive demand. The 'No Drunks' rule was partly why 'sober' family groups could and would visit. There are other yards in town where the racial groups mingle. Some of these are drunken associations with violence and careless trashing of the environment. We drew a line. When such visitations might be on the brink of occurring, it

Figure 7.2. ▼ Mrs Janie Whistle Raking the Yard
Note: Mrs Janie Whistle raking the yard after a windstorm, also showing fishpond and cement-rendered shed and workroom (Craig San Roque, with permission).

Figure 7.3. ▼ In the Company of Women and Play
Note: In the company of women and play in the yard, with Nakamarra minding two small children (Craig San Roque, with permission).

would be made clear, usually by myself with measured drama, that such carelessness was not welcome. This was especially so since my work in alcohol and petrol-sniffing prevention in Aboriginal circles was well enough known. (In extreme circumstances, police were summoned.) There are other households where generous reciprocity was maintained and where certain Aboriginal families knew that they would always find some kind of welcome, some kind of bed, some kind of respite. Much of the notable and successful intercultural work of the desert region is supported by such reciprocal relationships. In many such yards strategically placed around the town, implicit, quietly nuanced Black-White relationships have been lived and maintained through intimate domestic interchange. This is the 'practical reconciliation' of Alice Springs; a way to live and get one's work done.[5] There are, of course, many suburban Alice Springs yards characterized by security gates, savage dogs and 'attitude'. One can design for safety by exclusion and one can design for reasonable safety by inclusion.

Design Elements

The yard environment was put together with the intention to maintain interactive intercultural domestic areas that worked for adults and for children of the families who moved through the compound. While leaving room for the spontaneous clutter of play and ordinary domestic activities, it is worth noting a few elements that Jude Prichard insisted upon in her reconstruction of the original cattlemen's backyard so as to make it a viable indoor/outdoor living area for diverse activities. These elements came from particular observations of children's play patterns and behaviours of (Aboriginal and other) women and children in bush camps, communities and around the house/yard. Jude was influenced by observations of South East Asian compounds and her training in urban design. Local women's advice as to what makes a good living area was heeded and incorporated. The 'advice' emerged in thoughtful comments from friends and fellow parents including especially Sally Mumford (similarly trained in architecture and design), and some bush women, especially Jilly Nakamarra Spencer Nelson, Bertha Nakamarra Dixon, Marlene Nampijimpa Ross, Rachel Nakamarra Jurra, Samantha Jones and Elva Cook, all of whom lived in town camps or 'remote area' communities and outstations. Men contributed; Andrew Spencer Japaljarri walking round the yard on his first visit nodded approvingly as he looked at the trees, mostly fruit and old 'white cedars'. His comment 'plenty of firewood' may have reflected his bushman's interests but it also revealed different perceptions about the value of European garden trees. White cedars are not good firewood, and citrus has better uses. I could say more about Aboriginal male use of house structures – but my focus here is on child-and-mother's domain.

The matter of Aboriginal housing, traditional and contemporary, and how Indigenous people order the priorities of what makes a good place (*ngurra*), is too complex to detail here but some factors that were essential in Jude Prichard's thinking about our bicultural family compound can be summarized thus:

- boundaries
- location of water and ablution sources
- access to cooking areas and fireplace
- sleeping and play area
- locations of shade
- areas of seclusion and refuge
- areas for imaginative activity

Boundaries: a boundary system is naturally established by the compound design, a model observable in Mediterranean, Islamic and Indian dwellings with climates similar to Central Australia. This form allows for seclusion, surveillance, defence and limited access. Interior shaded areas were favoured for protecting children, and these were maintained as the key of the design. Significantly, *no vehicles* could drive into the back yard compound. This is an issue in Aboriginal communities where vehicular access can be chaotic and invasive.

Water: there were two outside water taps close to the living/playing/cooking area. There was later a fishpond which the ladies insisted had to be close to the camping area. (I am not sure if this was a borrowed Western aesthetic idea or nostalgia for the old days camping by water holes, or so that dogs could more easily drink.)

Ablution: there was an outside bathroom with toilet, laundry and sink separate to our family bathroom. This is a significant feature. Care of toilet and ablution spaces in Aboriginal houses on communities is a serious matter. Our system worked tolerably enough, given the demand, and it is a story in itself.

Sandpit: the outdoor fireplace/play sandpit, which could sleep six to ten people, was enclosed by the ochre rendered wall (Figure 7.4). Such a 'windbreak' is an essential element of Aboriginal desert architecture. It can be made of brushwood, tin sheets, and tarpaulin; in this case we see the *wiltja* (traditional round wet-weather shelter) -style cement blocks, a metre high and curved, along which one can sit or walk (if you are child

Figure 7.4. ▼ Ladies Camping, Breakfast

Note: See the fireplace and windbreak based on the concrete wall. The kitchen door of the house can be glimpsed in the background behind the makeshift windbreak tarps. It was August and cold winds were coming from the south (Craig San Roque, with permission).

wanting to balance). It served as the base structure for play huts, tents and encampments, 'castles', and family intimacies. This sandpit might be configured as the core location of the interaction between two cultural worlds – the heart of the yard. It was a living area formed by and adaptive to the bush women's relationships. It was where most of the cultural conversations took place.

Kitchen: the original house had a small, inconvenient (bachelor's) kitchen. It was never really very practical. Eventually we took down a wall and opened a window hatchway into the yard which then became good for surveillance of children who could come to the low window for goods. Bush-style cooking took place at the low, simple and easily removable grilling fireplace set into the sandpit windbreak. Here people could sit around the fire, stew 'billy tea' and cook kangaroo tail and chops. The site for many story exchanges, visitors could spread bedding and sleep by the fire, waking in the morning in a familiar bush camp configuration. They would make tea and breakfast from leftover kangaroo tail and bread, etc., and get cleaned up, shower and so forth and head off into town for work, conferences, health visitors meetings, funerals, shopping and whatever else the town demanded. The fire site is significant. The key to being able to run two 'households' concurrently, at times, seemed to be the two area options; the outdoor family fireplace configuration which could operate independently to the indoor (mostly White) family and work activities. Fire safety was always of interest. When the breakfast fire and bedding disappeared it became a children's sandpit again. Transience and flexibility were key elements. So too are patience, tolerance and a slow pace of interaction, boundary setting and unsentimental negotiation of diverse needs and demands.

Structures

Outside buildings: the old cattlemen's two rooms served us well – one on occasion as domicile for the older ladies, where privacy from hubbub was needed. And one was my workroom. The old corrugated iron garage, rebuilt in rendered concrete blocks with kitchen etc., housed friends, lodgers, and served for a period as a consulting room. I mention this because, contrary to expectations, a psychological consultancy activity could, for a period, exist alongside our shared living. Double doors opened onto the yard. It was a flexible space. Activity around this site also features in my story 'A Long Weekend in Alice Springs' (San Roque 2004: 46).

Inner house: in general the inner house came to be recognized as our family territory and understood as such. This took time and was easier to accomplish once the outdoor regions became usefully adapted. A region on the south side was the 'Whitefella garden' with a table, vegetables and chooks. The point being made here is about areas of differentiated regions, indoors and outdoors, which accommodates a diversity of activities when required, a keynote of Prichard's design ethos.

Shade/orchard: when the oranges and mandarins were in season, certain bush people would always turn up. The orchard was part of the known local resources for food gathering with a history that preceded our occupation. The compound had wires stretched across it to carry sail cloth and cane shadings. This gave the place a North African or Middle Eastern feel, matched by the lime wash colours, tiles and enclosing wall. Shade and self-cooling breeze access in arid land dwellings is an issue now – and may, with climate alteration – become more so.

Ground. The compound area was a hard-packed red clay laterite, a rammed earth composition developed by Tangentyerre Aboriginal Council Design and Landcare. Intended for large-scale pathways and environments (e.g., The Desert Park), Jude adapted it for domestic use. The clear, hard-packed ochre surface imparted an aesthetic unifying sensation as well as being functional for kids and easy to keep clean of rubbish. Before this, the area was a hodgepodge of old concrete slabs, grass, dog bones and failed gardens – a sight of depression, detritus and neglect in which many Aboriginal people are forced to live. When given a better option, women such as Mrs. Whistle and Mrs. Nakamarra Spencer responded with obvious pleasure and pride in place.

Attitude: the matter of the attitudes that people allow to suffuse a living area has to be thought about. It has to do with how one uses, controls and takes care of an area and allows reciprocal and differing private lives to go on, for tolerable time spans. Jude's attitude toward the yard over which she had control included the notion that this was a space where imaginative behaviour, play and humour could thrive and be firmly protected. Being a mother, she was supported in this approach by enough people to make it work. This goes straight to Katrina Tjitayi's rabbit warren story. There have to be enough people prepared to make a 'unified vision' work. What makes successful (or failed) living spaces in interracial towns and community settlements is a big issue for Central Australians.

Incidents

The way a place (or a stage) is set up is one thing, but what also matters is what goes on there, and so I come to a few incidents. Incidents such as those outlined below occur in many places where cultural groupings cross over. There must be hundreds of local domestic stories of how people manage to live together or fail. Many Central Australian households have found their own solutions. Each would have an interesting tale to contribute to a study on environmental design for remote area towns. To learn from these experiences seems significant: with the increasing movement of bush people to towns, it is generally anticipated that the Alice Springs population may become 50 per cent Aboriginal within ten years.

Lament

It is nightfall; the orange trees shimmer in a summer evening. Today's bad news is the suicide of a boy we know. Suicide is no surprise now; too many young people are losing the geometry of their lives. Two Warlpiri women sit by the fire, pensive, they are relatives of the boy. I turn to music and play a Spanish lament, flamenco. Nakamarra Dixon is sitting on the sand, her head resting loosely, beating time, unaware of the meaning of the language but following every move of the song's nuances, her eyes glistening. She asks: 'Where does that music come from?' 'It comes from Spain, Nakamarra, from the gypsy country'. 'I love that music, Jungarai, play it again!' After a while she asks what the words mean. (At that moment it is Carmen Linares singing a tango grandadinos, *De Color de Rosa.*) 'Nakamarra', I say,

> in this song she's not so sad, she is singing about the mulberry tree, that tree over there with the purple juicy berries you mob like so much. It's a love song. She sings that the mulberry is like a queen in her palace, a beautiful woman dressed in green, and all the mulberries are men. She sings that the mulberry men are in love with the queen, and each one wants to find the way to her. Now she sings she is lonely, she is winding beans into her long black hair; green and red striped beans in her hair and she's waiting for her lover to come. She says that she loves this city, Granada, she loves to wake in the morning and hear the bells from the church ringing. She is singing about mulberries and beans as love songs the way you mob sing acacia beans and bush plums. We all have country love songs, Nakamarra.

And I am glad that we are sitting together at night, among oranges and the mulberry. And can quietly remember the boy who died, and what has been lost. No culture is a stranger to lament.

Motorcar

Another evening and visitors from Europe, an Englishman's car is parked in the driveway. Sometime in the evening Nampijimpa's son, sixteen or so years of age, and his friend come through the driveway gate and sit for a while. Dark, slender, alive sort of boys. 'Uncle, can I borrow your car? Maybe some money for petrol?' I do not lend my car. I give him ten dollars. 'Can you drive me?' 'No, I am sorry, not tonight, I have visitors'. He says thanks and leaves. There are some uncle words from me about stealing cars and not to steal cars, like happened yesterday and what trouble comes for him out of stealing things. 'No, Uncle', and the two boys walk into the dark. The visitors keep doing what visitors do, talking, asking questions, and it is time to go home. The Englishman leaves. Where his car is meant to be there is an empty space. The car is gone. No one heard a thing. Jude and I look at the empty space. Someone says police. I say to the Englishman, maybe we'll go look for it. Jude and I calculate certain things about Nampijimpa's son. My own vehicle is still there. With the Englishman somewhat bemused, we head south to the town camp where I think Nampijimpa is staying tonight, out of town on the south highway. It is after midnight and two 'Whitefellas' drive into a darkened Aboriginal camp seeking out a particular house. The Englishman is maybe a little concerned for his life, as much as he is for his car. I do find Nampijimpa, and there is talk about cars. Nobody seems to know anything. But then someone comes up and says, 'A car like that is down there in the bush'. He shows us where, and I drive down the obscure track. Finally the headlights pick up the Englishman's car, as though it were lost in a jungle. The owner thinks it is a miracle, and I think, tomorrow I will have to tell Nampijimpa's son not to steal cars. Again. No one says it was he. Nampijimpa does not place the blame on her son. No one says anything. I guess everyone appreciates that we all know the story, and the protocol is 'understatement'. This incident was one reason for laying the crunchy gravel in the driveway. At least this way we would have a fighting chance to intercept Nampiimpa's son before an unsuspecting vehicle had again been silently rolled out the gate and into the street.

Playgroup

Another day. Children have come for the playgroup. It is the under-fives parent-run morning playgroup with eight or nine kids and bikes, mostly our children and the neighbours', who are self-reliantly forming their own legitimate and diverse play group. There was a dress-up box. This box was always there. Sometimes when bush kids visit, they go to the dress-up box and put on dresses, masks, colours and make-up and play and dance. Our children join in. This is a variation of when the Warlpiri women paint up our children with white and ochre and teach extracts of ceremony. The shared performance seems to bring especial and relaxing joy (*see* Figure 7.5).

Figure 7.5. ▼ Girls Dressed Up
Note: Winki, a Pintupi girl (left) and Inki, the author's daughter, who were playmates and 'sisters', both c. seven years old (Craig San Roque, with permission).

I like to watch this kind of two-way play; you can lose a lot of prejudice and fixed ideas this way. I remember one night in a camp with petrol sniffers: it was dark, the fire low; one of the boys slipped away, then returned dressed in woman's clothes and head scarf, cradling a 'baby'. He sat without a word by the fire for ten minutes cradling, as though crooning to the baby. All the boys were fascinated, spellbound. Then quietly 'she' got up and disappeared into the dark. He returned as though nothing had happened, dressed again nonchalantly in his New York macho style. Such a masterful performance. This performance is even more masterful psychologically if I tell you that this young man lost his mother when he was an infant. She died while carrying him. No one was present. When her body was finally found the baby was still with her, doing what he could to suckle.

Meanwhile, back in the yard, at the playgroup, Nungarai comes in with her two kids. They survey the scene; the bikes, the water hose and the slide. Children from two domains, two races, mingle with good humour and sandwiches. Jason, her four-year-old son from out bush, does not know how to manage a town-style toilet. He goes behind a tree. I have been asked to teach him how to climb up to the white ceramic bowl and sit there. He is not successful. Anyway, in his community, most of the ceramic bowls are broken, clogged, overflowing and dribbling sewered water into the yard. Trees are maybe safer, he probably correctly thinks. And dogs will clean it up. The same dogs who sleep with him at night, probably. He shits in the yard under a tree. Life cycles. This time it is not the dogs but myself who cleans it up.

Ladies Overnight

Ten Warlpiri ladies arrive wanting, politely, somewhere safe to sleep. They were heading south for women's ceremonies, and the vehicle ran into trouble. It will take a day or two to fix. They want somewhere far from drunks and distractions so they can keep their attention calm and stop young men from trying to grab their money. The old women are a part of the domestic economy, their dollars safely tucked away in beanies (knitted cap) and between breasts. The Toyota dropped them off in a bundle of sticks and bags, pillows and blankets and smiles. The truck kept going so nobody would notice where the grannies are staying. In the yard they relax, maybe ten or twelve people, and someone begins rigging up tarpaulin windbreaks. Somehow a shopping trolley was worked into the shelter, maybe to keep things away from dogs. Over two days these noted cultural women relaxed, cooked, slept, prepared and rehearsed their ceremony dance. Children came and went underfoot. The women painted children with children's designs; everyone had a good time. When the vehicle was ready, the Warlpiri women left in good spirits, their ceremonial discipline intact. I remember skin and stripes of red, white and yellow ochre, feathers, hair, songs, smoke and Black and White humanized bodies combining. Women and children danced, untroubled in a back yard in town.

Lonely Boy

In the shade, a small group are working on the Pintupi translation of an ancient mythological story. The story is about a mythic Crow who abuses and eats his own children. It comes from an old Mediterranean region but is being cheerfully adapted by these three Pintupi/Warlpiri women working out the translations of a style of storytelling that is familiar to them. Uncle Crow's/Kronos's brutish behaviour resonates with some of the more violent Aboriginal mythic stories, and everyone is enjoying the intercultural crossing of an old and strong story. Kronos's cannibalistic, rapacious behaviour is appreciated as an image of abuse of children by drunks. The women do not intellectualize these stories. They speak directly to 'bad things' done by men and women whom we all know but do not wish to publicly name. The conversation is being filmed for the documentary *Sugarman*. Another woman who is helping with the story comes into the compound with a child cradled in a blanket. She lays down the small child, limply drowsing on the sand. Later on being questioned by the filmmaker (David Roberts) she says: 'This is my daughter's son. She doesn't look after him. It's grog. Alcohol did that. I lost my family through grog'. She counts off on her fingers the men and women lost in this way. The boy lies there. He rests. As grandmother she takes care of him. This brings for her much trouble and consternation. There are tensions. I went with her one day to a town fringe camp and was caught up in a family argument. When it was timely I retreated with the grandmother, backing the vehicle out of the camp so I could see who might be coming after us, the tyres crunching broken glass and aluminium beer cans. The life of these children is surrounded with strife; but here today, at least no one troubles him. He is fed. He has some respite. He is not well. A lonely boy drowsing on the sand.

Conclusion

I have given you a glimpse of a family backyard and by this means have tried to make a case for valuing culturally interactive everyday life. In this I have followed a mentor, Donald Winnicott. It is a long way from Harley Street, London, to Mueller Street, Alice Springs, but what connects is the idea of safeguarded spaces between people. A backyard can be a place of interaction; it requires practical physical design to make it work. There *is* neglect in Central Australia but the location of the neglect may have been misplaced. Maybe neglect is to be found in the delicate spaces between persons of these two historically different peoples – the Indigenous Australian and the settling peoples who are mostly, so far, of European and traumatic origins. Between us is a vastly complex, still unexplored psychological space. Life is played out in streets, yards and living rooms, in locations which produce our Australian culture, places that materialize as tin sheds, concrete walls, swimming pools, wrecked cars, bodies. Different children come and go. Taken together, the layers of backyard experiences, sheds, walls, water, car wrecks, bodies will flow into the children's understanding of the world they can make. It is possible to work out a way of living close up to each other – there are instances of this in Australian cultural history, though the instances may be short lived and easily overwhelmed by various kinds of drunkenness. All I can say is this – effort was made by a family to make a place that worked. We sustained this for a few years. Some people remember it, some forget.

Notes

This chapter is dedicated, at Jude Prichard's request, to Mr Ian 'Ribs' Ward of Warburton, Western Australia, who tragically passed away on 27 January 2008 unnoticed in the back of a police custodial vehicle in 40 degrees heat. During 2000 Ms Prichard was associated with Tania Dennis (www.insideout–architects.com) at Warburton on the Tjulyuru Cultural Centre (www.tjulyuru.com) construction, landscaping and consultation process with Mr Ward – a definitive and generous man.

1. I do advocate for thoughtfully made environments where imaginative relationships can develop between Aboriginal and non-Aboriginal people in ordinary settings, especially the places where children spend their time. Housing environments are obviously significant factors in the way relationships are restrained or liberated in cities, as they are in remote Aboriginal 'settlements'. The dynamics of life in intercultural/racial townships such as Alice Springs, Yuendumu, Coober Pedy and Broome may have something instructive for planners to take into consideration.

2. For a distribution of language groups in the region *see* Horton 1996.

3. There is an intricate, abstract-conceptual language that describes intersubjective experiences that is part of psychotherapeutic theory and work. Some people have carried these ideas over into relations between people of different cultures (*see* e.g., San Roque in CARPA Manual 2003; Devisch 2007).

4. On only one occasion has there been a dangerous intruder, but this is a significant incident that for various reasons I will not describe in this chapter. On that night the dog was away.

5. The relationship of reciprocity established between successive generations of Black and White people in this region is indeed a social fact. It deserves serious attention, most especially by intelligent federal government operatives keen to make a realistic success of the 2007 interventions intended to facilitate children's development.

PART III

Youth, Identity and Social Transformation

CHAPTER 8

Organization within Disorder

The Present and Future of Young People in the Ngaanyatjarra Lands

David Brooks

External Perceptions

In light of the furore that has arisen since 2006 on the subject of remote Aboriginal communities,[1] it is timely to test some of the general proposi-tions typically put, against a particular ethnographic context. The debate as conducted in media and political circles tends to measure remote Aboriginal people in generic ways and to employ assumptions about their (failed) participation in a national polity. In contrast, in this chapter I focus on a particular remote group's youth as embedded in a social world. My aim is to show how the world of relevance to the life situation of these young people is primarily that of the body politic of the local Aboriginal region – the Ngaanyatjarra Lands.[2] In saying this I do not deny that the local world is itself heavily articulated with the nation-state, and that young people are increasingly to be found, on occasion, raising their sights beyond the local to wider horizons. The central message that I hope to convey in this chapter is that a high degree of social organiza-tion exists in that portion of the remote Aboriginal sector occupied by the Ngaanyatjarra. The youth population is largely a part of this organized regional world – albeit they do operate outside of it at times. I argue that the lives of local people, including the young, must be predominantly understood as unfolding within a distinct template that is generated from within Ngaanyatjarra society. Specifically, it is through ceremony that the Ngaanyatjarra create a real-life template of order. This template does contain some damaged parts, but overall it provides the people with a wide set of opportunities and constraints. Some of these we may judge as working to promote a rich and rewarding life for the individual and the group; others are best thought of as simply different from the 'main-stream' in a neutral sense; while still others are evidently inclined to militate against the achievement of good outcomes in a number of critical areas, including health and longevity, orderliness in many aspects of domestic and community life, schooling and employment.

It is the poor standing of remote communities across a range of measurable aspects of well-being that is at the core of the public focus on them. A potent idea has developed in many quarters that in essence it is not really possible to tackle these deep-seated problems of social, economic and psychological well-being by working within or in cooperation with local structures, because there are effectively no such structures. Thus, it is not only acceptable but also necessary for external parties to move in and begin a whole social and structural rebuilding agenda. However, even with the best will in the world, it seems very difficult to imagine how such an agenda could be successful, given the difficulty of adequately conceptualizing, let alone implementing, such an ambitious rebuilding task. But apart from this, how do we know – or on what basis do we judge – that the structures of such groups have in fact broken down so irreparably? Few would argue about there being serious failings in these communities – but on the other hand some aspects of life in the Ngaanyatjarra Lands unfold well, perhaps better than in the mainstream. What approach might we be able to find that would allow us to look in a more fine-tuned way at the state of social affairs, to determine more exactly where the sources of the problems might lie and how they might be tackled? Possibly as we look more deeply we might find some overlooked strengths as well, which could provide the basis for more effective 'collaborative', rather than interventionist, approaches to achieving change. In this spirit, I will explore in this chapter how the existence or otherwise of a lack of social cohesion and organization can be identified in the Ngaanyatjarra region, through an analysis of ethnographic material relating to youth. In this material I focus on several dimensions of local social and cultural life. Recurrent strands in the discussion will be the relationship of the people to their country and its *tjukurrpa* (Dreamings); and the norms and practices relating to kinship, marriage and the life cycle. Later in the chapter, I set out some case study material relating to male youth. In general, because of the gender divide in the desert – which influences anthropological work as well as the lives of the people – my material tends to be more focused around males than females.

Background to the Ngaanyatjarra People and Lands

The people now known as the Ngaanyatjarra, who are part of what has been termed the Western Desert sociocultural bloc (Berndt 1959), practised a hunter-gatherer economy in the environmentally harsh desert for thousands of years.[3] With its extremely low overall levels of food biomass coupled with frequent periods when drought conditions prevailed and almost no food was available, the Western Desert was 'possibly the most marginal example of permanent human occupation in the world' (Cane 1990: 156). The people lived mostly in small mobile groups of about a dozen persons, with overall population density at a lower level than that of any other known society. Human physical life, as well as the existence of the society as such, hovered at the extreme limits of viability. Under these conditions, it is remarkable that the desert culture reveals such a deep concern with human relationships and a thirst for understanding the nature of the world. A formidable body of mythology and religious song and dance was developed, along with rules for ritual practice and a sophisticated framework (outlined in a later section) for the socialization of young people.

However, the vicissitudes of life often undermined these achievements. For example, premature deaths and the general sparseness of the population meant that many children grew up without key relatives present. (It was very common for a child to suffer the early loss of the father, in particular.[4]) Thus in practice socialization was something of a hit-and-miss affair. Because of the absence of centralized political and juridical institutions, the maintenance of social order (or its corollary, disorder) was ultimately in the hands of individuals; it potentially gave physically capable people, mostly men, an inordinate amount of power over their fellows. Much therefore depended on the extent to which such persons behaved according to the values of obligation, responsibility and compassion that the culture emphasized, which in turn was likely to depend on the amount of effective socialization they had had. This was, as mentioned, variable. While the best long-term survival option was for everyone to behave in accordance with the cultural values, which for the most part encoded the most socially functional behaviour, they inevitably did not always do so. The ultimate social sanction on a recalcitrant individual was for a strong person to impose himself or herself on the offender by force. Thus through a burst of violence (*nganyirri purlka*) – not usually prolonged – the physically capable person would impose order on a particular situation. While this might be for the social benefit, such a person could also, if they were so inclined and if there was no one strong enough to resist, use the same means to indulge their own desires. Although inclusiveness and compassion were valued traits in the desert (Myers 1986: 113–16), countless stories of classical life[5] reveal that the self-interest of dominating persons was a very powerful social force. In general, it was to everyone's benefit to express the values of inclusiveness and compassion, because avoiding the unnecessary making of enemies was a critical survival strategy. But (to take the case of a man) it was the people immediately around him – particularly his wife and children and his brothers, and persons with high productivity – that the dominating individual would most want to be inclusive and compassionate towards. If times were particularly hard, or if the circumstances otherwise demanded it, such a person could and often would sacrifice the others, the more distant persons and the less productive. In these situations, those most needing compassion might be the least likely to receive it. It is important to understand these dimensions of classical desert society, as they continue to have a strong influence on many aspects of present practices. Physically capable persons still often make use of their strength, or the threat of it, to obtain more than their share of resources, or even things they are not entitled to at all. Even the much-vaunted regard for 'family' is not necessarily a bedrock value, for it is the protection of what is useful to a person and the sacrifice of what is not useful that may be the actual determining consideration in how a person acts. Some of those who offend along such lines are young people.

The culture of the region, like that of other Australian Aboriginal groups, is based on the Dreaming (here called *tjukurrpa*). In the Western Desert, the Dreaming complex is famously informed by a spectacular network of Dreaming tracks, many of which travel hundreds of kilometres, criss-crossing the landscape. The major beings who established these networks include the Kangaroo Man, the Emu, the Two 'Clever' Men (*wati kutjarra*), the Zebra Finch flock, the Dingo and scores of others. In their travels these beings are understood to have created the animals and plants of the desert that provide food for the people. Despite such worthy acts, in the mythology the beings often come across as capricious, deceptive and both violent and playful. The great tracks of the Dreaming Ancestors are associated with a vast and intricate social structure, through which a web of personal and group connections have been established to particular places – many of them sites of sacred creativity – over great areas of the landscape. This structure helped to build commonalities over great distances in an effort to overcome the otherwise largely dispersive tendencies of the economy and way of life. Distance and the attempt to conquer its vicissitudes through a panoramic perspective on the landscape and a voracious appetite for travel, are threads woven through desert life. Central to cultural practice is the veneration both of *tjukurrpa*-related knowledge – connected with the monumental travels of the Ancestors – and of the older members of society who were regarded as being the particular repositories of this knowledge. This point is germane to some of the arguments in this paper.[6]

Since the beginnings of their contact with the Australian settler world, the Ngaanyatjarra people and their forebears have continued to reside in, and to constitute the dominant population within the 200,000 sq km of desert that comprise their traditional lands. This area has become known colloquially as the 'Ngaanyatjarra Lands'. The Warburton mission, established in 1932, was the first outside agency in the area and until the late 1950s the only one. The mission itself had a relatively light impact, in comparison to the impact that settlement had in most parts of the continent, and for many years it affected a limited proportion of the overall area of the Lands and its people. In effect, the people were able to pace their own adaptation to the settler society over a twenty-five-year period, something that has been immensely to their benefit in terms of social and cultural integrity. To the present day, the region remains by most standards distinctly 'remote' – though to the Ngaanyatjarra it is of course at the centre of the world. The nearest urban centres, Alice Springs and Kalgoorlie, are both over 1,000 km away by road, to the east and the west respectively; there are no industrial developments or significant infrastructural links to other regions or centres of Australia; and the 1,600-plus Ngaanyatjarra people remain the sole occupants of the Lands other than staff and service providers. Associated with this isolation and lack of economic developments, the Ngaanyatjarra Lands not only has one of the lowest per capita income levels in Australia, but also some of the most expensive consumer articles. A particular impact arises from the high price of fuel for the motor vehicles that the people's intense desire for movement causes them to prize so highly. The effect is exacerbated by the amount of damage caused to vehicles by the unpaved roads of the region. The people now live in ten small communities that are spread widely across their Lands, but are highly interconnected in terms of kin and marriage relationships. Nine of these are 'new' communities that developed from the 1970s onwards as a result of the so-called homelands or decentralization movement that was taking hold in Central Australia and other remote regions at this time. This movement saw the return to their own particular traditional localities of people who since the early 1930s had been gradually gathering at Warburton mission. Warburton, now administered not by the mission but by its own local Aboriginal Council, remains the largest community and the regional centre. Since 1980 the people of the area have formed the Ngaanyatjarra Council, and subsequently also the Ngaanyatjarra-ku Shire, through which most services and programs affecting the area are run, and through which political and strategic interests such as those related to land tenure are pursued. Notwithstanding the chronic government policy and service delivery failures that have severely limited the development of the whole remote Aboriginal community sector for decades, the Ngaanyatjarra communities have a record of stability and continuity in administration that is widely recognized. An important factor in this is an unusually high level of longevity and stability among staff. Also, and largely due to the long-standing 'dry area' legislation, there is little alcohol-related social disruption on the Lands, and for the most part everyday public life unfolds in a peaceful and constructively focused way.

The Ngaanyatjarra share in the fundamental features that character-ize the people of the Western Desert bloc, which include the *tjukurrpa* culture alluded to above with its stress on links between people and land, and a strong preoccupation with kin connectedness among people both nearby and far afield. As with most of their desert fellows, Christian beliefs have also come to figure prominently in their lives, first through the long mission influence and more recently from other, Indigenized Christian influences, particularly those with an emphasis on charismatic evangelism.[7] Also characteristic of the desert is their self-confidence in their identity as Aboriginal desert people, which causes them to dem-onstrate less overt ambivalence or hostility towards 'Whitefellas' than is sometimes found in other more urban or rural areas. At the same time, the modern-day social and cultural system of the Lands is not generi-cally 'Western Desert' but rather is distinctively Ngaanyatjarra. It would be surprising if there were not significant differences across the Western Desert area, given that historical forces arising from settler society have impacted differentially across the desert as a whole. Some of the differ-ences have deeper roots: for example, their classical land-owning system, while containing the common desert ingredients, has its own emphases and preoccupations. During the last seventy-five years, a characteristic Ngaanyatjarra worldview and ethos have emerged through their own experience of engagement as a group with the particular 'Whitefella' parties that have come their way. This has produced a polity divergent in many ways from that of their desert neighbours, such as the Pitjantjatjara and the Mardu (*see* chapters 2 and 5, and 9 respectively, this volume), who have had their own separate, if structurally similar, experiences over the same period. The Ngaanyatjarra Council, too, has acquired a char-acteristic style of engagement and preoccupation that differs markedly from many other desert councils. The minutes of monthly meetings held since the council's inception show that the Ngaanyatjarra self-perception is strongly coloured by notions of self-help, pragmatism and cooperation with outside parties. This is not every council's outlook.

The main orientation of the Ngaanyatjarra, as I have observed it over the last two decades, is towards their own internal social and cultural affairs. Finding enough stimulation and interest in their own world to satisfy them, they seem to have felt no great need to look beyond. Yet this has recently started to change. Not that the local scene has lost its zest. Rather, people realize that in the 'globalized' world, nonengagement is the road to extinction. In some ways, as we shall see, for all the troubles that beset them, young people are leading the way in terms of the increased engagement that is occurring.

Youth Demographics and Social Problem Areas

Identifying the age groupings that 'typically form the target of social policy initiatives' in Australia generally, demographer John Taylor (2002: 13) denotes the 15–24 grouping as 'the years of school-to-work transition', followed by the 25–44 grouping which he terms 'the years of family formation and employment'. But for the Ngaanyatjarra, it is more relevant to group together the 15–29 year olds. Under about 15, Ngaanyatjarra people, in common with the broader population, are considered to be children. But unlike the mainstream, not until they are about 30 are they effectively 'adult' – particularly in the case of males.[8] The Ngaanyatjarra refer to the 15–29 year old male group as 'youngfellas'. The background to what seems to be an unusually extended age of the youth category will emerge below and in subsequent sections.

In a recent count (Brooks and Kral 2007), the total Aboriginal population of the Ngaanyatjarra-ku Shire Lands (minus temporary absentees and prison inmates) was found to be 1,589, of which five hundred were in the 15–29 age grouping.[9] It is basically these five hundred young people who are the subject of this chapter. The figure represents 31 per cent of the total population, which is a much higher percentage than has been found for the same age group across the whole of the Indigenous Australian population (25.5 per cent) or for the Australian non-Indigenous population (24.5 per cent).[10] Noteworthy in terms of the issues discussed in this chapter is the fact that 222 or 44.4 per cent of youth reside in the largest community, Warburton, whereas the proportion of the total Ngaanyatjarra population residing in Warburton is 38.9 per cent. Against a general Ngaanyatjarra background of conformity between country connections and community residence – and conformity with classical ways of life such as living with close family and undergoing initiation procedures – Warburton is to some extent a 'town', in which young people have the 'freedom of the streets' at night. Entertainment and sporting resources are available. The Warburton Youth Arts Project has established a unique 'youth culture' program that interconnects with global youth culture and where filmmaking, hip-hop music, youth fashion events and the like are flourishing.[11] Also, young unmarried persons are able to come here from other Lands communities without their parents to look for sexual/marital partners – though they still comply with the older standards to the extent of 'stopping' in a household with which they have an extended family connection. The increased presence of young people at Warburton is reflective of the degree to which youth, as I put it in my opening paragraph, are raising their sights beyond the embrace of Ngaanyatjarra culture. (By comparison, only 37 per cent of the 0–14 age grouping resides in Warburton.)

A very high proportion of Ngaanyatjarra 15–29-year-olds are 'married'.[12] Most of the partnerships are between persons of very similar age. Both of these facts represent a significant change from classical times, when men did not marry until they were around 30, after they had completed lengthy initiation procedures, and girls married at or shortly after puberty. (So if anything females are remaining unmarried for slightly longer now.) The age difference between partners used to be generally more than 15 years. Just as with young people in the same age group in mainstream Australia – but unlike what happened in classical times with the Ngaanyatjarra – many individuals have a string of romantic/sexual relationships before finally 'settling down'. However there are two interesting differences from the mainstream. One is that Ngaanyatjarra people less clearly distinguish early ephemeral or experimental relationships from the later more long-lasting ones that are unambiguously marriage, and that always involve having children (adopted ones in the absence of biological progeny). In line with classical usage, all people in sexual relationships are referred to as 'married', though some informants do put verbal quotation marks around the term when a given relationship very obviously lacks much substance. The second difference, and an important one, is that unlike in mainstream Australia, 'getting married' for this age group does not involve the notion of setting up a separate domestic unit. Young Ngaanyatjarra 'marrieds' do live together, but they cohabit in a parental or other relative's house. (Statistically, a young couple is about equally likely to reside in the household of the parents of the husband or wife.) This is partly a matter of a lack of available housing,[13] but in some ways it also follows long-standing practice. The contemporary household of around a dozen people is about the same size as the 'band' (Peterson 1986) in which people used to live in classical times. In the band regime, a married couple would only become the centre of a domestic unit after many years and after the death of the older people in the band. This is still the case now. However, in classical times the band worked as a unit in many situations and had a structure in terms of the roles of its members, whereas there is much less reason (in a social and survival sense) for the contemporary household to pull together as a unit, and in fact it does so rarely. At the same time, the nature of the household as it now is reflects the fact that some members are not enacting role obligations that once were mandatory. For example, a present-day daughter-in-law living in her husband's parents' house will now rarely cook regularly for her husband, or assist her mother-in-law with food preparation. Some are even able to off-load the responsibility for caring for their own children, with the mother-in-law or other older women filling this gap too (*cf.* Tonkinson, this volume). Conversely, a mother-in-law will often act in a controlling way towards a daughter-in-law who is residing with her, actively preventing her from taking on any useful role while complaining about her failure to do so. As for the young man, the contemporary reality is that his hours per week in employment are almost certain to be short and the work essentially undemanding, a situation that does not change when he becomes a husband and father.[14] Neither he nor his wife will contribute, or be expected to contribute in any significant way, to the finances or maintenance of the household. (Indeed, households have very little in the way of finances, but the essentials, mainly food, are usually provided by the older core household members.) Classically, young men (both pre- and post-marriage) worked very hard to produce meat for the whole band, while young women did more than their share of tasks among the older women, mothers-in-law, mothers and older co-wives, as well as caring for their children. The contemporary contraction in the social parts played by both males and females through their teens and twenties is linked to the observable fact that the relationship of a young married couple now tends to remain largely based around the bonds of emotion and shared youth interests that it was initially founded on. (Young Ngaanyatjarra people have been selecting their own partners on a 'love' basis for nearly half a century now, as opposed to having them selected by their elders. But this does not mean there is no structuring to the selection process, as we shall see below.) As indicated, even the coming of children does not bring much of a change in terms of any increased focus on the domestic side of life, the need to work both within and outside of the household, or the development of a broader sense of being part of the community and the world. These features typically do not emerge until the post-thirty years. Thus young men and women tend to live in what is in many ways a 'floating' state, where youth-type preoccupations continue to prevail, for an extended period. The negative behaviours associated with this state include an egoistic orientation and a focus on relationship dramas, including family violence; a high level of substance misuse; a high accident and injury rate; casualness with money, including gambling at cards and the making of 'windfall' purchases such as second-hand cars, without the capacity to maintain these items; a casual attitude towards the care of material items without regard to their replacement cost; frequent wilful destruction of personal and community property; and a life that is habitually 'on the edge' and lacks many stable elements or calm periods. While much of the reason for this scenario arises from contemporary conditions and circumstances, certain continuities with the past are apparent, such as the egoism and violence.

A very significant number, 54 according to the 2007 population survey (Brooks and Kral 2007), of Ngaanyatjarra men are in jail. Nearly half (23) of these are in the 15–29 age group. The figure of 54 from a total of 16-year-olds in the Ngaanyatjarra population of 1,143 represents an incarceration rate of 4.7 per cent, as compared with a 1999 ABS figure of a national 1.7 per cent incarceration rate of Indigenous people over 16 years old, itself a figure 14 times higher than the non-Indigenous rate of 0.12 per cent (Australian Crime: Facts and Figures 2000). Most of the offences of Ngaanyatjarra prisoners relate to domestic and sexual violence and driving offences, though a significant number also stem from fines enforcement matters. The issue of the incarceration rate deserves a comment here. It would certainly be desirable for the rate to be lower, but (apart from the fines enforcement matters) the prisoners concerned were all charged and convicted on the individual circumstances of serious offences committed. It would be the very opposite of responsible to try and achieve a lower imprisonment rate through a failure to either respond to offences that have been committed or to prosecute offenders. Indeed the Ngaanyatjarra people have consistently lobbied for a greater police presence – in the last three years, as a result of these efforts, permanently staffed police stations have been established in two communities – in order that the commission of offences, particularly offences of violence, should be made more accountable. It is partly because of this that public life in the Lands is predominantly peaceful, as noted earlier.[15] As for the fines-related matters, the people have long pushed, through the Ngaanyatjarra Council, for alternatives to prison in these cases (*see* e.g., Ngaanyatjarra Council 2003: 103).

While some of the preceding observations paint a bleak picture of youth affairs, this is far from the whole story. As we shall see, during their youthful years most people are in fact imbibing the basic set of values of their elders; they are obeying many of the key cultural rules; and they gradually come to read life through the lens of the *tjukurrpa* as the generations have before them. They are not rebellious, and they unfailingly express their attachment to family and kin, and to their home in the Ngaanyatjarra Lands (Inge Kral, personal communication 2007). Whether or not all of this is desirable, or is sufficient to meet the contemporary challenges, is another matter, which I take up later in the chapter.

Is There Social and Cultural Trauma among the Ngaanyatjarra People?

Given the concerns of this chapter, the issue of trauma seems an important question to at least touch on briefly. A considerable body of literature asserts that because of the nature of the history of European occupation, Australian Indigenous people are in a state of trauma that 'can be likened to the symptomatology [*sic*] of Post-Traumatic Stress Syndrome' (Halloran 2004: 6). For example, psychologist Michael Halloran writes:

> There is little doubt that in real and symbolic terms, Australian Aboriginal culture has been traumatized by the 'European invasion'. There is also little doubt that Aboriginal Australians suffer a poor state of social, psychological and physical health reflecting a general state of anxiety … there is strong evidence to support the relationship between cultural destruction, cultural trauma, and the situation of Aboriginal people today. (2004: 9)

Halloran (2004: 4) defines cultural trauma as 'a state wherein cultural knowledge and practices have been weakened to the extent that they fail in their capacity to imbue individual existence with meaning and value'. I would argue strongly, and I am sure that most Ngaanyatjarra people would also, that this definition most certainly does not apply to them. On the other hand, harrowing and traumatic experiences are part of everybody's life here. Ngaanyatjarra people regularly see family members dying prematurely from poor health. While as I previously noted, the atmosphere of daily life is largely peaceful, individuals and families have over the years experienced many episodes of violent argument, assault and the like. Between the 1970s and the early 1990s when leaded petrol was available at the pumps and sniffing was at its height, some parents lost three or even more children in the teen and twenties age group. A series of horrendous multiple-death car crashes in the 1980s decimated some families and communities. The death toll from these and other causes has left gaping holes in the genealogical structure. Almost everyone bears a variety of physical scars from fights, car accidents, burns and the like. (In the case of the oldest people, their scars were mostly inflicted decades ago, when interpersonal violence was equally as common but arguably more predictable in its occurrence [Brooks and Shaw 2003].) Virtually every person old enough to have a marital partner has been either the perpetrator or recipient of marital violence, and everyone has lived with it occurring regularly in and around their household. Many children have experienced abuse, including sexual abuse.

Then there is the matter of the extremely high rate of imprisonment mentioned above. Not only does this imprisonment rate clearly indicate a great deal of social disruption, but the absence through incarceration of so many persons in distant detention centres itself causes much distress to members of their families.

There are other less obvious sorts of trauma, arising from the domains of cultural misunderstandings and dependency. As an illustration, a study undertaken in 2002 found that it is common for persons taken as patients to Kalgoorlie or Alice Springs hospitals for major operations to experience serious fear arising from culturally founded gaps in their understanding of what is happening to them (Brooks and Shaw 2001). For instance, several persons told stories about how when they were going under a general anaesthetic they feared that hospital staff, standing in a knot conferring in whispers, were engaged in a plot to kill them. Other examples involved the common situation where a person with an ailment is suddenly evacuated (by Flying Doctor plane) from the Lands. Sometimes the ailment as identified at the time is not a life-threatening one, yet the patient may die in hospital shortly afterwards. The explanations that relatives receive of the chain of events, and of why the official cause of death is often very different from the original symptoms and diagnosis, tend to get lost in the cultural gaps. Years after the event, many people still do not understand why their loved one died. Sometimes they entertain ideas that misadventure might have occurred. In such ways, life often seems out of control to Ngaanyatjarra people. In the context of discussions about youth suicides and suicide attempts, Aboriginal informants have told me that young men, pursued by police for some offence, perhaps a serious one like assault or dangerous driving, will often look around, see others who have done the same things and think: 'Why are they after just me?' The alienation and paranoia evident in these scenarios point to the kind of damage that can go on being generated when a social environment contains a major culturally based gap in understandings about the nature, causes and intentions of events.

Apart from these traumas, there is of course at a broad-scale level an element of dependency in the situation of Ngaanyatjarra people vis-à-vis the Australian state, which can be expected to give rise to social disadvantage and difficulties. A proper exploration of this complex subject would require an analysis of historical relationships over three quarters of a century as well as of contemporary structures.[16] However, I would make the general observation that the dependency experienced by Ngaanyatjarra people is mitigated by the high level of control that – notwithstanding the commentary above – they have always exercised over many important aspects of their lives at the local and regional level. In contrast to the situation outlined by Moisseeff (this volume) for rural and urban-based Aboriginal families, I do not think that, on the Lands, the underlying dependency on a public service infrastructure or the problems of racism can be counted among the primary causes of the social difficulties among youth, though these doubtless play some part. The sorts of traumas that I have pointed to undoubtedly contribute to poor outcomes too. But I would assert that not just one but *the* major issue driving these outcomes is the lack of an economic base that would create jobs and opportunities for the youth, particularly for the young men. As I write, a major mine is being planned for the region, which along with some other mining prospects has the potential not only to infuse some much-needed money and general development into the Lands, but to provide a means for young Ngaanyatjarra men and women to again take on the kinds of active social roles they once had as providers and carers.

Further Comments on Age Categories

I have mentioned some of the reasons, rooted in postclassical changes, for why the category 'youth' extends to such a late age, particularly for males. To complement this it is necessary to consider the age issue in the context of Ngaanyatjarra (as opposed to European) understandings of the progression through the life cycle. The situation here is similar to that described by Myers and Sackett for other Western Desert peoples, the Pintupi and people of Wiluna respectively. For males, initiation at the age of approximately fifteen or sixteen transforms male *tjilku,* children, into *wati,* which in Aboriginal English is rendered as 'man'. This does not necessarily equate to what Europeans mean by 'adult'. We have seen how under contemporary circumstances the active role of postinitiated males has been truncated, but even the Indigenous system itself envisages very little authority for the 'youngfellas' below about thirty years old. As Sackett (1978: 121) has described, young men should behave with modesty and avoid the appearance of making too much of themselves, their status, or what knowledge they have (which may in fact be more substantial than it seems). Over thirty, a *wati* gradually acquires some credibility in the public domain, but in the Ngaanyatjarra area it is a rare man under fifty who is regarded as having the knowledge and experience to be taken very seriously. Even men in their late fifties commonly make statements to the effect that they are only privy to a limited amount of the *tjukurrpa,* the knowledge that allows a man to be treated as a *wati yirna,* or *tjilpi* (respected elder listened to as of right). Acquiring acceptance into this highly valued category is hotly contested and monitored closely.[17] Men well into their sixties may be scoffed at for having the temerity to claim this status prematurely.

Considering the low life expectancy of desert people in classical times and now (albeit the causes have changed), it may seem somewhat odd or socially unbalanced that the social progress of maturation should be so delayed in this way. But it makes sense against the background indicated earlier of the singular importance attached to *tjukurrpa*-related knowledge and to the old people who hold it. So critical is the social function of this nexus of knowledge and old people that its credibility must be protected whatever the cost. (Not surprisingly, the old people manipulate these notions to their own advantage at times.) On the other hand, or perhaps because of the 'skewing' of the maturational cycle that follows, there are a number of implications and consequences that flow from such a prioritization. For instance, the long-delayed social recognition extended to 'youngfellas' can be very frustrating for them. In the lead-up to their initiation, they are primed to believe that their status is about to change in a monumental way and that, as *watiya* ('men'), they will be held in great respect within the community. The symbolism of the ceremony itself announces the idea of a radical separation from childhood. But when the initiates emerge, newly wearing the red headband, proud symbol of the male brotherhood of Western Desert *watiya*, they find themselves in something of a social no-man's-land. In earlier times, they would at this stage have embarked on a long phase as one of a group of postinitiates (*tjawarratja*), essentially located outside the flow of everyday life. Physically camping off to one side of the band, and restricted in their contact with women and children, they would spend their time under the rigorous authority of the older men, acquiring and practising the skills of physical survival – particularly hunting – and becoming learned in the *tjukurrpa*.[18] This would involve immersion in the stories, songs and dances of the *tjukurrpa* beings, and undertaking journeys following the tracks of the beings and visiting the places they created. By the end of his time, a young man would have earned himself a wife (through providing meat to his future parents-in-law for an extended period) and the freedom to begin to make his own plans and determine his own movements. He would have matured to adulthood, in both a social and a personal sense. Now however, this whole induction regime comes into play sporadically at best. It is not so much the loss of the content that is significant, but the loss of a distinct and calibrated process of maturation; and of a socially specified set of activities to effectively occupy a person's time during the years between childhood and full adulthood. There is no longer a defined pathway, clearly articulated with the goals of later life, for the 'youngfellas' to follow.

It could be said that this loss or shift simply brings the Ngaanyatjarra more into line with most of the rest of us. However, Western society has had a very long time to adjust to a generally more fuzzy and individualistic paradigm for the maturation process (*see also* Moisseeff, this volume), whereas for the Ngaanyatjarra it has all happened in the lifetime of the extant older generation. Perhaps an even more important difference is that, unlike most Westerners, the Ngaanyatjarra live in a setting where very little employment of the meaningful and well-paid kind exists. The local jobs that could serve as pivotal building blocks in the lives of the young people – and in so doing bring a significant injection of order to this society – have so far been lacking.

Evidence for the Existence of Order

When one focuses on standard indicators of health and prosperity, the picture for Ngaanyatjarra youth does look mostly bleak. Yet there are other measures of social order that take into account the particular nature of the sociocultural world the Ngaanyatjarra inhabit, and these can tell a different story. For example, one could look at the way in which ritual is organized. Critical to ritual are the lifelong labels that every Ngaanyatjarra person has, often called their 'skin' in English.[19] There are four of these labels in total and they are all logically interrelated according to kinship categories.[20] Thus, if my father was an A, he must marry a B, and I will automatically be a C and must marry a D. My brothers and sisters will be C like me. Everybody in the society fits together like a jigsaw puzzle in terms of this system. There is a generational moiety system too, which meshes with the 'skin' system, and that divides everybody into just two categories, sun side and shade side. Like the skin designations, these identities are life-long. Every Ngaanyatjarra person is known as either a sun side or a shade side person, with the total population splitting roughly half in each category. If I (a C) am a sun side person, my wife and potential wife, and my brothers-in-law (all D), will be sun side also; while my father (and his siblings) and mother (and her siblings) will be shade side. Not only is everybody in my generation a sun person, but everyone in my grandparents' and grandchildren's generations are sun people too. Likewise, the children of my own generation are grouped together with everyone in my parents' generation as shade side people.[21] At ceremony time, all the people present will be organized on the basis of this system, both spatially and in terms of roles played – and even in terms of emotions expressed. Sun side people will sit on one side of the ceremony ground and will do certain things at certain times, and likewise with shade side people. There is much more complexity than this, but everything fits within this basic framework. This organizational framework applies to all Ngaanyatjarra ceremonial gatherings, whatever the particular nature or focus of the ceremony. Funerals come within the same ambit. From classical times, everybody who is geographically close enough is expected to attend all the ceremonies that are performed (except in the case of the smaller gender or age-restricted ones), and still today the great majority of people do attend, even though the schedule is an onerous one. The maintenance of these complex systems, the capacity to mount such large-scale events, usually involving participants from widely spaced communities, and the near universality of the attendance all point to the presence of considerable integrity in the overall social order.[22]

However, I now want to go a step further and look at what all this means for marital unions. I indicated earlier how during their early years, contemporary marital partnerships tend to lack a solid social backbone and functionality. This is a genuine problem that requires a solution – and the only realistic solution, in the world of the twenty-first century, appears to be jobs. But quite apart from the issue of how well marriage is working in its aspect as a partnership, there is the question of the reproduction of children. In terms of my account of ceremonial organization, if even a small number of Ngaanyatjarra people had married incorrectly at some time in the past – or more accurately if there had been any children born to incorrectly paired parents – then the attendance at ceremony of these progeny would seriously disturb the structure. There would be disorder in the schema of where people should sit, what they should be doing, and what emotions they should be displaying. I argue that this is particularly significant because it is in and through ceremony that the Ngaanyatjarra create a real-life template of order, through the deployment of people in effect as chess-pieces. Every 'player' participates in a finely organized sequence of set pieces leading towards a climax. With everyday life so often having an unstructured and haphazard quality – in classical times it could hardly be otherwise with the extremely small and dispersed population – ceremonial occasions are the vital times when an image of a larger, more enduring and perfectly ordered world is conjured up, and through the drama and excitement of the performance, stamped upon the minds of the participants. People can clearly be observed in contemporary times going home from ceremonies with glowing, larger-than-life impressions of what they have been through. These arise from and celebrate not only the major elements but also, crucially, the totalizing nature of the event. Critical to this holistic template is the way that all participants – those in the category of witnesses and minor players as well as those who are the focus of the ceremonial activity – are configured throughout the proceedings in terms of the integrated framework that the skin and moiety systems provide.

In practice, it would be far too much to expect that all the hundreds and thousands of past marriages had complied with the rules, and that the social fabric was therefore free of disruption. But it is statistically remarkable how few wrong marriages there have actually been in the historical record.[23] I am aware that in some other regions, Aboriginal groups who possess the same kinds of categorizing systems, having experienced many infractions, have devised 'solutions' to the problem of a lack of compliance, such as the rule expressed as 'throwing away the father'. If only one parent's skin (or generational moiety) affiliation is taken into account, the problem is sidestepped. It is telling that the Ngaanyatjarra have not opted for any strategies of this kind. In the rare instance where a wrong marriage has occurred and a child has a dual or contradictory affiliation, they do not resolve the issue at all. Relatives on the father's side continue to treat the children as possessing the skin that flows from his affiliation, while relatives on the mother's side do likewise. Whenever the two are present at an occasion (i.e., a ceremony) when the contradiction is made apparent, uproar ensues. I am in the process of compiling statistics on the percentage of noncomplying marriages (that have produced children) of under thirty-year-olds that have been transacted in the last ten years, and although I have not yet completed this task, I expect the figure to be less than 5 per cent. Incidentally in one project undertaken in 2003 (Brooks and Shaw), I analysed a number of marital relationships within the 'youth' age group in which there was a high incidence of domestic violence. Though a correlation might have been expected between practical malfunction and socially invalid partner selection, this was not borne out by the research.[24] Even in these cases there had been close conformity with the skin rules. In general, it can be said that for all the faltering status of their marriages, Ngaanyatjarra young couples are obeying the partner selection rules and in the process are making a constructive contribution to their social polity, by producing children whose existence serves to enhance rather than disrupt the holistic nature and appearance of the body politic.

The Tjukurrpa

I have already sketched in the central role played by the Dreaming as a medium that infuses so many dimensions of life – including the way the landscape is seen, spiritual and social connectedness to this landscape, the environment as a provider of resources, and group and personal identity. It is also a system of philosophical enquiry and knowledge. As such, it carries the imprint of the past, redolent in the identities of the great beings that animate it – Kangaroo Man, Emu, Seven Sisters and all the rest. In many ways the *tjukurrpa* in this classical sense appears as an edifice of interconnectedness, developed over centuries or millennia and still universally accepted and revered by the Ngaanyatjarra. But now I want to point out another, perhaps less obvious aspect of the *tjukurrpa* realm. This is that the Dreaming, apart from being an edifice emanating from the past to inform the present, has always also been a medium through which people in the present imagined their world in a language shared by their fellows. Through their own dreams and other mechanisms such as their personal *tjukurrpa* stories, which became elaborated in the course of their life times, people have always added to the compendium of general *tjukurrpa* knowledge, sometimes sending parts of it off in new directions (*see also* Tonkinson 1991a: 123). One could use the term '*tjukurrpa*-thinking' to describe this feature of the Ngaanyatjarra world. Ngaanyatjarra people are not and never have been 'locked' solely into a *tjukurrpa* perspective – many aspects of life, like the practical domain of food collection, are seen by them in appropriately practical terms – but much of their habitual thinking about the world does take place through the lens of the *tjukurrpa*. This 'habit' is something that they share in common and that distinguishes them from 'Whitefellas' – not only from distant 'government' or 'mining' Whitefellas, but even from (almost all of) those who live and work among them. I will provide some illustrations of the extent to which *tjukurrpa*-thinking still pervades the Ngaanyatjarra world. My purpose in doing so is firstly to give an idea of how much shared meaning there actually is, for Ngaanyatjarra people, in the circumstances of the world around them; secondly to show how many ideas and events that might seem random or baseless to an outsider are actually part of a systematic perspective on the world; and thirdly to provide the material that can shed light on a question that is sometimes raised about groups like the Ngaanyatjarra – the question of whether in some respects 'culture' could be considered a driver of poor outcomes in well-being, achievement and the rest.

I have pointed out that the Dreaming tracks of the desert create interconnectedness over great tracts of country. They do this both by imprinting the landscape with common associations and by providing a framework that caters for the connectedness of human beings. Each and every person in this classical Ngaanyatjarra vision has a 'place'. This place is linked with both a particular Dreaming entity and a particular geographical site, while at the same time and at another level, the significance is less in the particularities than in the fact that the person participates in a holistic edifice that embraces all known people. The main mechanism, in classical times, by which each person obtained a 'place' was through birth. Every person was born at a site that lay along a Dreaming track, or at least in an area that was regarded as the country of a Dreaming being. Since all Ngaanyatjarra country came under this rubric, it was not possible to be born in a non-Dreaming place. A person's 'place', normally their birthplace, was their inalienable, intrinsic home, their place of origin, which they would refer to as 'my *ngurra*'.[25] In the classical past, then, it was normal for a person to acquire their intrinsic association with a Dreaming entity through being born along the Dreaming track of the being concerned, i.e., at a place understood to have been created by the being. As well as the association with the being or species, the birth event also created an association – regarded equally as of an intrinsic nature – with a particular place in the landscape. (These two links are central to 'totemism' [Elkin 1934; Lévi-Strauss 1963; Leach 1968] in the Ngaanyatjarra region. However, as I explain below, there are many indications of the existence of a totemic principle that is not tied so closely to the Dreaming framework.) When one considers the population at large, the net result was a landscape both criss-crossed by Dreaming tracks and dotted with sites with which individuals were indelibly linked. And since the significance of the connections lies not only in the individual cases but also in their holistic connectedness, in a sense everybody alive at any given time shared a 'combined inheritance' of all the associations that had arisen among all the people through these birth events and similar processes. Over time, too, the associations were multiplied, again in an interconnected way, by successive generations of people. All of this taken together amounts to the 'edifice' of connectedness I have referred to.

This is the background to what is still meant today when people who were born under classical conditions refer to 'my *ngurra*'. The other ingredient for such people is that while they may have other connections to country as well, the core of their link to country, as connoted by the *ngurra*, is the place where immediate, personal feelings of connection, usually bound up with actual life experience, are concentrated. As understood now, forty years after Ngaanyatjarra people effectively completed the transition to settlement life, *ngurra* implies an origin place deriving from the time when life was lived in the bush and everyone's birth was part of the *tjukurrpa* being/site schema. Present-day birth events lack elements of this schema. People born in contemporary times do not have a *ngurra* in the sense that the old people did. (Since the early 1980s, births have been taking place in hospitals in distant centres.[26]) Most young people still acquire a *tjukurrpa,* but its connection to the Dreaming track framework is usually tenuous at best, and in some cases the nature of the association is evidently less a link into this framework than a manifestation of a general sort of totemic principle. (For instance, one young woman has a rabbit *tjukurrpa.* Rabbits of course are an introduced species, and are not part of the classical Dreaming compendium. The 'story' for the woman concerns a rabbit that was hunted at the time of her birth, and which when eaten by her mother, made her sick – indicating its nonordinary nature. This is the same kind of story that is often found in the classical '*tjukurrpa* framework' cases.) Certainly, young people are still understood to have connections to particular places and areas in the landscape, normally (now) connections that are not direct but that derive from the more directly obtained connections of their parents and other antecedents. And as these antecedents did, contemporary young people also share in some ways in a 'combined inheritance' of a multiplicity of past associations. The nature of the connectedness of young people to country is a very important topic. Firstly, related to the totemic component, there are significant identity issues involved. Secondly, how young people come to see the meaning, strength and overall relevance of their relationship with the land is going to determine many aspects of their general attitudes and perspectives, including basic questions such as whether they maintain a commitment to living in their desert homeland. Thirdly, the nature of their connectedness will be – and already is – important because of the way that 'rights and interests' (to use the language of native title[27]) associated with country connectedness have in recent decades been acquiring new kinds of value as resources.

At present the whole question of where people of the postclassical era stand in terms of these issues is largely unresolved. It would be easy to say that the connection of these people to country is now merely one of descent, and this formulation is sometimes expressed even on the Lands. But while most people including the young persons themselves tend to be uncertain yet about how to fully understand contemporary connectedness, aspects of the responses by James and others – appearing later in the chapter – show that the ideas and feelings related to country still run very deep for them, deeper than the notion of descent suggests. At any rate, no paradigm has yet emerged to specify rules relating to the 'updating' of traditional sorts of associations like the totemic association, or to redefine matters to do with the nature of connectedness to country. But, as I have indicated, the habit of *tjukurrpa*-thinking goes on apace, with new ideas and possibilities being thrown up constantly on this subject, as on so many others.

An example is provided by a man F. in his forties, talking about his youngest son, born in 2006. F. said that this baby did have a *tjukurrpa,* and gave the following explanation in relation to it:

> When my wife was 'waiting' [for the birth] in Kalgoorlie, I was here in Warburton. We had been talking [on the phone] about whether we would have a boy or a girl. A *walawurru* (eagle) landed on our house, then hopped down to the verandah, and walked right up to where I was sitting on the bonnet of my car, having a cup of tea with my brother-in-law. The eagle – it was a male one – looked me straight in the eye, then it looked to the north. [There is a major *walawurru* site to the north, located within F.'s general area of country.] When it flew away, it went northwards. The next day my wife had a baby boy.

The eagle's visit revealed to F. that he was to have a boy child, and it was implicit that the boy had a strong association with the *walawurru.* The way that the eagle signalled his northerly origin established its own connection with F.'s country, 'proved' that its appearance was not a normal natural event but constituted a message from the *tjukurrpa* world about F.'s child, and revealed that the child had a connection with that northerly country (via F.). Thus although the child's birthplace is Kalgoorlie, the existence of an intrinsic connection with a particular traditional area of country, that of his father, was both made apparent and validated through the incident of the eagle's visit. Leaving aside the question of how enduring this act of identification by F. is likely to be,[28] the example has a mythopoeic aura in its own terms, illustrating the continuing vitality of the notion of both personal totem and connection to country, and showing both the persistence and the creativity of *tjukurrpa*-thinking in relation to these matters. However, I repeat that at present, a specific paradigm to cover these issues of identity and connectedness in the post-classical era has not emerged. This leaves a gap for displays of creativity of the type shown by F. – and out of such efforts, a consensus will presumably eventually evolve.

Tjukurrpa-thinking manifests itself not only in the realms of identity, origin and connection to country. Now that people are no longer continuously travelling the landscape in pursuit of a living as they once did, the kinds of issues that tend to occupy their minds have changed, but these new issues are looked at through the same basic prism as before. For example, since mining exploration has become part of local life in recent decades, Ngaanyatjarra people are not surprised[29] when mining companies look for, and sometimes find, mineralization along Dreaming tracks. (It is rather when the exploration occurs in non-Dreaming areas that the people are sceptical about the likelihood of success.) After all, it is the activities of the Dreaming beings that have created the special, the interesting and the valuable within the landscape. As an illustration of the versatility and scope of *tjukurrpa*-thinking in this area, I will make some comments about one major Dreaming track ('X') that is associated with mineral discoveries. This Dreaming, which traverses perhaps 1,000 km of country to the west of the Lands before coming to the Ngaanya-tjarra Lands, is owned by men. Much of its mythology deals in complex ways with gender questions such as: who came first, men or women? Who possessed power in the first place? Many of the stories relating to the Dreaming explore the disconcerting possibility that women may have originally possessed the means of initiating males. Gender issues still preoccupy Ngaanyatjarra people enormously, and this is part of the reason why the mythology of this Dreaming retains the high level of general interest that it does. However, the sorts of comparative questions that arise in this mythology can also be transposed from the gender context to other contexts, such as a geographical one. Thus this *tjukurrpa* is adaptable enough to be useful when, for instance, Ngaanyatjarra men wish to evaluate themselves not against women but against their fellows in other parts of the desert. Who can be said to have the most potency? Who is dealing more successfully with the challenges of modern times? Such questions, for Ngaanyatjarra men, tend not to involve the sorts of issues that interest outside commentators, like prevailing indicators of health and longevity, education and employment, and the like. They are much more likely to concern a whole series of completely different questions, ones centring around the *tjukurrpa*. The people of Kalgoorlie and Wiluna to their west are seen by Ngaanyatjarra men to have profited from the development of mines that extracted the substance of the *tjukurrpa* being X as it came through those areas. But in the Lands, the valuable material left by X has not (or not yet) been mined. At times the Ngaanyatjarra view the westerners' presumed gains with envy, and at times they think in terms of their counterparts having given away something important that they retain. But whichever way they take it, they are both fascinated and indignant at this difference – by the fact that the valuable places have been exploited to the west, whereas in the Ngaanyatjarra Lands they remain intact and untapped. Ideas and comparisons along these lines are among those that most intensely preoccupy Ngaanyatjarra men.[30]

Tjukurrpa-thinking in Everyday Life

But *tjukurrpa*-thinking is much more extensive than even these cases reveal. It can almost be said that every unique or unusual event, small or large, that happens in the Lands is sooner or later given an explanation arising from *tjukurrpa*-thinking. I will give just three short examples among hundreds that I have recorded. When a young man recently became mentally disturbed and refused to leave his grandmother's house for several months, community residents divined that one of the Seven Sisters had (literally) entered his head. The Seven Sisters Dreaming (the Pleiades) inhabits much of the landscape around the community concerned. Over a year later the young man was taken to a spiritual healer in far-away Wiluna who is said to have 'scared away' the interloper – and the patient has since returned to normal. The Sisters are always being interpreted as interfering or helping in local people's affairs in one way or another. For example they are considered to make cars break down at the point where their track crosses the main highway. It is not that the Sisters are malevolent, but that (in the mythology) they are endlessly pursued by a lecherous man, and hence are always hiding and in a state of agitation. Thus the Sister who became entrapped in the young man was simply behaving true to form.

In connection with this same Dreaming, and illustrating how even young children engage in creative *tjukurrpa*-thinking, an eleven-year-old girl from the same community wrote a story recently in which she depicted the Sisters as having television sets in the caves in which they live in the nearby landscape. Unlike some residents of the Lands, who have access to Foxtel, the Sisters were limited solely to the ABC. 'Poor things', the girl said! Incidentally the community is actually now sometimes called 'Seven Sisters' rather than its normal name, in another example of the application of *tjukurrpa*-thinking in a new area.

Two young women who are close cousins were born a few weeks apart, in 1978, at Blackstone, a community strongly associated with the *wati kutjarra* (the Two 'Clever' Men) Dreaming. This Dreaming is imprinted on the adjacent Blackstone Range. Among other things, this inseparable pair of beings spends a lot of time in the mythology playing around with the concept that they are at once similar and different. They are usually represented by two varieties of goanna that have various differing characteristics. One aspect of the contrast is that one is a dark colour and the other a light. Like these two beings, the two girls, who spent a lot of time together as children, were seen by their family as physically similar, but with one having a lighter skin than the other. It was inevitable that the idea would be coined[31] that they were actually manifestations of the Two Men – that is, that they both possessed the *tjukurrpa* of the Two Men, one being the light party and one the dark. Thus the language of the *tjukurrpa* served to express publicly and to cement the close personal relationship that existed in the everyday world between the girls. (The fact that the *tjukurrpa* was a male one was no bar whatsoever to this association being made.)

Perhaps the most striking feature of life in the Lands is the fact that there is so much interconnectedness. Not only is each person connected to everyone else through kin and family relations and a web of links to country, there is also the *tjukurrpa*-thinking, shared by all, through which, as we have seen, people interpret many aspects of the world and conceive many further types of linkages between people, country, events and phenomena both perennial and new. They may apply elements of the Dreaming infrastructure to give further meaning to existing connections (as with the two cousins whose closeness was likened to that of the inseparable Two Men of mythology). Every day in the Lands brings new stories and revelations that illustrate and further build on the web of connections.

Transmission of the *Tjukurrpa* to Young People

However, as the following case study material involving a young Ngaanyatjarra man shows, connections and especially rights to country and authority need to be acquired; they are not just given. Today as in the past, the structural conditions of the transmission of the Dreaming from the older to the younger generation are inflected by the particular family situation and life experiences of individuals. In the contemporary setting, this includes engaging the non-Ngaanyatjarra world, and it involves insecurities in relation to the way in which young men can establish links to the country of their ancestors.

The Case of James Park

James Park (born 1978) is trying to pursue a career that relates to country. He is the grandson (a daughter's son) of one of the most respected traditionally oriented elders (*tjilpi*) of the Lands, Jack Palmer (born 1923). James is married to a woman from another Ngaanyatjarra community. They are correctly related to one another, and they live in the house of his mother and father. In 2006 James told me he was interested in a job with the Land and Culture unit of the Ngaanyatjarra Council, but said he also knew that the (older) men would laugh at him if he pursued it – because of his youth and inexperience. He has work credentials, having held other council and community positions and shown himself willing to work on community projects. To my knowledge he had not established a reputation among the men of being interested in the country and *tjukurrpa*-related sphere, though given his age there would have been few opportunities for him to have done this.

I asked him whether he had learned much about country from his grandfather, and he replied that he had been shown some sites, but that his grandfather tended to laugh when he asked him about such things. This sounds harsh, yet it is not indicative of any animosity – it is clear that the relationship between the two is affectionate enough. The problem is that there is a great gulf between them in terms of understandings and expectations. James treats Jack with respect according to his lights, but in Jack's day a young man wanting to acquire knowledge of the *tjukurrpa* would have to spend years supplying hard-won game meat and similar resources to his elders. Myers observed the same for the Pintupi. He comments on the age hierarchy thus: 'As the Pintupi say, ritual knowledge is "dear." Older men "give" knowledge and instructees [*sic*] "pay" with pain, meat and obedience … As a result of the transaction, there is an increase of "value" on the part of the junior' (Myers 1980: 210).

As this suggests, knowledge had to be prised from its holders, the *tjilpiya*, bit by bit, and with a lot of effort. This holds true just as strongly now. People like Jack carefully dole out bits of knowledge to the young – and when it benefits them to do so. Thus they ensure that they keep sufficient to themselves, maintaining prime control over country and its *tjukurrpa* until their last gasp. If they did not, they fear they would soon be bypassed and perceived as useless. (It should be acknowledged that the elders can often be very generous with their knowledge to certain people. Jack, for instance, has provided valuable information about connections to family and country and the like, to Ngaanyatjarra persons who through historical circumstances were raised in distant places and returned to the Lands in later life.) If young men are not making progress in the 'arm wrestle' associated with the life cycle, as seems to be the case with James, several explanations are possible. It may be because they do not fully appreciate the 'rules of engagement', or because the prospects of gain no longer equal the dedication required. It would no doubt have been easier if, rather than trying to engage directly with Jack, he had approached somebody in the intermediate generation – ideally an uncle (mother's brother). However there is no suitable person available to him in this category. James might not have made much progress yet in terms of getting a job working on country, but he does make efforts to demonstrate his interest: he recently composed and recorded a song, released on a local CD, entitled 'Blackstone – My Grandfather's Land' (the reference is specifically to Jack). The lyrics contain the lines, 'Blackstone is where I come from, where I live, and where I belong'.[32]

It is worthwhile exploring a little further the notion of the contemporary community as an object of enthusiastic identification, as revealed in
James's song. The notion is apparent among young people of the Lands
in a number of ways. It appears in the graffiti on the walls of local buildings, and it is the mainstay of much of the artistic production that goes
on in the Youth Arts centre. This art also engages extensively with the
broader modern world both through the new 'tool kit' (guitars, 'Garage
Band' software on the computer, clothing as a fashion statement) and in
ideas and imagery (hip-hop, rap, gangsta music and accompanying Afro-
American styles). But the identification with the local community shows
the continuing power for young people of themes rooted in their own
background. These themes include identification with kin and locality,
and, probably increasingly, they tap into the *tjukurrpa* realm as well. In a
development that has started quite recently, communities themselves are
becoming more identified with whatever particular Dreaming features in
the nearby landscape; and via this channel, such Dreamings are finding
their way into the thinking and the art of the local youth. The case of the
young girl of 'Seven Sisters' community with her drawings of these *tjukurrpa* beings watching Foxtel shows similar aspects of innovative continuity, as does the example of F. and his son, where a rather ingenious
specific connection into the Dreaming 'edifice' was posited for a young
child in the story involving the eagle.

Conclusion

I made the point early in this chapter that in the Ngaanyatjarra region,
the overall impact of settler society has been comparatively light. The
people were not moved away from their country, the mission era was
relatively benign and through the decades up to the 1960s, most of the
population was able to adjust to the new circumstances at its own pace.
Of course, objectively speaking the Ngaanyatjarra have been forced to
radically adapt their way of life from the hunter-gatherer past. But this
has not created a disjunction, a yawning gap between a classical past
and a compromised present. This is certainly how Ngaanyatjarra themselves see the situation. Despite this, the Ngaanyatjarra fare no better on
most of the main indicators of social well-being than the people of other
areas where the encounter with the White world has been more difficult
and various aspects of life are less stable and less well knit. And yet, the
Ngaanyatjarra surely have benefited from the relatively benign history
and their well-being is surely enhanced by the many positive aspects of
the life of the region that we have seen – the social interconnectedness,

the pervasive presence of organizational principles, the multilayered relationship to country and the vitality of the collective intellectual life as shown in the way that country and the *tjukurrpa* are continually being harnessed and reimagined in new situations and to new ends. There are many signs that young people, while having a keen interest in global youth culture and the like (something that could hardly be wished away), are also following their elders, actually to a surprising degree. One thing they make very clear is that they are living where they want to be. Their replies to questions, the graffiti that they draw, the songs they write and sing – all unanimously and emphatically declare that they have not the slightest intention of leaving their home in the desert.

What about *tjukurrpa*-thinking? I have given this close attention in the chapter not only because it is so pervasive in the Ngaanyatjarra world that it cannot be ignored but also because it shows just how much life and vigour there is here. As such, I have presented it as basically a social benefit that among other things knits Ngaanyatjarra people together at an intellectual level. Some commentators, though, have argued that 'culture' is a blind alley for Aboriginal communities, in that it provides a shield for the perpetuation of undesirable behaviours – such as those associated with the domination of local life by exploitative leaders – and inhibits the development among the people of ideas and behaviours more attuned to a healthy and prosperous life in the modern world. Violent behaviour and intimidation does occur in this region, and it is associated with the exploitation of the weak by the strong. But its exercise, in the desert, is not in the nature of a privilege emergent from a leadership role. It is not founded in or supported by 'culture', but is purely a matter of some people being stronger than others and exerting this superiority in strength, sometimes for their own benefit, in the absence of any means to prevent them. Persons overusing their capacity selfishly were (and are) actually less likely to be accorded the respect that goes with the notion of leadership, with others avoiding them as much as possible. In any case, any institution of leadership, whether for good or for bad, was mostly lacking in the desert (*cf.* Tonkinson 1991b).

Similarly, there is no evidence that systematic abuse such as child sexual abuse was present in classical times in any patterned way, as a right or privilege, but only that it occurred occasionally and randomly, again as an act of indulgence by someone who had the power and the opportunity. This in the very way it was constituted was not the kind of society that could create such patterns. Even now this largely remains true, though sedentary conditions do allow for a degree of entrenchment of power in some quarters. But by and large, the child abuse and the other forms of violence that occur contemporarily have to be seen in the light of the persistence of the classical *nganyirri purlka* syndrome as I have described it, not as any function of a society that contains malevolent strata or that is distorted or disordered. This is certainly not to condone the violence and abuse that does occur. To tackle this, it first needs to be recognized that some undesirable elements existed in the past and that they persist – *nganyirri purlka* being one of them. To do this does not imply a denigration of the classical inheritance as a whole. Far from it, the sophisticated organizational templates for ritual, and the phenomenon of the *tjukurrpa* in all its richness are achievements that no one could fail to admire.

But, and this is the last question, is it true that *tjukurrpa*-thinking and some other elements of desert culture, for all their elegance and social efficacy, are going to hinder young Ngaanyatjarra people from becoming more successful citizens (and consumers) in contemporary Australia? In some ways, yes. Clearly, if much of your fundamental thinking about the world starts from a different premise, you are going to have many different values and aspects of your life proceeding along very different lines. I think this can be accommodated. To my mind, there is no way of changing the culture radically even if it was thought desirable – and who would seriously think so when what the Ngaanyatjarra have retained of human value far outweighs the problems they bear?

Notes

1. *See* e.g., papers for the 2006 Bennelong Society conference entitled 'Leaving Remote Communities'. http://www.bennelong.com.au.
2. The Ngaanyatjarra Lands comprise a region some 200,000 sq km in extent, in the desert zone of the central part of Western Australia, abutting the Northern Territory and South Australian borders.
3. Archaeological research has shown that the outer margins of Australia's arid centre were inhabited from before 30,000 BP (Mulvaney and Kamminga 1999: 206). Such research remains to be conducted for the more central Ngaanyatjarra area, but there is no reason to doubt the longevity of their occupation.
4. Although children who had lost a father would still be brought up in a group containing close relatives, it was not necessarily the case that the mother would remarry, thus providing a new 'father'. Often a brother of the widowed woman, an uncle to the child, would effectively take responsibility for the family.
5. Following Sutton (n.d.) I use the term *classical* in this chapter in preference to *traditional,* to refer to the previous distinct way of life under the old hunter-gatherer economy and conditions of autonomy from the state. Confusion may arise with the term *traditional* as it can refer to certain cultural and behavioural elements that continue to exist in the present.
6. Except where otherwise indicated, the ethnographic observations about the Ngaanyatjarra throughout the chapter are based on my own anthropological work in the region over a period of more than twenty consecutive years.

7. The story of Christianity in the Lands is a complex and interesting chapter waiting to be told. For background *see* Blackett 1997. It should also be noted that differing denominational affiliations of missions in different parts of the desert have coloured the Christian impacts in differing ways. For example, the Presbyterian mission at Ernabella pursued significantly different policies from the Warburton mission, run by the more fundamentalist 'interdenominational' United Aborigines Mission (UAM). *See* Hilliard 1968; Plant and Viegas 2002.

8. In the case of females, the general view, at least of the contemporary older generation, is that a girl (*kungka*) becomes a woman (*minyma*) after she has had her second child.

9. The ABS census figures for the Ngaanyatjarra Lands are not utilized in the current chapter, for reasons of inaccuracy, as discussed in Brooks and Kral 2007: 5.

10. National figures retrieved 7 January 2007 from the 2001 ABS census. *See* http://www.healthinfonet.ecu.edu.au.

11. *See* Kral 2007; and entries by Janet Vost and Seema Sanghi at http://www.warburtonyoutharts.blogspot.com/.

12. No formal betrothal ceremonies or legal contracts of any kind, whether grounded in Indigenous or Western traditions, are normally associated with modern 'marriage' in the desert.

13. As in almost all remote Aboriginal communities, housing is in acutely short supply in the Ngaanyatjarra Lands.

14. Most young people work under the Community Development Employment Projects (CDEP) program, created by the Australian Government in the 1980s to cater for remote communities where few jobs as such were available. The program effectively pools individual unemployment benefit entitlements and channels them through locally controlled organizations, which then administer work and payment regimes in relation to them.

15. I am indebted to Damian McLean, long-time community development adviser for Warburton community, and president of the Shire of Ngaanyatjarra-ku, for the observations in this paragraph.

16. I have previously considered some of these matters in Brooks 2002.

17. *See also* Keen 1994. For a comprehensive discussion of knowledge, authority and intergenerational transmission in a related society, *see* Myers 1980: 197–214.

18. During the seclusion period it was – and still is – the role of younger brothers and even sisters (*tjilku,* children) to bring food for their postinitiate siblings. Making sure that neither party sees the other, the child places the food in a spot where it can be collected later (Damian McLean, personal communication).

19. There is an extensive literature on the so-called section systems and their derivatives, but most of the issues addressed in that literature are not germane to my analysis here.

20. Strictly speaking, the Ngaanyatjarra have six labels, but two of them are functionally equivalent to two others. Systematically, it is a four-section system.

21. The generational moiety system actually has a much greater antiquity in the desert than the section system, which arrived in the Ngaanyatjarra area only in the early twentieth century – though contemporary Ngaanyatjarra people are

not generally aware of this. But as indicated, the two systems logically fit together seamlessly.

22. It might be remarked that the Ngaanyatjarra, like many remote Aboriginal people, are also very effective in organizing football carnivals that involve communities from far and wide.

23. Richard Gould (1969: 108) says that out of ninety-four marriages, he recorded only three that broke the rules. A similar level of compliance is revealed in the genealogies that I possess for the Ngaanyatjarra polity.

24. Many senior Ngaanyatjarra people have insight into their society, and older women in particular, who monitor and nurture society on many fronts, know the places where the 'glue' needs to be applied and what threatens its efficacy. For example, they exhort the young girls who are approaching marriageable age to 'get the right man' – meaning a man with the right skin (and who is also sufficiently genealogically distant). They promote sayings like the following: 'When two people marry wrong way, they will have sickly children. But when they marry right way, the children will be healthy'.

25. Myers (1986: 54–57) provides an extensive discussion of the *ngurra* among the Pintupi, which, in his contribution to this volume, he links to the experience of 'ontological security' deriving from the extension of the child-parent bond to country.

26. Nowadays, the Ngaanyatjarra Health Service effectively insists that expectant mothers go to town to have their babies, as the remote conditions and other factors mean that the NHS cannot ensure the presence of a doctor at an accessible distance at any given time. The Health Service's position is that managing local births in these circumstances would place too much of a demand on existing health staff, especially with the less-than-ideal health status of many mothers.

27. Native Title Act 1993.

28. The connection to country that has been 'coined' here by F. for his son is an extremely flimsy one at this stage – more in the nature of a father's hope than anything else. Not grounded in a concrete event like birth, it also may not acquire the sorts of reinforcement and accretions that in earlier times used to flow naturally from residence in the area and from the events and discourses of bush life. To nurture it, F. will probably need to arrange special trips to the area so that bonding occurs to place and associations.

29. It should be noted that at the same time they are likely to be fearful of the *tjukurrpa* being threatened by these discoveries.

30. Thus although Ngaanyatjarra people might have a limited input into issues that are important in the wider world, they by no means see themselves as helpless or apathetic or bereft of meaning and aspiration. Just like anybody else, they measure themselves against the people and issues that they consider to be relevant.

31. Of course the Ngaanyatjarra do not see this as a matter of an idea being coined, but rather as the preexisting but hidden reality becoming revealed.

32. Similar themes are expressed by other young male singer-songwriters who commonly make reference to the significance of kin and country in their contemporary worldview.

CHAPTER 9

Being Mardu

Change and Challenge for Some Western Desert Young People Today

Myrna Tonkinson

Multiple Sources of Identity and Social Stress: Scope of Discussion

A commonly stated cliché is the claim that Aboriginal Australians are caught between two worlds: the beliefs, values and attitudes of their 'traditional' culture, and those of the dominant society, which has as its foundations European traditions and worldview. Statements of this type are common in the mass media and among lay observers of Aboriginal people and their communities, and they can also be heard among Aboriginal people themselves.[1] There is, in the case of the young Mardu people with whom I have conducted research, some factual basis for this unsubtle generalization. The metaphor has validity insofar as people perceive themselves, or others, as having to choose between, or being confronted by, behaviours, values and worldviews that are, at least potentially, incompatible. The young people I discuss here often describe their actions as doing things 'Mardu way' in contrast, at least implicitly, to 'Whitefella way'; they also sometimes invoke Whitefella law or way to explain or justify behaviour. These contrasting labels are comparable to those invoked by Navajo youth: 'Navajo ways' versus 'Anglo ways' (Dole and Csordas 2003). Dole and Csordas argue convincingly that there is no analytically valid dichotomy in such cases: while the people themselves routinely speak of 'Navajo ways' versus 'Anglo ways', and the distinctions have 'considerable social weight', the views and behaviours of Navajo youth do not fit neatly into the simple categories suggested by these labels (Dole and Csordas 2003: 369).[2]

Young Mardu experience competing values and expectations. They live in communities where Mardu constitute a majority, but are also part of a wider Australian society in which they are increasingly expected to participate in school, employment and other activities for which their

213

Mardu upbringing does not necessarily prepare them.[3] They identify primarily and strongly as Mardu, and it is close relationships within the Mardu community that remain the major sources of identity, stability and conflict for young people. They speak Marduwangka (*see below*), though they often incorporate English words and phrases into their speech. They hold beliefs, values and practices that appear continuous with their ancestral traditions, yet young Mardu also embrace characteristics of the culture of the wider Australian society, and indeed 'the West' more generally. The 'worlds' they inhabit are not discrete but overlapping and interacting; they generate attitudes, values and behaviours that may closely resemble Mardu ways, or may be more like those prevailing in 'mainstream' Australian society, or may be observably distinct from the predominant features of both of those groups.[4] The condition of young Mardu is certainly not a simple aggregation of attitudes and behaviours freely selected from an array of options; rather, we might say that their habitus emerges from experiences in a largely Mardu domain, but situated within the greater Australian society.

These young people encounter hindrances to the realization of their potential in both mainstream and Mardu social arenas: they cannot emulate fully the lives of their antecedents by drawing on the cultural wealth that their grandparents and even many of their parents possessed; and for structural, customary and attitudinal reasons, nor can they participate fully in the wider Australian society, or gain access to many of the opportunities that, at least notionally, are available to them as Australian citizens. Most can speak English fluently but, owing to limited education and experience, tend to have restricted knowledge of concepts and vocabulary. Like the Aranda described by Austin-Broos (1996: 4), Mardu of all ages usually explain illness, accidents and some instances of violence in terms of sorcery. Yet, their exposure to, and involvement in, the larger non-Mardu Australian and global world mean that younger Mardu are assimilating aspects of the outside world and defining themselves as distinct in ways that are different from, and sometimes in conflict with, those of their elders. The groups with which they might compare themselves are no longer solely other desert people, or coastal Pilbara Aboriginal people, or the missionaries and pastoralists with whom Mardu interacted in the past, but an array of others, whom they encounter directly and via the mass media. Among other things, younger Mardu are beginning to call themselves 'Aboriginal', linking into an expanded universe of connection, and they express some affinity with Aboriginal people beyond their own widely dispersed Western Desert relatives and countrymen.[5] Some also invoke the label 'Australian', though this is less common. Recognition of Australianness also entails intimations that the Mardu's difference is something that separates them, often uncomfortably, from White Australians. One middle-aged Mardu man commented on the extreme shyness of some of his teenage relatives thus: 'I tell them "don't be shy; this place doesn't belong to White people, we were here long before them."'[6] Such self-perception suggests the acquisition by young Mardu of an 'out-group' identity that Austin-Broos (1996: 5) sees as occurring in the development of an ethnic identity.

The Study

The material presented here is drawn from a larger study of the effects on Mardu people's identity and worldview of pervasive problems they experience in the changing circumstances of their lives, particularly those related to health and well-being. In addition to this recent study, I also draw upon my long-term research with the Mardu. This is not a definitive account; rather, I provide some glimpses of their lives with special attention to difficulties and challenges.

I examine aspects of the behaviour and views of adolescents and young adults from three related communities in Western Australia. The study on which this paper is based was conducted in Jigalong, Punmu and the town of Newman; supplementary material was gathered in Perth and Parnngurr. The young people who are the major focus of this chapter range in age from about fourteen years to about thirty years; all were born after the Mardu had adopted a sedentary existence. Between us, Bob Tonkinson and I interviewed thirty-one people in this age bracket, and had less-structured conversations and observations involving people of similar age and older; a research assistant also interviewed eight young people at Parnngurr for the study. The combined population of the Mardu communities from which we drew participants is approximately five hundred; the greater Mardu population is in excess of one thousand.

From among the numerous possibilities for exploration of challenges and dilemmas faced by Mardu youth, I focus on three areas of behaviour that are perceived, within their own communities as well as by outside observers, as troublesome: 1) marriage and sexual relationships – including teenage child bearing and family formation; 2) alcohol and drug use; and 3) violence. These are areas in which the options available to young people differ markedly from those that prevailed in previous generations, hence rules are in flux and models for behaviour are scarce or inappropriate. These conditions present dangers to young Mardu, but also opportunities for innovation. The changed circumstances they face stem from the transition made by earlier generations to sedentary life, causing an attenuation of the traditional economy and the rupture of many social structures, rules and customs. Successive governments imposed restrictions upon, or facilitated radical changes to, Mardu existence. However, these changes did not extend to full participation in the wider Australian society; their options were, and continue to be, limited in comparison to those available to the majority of non-Aboriginal Australians. For Mardu, the psychological effects of this situation have not been assessed, but some inferences may be drawn from statements made by young people and from behaviours they display. In addition to many obvious social consequences, there are potential ones on which we may speculate.

Mardu Society in Historical Context

The Mardu are part of the much larger Western Desert cultural bloc, whose members are speakers of one or more mutually intelligible dialects of the Western Desert language. They speak primarily Manyjilyjarra, but also Kartujarra, Warnman or other dialects linked to particular areas of land from which they originate. Today, following some decades of living in large settlements where several Western Desert dialects are spoken, a more inclusive language label, Marduwangka, is used, and the people refer to themselves as the Mardu.[7]

Over several decades, beginning in the 1930s and continuing until the 1970s, most Western Desert people moved out from their homelands to a number of missions and settlements in Western Australia, the Northern Territory and South Australia. The majority of those now known as Mardu initially made their home at the former fundamentalist Christian mission station of Jigalong, but have close relatives in a number of other locations. Jigalong, which remains a major centre for Mardu people and the practice of their traditions, is near the western edge of the Gibson Desert and not part of their traditional homelands. In the 1980s many Jigalong Mardu, especially Manyjilyjarra and Warnman speakers, moved back to their traditional lands in the desert proper.[8] These were, at first, satellite outstations, but later they became permanent, with similar services and amenities as the older settlements and missions. Today there are small, thriving communities at Parnngurr, Punmu, and Kunawarriji as well as at Jigalong. Smaller Mardu populations also live in the towns of Newman, Marble Bar, Nullagine, Port Hedland, Perth and other urban areas.[9] The residents of any one of these communities have members of their extended families living in one or more of the others, and in other Western Desert settlements, such as Wiluna, Warburton Ranges, Kiwirrkura, Yandeyarra, Bidyadanga and Fitzroy Crossing. Mardu travel frequently to these and other localities for funerals, ceremonial activities and to visit relatives; they often stay for extended periods in places other than their home bases. Children usually accompany their parents and sometimes remain with relatives for longer visits. Young people generally tend to be highly mobile, visiting relatives in various settlements and towns.

The shift to a more sedentary existence in large settlements controlled by missionaries and other agents of the state is associated with numerous and continuing impacts on the lives of at least three generations of Mardu (*see* R. Tonkinson 1974, 1991a, 2007a). Among other things, schooling and years of compulsory residence in dormitories placed children under the control of non-Mardu missionaries and teachers – never exclusively, but for significant periods. Adults were dependent on the state and its agents for their livelihood. A significant minority of the Mardu population was engaged in seasonal employment on cattle and sheep stations, but freedom of movement was restricted. Over many decades since initial contact, starting for some as early as the 1930s, changing government policies have dictated the parameters within which Mardu operate. The results have been mixed: adaptation, innovation, confusion, calamity and resilience are among the descriptors that apply (*see* R. Tonkinson 2007b).

Tenuous Identifications: 'Mardu', 'Aboriginal' and 'Mainstream'

As I mentioned earlier, young people identify themselves first and foremost as Mardu, and distinctive cultural features they share with older Mardu are prominent. They seldom express identity in terms of being part of the Australian nation. However, there is a growing tendency among young Mardu to identify as 'Aboriginal' as well as Mardu, and to thus see themselves as part of a wider category of Aboriginal persons. This is most apparent in sport: Aboriginal footballers, for example, are pointed out and admired; boys and young men know which teams have Aboriginal players, how many, and what their names and backgrounds are. They also admire Aboriginal bands and singers, and aspiring Mardu musicians imitate their styles. Young Mardu also share many of the interests and activities that characterize their non-Aboriginal counterparts, although there are significant divergences in the worldview and behaviour of the two categories of youth.

Young Mardu are not unique in forging their identity from different sources, but they do so in locally specific ways. The complexity of meaning of the deployment of oppositional rhetoric and behaviour that Robinson (1997: 128–9) proposes for Tiwi youth in the far north of the continent has no readily discernible parallel among the Mardu. They occasionally remark on their differences from, and disadvantage vis-à-vis

'Whitefellas', but this is unusual. In fact, most young Mardu we spoke to showed scant knowledge of, or interest in, White Australian society or the views and opinions of non-Mardu.[10] When people display rage, the frustrations they feel may well have to do with problems that arise in relation to the outside world, but the proximate cause is usually local and personal. I have no evidence that they are opposing White society and authority, nor can I claim that youth engaging in rebellious behaviour are attempting to play off internal and external forces of authority as Robinson suggests (1997: 129). It is possible, however, that youth play on their elders' concerns about the opinions outsiders hold of Mardu in cases like the following, recorded in my field notes.

> After a break-in at the local store one night, a number of teenage boys were hauled before a community meeting, where they were verbally and physically chastised by older men and women of their families. One woman said to me: 'They make us shame in front of White people'. The store operators, a White couple, had made their exasperation clear, having had the same experience, at the hands of mostly the same perpetrators, only a couple of weeks earlier.

I could speculate that the boys were issuing a challenge of some sort to their elders, but their actions could as easily be attributed to the desire for the stolen goods, or the thrill of planning and effecting the burglary.

Youth Culture

Despite being part of the poorest segment of the Australian population, and mostly living in small, remote communities, Mardu adolescents and young adults are keen consumers of global youth culture. They enjoy many of the same products and pastimes as their peers in Australia and elsewhere. Many drink alcohol, and some indulge in recreational substance use; they wear clothing that mimics the styles of hip-hop and sports stars. In their homes they watch television and DVDs, listen to CDs, and play electronic games. They express little curiosity about the origins of these goods or the people and places portrayed in them. Young Mardu take advantage of technology to maintain and extend links with family. Few homes have telephones, but there is heavy use of public phones, office phones and fax machines, and many people acquire mobile phones when they are in towns where reception is possible. They also take a keen, if sporadic, interest in sport. Young men in particular admire sport stars, especially in football, and also enjoy playing. Western Desert people hold intercommunity sports carnivals, featuring Australian Rules football for boys and men and, for women and girls, softball. People travel great distances to be participants and spectators at these competitions. Skilful playing is admired, and occasionally family members might complain, or fight, if one of their own is not selected to play or travel to an event. Yet a tendency to abjure the limelight is apparent: individual prize winners are diffident about accepting their honours, and such awards are not displayed as they might be in other Australian contexts; indeed, the recipients treat them, as they do most possessions, with apparent indifference.

Local Orientations

Almost without exception, when asked what makes them happy, young people reply 'being with family'. The most common cause of sadness mentioned was 'losing family' (the death of kin). They express strong ties to their communities and families, and little desire to separate from them. At the same time, however, in rejecting many of the strictures that used to be imposed on the young by their elders, they seek to make decisions for themselves that were once the prerogative of parents and other senior relatives. However, this does not mean that other forms of regulating young people's lives have replaced previous forms of restraint. Notably, young Mardu have not embraced schooling with much enthusiasm or success, and their participation, both potential and actual, in the workforce is extremely limited. To a considerable degree, young Mardu are in an ambiguous position: on the one hand, their identity as Mardu is strong, but their incorporation into the traditions of their elders and forebears is tenuous; on the other hand, while invoking concepts like free choice of marriage partners or practices such as the consumption of alcohol and other substances, their understanding of, and involvement in, 'mainstream' Australian society is rudimentary. Much of the knowledge and assumptions acquired by children in the dominant society, via socialization in the family and at school, is not necessarily part of the worldview, expectations and behaviours of young Mardu (*cf.* Burbank 2006). Furthermore, the low investment by Mardu in formal education suggests that they do not perceive value in trading off priorities such as being with family, attending funerals and ceremonies and protecting children from teasing or bullying, for participation, and potential success, in school. The benefits of education that most Australians expect, and some Mardu articulate, such as gaining 'good jobs' or taking on leadership positions, are not sufficient inducements to either children or parents – at least partly because the evidence to date for attainment of such rewards is slight. Negative and positive orientations towards formal education appear to be deeply embedded in local cultural histories and perspectives, rather than merely commonplace among disadvantaged youth.[11] A comparison with an African example is instructive here. In his account of the lives of young men in Jimma, a city in southern Ethiopia, Mains (2007) provides striking contrasts with what I have found among Mardu youth. While idleness characterizes both groups, it is perceived differently, and the alternatives to unemployment are quite different. Mains states that the Ethiopian young men he studied have a high regard for education, which has taken the place of military activity in facilitating social mobility; they want to have jobs but abjure the available low-status employment, regarding it as shameful. They prefer to remain unemployed rather than take on menial work at home, but dream of going abroad to make their fortune, even if that entails menial work (Mains 2007: 661–63). For young Mardu, education is not greatly desired, and involvement in production is not a significant component of identity, there is no stigma attached either to menial work or to unemployment, and emigration is not a goal, at least not as an avenue to employment and status enhancement. There may, however, be the beginnings of change as some young men and women are now being trained or employed, usually on rotation, in mines near their home bases.

Beliefs and Practices

There are strong similarities between the beliefs, attitudes and social values of young and older Mardu. At the same time, there are significant differences in the extent to which younger Mardu and their elders perceive the importance of conformity to traditions such as marriage rules, acceptance of parental stipulations, and participation in ritual life. Youth offer little challenge to their parents and elders in terms of beliefs; for example, they share with their elders theories about human motivation and action, illness and death. Like the young Ngaanyatjarra described by Brooks (this volume), they also share a firm belief in the Dreaming – mythological creatures and events in stories that explain the natural world and customary practices. While making use of medical services and pharmaceutical remedies, and often attributing certain illnesses, such as diabetes, to introduced foods and alcohol, they explain many conditions and events as resulting from sorcery or spirits, and they believe that such conditions can be effectively mitigated only by traditional healers. Young and older Mardu have similar attitudes to family and community, and similar levels of understanding of the structures and operation of Australian institutions such as government and its agencies, education and employment.

Childrearing

In bringing up their children, the maintenance of Mardu values, attitudes and beliefs is strong even while many elements are being eroded by young people's embrace of new behaviours. Breastfeeding is the norm, and mothers are usually the primary carers, at least of infants, but child-rearing is a shared responsibility. Despite changes to marriage, fertility and household arrangements, childrearing involves many members of the extended family. Young Mardu of both sexes are involved in the care of children to an extent that is noticeably greater than among their non-Aboriginal peers. Younger siblings are often left in the care of older ones, and both boys and girls commonly carry small children around and take responsibility for them. Fathers are never primary carers, but tend to be attentive and affectionate to their children. Children are almost always dealt with indulgently by their parents and other adults. They are accorded considerable autonomy while maintaining close attachment to their parents/guardians, which endures into adolescence and adulthood. As is the case in other Aboriginal groups (for example, the Lajamanu Warlpiri described by O'Shannessy, this volume), children are thought able to make decisions of their own, such as whether to attend school. This puts Mardu practice at odds with the requirements of the state and the expectations of teachers and others. The liberty that young children enjoy used to be reined in once boys embarked on the long process of initiation, or girls joined their promised husband's household. However, these practices are no longer observed to the same extent, so it appears that, in many families, parental influence on their teenage and adult children is less than effective, and social sanctions are inconsistently applied.

Although there are many cases of parents failing to care for their own children (most commonly because they are alcohol misusers), the majority of children receive loving care from some adult or other. Most Mardu households experience shortages of food and other necessities at some point. Children may, therefore, go hungry or be insufficiently fed at times, but the ethos of sharing is powerful, and someone can usually be relied upon to help out. When funds are available, even quite small children are given money to spend as they wish. Many parents, including surrogates, go to great lengths to protect their children from perceived dangers related to drinking and fighting (*cf.* Sansom and Baines 1988). It is common for parents to travel to towns where their teenage or young adult children may be drinking, and take them back to their home community, or delegate a relative such as an uncle or aunt to take charge of the youngster. Parents also sometimes intervene to stop their teenage or adult children driving while drunk, or travelling in vehicles with drunken drivers. Even when parents have their own problems with alcohol or violence, they seem anxious to quarantine their children from these dangers. Such measures often prove futile, but the desire of parents to keep their children safe and alive is much in evidence.

Many older people explicitly worry about the preservation and continuity of 'the Law' or 'culture' in the future. One woman put it this way:
'[Our] language is alright, it's strong, but I worry about culture because
young people not learning [many of the ceremonies]; and so many of
them have *nyakaji* (irregular or 'wrong' marriage partners)'. Maintaining
the Law and ritual life rests on the possibility of passing it on down the
generations; the young gradually acquire knowledge in this domain as
they work towards adult status. This process of attaining adulthood has
altered as a consequence of changes in the way Mardu live.

Attaining Adult Status

Still today, attaining social recognition as an adult in Mardu society is
only possible, for males, and to a lesser extent for females (for whom
motherhood is a major marker of adult status), by 'being put through the
Law'. While only males undergo physical operations, members of both
sexes need to be incorporated in the ritual status hierarchy to be 'proper
Law people'. Virtually all young people participate in 'Law business',
which is carried out at regional gatherings of people from widely scattered communities throughout and beyond the Western Desert. These
meetings, held predominantly around the holiday season in the summer
months amid great excitement, involve hundreds of people in intense social and ritual interaction, mostly away from the gaze of non-Aboriginal
people. Ritual life entails extensive travel as members of several communities gather in one place to 'put through' a group of teenage boys. The
large encampment may continue over a period of several weeks, with
rituals and other ceremonial activities performed daily, before the dramatic culmination (*see* R. Tonkinson 1991a). Over the summer, a series
of such gatherings may take place in different communities. Attendance
at ritual events requires many participants to be away from their home
communities and sometimes protracted absence from work and school.
While this appears not to be a major deterrent, it does contribute to the
reduction in time available for ceremonial activities.

Elders control ritual life, but young people are enjoined to participate
and learn. At times, this domain, too, can be a source of tension between
older and younger people. The revelation of ritual knowledge that used
to occur gradually over more than a decade prior to marriage is now
attenuated, and older people bemoan the fact that important rituals are
no longer being performed. At the same time, many young Mardu blame
their elders for failing to pass on the Law properly. The ramifications
of this situation apply to Mardu society as a whole because these rites
are not only important for transmitting culturally vital knowledge to the

next generation but are the basis for individual advancement through the ritual status hierarchy. Although young people show enthusiasm about ceremonial events, and some express worries about the Law weakening, others, and sometimes the same ones, also say they are not very interested, although they go along, because '[all the repetition] is boring', in the words of one young man, or because, as one young woman said, 'I don't like getting up to dance'. A few express fear of ritual activity in the bush, and some report tension between the maintenance of ritual traditions and their commitment to Christianity. Thus, ambivalence about ritual and its maintenance is apparent among young adults, despite their tendency to aver a strong belief in their 'Law'.[12]

Three Arenas of Challenge

I now examine in more detail some areas in which young people's behaviour presents particular challenges to, or are perceived as problems by, their elders and/or members of the wider society: marriage, sex and reproduction; substance misuse; and violence. The concerns of older Mardu are not identical to those of 'Whitefellas', but there is some coincidence insofar as youthful behaviours that trouble Mardu parents have parallels among other young Australians, and that, more significantly, may cause young Mardu trouble with the justice system or other non-Mardu authorities. In the discussion that follows logically from these interrelated challenges, my particular focus will be on the behaviours of young Mardu that may be seen as constituting a high level of risk.[13] These behaviours are not only potentially harmful to individuals; they also have implications for social cohesion and community viability in the face of external threats, such as the policies of governments that would impose punitive sanctions, even to the extent of closing remote communities, but these cannot be considered within the limits of this paper (*see* R. Tonkinson 2007b).

Marriage, Sex and Reproduction

For young Mardu, sex, marriage, parenthood and family formation are aspects of life characterized by conflicting ideas and practices. Young people's practices do not fit neatly within either traditional Mardu or contemporary Australian norms. These most fundamental human activities are observably changing and constitute sites of potential conflicts, both within and between the generations. When young people challenge or break the rules, they may provoke alarm, anger and intervention from their elders.

Marriage[14]

According to Mardu tradition, marriage should always be between a man and a woman who are 'straight': related as 'spouses' in their kinship system (any individual will have many potential spouses). Marriages are also the result of arrangements made, or at least approved, by parental and grandparental elders of the prospective spouses. In the past, betrothal most often occurred at the time of male circumcision, when persons in the appropriate kin category would promise a wife to the initiate; in such cases, the *pilyurr* (promised wife) would be an infant or small child, who would be given to her husband when he had attained full social adulthood up to fifteen or so years later. Sometimes, younger women were bestowed on older men by their parents or senior relatives; and betrothals were sometimes arranged between parents of a boy and a girl of similar age. The remarriage of widows required the sanction of certain relatives, although the woman concerned could express her views (*see* R. Tonkinson 1991a: 105). There was no form of marriage that did not involve the consent, at least, of people other than the spouses. These arranged marriages were not free of contention and conflict, and Mardu tell many stories of unsanctioned relationships, elopements and other infractions that attracted severe punishment, although they might eventually gain acceptance. On the whole, people conformed by marrying the chosen spouse, while sometimes conducting discreet extramarital affairs. To some extent, these practices persisted up until the 1980s, although resisted by many young people; young women in particular increasingly rejected arrangements entered into by their parents and senior relatives, failing to go to promised husbands, or running away from them (R. Tonkinson 1990, 2007a: 239).

Marriage demonstrates well the conflict between ideals and actual behaviour among young Mardu today. Having internalized their elders' beliefs that marriage is appropriate only between certain categories of kin, they invariably state the ideal, even if they do not abide by it. Defiance is clearest, and most unapologetic, in their rejection of arranged marriages. Decades ago, missionaries abetted young people's resistance to arranged marriage and desire to select mates who were closer to their own age. Partner selection has become almost entirely the prerogative of the individuals seeking to become a couple, but, while conceding arranged marriages are no longer tenable, many parents remain influential in delaying, vetoing, encouraging or endorsing their children's marriages. Acceptance is usually gained, provided the pair is 'straight', not 'wrong' (*see below*). At one community, adult residents of all ages spoke with pride of the fact that all marriages there were 'straight', that is, in the right kin relationship.

When a society undergoes rapid change, sexuality and marriage are among those aspects of life that are bound to be affected strongly as social conditions and the rules governing these areas are challenged by new ideas and conditions (see, e.g., Ahearn 2001). For the Mardu, one factor that has had an obvious effect on sexual behaviour and marriage is sedentary life in missions and settlements. The large aggregations that resulted brought people together for protracted periods and created many more opportunities for sexual attraction and liaisons than would have been the case in the nomadic past. Unlike the Ngaanyatjarra described in Brooks's chapter, the Mardu have for at least a generation increasingly formed 'wrong' relationships, which include couples who insist on staying together as spouses and raising children. Although they are invariably punished by relatives, some of these marriages have endured. Today, some children from these 'wrong' unions are also marrying wrongly, thus compounding the problem of muddled social category membership created by their parents.[15] A typical comment about marrying correctly was made by one young woman: 'It's good to marry straight, otherwise the children won't know who to follow' (i.e., in deciding 'section' membership, or kin terms to use with relatives; and, importantly, in establishing their roles in rituals, funerals and other contexts). The Western notion of choosing a partner on the basis of romantic love is now entrenched and is sometimes invoked to justify wrong marriage. One middle-aged man told me this about his marriage, which had been bitterly opposed by both families: 'We fell in love with each other and we wanted to be together'. He and his wife left their community temporarily, but their relationship eventually gained acceptance. Many wrongly married couples live in towns because they can thereby escape some of the opprobrium that is the lot of offenders. Even in town, though, reference to wrong marriage is one of the insults than can provoke fights when people are drunk.

In addition to rejection or modification of traditional practices, Mardu have made innovations regarding marriage. For example, although bestowal has all but disappeared, there is effort to introduce young people who are 'straight' for each other and encourage them to become spouses. In a growing and significant number of cases, a young person chooses a partner who is the sibling of their opposite-sex sibling's partner.[16] Thus, a young man explained his marriage in these terms: 'I got her because my sister is married to her brother'. Another young man said, 'Her [his wife's] brother has my sister, see?' These marriages have the virtues of satisfying the rules as 'straight' and continuing the tradition of reciprocity (*puntaju*) between families in the provision of spouses. Also, they tend to be between young people from different communities and are seen to be strengthening ties between those, as the couples tend to spend time with each spouse's family. A middle-aged woman spoke approvingly of this practice, saying: 'It helps bring families closer together'.[17]

Although reported as common among related Aboriginal groups, such direct sister exchange is a form of marriage that departs from the Mardu conventions observed in the recent past. R. Tonkinson (1974: 49) reports that bilateral cross-cousin marriage was the norm, and that sister exchange was possible, but rare. A form of delayed reciprocity occurred whereby the 'sons' sons of a family, which gives one of its females in marriage, will eventually receive a wife from the recipients when circumstances permit' (R. Tonkinson 1991a: 64; see also Sackett 1976).[18] Perhaps what occurs now is an innovative modification of existing rules to permit young people to choose spouses rather than have them bestowed, while controlling the range of people from whom they may choose. By encouraging direct sister exchange in which the spouses have a say, families ensure reciprocity without enforcing arranged marriages. Moreover, one's spouse's sibling is almost certain to be a 'straight' spouse for oneself, so the result is two correct marriages that would satisfy the families' wishes.

The tactical use of church marriage to legitimize liaisons that do not conform to Mardu tradition is another innovation. While some young people who are affiliated with a church choose to have a church wedding, in other cases, people go through a church ceremony in order to make their choices legal under Australian law, even as they breach Mardu Law. There are also examples of people innovatively bending the kinship rules in order to make a 'wrong' relationship less offensive, but this tends to engender disapproval.

Teenage Pregnancy

Some ethnographers have argued that it would be limiting to perceive only negative outcomes of teenage parenthood. For example, Burton (1990) describes the 'accelerated family timetable' among some urban African-American families in the United States as 'an alternative life-course strategy', which is a rational response to conditions of poverty and inequality. In Australia, Pauline Fietz (personal communication) observed in another Western Desert community that teenage motherhood is a deliberate lifestyle choice often avidly aspired to by young women, as it enables access to the valued social role of childrearing. She suggests furthermore that for some young women, motherhood may be an exit strategy, enabling them to remove themselves legitimately, even if only temporarily, from the social pressure to engage in drinking, substance misuse, life in town camps and associated behaviours. Motherhood may also have integrative potential where young women have become alienated from their families, as it tends to strengthen ties of maternal relatedness as mothers, grandmothers and other female kin renew their involvement in the life of the young woman and her child. Similarly, Robinson (1995b: 260), while recognizing the difficulties involved, demonstrates that teenage motherhood among the Tiwi reflects continuities with patterns of 'female cooperation and interdependence in childrearing and domestic activity within the maternal collectivity'. There are several examples of this type of cooperation among Mardu women. However, the positives must be balanced against the negatives: for many mothers, grandmothers, sisters and other female and male relatives, the care of the children of their teenagers can be onerous, if they take it on, and worrying if they leave it to the natural parent(s). There are numerous examples of teenage mothers whose babies' health has been compromised by their behaviour during pregnancy or as mothers, or who are unable to care for one or more children. Not acting as primary carer for your child is also a departure from customary parenting that is deplored by some Mardu (*cf.* Lewis, this volume, who describes the same for certain Anangu families).

The rate of early teenage pregnancy has been rising. As noted above, in the past girls would be given in marriage to their older promised husbands around the onset of puberty. From this it might be assumed that motherhood commonly occurred at a young age; however, it is likely that menarche was reached later and fecundity was lower then than it is now (*see* Burbank 1988). Older Mardu claim that the prevalence of early-teen pregnancy we observe today is something new, and troubling; perhaps the change they are noting is that many young mothers are single, a condition unheard of in the past. It is important to consider also that teenage fatherhood is a relatively new phenomenon: in the past, the social role of pater was limited to fully initiated men, i.e., those in the region of thirty or more years of age, though a youth could have been the genitor.

In accord with Moisseeff's observation (this volume) that the capacity for, and recognition of, having children is paramount in attaining adult status in many non-Western contexts, many young Mardu of both genders appear keen to establish families of procreation. Despite the views of many of their elders, in today's circumstances becoming a parent is one of the few ways in which adulthood can be experienced and demonstrated by young Mardu, who leave school early, seldom gain enduring employment, and do not advance in ritual status. Parenthood is a respected role in Mardu culture and a young couple's elders tend to accept their marriage if they become parents. They can also gain some independence through supporting parents' benefits provided by the federal government. However, many young parents remain largely dependent on their own parents for shelter, childcare, and often money as well (as Brooks, this volume, also reports for the Ngaanyatjarra). While parenthood may be a route to adult status, and some young parents embrace responsibility, in a number of cases, young single mothers and some young married parents neglect or abandon their children in the knowledge that they will be cared for by other family members, often the infant's grandparents. One man, who with his wife is raising the child of their teenage granddaughter, told me: 'We can't leave him with her because she goes with her friends, playing, and forget[s] about him'. And a young grandmother said of her teenage daughter and son-in-law: 'They stay up late playing computer games … [so] they can't get up in the morning and I'm stuck looking after their kids'.

Today, reliable contraception is available but not taken up by all young women of childbearing age. There are many potentially detrimental consequences of teenage pregnancies and births. These cannot be examined in detail here, but include premature and low birth weight babies, who usually suffer lifelong vulnerability to a number of serious illnesses and social problems (*see* e.g., ICHR 2006).[19] The young mother's education usually ceases, if it had not already. Often, primary responsibility for the rearing of the child must be borne by grandparents or other relatives. Indeed, the fostering of children, typically by close relatives, is a common practice. Fosterage may be temporary or permanent, and nowadays the authorities are usually advised and parenting allowance paid to the foster parents. To varying degrees, the actual parents may continue to be involved with the child, who always knows who his or her actual parents are. Fosterage normally results when concerned relatives intervene, with the acquiescence, or at the request of, the parent(s) to take over the care of a child or children suffering, or at risk of, neglect.[20] The precipitating conditions include alcohol misuse by one or both parents, or the mother's chronic or acute illness, such as renal failure, that requires living away from their home communities for extensive periods, or indefinitely (*cf.* Sansom and Baines 1988). The prevalence of premature death has also contributed to an increase in fosterage. One consequence of the current pattern is that the models for parenting to which children are exposed include significant evidence that an offspring's biological parent(s) need not have sole or ultimate responsibility for the child's upbringing. This situation bestows advantages in that most children and young people have a number of adults on whom they can rely for care and support. However, it often also entails a high degree of uncertainty and instability in the lives of children.

Substance Misuse

While many senior adults disapprove, drinking alcohol is highly desirable in the eyes of many young people. The communities under Mardu control are all 'dry', that is, their councils impose penalties on anyone bringing alcohol into their areas. In a number of interviews, however, teenage Mardu listed drinking as one of the things they like or hope to do when they visit towns like Newman and Port Hedland. The young people associate alcohol consumption not only with adult status but also with celebration: getting 'sparked up' is desirable, a way to enjoy oneself, join in fun with others and escape tedium. However, many drinkers, including some young adults, are alcoholics who live in towns to ensure access to alcohol; they regularly drink large quantities of beer, port and premixed drinks based on spirits. These drinkers gather in groups, share drinks and typically consume all the available alcohol in a single sitting.[21] It is impossible to overstate the social nature of drinking. It is almost always a group activity in which drinks are shared, and there is considerable pressure on spouses and others to join with their drinking companions. While these events can be amicable, quite frequently there are adverse outcomes as people become drunk, speak offensively, engage in fights (*see below*), have sexual relations with inappropriate partners and so on. Such drunken behaviours are widely disparaged, even by some who indulge in it. By no means do all young people drink, and those who do may not necessarily become inebriated, but drinking for recreation and celebration is well established, and drinking to excess is the habit of a significant number of young (as well as older) people.

Collmann (1988: 149–68) argues persuasively that drinking behaviour among the Aboriginal people with whom he did research in Central Australia is an important aspect of exchange relationships; drinkers observe rules about sharing, generosity, social solidarity and other Aboriginal values. He also claims that drunkenness enables people to 'shed shame' and experience personal power (1988: 164–65; *see also* Brady 1992b). This has resonances with the situation prevailing among Mardu, including youth. Many people participate in conduct they characterize as dangerous, but the fact that they have seen examples of disastrous consequences does not seem to inhibit most drinkers. Some say they can stop any time they want. In interviews and conversations, alcohol is invariably mentioned as a source of trouble. As one man in his thirties put it, 'Alcohol is the number one problem' causing conflict, illness, death and disability.[22]

Cannabis, mostly called 'ganja', is also a popular drug used by Mardu youth; both male and female young people report smoking it (some older people also smoke ganja). Its calmative qualities are sometimes cited in opposition to the effects of alcohol – 'Ganja makes you feel relaxed', but there is ambivalence about its use. While some people see its effects as more benign than those of alcohol, other people blame it for violent or reckless behaviour in some users: 'Ganja makes them mad', one woman said. Petrol sniffing is not a major problem in any of the Mardu communities discussed here, but a few boys and young men do indulge in this practice. Few interviewees report having tried it, and there is consensus that it is dangerous, and suicide or *ngakumpa* (mental incapacity) are cited as evidence of its danger. Smoking is prevalent among young Mardu, and awareness about its potentially harmful effects is limited.

Violence

It is impossible to discuss the lives of young Mardu without considering violence.[23] Although there are communities noted for their tranquillity, violent events occur from time to time, sometimes with lethal consequences. Residents of remote places are occasionally involved in violent incidents when they spend time in towns where drunken fights are common. Although some people are particularly notorious for violent behaviour, no extended family is immune.

Children almost never experience violence from adults; as a rule, Mardu adults do not hit young children and, should such an act occur, the offending person is usually severely criticized or punished. However, young children are encouraged to express their anger physically, towards adults as well as their peers (*see also* Musharbash, this volume), and children observe violence between adults, if not in their own households then in others around them. The village-like living arrangements and the often public nature of violence ensure exposure, and discussion that children overhear or participate in. They learn from observation that fighting is a legitimate way to settle disputes, and that corporal punishment for wrongdoing is acceptable; for example, teenagers and adults are sometimes publicly beaten for a variety of serious infractions. It is noteworthy, however, that young Mardu are not inured to conflict and violence. While fighting is common, it was often mentioned by young people when they were asked what things make them sad – only the deaths of loved ones was more frequently cited.

As noted earlier, when people drink, they tend to do so in small groups of individuals who are related or know one another well, and it is common for arguments and fights to occur within such groups when individuals are drunk, sometimes over the distribution of the drinks (*cf.* Collmann 1988: 168–204). The Mardu case has other resonances with elements of Collmann's analysis, in that violence is a legitimate way of resolving conflict. It usually takes place between adults, and its incidence is high among members who share residence and domestic resources, with male-female violence being common. Certainly, there are conflicts over resources (money, liquor, secret knowledge) and over issues of autonomy, between men and women or between older and younger family members. However, the violence that occurs among young Mardu cannot adequately be explained neatly as the outcome of threatened or ruptured exchange-based relationships. Rather, it has many and complex origins and meanings that might include the kind of moral justification that Sansom (1980) reports, in which perpetrators of violence claim an obligation to act to remedy wrongs. Another important aspect of violence among Mardu accords with Myers's (1988a) description of Pintupi acts of violence in which both anger and compassion are implicated.[24]

Fights between spouses or lovers are common, with jealousy as a major precipitator. There are numerous accounts of 'jealousing' between men and women, and these arguments sometimes result in violence, especially if one, or both, partner(s) is drunk. There are also examples of men lashing out at women who have been baiting them in an effort to provoke jealousy. Striking with fists or with clubs and other weapons occurs frequently, and stabbing with knives, screwdrivers and other weapons has become alarmingly common. One teenage woman, explaining that she had broken up with her boyfriend, generalized about the behaviour of young men like him: 'He'll get jealous for you. Come to town and give you hiding. I don't know how … Some people follow their father. When they was young they been see from their parents' (as children they saw their behaviour and adopted it). Other girls and young women also complained about violence by their boyfriends. One said she left the father of her baby because he would go off with his friends returning drunk and violent: 'Start fighting with me, I fight right back … You got to learn to fight back. You can't just let a man hit us one side. You got to fight back somehow … Can't just let ourselves get busted up'. Yet a degree of tolerance for violence prevails. Some incidents are treated with wry humour, including comments such as 'that was a love fight'. While violent conflict is not limited to young people, its incidence among them is high. Many have been arrested and charged, and some, more males than females, are repeat offenders (*cf.* Brooks, this volume). Although it is culturally acceptable for women to fight, they often fare badly in fights with men. Over many years, there have been numerous deaths and disabling injuries, with female victims disproportionately greater than male. Sometimes, families try to encourage women to leave their violent spouses, often to no avail. Yet, there are also cases in which families, especially mothers, defend their violent sons, and some in which an abused woman is afraid to leave her partner for fear of criticism or even violent retaliation from her in-laws. Some comments from young women indicate changing attitudes. Regarding an age-mate who had left her abusive husband, a young woman remarked, 'She's free now, she can start a new life'. Another said of a young man who is in prison for violent attacks on his partner: 'He *should* be in jail, he's cruel one, too rough'.

Feuding, which is reported among a number of Aboriginal groups across Australia, is not a feature of Mardu society, although fights between groups of young men from different families occur from time to time and sometimes lead to intervention by parents, siblings and other supporters, of both genders, on either side, and a tit-for-tat series of confrontations ensues.

The incidence of self-harm appears to be increasing among young adults and adolescents. Both sexes engage in it, but the forms it takes among young men is usually more lethal than those practised by young women. Some young women cut slashes along the inner surface of their forearms; this is the most commonly visible form of self-harm, but some burn themselves on the hand or arm with cigarettes. Young women have also been reported to have threatened suicide, but I know of only one case where it can be argued that a young woman's death, in a car accident, might have been a deliberate act. Young male Mardu tend to use more violent means, such as stabbing, hanging, shooting or setting fire to themselves. Young men sometimes drive cars dangerously around settlements when they are angry. This is a recognized way of expressing anger, though it is viewed with disapprobation especially because the behaviour endangers not only the driver but children and others who might get in the way. In one recent case, a young man died after driving at high speed after an argument.[25] Such acts tend to occur during or after arguments with a spouse or lover; death has sometimes been the result, although not all have been intentional suicides. Self-harm can be the result not only of rage but also of grief. The following remarks by a young man indicate the kind of thinking that might lead to this: 'When people you love die, they stay in your head, but you try not to think about them too much. You tell yourself you can handle it and move on with your life; otherwise you might get stupid and go and kill yourself, follow your lost [loved ones]'.

Conclusions

My recent research, set against the background of earlier fieldwork, provides considerable evidence that young people, along with the entire Mardu population, are experiencing a variety of pressures resulting from both change and resistance to change. Young people are particularly affected, not least because there are increasing external expectations, from government and a variety of commentators, that they should participate in education and the workforce and embrace 'Australian values'. These young people, while having their Mardu identity firmly grounded, are subject to pressures that engender conflicting feelings and behaviours. Mardu youth who are confident of relating to the wider Mardu society seem less troubled by feelings of isolation from their communities/families than the young Navajo described by Dole and Csordas (2003). They have learned to navigate adequately aspects of Australian society, but cannot be said to be at home there; they participate in global youth culture, but their horizons remain narrow, bound to a principally Mardu universe where familiarity and connectedness afford them self-assurance.[26]

Having surveyed some of the current experiences, conditions, behaviours, beliefs and attitudes of young Mardu, it is difficult to draw definitive conclusions, but it is possible to speculate on some trends and their possible effects, and several lines along which further research can be conducted. Young Mardu today, while identifying strongly with their ancestral culture and heritage, are increasingly participating in a broader sociocultural milieu that embraces aspects of Australian and global ideas, values and behaviours. They appear to be partial members of parallel worlds: fully Mardu in their beliefs and values, yet not in their day-to-day practice; more comfortable than their elders in the non-Mardu world, yet far from fully conversant with it or at home in it. I have focused here on three areas – marriage and sexuality, substance use and violence – in which young Mardu encounter challenges as they attempt to realize adulthood informed by both Mardu and Australian ideas and values that are, to a considerable extent, conflicting or contradictory.

Young people are faced with conditions for which their elders have not developed clear norms and values, and they are influenced by the wider Australian and global culture, but insufficiently familiar with the underpinning assumptions, strategies and techniques to ensure success. Thus, for example, parents send their children to school because they have been told it is a requirement and that it is a good thing, but although those parents went to school themselves, their experience, in school and subsequently, provided no compelling aspirations for themselves or their children. Parents, even when they encourage school attendance, can provide virtually no meaningful support for those children as models for studious behaviour, tutors to aid their school-based learning or enforcers of rules and behaviours that reinforce or complement those of school. In other areas, such as drinking, handling motor vehicles or gambling, the absence of information and constructive models from older people often leaves adolescents and young adults either devising their own norms, which may or may not be effective, or replicating hazardous or inappropriate practices.

Values based on the hunter-gatherer experience militate against accumulation and delayed consumption of material resources, and against sacrificing immediate returns in anticipation of greater future rewards. I do not mean that Mardu, or Western Desert people more generally, are incapable of planning and preparing for the future – their ceremonial life is replete with examples of just this. Rather, their future orientation is of a sort that has not tended to motivate them to save, endure the rigours of school, engage in seemingly unrewarding work and so on.

The behaviours that adolescent and young adult Mardu engage in are often potentially harmful, and I have raised the possibility that an absence of the kind of future orientation characteristic of Australians in general may be a reason young Mardu tend to indulge in risky behaviours to a greater extent than their mainstream Australian peers. The rates of mortality, morbidity, disability and teen pregnancy and its hazards, both for the resulting children and their mothers, are challenges that confront young Mardu in ways that their predecessors did not experience. At the same time, young Mardu are largely unable to avail themselves of the resources, privileges and supports that many of their Australian (and global) peers take for granted. Being Mardu today means performing identity, personhood and relationships in ways that differ sharply from those of earlier generations. Among the changes is what might match Austin-Broos's notion of an emergent ethnic identity. Whether this changing identity will assist them to gain a secure foothold in Australian society and transcend the daunting pressures which they currently confront is impossible to predict. However, I would like to think that the Mardu capacity to endure hardship, to innovate and to be resilient, which is prodigious, will ultimately enable younger Mardu to forge new and rewarding paths to fulfilment in the greatly changed world they inhabit.

Notes

This research project was funded by ARC Discovery Grant 35012000. Eight months' fieldwork was conducted in two remote communities and a regional town in short seasons between 2002 and 2005. The research was done collaboratively with Bob Tonkinson, who has made his data available to me for this paper. I began anthropological research among the Mardu in 1974, aided by grants from the Australian Institute of Aboriginal and Torres Strait Islander Studies in 1974 and 1978.

I am grateful to Ute Eickelkamp, Victoria Burbank, Bob Tonkinson and Pauline Fietz for valuable comments on earlier drafts of this paper; any remaining faults are entirely my responsibility. Thanks to Brooke Scelza for interviews she conducted on my behalf with young people at Parnngurr. My heartfelt appreciation goes to the Mardu people of the East Pilbara, and elsewhere, for hosting my research, and for their willingness to share their knowledge, experiences and views with me. Special thanks to Patricia Fry Burungu for her passionate commitment to Mardu culture and traditions, and her keen insight.

1. There is also scholarly examination of the cultural contrasts perceived by Aborigines and other lay observers. Austin-Broos (1996) reviews the extensive Australian Aboriginal anthropological literature on what she labels 'two laws talk'; she posits the emergence of new identities among Aboriginal people (in particular, the Aranda people whose case she presents) stemming from their experience of transformations in their society. Austin-Broos's argument that this new identity can be conceived of as constituting an ethnicity, not just affiliation based on descent, may well apply to what appears to be occurring among younger Mardu people.

2. Dole and Csordas (2003) make many observations about Navajo youth that resonate with those I offer here about Mardu. In particular, they point to the differences between young Navajo and their elders regarding the extent to which 'tradition' is observed by the former, and worries among the latter about the cultural competence of youth. Importantly, however, Mardu youth tend not to distance themselves from 'tradition' or objectify it as 'things'/'stuff' as Dole and Csordas say Navajo youth do; rather, most express respect, even awe for their 'Law'.

3. It is tempting to speculate that these changes and challenges introduce uncertainty and insecurity that might account, in part at least, for the high level of risk-taking behaviour that occurs among young Mardu. The rate of accidents, self-harm and substance misuse among Mardu is of catastrophic proportions.

4. Mardu see themselves as a unified and distinct population, as opposed to all others: non-Mardu Aboriginal people, and more saliently today, to 'Whitefellas', their generic label, not only for Australians of European ancestry, but for non-Aboriginal Australians more generally (*see* M. Tonkinson 1990). I use the term *mainstream* as a kind of shorthand to denote the greater Australian population, fully aware of the limitations of such a designation. Australian society is complex and diverse, and homogeneous labels obscure this; Mardu are not homogeneous either, of course, although they are more readily classified as a group in terms of socioeconomic status and several other social indicators.

5. The adoption of Aboriginality by Mardu illustrates some of the complexity of changing identities. Mardu sometimes contrast themselves with coastal Pilbara Aborigines, such as Yamatji, or with urban Nyungars they encounter in Perth, but they also find models among non-Mardu Aboriginal people, for example, the incorporation of the Aboriginal flag and colours in dress and displays or the elaboration of funeral practices drawing lessons from Nyungars.

6. Sutton (2009) has commented on acute shyness among some young Aboriginal people today, in contrast with earlier generations. In my view, this is a symptom of awareness of difference as inequality.

7. Mardu take a keen interest in language differences. Older people distinguish Marduwangka from the dialect they speak or used to speak; they point out that children are speaking a variety that is a mixture of dialects of the Western Desert

language. In addition, people of all ages use some English in their speech, and this tendency is more marked among younger Mardu. Neologisms in which English words are modified to conform to Mardu grammar, for example, are widely used.

8. This was a consequence of a change in government policy, in recognition of the fact that large aggregations of people in missions and settlements had had unintended negative, sometimes catastrophic, consequences. The shift from small bands of closely related families, moving over large tracts of land, to sedentary populations of hundreds of people, often unrelated and sometimes even speaking different languages, resulted in tensions and conflicts. Furthermore, the economic life of the inmates of such settlements was radically changed; their hunting and gathering activities were curtailed and the available work, such as on pastoral properties, was not enough to occupy the majority of adults, so idleness and boredom became entrenched, with many adverse consequences. In the late 1970s, the 'outstation movement' was encouraged as it was thought that permitting people to return to their ancestral lands, live in smaller family-based groups and engage in their traditional economic and cultural activities would result in an improvement of their lives and a reduction of the problems they and their custodians faced. As is well known, the results have been far from an unqualified success.

9. While there is a sizeable Mardu population permanently settled in Newman, and the people living there designate it as their home base, no ceremonial life occurs there. Mardu residents speak of Jigalong as 'country' where they have strong ties, visit often and expect to be buried.

10. The Mardu certainly see themselves as belonging to a separate category from 'Whitefellas' but, for them, the latter category includes not only White people but a variety of other non-Mardu, including people who may identify themselves as Aboriginal. While the latter are of mixed descent, it is not a simple question of colour: The Mardu also use the label *martamarta* in their own language (or 'half-caste'), or sometimes 'Whitefella/*mijiji* (White woman) for a category of urban Aboriginal people distinguishable by colour, behaviour, status, etc., but Mardu of mixed descent are never included in the non-Mardu category (*see* M. Tonkinson 1990).

11. To some extent, this may be explained in terms of noncongruent schemas that underpin practices of learning. Strauss and Quinn (1994) define schemas as 'the generic versions of experience that remain in memory'; these 'learned prototypes' mediate our experience of the external world. It appears that in the schemas of most Mardu children and adults, school lacks strong positive emotional associations while not necessarily having negative associations.

12. It is important to note here that while some young people, and a few older Mardu as well, claim to be Christians, their knowledge of Christian theology and tradition is shallow, at best. Some Mardu claim that the Christian God (*Mama*) also gave Mardu their 'Law' and therefore there is no real conflict between that Law and Christianity. Church services are irregular, and participation in them is derisory. Funerals are frequent and almost always involve one or more Christian ministers; they are well attended. Christian weddings are rare and attract little attention or attendance by Mardu.

13. A number of North American researchers have noted that among poor and marginalized young people, there is a relatively high prevalence of risky behaviours including smoking, the use of alcohol and illicit drugs, accidents, suicide, violence and teenage parenting, with consequences for life expectancy, morbidity, etc. (see e.g., Dryfoos 1998; Moore 1995, especially the chapters by Burton, Lewis and Ooms; Wilson and Daly 1997). These and other social scientists suggest that the tendency to indulge in such behaviours is a consequence of limited options for attaining adult status and therefore limited expectations for the future (see also Aronowitz 2005). While conditions in Australia do not match exactly those described for the United States and Canada, and my data for the Mardu are only anecdotal, my observation that these high-risk behaviours are common among them is supported by available epidemiological findings for the larger Aboriginal population (e.g., ICHR 2006).

14. Because Mardu rarely contract legal marriages according to Australian law, most unions would be classified as de facto. Although strict Mardu rules regarding marriage do exist, they are frequently flouted. The term *nyupa* (spouse) is applied only in cases that meet these rules.

15. While people continue to cling to the ideal of correct marriages, there is high incidence of irregular marriages in adults of the generation who married since the late 1960s and 1970s. When such unions produce children, this results in embarrassment and confusion over which social category to assign them to. There are degrees of wrong relationship, and the more egregious breaches attract criticism and scorn and engender shame in the offenders.

16. Here, siblings include the children of same-sex siblings.

17. Similarly, Frances Morphy (2006: 27) observes that '[m]arriage in the Aboriginal system does not create bonds of kinship: it reinforces and reaffirms already existing kin relationships'.

18. While there is a strong notion of families 'exchanging' wives, the situation among the Mardu is not the direct sister exchange reported by (Radcliffe) Brown for the Kariera (1913: 156). As Laurent Dousset (personal communication) suggests: 'The terminology does allow for close cross-cousin marriage such as mMBD, mFZD, fMBS, fFZS, [but] … because it is allowed in the terminology [does not mean] that it actually happened … the "system" does allow for it, but is very unusual. Western Desert alliance strategies tend rather to marry distant cross-cousins … and people still try to marry "long way" so as to establish access to distant resources'.

19. In its report on a comprehensive survey of Aboriginal children's health in Western Australia, the Telethon Institute for Child Health Research states that low birth weight affects over 11 per cent of Aboriginal babies in the state, which is double the rate for the population at large. The Report points out that '[l]ow birth weight infants are more likely to have health problems than infants of normal birth and more likely to develop chronic diseases in adult life' (2006: 107). This claim has been well demonstrated in a number of international studies conducted in recent years (see Kuzawa 2008).

20. It is worth noting, however, that Mardu have a system that permits a relative to lay claim to a child and become its parent with the approval of the biological parents.

21. In addition to other sources cited, Brady (1992b); Gray and Saggers (2002) and Saggers and Gray (1998) provide useful, relevant descriptions of patterns of alcohol consumption among Aboriginal people.

22. A recent report reveals that alcohol-related deaths among Aboriginal Australians occur at a staggering rate. The figures suggest that there has been an increase in alcohol consumption overall, and that its prevalence among women is steadily approaching that among men (Chikritzs et al. 2007). For an anthropological interpretation of drinking and related social problems in a northern Aboriginal community *see* McKnight 2002.

23. Indeed, violence is a feature of many, if not most remote Aboriginal communities (*see* e.g., Burbank 1994; Robinson 1995a). It is also, as Brooks (this volume) explains, part of longstanding cultural traditions, although prevalence varies.

24. Robinson's (1995b) argument that the conventions of nonstate regulatory systems like those of the Tiwi and the Mardu are incompatible with state regulatory systems and have eroded in the colonial context, exacerbated by the availability of alcohol, is also apposite.

25. Burbank includes fast driving of vehicles in the category of behaviour resulting from anger that she labels 'aggressive displays' (1985: 48–50), in which property may be destroyed or damaged or other acts committed against things rather than persons.

26. Note however, that young people are very sensitive about exclusion. Threats to their dignity from perceived rejection by family/kin/friends sometimes engender violent responses, including self-harm.

CHAPTER 10

Invisible and Visible Loyalties in Racialized Contexts

A Systemic Perspective on Aboriginal Youth

Marika Moisseeff

We heard quite late that the funeral would take place the following day in Coober Pedy. Having left Port Augusta soon after, we arrived in the middle of the night at the mourners' house. After solemnly shaking hands with everyone as is expected on such occasions, one old man held on to my hand saying: 'Who the hell are you?' Indeed I was the only non-Aboriginal person present, and obviously a foreigner. It would have been quite embarrassing to explain then and there that I was an anthropologist and so forth, and so I just answered, 'I am a half-caste Jew!' The man burst out laughing, joined by others, and nobody asked me again, that night, who I was. Of course, nobody could pretend they now knew who I was, but in using this condensed formula one might think that I had conveyed who I was at that very moment: someone trying to clarify her identity problems while undertaking an anthropological study among people having not the same problems as I, but related ones.

Adopting a systemic perspective, I want to propose the following two-fold argument: in Central Australian Aboriginal societies, well-established cultural forms of individuation rely on two functions, the female nurturing and the male filiative. The crucial shift from nurture to filiation – distancing from maternal influence while forging new social ties – that underlies the process of constructing adult identity has been thwarted in the course of colonization and through ongoing racial discrimination within a system of welfare dependency. For Aboriginal people, nurture and filiation have merged into one. Having been divested of their parental roles and treated as a society of children, Aboriginal people's capacity to assume a filiative function by providing viable role models for younger generations has been undermined. Under these conditions, Aboriginal youths, and more especially young men, struggle to demonstrate their allegiance to the Aboriginal community and to attain a degree of autonomy on their

own. Often, paradoxically, this takes the form of self-destructive practices. In this chapter I consider the pervasive effects of what has been from
the beginning a hierarchical encounter between two 'racialized' cultural
groups on the experience of Aboriginality during the formative years of
adolescence and young adulthood.

My approach is based on anthropological field research since 1991
with Aboriginal families in urban and rural milieus in South Australia
that have strong links with communities in the centre, on the classic
ethnographies of Central Australian Aboriginal societies and on my clinical experience as a psychiatrist having worked as a family therapist in
France for over twenty years. Like Gary Robinson (1992a, 1992b), I am
convinced that the difficulties that many young Aboriginal people share
with other colonized Indigenous groups and marginalized ethnic minori-
ties can be better understood in their specificity if they are approached
through the analysis of individual and family itineraries. Disclosing personal material, however, raises ethical issues of confidentiality. While
I have changed people's names, in this case, doing so is certainly not
enough to guarantee the anonymity of those concerned. In order to
lessen the concerned persons' possible impression of being treated as
objects under the distancing lens of the scientific eye, I will try to relate
the particularities of Aboriginal cultural ethos to that which is usually
implicit in descriptions of Aboriginal societies, namely, certain overrid-
ing ideological tenets of contemporary Western society. I will share some
of my own experiences as a French person of mixed origin, and make
reference to personal dilemmas of identity drawn from other, equally
complicated cultural contexts.

Childhood Memories in Special Cultural Contexts

A young person has first been a child, and as such may have already
experienced discrimination, either towards him/herself or towards members of his/her family, especially if he/she lives in a mixed social environment. This is sure to affect how he/she enters into adulthood. Consider
the following example.

Peter, an Aboriginal friend, was raised on a settlement taken over by
a mission and where the use of Aboriginal language had been banned.
He remembered how, at the beginning of the 1960s when he was a young
child of about four years of age, he had met up with the missionary, a
tall White man, and had happily greeted him using the local language.
The man's face blushed deep red and he rushed angrily after the boy.
Peter, not grasping what was happening, was terrified. While running

away, he looked back at his mother, searching her face for some sort of understanding and support. At that moment he discovered the reality of being an Aboriginal child; although looking directly at him, she made no move to protect him. Indeed, if she had tried to stop the missionary, the situation could have turned out very badly, the worst case being that she could have had her child taken away from her. This scene epitomizes the relational context of interactions between Aboriginal and non-Aboriginal people at the time, a context which Aboriginal children were made aware of from very early on. In those days, Aboriginal adults and parents were themselves treated as big children placed under the guardianship of State Aboriginal Affairs Boards. They could not travel outside the settlement premises without a permit, and their activities and expenses were closely supervised. And above all, what is until today felt to have been the most powerful factor in the altering of their culture, they were not granted full responsibility for their children's upbringing and ran the constant risk of being stripped of their parental role, as has been the case for other Indigenous peoples (see e.g., Hughes 1987). This is the lesson learned all through childhood by Aboriginal children of that generation living on missions or reserves. It made them fully aware of the inferior position they would be led to occupy as a grown up person of Aboriginal descent in a White man's world.

Peter was a mature man when he told me his story. However, this baffling encounter with the missionary remained very vivid in his mind, as it most probably was at the time he became an adult. In internalizing this type of interaction, he learned to see himself from an outside, White-fella perspective. Such internalization implies identification with each of the parties involved: his own position as a helpless infant, that of his powerless Aboriginal mother, and that of the powerful and domineering White man. Here, three types of hierarchical relationship – adult/child, man/woman and White/Black – are condensed into one, such that the missionary, who wields power over the other two parties, appears as the only adult in the scene. The Aboriginal mother, like the Aboriginal people as a whole, is situated at the same level as her child, and indeed, Aboriginal mothers were under the authority of White men who defined the law within Australia and had the right to manage Aboriginal life and relationships. At the time, relationships between men and women in general were unequal, if in different ways, among Aboriginal people and in the rest of Australian society.[1] However, Aboriginal men were relegated to a highly peculiar position: on the one hand, they were held by the White society to be inferior to White men and in this respect were located on the same level as women – White or Black, but usually at a position lower than White women; on the other hand, they were placed on the same level as children. It is usual for a child to want to grow up fast in order to do the prestigious and important things that only adults are free to do. But in these special conditions, one may expect that growing up and becoming an adult is considerably less desirable, especially for boys, a point I will return to.

As the Afro-American writer Toi Derricotte has noted: 'racism's most damaging insult is internal, to "self" as perception' (1997: 20). And it is precisely because racism is internalized through repeated experiences of awkward relational situations that, for the victims, it cannot be thought as something 'out there' that one can set aside in order to consider or resolve. In short, it is incorporated (Bourdieu 1980) and, as Derricotte suggests, should be understood as a 'form of child abuse' (1997: 17). Derricotte is Black but because her light skin colouring allows her to pass for White, she is constantly wondering if what is happening to her is due to the fact that people believe she is White, or if it is because they know she is Black. Consequently, she is continually questioning herself about what to do: should she claim her Blackness or let it ride? Throughout her book, she constantly articulates her childhood memories and her family and community histories with her adult life and the difficult personal choices the latter entails regarding the assertion of her identity. A 're-creation and revision of the self', which for Derricotte took the form of writing a book about her experiences of racism and their consequences on the most intimate parts of her life, was, in spite of the overwhelming feelings of shame it occasioned, a necessary process. Without it, she would not have been able to make sense of these experiences and to free herself from feelings of depression: 'I have come to realize that we negotiate a very complicated reality, and that we do the best we can, and that there is no perfect past to go back to. It is at this point of understanding that I think we develop compassion for ourselves and each other' (1997: 202).

Peter's experience, both as a child and as an adult, shows certain similarities with hers. His ability to disclose painful memories with grace and generosity bears witness to his self-reflexivity: he also knows *there is no perfect past to go back to,* and has learnt to negotiate the highly complex reality in which he has been living. Like a number of other Aboriginal people I met during my fieldwork, Peter was a successful person, with a permanent job in the public sector where he acted for his own Aboriginal community from which he had never parted. At the same time, he had been able to develop good relationships within the non-Aboriginal community of his country town. However, as for Derricotte, this exceptional achievement – a balancing act between two worlds – can never be taken for granted. It is the result of an ongoing and at times agonizing endeavour. Yet this still in no way guarantees immunity from stressful experiences, and a positive outcome is never definitively assured, either for oneself or, even less so, for one's children who will have to bear the consequences of their parent's success or failure.

The Importance of Being a 'Loration'

We were heading to Ceduna to attend yet another funeral. Helen, who was driving, had generously offered me the desirable front seat next to her, which her youngest daughter, Madalynn, was usually entitled to. Madalynn reluctantly complied, but after a while started to whine. Finally, she used what, for her, was probably a clinching argument: why was I to be favoured like this when 'she is not even our loration' [*sic*]? Her mother, aunt and uncle, embarrassed for me, burst out laughing: 'She is your auntie Marika!' Of course, Madalynn meant to say 'relation' and since that time I have remained the family's French 'loration'. My peculiar status within the community where I was doing my fieldwork had already raised questions among the youngest children. Some asked me how it was that while everybody was related to everybody else in the community, I was the only one who was not. It looked as though I was sharing everything else but kin relations. Didn't I feel lonely to be the only one of my kind? To diminish the loneliness I was supposed to be feeling when my husband was away, adults offered to send me their children for company at night. One of the teenagers with whom I worked closely considered me to be the first and only 'friend' she had ever had. She told me that this made her realize that only White people may have or may become 'friends', that is, close persons who are not kinsmen: 'You see, we [Aboriginal people] have no friends because we are all relatives'. And indeed, even when Aboriginal people from distant communities meet, in my experience they usually try to trace their connection through their in-laws or other relatives. Section and moiety systems have also been used in this way, to offer a kinship position to an Aboriginal stranger from another community. Aboriginal kinship systems are classificatory and founded upon the interrelationship of sibling sets both within and between generations. In such a cultural setting, family ties mediate the individual's insertion within the complex network of relationships between extended families, between various 'tribal'[2] groups and between the Aboriginal and non-Aboriginal communities.

It is the emphasis Aboriginal people place on being part of a family and community network and the consequences this has on individuals' strategies for working out their identity within the society at large that I want to address next.

Racism Continues

One might consider that Peter's unfortunate experience, now that he is an adult and not a helpless child, belongs to the past, his own personal past and his country's historical past: missionaries or superintendents do not manage Aborigines' lives as they did before. However, the hierarchical relationship between the two cultural groups in question persists because they continue to be assessed in terms of their respective places on the sociocultural evolutionary ladder. In this now unofficial, yet still lingering scheme, the one, the so-called 'native' of Australia, supposedly belongs to a primitive, stone-age culture and lags 'behind', whereas the other, as part of European, Anglo-Celtic 'civilization', is presumed to represent the apex of sociocultural achievement (Moisseeff 1999b, 2005). From this ideological viewpoint, the coexistence of these two groups on the same land has always been problematic: they are alleged to belong to different eras – the one set in a prehistoric past, the other heading towards a highly sophisticated technological future – and yet they are copresent. Within this pervasive, all-too-often overlooked ideological framework, cultural differences – those between 'primitive' populations of the New World, the Pacific and 'deepest' Africa on the one hand, and their 'evolved' Western ex-colonizers on the other – are biologically grounded. Consequently, and while nowadays this is usually not openly discussed as such, the cultural differences between these two types of societies may still be presumed to be connected to distinctive essences, all the more so that these differences tend to be correlated with visible morphological disparities such as skin colour or other physical features. Indeed, the cultural specificities of Aboriginal people are easily linked to morphological characteristics which in turn, in keeping with a widely internalized neo-Darwinian perspective, are related to biological (DNA-related) inferiority: they don't look the same as 'us', their culture is primitive compared to 'ours', and therefore they are, by essence, behind 'us'.[3] The dramatic consequences of this type of reasoning for Indigenous peoples are well known: segregation either to protect them from the damaging influence of civilization, and/or letting them die out so as to leave place for those who are more evolved and better fitted to the modern world. The alternative has been to try to help them to progressively attain 'our' level of development. In short, if they want to live with us, they have to assimilate, that is, to disappear as a distinct cultural and ethnic group.[4] This 'is clearly illustrated by an address by South Australia's Governor Hindmarsh (1785–1860) to the natives of that state: "Black Men, … you cannot be happy unless you imitate white men. Build huts, wear clothes, work and be useful. Love white men … Learn to speak English"' (Behrendt 1994: 69).

To the puzzled amazement of many Westerners, cultural groups all over the world who have been discriminated against because they were considered inferior have resisted assimilation. Why is it, some Westerners have asked, that when they are offered the possibility of attaining a higher level on the evolutionary scale, they are so reluctant? This perplexity reveals the difficulty people from the dominant Western culture have in recognizing the all-important role of kinship ties and relatedness as the grounds for the construction of personal and collective identities. Such a lack of comprehension is illustrated by the views of an Australian physician I once heard on Australia's national ABC radio. She had strongly encouraged a very bright young Aboriginal woman she had met in Sydney's Redfern to leave her community behind in order to fulfil her potential. To her surprise, the young woman refused and gave her to understand that this was not an option. Bewildered, the physician sadly concluded, 'You see, it's simply not their ways'. In order to make sense of this vignette, it is necessary to accept the fact that individuals are not simple physical entities able to graft their bodies onto another cultural 'phylum', stripping themselves of the ties to family and community through which the elements from which they constitute their identity are transmitted. They are above all relational beings within a social fabric based on kinship.

Between Relational Being and Stereotypes

I felt that a number of the Aboriginal children and youths I met in the town of Port Augusta clearly had the potential to pursue a successful career in sport, dance or fashion. When I asked them why they didn't try, they explained that they simply could not envisage leaving their family behind in order to join a world they did not belong to. It would be too hard, they said; they would continuously miss their relatives. This sense of relational belonging goes together with a strong attachment to 'country', that is, those places each Aboriginal person feels personally affiliated with through his/her family ties (Moisseeff 1999a). Travelling all over Australia with members of the community is highly enjoyable. But going to Adelaide, Canberra, Sydney or elsewhere in order to study or work in isolation from the family means estrangement from the community and to be on shaky ground.

In all cultural settings, the reworking of family ties plays a dominant role in the process underlying the achievement of adult identity because the latter implies gaining autonomy from one's parents. It is necessary to distance oneself from one's first intimates in order to become intimate with those who were, until then, more distant others (friends, sexual partners and/or spouses, in-laws and so forth). In contemporary Western societies, the substitution of first intimates by new ones is linked to the ability to develop friendship among peers during childhood and later on. An individual is expected to choose among those he/she associates with within the education system, in leisure activities, at work and in the neighbourhood. The latter settings are not supposed to correspond to a person's kinship network. Rather, friends are the people one chooses to become close to in addition to or in place of family intimates; as a rule, they are therefore at a certain remove from the family of origin. And the network of relationships an individual builds up in this way contributes to his/her integration within society at large. It determines his/her adult identity in relational terms and underlies the singular nature of this identity.

In the Aboriginal communities where I have done fieldwork, the process of growing up comprises a constant reworking of a network of relationships by choosing whom to be close to from among the different sets of siblings at different generational levels. This process continues throughout a person's life (see Myers, this volume). Everybody is expected to make relational choices according to whom they feel themselves to be; this is an important 'business', to be pursued in an assertive fashion. An individual's sense of personal relatedness is not supposed to correspond exactly to that of his/her parents, siblings or other relatives. Thus, from a very early age, everyone is urged to constitute his/her social network in an egocentric way and to bear responsibility for it. In case of conflicts, one has to decide for oneself whom to give support to or not. I remember how impatient and ill-at-ease people were when, placed in difficult situations, I would ask them what I was supposed to do: 'Do what you want, Marika!' Once my indecisiveness led one of my best friends to become so angry as to be on the verge of hitting me. 'You are a sook, Marika!' he exclaimed. Indeed, to be a respectful person, that is, from an Aboriginal perspective, to be a real human being, is to decide for oneself. I thus had to learn to choose, for different situations, on what grounds I wanted to stand, having been taught that there would always be people to back me up, others who would fight against me and still others who would refuse to take sides. However, they could only intervene, in one way or another, once I had taken the first step; nobody could do it for me or even speak on my behalf. While I had to learn such Aboriginal ways as an adult, Aboriginal people, of course, had learned them within the communities they had grown up in, through their experiences with various family members. In this sense, Aboriginal culture places a strong emphasis on individual autonomy (see Myers 1986; Brady 1992a; Martin 1993). However, this autonomy is acquired through the reworking of family ties. The situation is not the same for non-Aboriginal people, most of whom are expected to build their social network outside the family and beyond the web of kinship. In both cases, achieving adulthood implies gaining some sort of autonomy from parents. But for most Aboriginal people, this does not entail substituting strangers (friends) for relatives. Instead, family ties remain the building blocks of an Aboriginal person's adult identity; while he/she may develop other types of relationship outside the Aboriginal community, connection to it and with a person's Aboriginality rely heavily on the kinship network of parental affiliations (*see also* Barwick 1964).

Children raised in an Aboriginal community learn to adopt Aboriginal relational patterns appropriate to different situations as a function of the degree of closeness they have or wish to develop with such and such a person. In doing so they internalize a specifically Aboriginal ethos which entails behavioural rules for different ways of expressing emotions in a variety of relational contexts. The people I worked with, for example, distinguished between 'domestic' and 'public' settings. The former entail sharing a place on a daily-life basis and implies intimate interpersonal knowledge; in this case, expressing anger is a way of allowing distanced relationships to become closer. The latter pertain to more impersonal contexts, such as a political meeting; here, showing anger is a strategy for claiming a distinct collective identity. Another example relates to crying: while looked favourably upon in circumstances of public mourning, it is considered inappropriate as an overt expression of everyday personal distress. Such emotional grounding of social requirements shapes children's ideas of what it means to be an Aboriginal person in an Aboriginal setting (*see also* Andrews 2008).

However, because Aboriginal culture is embedded in a dominant non-Aboriginal culture, children are at the same time learning what it means to be an Aborigine within this wider framework. As Peter's story in the previous section showed, this latter learning process is grounded in encounters with non-Aboriginal people. It is also founded upon an awareness of such encounters as transmitted across time and by more distant relatives as well as by non-Aboriginal media (at school, on television, etc.). In this way, a child forms another idea of what it means to be an Aboriginal person, including being assigned a racialized, collective identity by the dominant, White social environment. Within the Aboriginal social network, which encourages speaking and acting for oneself as an individual, social identity is highly distinctive and differential. This stands in striking contrast to the other understanding of his/her identity that he/she has also been integrating while growing up, namely an externally assigned, depreciatory one in which personal identity is subsumed by non-Aboriginal stereotypes of what an Aborigine is supposed to be.

These stereotypes are fairly diverse; they may be extremely negative ('They are all drunken lazy bastards'), empathetic yet patronizing (Aborigines as the helpless victims of colonization), founded on selective, visible cultural traits supposed to characterize Aboriginal culture as a whole (dot paintings, didgeridoo, etc.), and so forth. However, these stereotypes also have a number of communalities. First, they all postulate a broad, general definition of Aboriginality in which an Aboriginal person's identity is gauged through the lens of an evolutionist ideology. Second, none of them is able to account for the extremely sophisticated Aboriginal ethos that allows Aboriginal people to be evaluated both as distinctive individualities and as relational beings. And finally, for Aboriginal youths in the course of becoming adults, they cannot be ignored.

Having to Choose and the Hazards of Cultural Identification

Within the context of hierarchical Aboriginal/non-Aboriginal relationships, an individual has little power to change the way he/she is perceived as a member of a discriminated group. As paradoxical as it may appear, one way out of this situation of having to face dominant group members holding such massive presuppositions is to explicitly claim to be what one is supposed to be: a Black bastard who does not follow the White man's rules, for example, or a savage with supernatural powers, etc. Transforming an imputation into a claim is a way of regaining power. Such a stance becomes particularly relevant during adolescence, when the urge for more autonomy and increased assertiveness intensifies (*cf.* Martin 1993). However, being identified as a member of a subordinate, disparaged group – eternal children whose needs are held to be catered for by the only 'real' adults who are members of the dominant group – is problematic (*see also* Samson 2004). Indeed, in the eyes of many non-Aboriginal adults, Aboriginal youths are doomed to become unemployed and/or delinquents. On the other hand, as I will try to show in this section, it is even more costly to seek distance from the discriminated group as this entails exiling oneself from family, deep-felt shame and a potential loss of self. Thus, for members of a discriminated group, the transition from childhood to adulthood is marked by a growing consciousness that they must assume responsibility for the collective identity assigned to them. The question of whether such a responsibility is desirable is not an option – they do not have the choice not to make a choice.

One can pretend not to be an Aboriginal person, especially if ties with the Aboriginal family are shaky (for instance, if one has been taken away and/or fostered out to a non-Aboriginal family or placed in an institution) and if one's physical features (light skin for example) allow. This may be a good strategy to avoid the damaging consequences of being associated with an assigned, negatively connoted collective identity: racist attitudes, difficulties in getting a job, a higher risk of being arrested, etc. However, it also raises a number of problems. Indeed, to the extent that a person's collective identity is intimately interwoven with family ties, breaking off from the social group also implies cutting oneself off from parents and kin. This is of course all the more difficult when the latter's bad living conditions cannot be ignored or forgotten. Psychotherapists are well aware of the conflicts of loyalty that decisions of this nature generate (Boszormenyi-Nagy and Spark 1984). Such individuals constantly question their right to be better off than their ascendants and community members, and the viability of having entered a world which, by virtue of the ambient hierarchical ideology, they know that they are not supposed to be entitled to. Thus, the choice of becoming a renegade by cutting off ties with family and community can only be exceptional or temporary. This is what was required by the granting of certificates of exemption or citizenship[5] that state governments introduced in the 1940s. Aborigines could seek exemption from the Protection Laws if, as Howie-Willis (1994a: 298–99) writes, they were 'deemed to have been "civilized," i.e., those who had adopted a "European lifestyle."' Their exempt status entitled them 'to vote, drink alcohol, use hotels and otherwise exercise the rights enjoyed by other Australians' on the condition that they refrain 'from "consorting" with [their] own parents and siblings'.

Choosing to integrate this other, dominant social world by accepting one part of one's identity at the expense of the other requires a lot of energy and effort to disguise what one 'truly' is. To succeed one has to be exceptionally strong and determined, all the while being agonizingly aware that this in no way guarantees a happy ending. Derricotte, the Afro-American writer already mentioned, and the Jewish-American writer Philip Roth, in his novel *The Human Stain* (2000), bear witness to the dilemmas involved. They describe how turning one's back on the family through which one is connected to a racialized, negative identity is not only extremely painful and isolating but can also be a dead end. Interestingly, Roth's main character chooses to adopt this strategy when, as a young man on the road to adulthood, he fully grasps what assuming his unapparent Blackness would entail: he would be unable to attend a prestigious mainstream university in order to pursue the professional career he desires, and he could not marry the White woman he has fallen in love with. Indeed, identity issues become critical upon reaching adulthood because in this difficult period, there are mounting pressures to personally assume responsibility for constructing an adult identity or persona. At that time, the identification process undergoes a radical transformation: from a child learning to behave in different sociocultural settings in accord with a distinctive sociocultural identity, to the adult position of assuming responsibility for this identity and having to bear the consequences of doing so. Although the character I am referring to here is fictional, the novel realistically describes how a collective identity sharply constrains intimate choices, which are part of the way a person constructs an adult identity. Being attracted to certain sexual partners, the decision to marry them or not, as well as professional choices are sustained by deeply rooted, personal motivations; at the same time, marriages and careers are means of achieving social status and, as public declarations, expressions of the way one wishes to be socially perceived.

Shameful Aspirations

As I have suggested, while the social status a person seeks to attain may appear to be an external aspect of personhood, when this involves a constant effort to expunge the links between self and family of origin, it entails a momentous inner struggle. Suffering incurred by what one is gives rise to a resolve to keep one's disavowed identity secret. However, to persistently pretend to be other than who one knowingly is adds to this suffering, combining it now with the shame of treason; also, there is the constant threat of being unmasked. Yet at the same time, wanting to attain a social status held to be reserved for members of the dominant group is often sustained by a strong desire for regaining self-esteem. Thus, achieving a preeminent social position or marrying a person of higher status is a way to acquire power or authority that is otherwise denied. Such power and authority may, in turn, give rise to increased autonomy, and is this not precisely what young people often yearn for? However, most of the young people belonging to discriminated groups are not in a position to fulfil such understandable desires. Their options are far more modest and consist, for the most part, in taking on features of the worldwide 'youth culture' as embodied in music and movie stars, sport heroes, fashion clothing or other commodity items.

Adopting elements of the sovereign Western 'culture' may give Aboriginal young people the temporary impression of having incorporated the power these elements connote. This is all the more so as most Aboriginal youths do not have the opportunity to cross the boundaries that separate their world from the Western, White one. For example, none of the Aboriginal children and youths I worked with had ever been invited to their non-Aboriginal schoolmates' homes. Their ideas of the latter's way of life were shaped by American TV series in which rich Californian adolescents live an enchanted, glitzy lifestyle. Reciprocally, none of their non-Aboriginal schoolmates had been invited into Aboriginal homes ('shame job!'). This, I suspect, is the norm. Consider, for example, the case of a well-known Australian anthropologist whom I had invited to our house-warming party in Queanbeyan near Canberra, where he met our Aboriginal neighbour and friend. While he cannot be suspected of racism, he told me afterwards that, although he had been raised in a small country town of New South Wales where there was an Aboriginal community, it was the first time he had socialized closely with an Aboriginal person. He was around forty and somewhat baffled by this.[6] Aboriginal youths are thus led to believe that, beyond the invisible boundaries that continue to set limits to their view, there is another world they picture as a cavern of Ali Baba, the 'open sesame' to which is denied them; it abounds with riches which they long for and which they are made to believe are not for them. The 'riches' I am referring to here are, of course, not so much material objects as the enviable lifestyle these objects are associated with. Like the tale's forty thieves, for Aboriginal people, getting their hands on the valuable objects in question may not provide them with that which, for a White person, is supposed to naturally follow. It gives them just a glimpse of what they are missing.

Dreaming to be White is at once shameful and at times tempting. The desired invisibility, in the sense of being treated as normal, is something only Whites are free to have, which means that possible success of an Aboriginal person is likely to be systematically called into question. The dream of being White is even more tantalizing if, like Derricotte who has deliberately chosen to share such a shameful temptation, one can pass for White:

> By the time I was in second grade, I already knew that white people had something special, desirable, a world I wanted to enter. On the first day of school, when the nun put the index card on my desk on which we were to neatly pen our names and addresses, and check the appropriate box – Negro or White – I hesitated as long as I could … I had a sense that checking 'Negro' would mean I would become something confusing … But they taught us that the eye of God sees all. 'Negro', I finally checked. (Derricotte 1997: 89)

The 'eye of God' in this passage bears witness to the intrusion of the self by the outside, domineering perspective that Whites have on Blacks or other ethnic groups they tend to classify as inferior. Once this perspective has been interiorized, it can never be extracted. One can only pretend that it is not there. Racism's most powerful damage is related to these inescapable, shameful thoughts about being Black and therefore inferior, or about wishing to be White and therefore implicitly accepting the superiority of Whites over Blacks. To be judged to be inferior in essence, by virtue of one's outward appearance, means that he or she who judges is able to see right through the person. It is as though one's inner privacy, no longer hidden, is blatantly exposed. In this light, concealing whenever possible what one truly is from members of the dominant group may be a positive strategy of empowerment. On the other hand, doing so may be interpreted as a betrayal of the discriminated group to which one belongs and, above all, a betrayal of those closest persons through which one is connected to this problematic collective identity.

Accountability

I cannot easily be identified as a 'half-caste Jew' because my body does not 'say' it. However, the fact that my father was Jewish has had important consequences for my life, not the least of which is my preoccupation with the study of problems of identity. At first, I had no choice but to become aware that I was affiliated with a group who has been discriminated against and that this affiliation had its cost. It meant, for example, that the words I spoke could amount to acts of claiming or disclaiming this part of my identity, my connection to my father's family and, through the latter, to the Jewish community. As I grew older, I learned that making choices in this regard would be my unavoidable, personal responsibility.

My father was a political refugee from Bulgaria whose family had moved to Israel after the creation of the new state. My mother, who was not Jewish, had been raised in the centre of France as part of a low-income peasant family who had become factory workers. I myself was raised in a middle-class suburb of Paris. I must have been around eight when a neighbour I was visiting asked whether I received letters from my Bulgarian grandmother. I answered, 'Oh, no, my grandmother sends letters from Israel'. When I reported this to my mother that evening, she screamed at me: 'Don't say your father's family is in Israel! You should have said they were in Bulgaria!' The following day I rushed to tell the neighbour that I had made a mistake: my grandmother lived in Bulgaria, not Israel. Of course, this was somewhat silly, but I was so puzzled by the importance that was given to what I had said so naturally – after all, I was just telling the truth – that I felt compelled to repair the damage I had obviously done. Several years later, a plumber came to do some work in our house while I was alone. He said to me: 'Everybody in the neighbourhood says that your father is Jewish, but I myself know that he is Bulgarian. He is Bulgarian, isn't he?' I answered 'Yes', but felt uncomfortable and bitter about it. However, I had learnt by then the importance of distinguishing between those to whom such matters may be disclosed, and those to whom they should never be revealed.

These anecdotes illustrate the self-consciousness that people who belong to a discriminated group are likely to acquire. It goes together with a heightened awareness that others may evaluate the way in which I take responsibility for who I am. Choices of what to say or do bear witness to my sense of integrity with respect to my identity. This, I suggest, is exactly what adolescents affiliated with a discriminated group cannot disregard – their accountability. They must leave behind the innocence of their childhood and embrace full responsibility for claiming who they are. Another example, also drawn from outside the Aboriginal community, illustrates further that this issue applies to persons belonging to any ethnic or cultural minority group.

I once heard the story of an Australian woman from India who was married to a Cambodian. One day, their son, who may have been around five years old, came back from school and announced, 'I hate Cambodians'. She asked him: did he love his dad? 'Sure', he answered. 'And what about so and so?' she continued, citing some of her husband's Cambodian friends. 'Yes, I like them very much!' She then explained to him that they were Cambodians. This story may cause one to smile: it is clear that this small child was simply repeating what he had heard at school, probably in order to be accepted by his peer group. But let's imagine he is a thirteen or fourteen-year-old. The story is all of a sudden not so funny. It will now be assumed that the youth is making a negative claim about his father's origin and where he wants to stand within society, denying an aspect of his own background. Although the frontiers between childhood and adolescence are not clearly marked, there is an impalpable sense for all concerned that something important has changed. It may concern the young person's sexual identity or the way he/she deals with intimacy and his/her transforming body. However, it also has to do with acquiring a sense of belonging to a group larger than the immediate family and local community. Thus, the whole image of a person's identity is being transformed during the transition towards adolescence.

'Coconutism'

During adolescence, young people come to realize that they have become liable for the way their parents are perceived, not only within their local community, but also vis-à-vis the society as a whole. For Aboriginal youths, it means becoming accountable for being related to people who are not considered to be of the same standing as other Australians. Members of their own community as well as those of the opposing, dominant group are prepared to interpret their behaviour and actions as so many instances of the way these young people assume their identity. They may even be pushed to make clear statements about where they stand. To be vague about this will be read as a sign of shame for oneself and betrayal of the group one belongs to, which in turn can lead to a rejection by the family and community.

Before the 1967 referendum and the self-determination policies that followed, a number of Aboriginal people of mixed descent who had been raised outside the Aboriginal community and who could pass for non-Aboriginal were encouraged not to claim their Aboriginality. The hope was that they would be able to have a better life than their ill-regarded counterparts. And, indeed, a number of them were able to study and obtain jobs in the public sector. Some have become eminent political figures or influential in other fields, especially during the period following the bicentenary in 1988. However, in those communities where their life stories are well known, they were qualified as 'Johnnies-come-lately' or, worse, 'coconuts' – Black outside, White inside.

Accusations of being a 'coconut' are multilayered. On the one hand, they seem to suggest that the Aboriginality of the accused is but skin deep, that his/her real, inner self is White. At the same time, however, as uttered by one Aboriginal person regarding another, they emphasize the inescapable Blackness, making attempts to adopt White people's ways appear as a vain and superficial veneer. In order to fully understand the meaning of such insults, it is helpful to consider them in light of a series of stances with regard to the identity that the persons in question are alleged to have adopted. Their inner Whiteness is first of all related to a suspected past determination to assimilate, that is, to forget where they came from. Those proffering this insult did not deny the Aboriginality of such persons,[7] but rather, they were accused of having kept hidden within themselves their Blackness when it suited them, in order to acquire higher status reserved, at the time, for Whites alone. Having subsequently made their 'coming out' as 'Blackfellas' before the White community – once again, according to rumour – they were then accused of concealing from their Black community the Whiteness that they were supposed to have acquired through their betrayal: they externalize their inner Blackness which they had until then kept hidden in order to acquire political positions made newly available for Aboriginal people. Thus, within the Aboriginal communities where they were known, people who disliked such persons or who contested their actions on the grounds that they had been unfairly privileged used this insult to express their distrust. Accusations of being a coconut, by exposing such person's 'true', inner White self, locates them on the opposing political side, that of the White enemy: 'They can't speak on our behalf!' In the 1950s world-renowned (French Caribbean) Black activist and psychiatrist Franz Fanon (1952) used in similar, albeit inverted fashion the phrase 'Black skin, White mask' to evoke the subordinate attitudes of French Caribbean Blacks towards the Whites of France. The use of such terms makes us aware of the divisive effect that an assigned, racialized collective identity has on a minority group encompassed by a dominant one.

Such conditions compel minority group members to clearly assert the collective identity they have chosen to assume. This is especially true when political issues are at stake and in intercultural contexts. If they want to be trusted, they must actively and consistently demonstrate the side on which they stand. Thus, merely being successful in school or at work when the majority of one's community has failed in both areas places a person at risk of being accused of 'coconutism': 'Who do you think you are? A Whitefella? A brainy one?' Such an insult is easily transferred to this person's children, who will have to make an even stronger claim about their identity. Thus, among Aboriginal youths living in a mixed environment and/or going to a mainstream school, one of the worst insults is indeed to be called a 'coconut' by Aboriginal peers. In such contexts where Aboriginal and non-Aboriginal communities overlap, one cannot afford neutrality because being neutral is taking the side of the dominant White culture. In the present-day French Caribbean, the equivalent insult is 'Bounty', the coconut candy bar covered with black chocolate; among the Japanese of Hawaii, it is 'banana', (yellow outside, white inside); among the North American Amerindian community, it is 'apple' (red outside, white inside). These strange fruits tell a great deal about the peer pressure exercised on those who belong to a discriminated group.

Becoming an adult, then, means becoming consciously accountable for the construction of one's identity as a member of a larger collectivity. Under the conditions we are considering, this entails making clear the chosen affiliation with one cultural group to the exclusion of the other. The alternatives are assuming full responsibility for an externally assigned identity or becoming a renegade. Doing the former implies explicitly taking on both the positive *and* the negative aspects of the identity that is externally assigned. Acquiring autonomy consists in transforming such an assignation into a claim: I am Aboriginal.

We are now in a position to better understand the peculiar constraints that bear upon youths who belong to a discriminated group such as the Aboriginal people of Australia. They are supposed to gain autonomy from their family. However, because their family connects them to the Aboriginal community and to the racialized identity which is assigned to it, they do not have the same leeway as youths of the dominant group, namely, of being able to distance themselves from their kin without having to explicitly assume a stance with respect to their collective identity. And if they want to put forward their Aboriginality, they must demonstrate their loyalty towards their community by maintaining their remoteness from the dominant group. Thus, among the few Aboriginal people who succeed in school, in spite of their family's economic and sociological handicaps, the great majority choose jobs that allow them to support the Aboriginal community, either directly (as Aboriginal aids or facilitators in different public sectors) or indirectly (by promoting Aboriginal pride in the fields of sport or art for example).

For Aboriginal people, as among many minority groups, family ties remain the cornerstone upon which sociocultural identities and differences are claimed and worked out. The disparaging, hierarchical relationship between the Aboriginal and non-Aboriginal communities, transmitted from generation to generation, contributes significantly to their shared sense of identity. In order to better understand how such a sense of relatedness founded upon the intergenerational transmission of negative experiences of racism intervenes in the lives of today's Aboriginal youth, I next consider what is at stake in the relationship between parents and children.

Nurturing and Filiation: The Two Sides of Parental Roles

I studied anthropology while I was a medical student, and one of my main concerns was to compare the means that different types of societies provide for individuals to achieve autonomy and adulthood. I started by re-examining Strehlow's and Spencer and Gillen's data on Aranda puberty rites and initiation rituals (Moisseeff 1992, 1995). When I began family therapy as a trainee in psychiatry, I found it useful to draw on this work in order to develop a cross-cultural perspective on parental roles that could make sense of the growing difficulties faced by families of adolescents in France and more generally in the West. I believe such a comparative perspective may also help to clarify the specific problems faced by Aboriginal youths who live in the culturally heterogeneous context of contemporary Australia.

In more traditional settings, parental roles tend to be formally differentiated according to the degree of dependency they imply. Being a parent of prepubescent children who depend upon adults for their basic needs differs markedly from being a parent of a young person on the road to becoming an adult. Puberty is explicitly related to the transformation of the individual into a potential or actual parent. The formal acknowledgement of children's right to assume responsibility over children themselves sustains the process whereby adulthood, that is, autonomy from parents, is attained. In this way, parents of adolescents are required to take on a new role – that of transmitting parenthood itself. This stands in striking contrast to the characteristic trend in contemporary Western societies where puberty does not imply an explicit, institutionalized redefinition of parental roles. The parents of young people know that they are supposed to change their behaviour towards their offspring, but they do not necessarily have a clear idea of what this new role they are expected to play involves. Society strongly encourages them to allow their children greater freedom so that they may attain personal fulfilment, and interestingly, this goes together with discouraging them from having children too soon; becoming a parent is seen as a potential obstacle to professional and/or sexual achievement. The only legal definition of parental responsibilities concerns the nurturing role parents must fulfil towards a dependent child and what material items they may transmit to their children. The question of what else they should impart to them, that is, those immaterial elements that define the relationship between parents and their adult children, remains largely a matter of personal choice rather than institutionalized norms. The situation is very different in those societies where having children is seen as the way of transmitting familial, social and cultural specificity. Here, children's accession to parenthood is considered to be a process of transmission that engages the responsibility of parents and of society as a whole; it is the privileged channel through which sociocultural identity itself is passed on.

Assumptions about what adult status and parental roles mean inevitably affect the way in which individuals experience their accession to adult- and parenthood. Similarly, the means individuals are provided with in order to fully assume their parental roles surely influence their capacity to become adults. Elsewhere I have discussed the link between difficulties encountered by adolescents and their parents in the West and the absence of a redefinition of parental roles around puberty (Moisseeff 1992, 1995, 1998, 2004a, 2004b, 2006). Here I want to consider the consequences, for today's Aboriginal youth, of the fact that Aboriginal people have been stripped of their parental responsibilities (in the past) as well as hindered (in the past and the present) from sustaining viable parental roles towards their children, all the while being kept materially

dependent, as adults, on alien – Western – welfare institutions. Such requires a closer look at what is involved in the parent-child relationship.

The Two Sides of Being a Child

The transition from childhood to adulthood, defined in our culture as
the period of adolescence, entails a shift between two states of *being a
child.* During the early years, to be a child means emotional and material dependency on other individuals for survival and development; this
is supposed to be a transitory state. But to be a child also means being
the offspring of parents, a state which relies on kinship ties and enables
individuals to continue to be their parents' children beyond childhood
itself. These two senses of the word *child* correspond to different sta-
tuses founded upon distinct types of dependency. In the first case, dependency refers to the *nurturing function* that is exercised by parental
figures in accordance with socially defined parental rights and duties
towards under-age children (feeding, socialization, emotional sharing
and so forth); it refers to parenthood. In the second case, dependency
refers to a *filiative function* whereby an individual is located within a
kinship system that extends well beyond the immediate family to define
a larger set of relational categories ('cousins', 'aunts', 'nephews' and
so forth) and associate patterns of interaction. Situating the individual
within a genealogical grid that includes members of preceding and following generations, as well as collateral relatives (parents' brothers and
sisters, their spouses, cousins and their spouses and so forth), this system
mediates the ordered succession of generations through which particular norms, attitudes, symbolic representations and areas of expertise are
passed on. For it is not only kinship that parents transmit to their children; in doing so they also hand down collective values and a distinctive ethos underlying particular kinds of social and affective behaviour
in different types of contexts. In short, they pass on the premises of a
characteristic sociocultural identity. And when these children become
parents in turn, they pass on to their own children the constituents of the
cultural identity that their parents bequeathed to them. In this way, by
having children, and by allowing one's children to have children, one
participates in the perpetuation of culture. What I have called the filiative function consists in transmitting to children not only the underlying
features of a distinctive collective identity but also the ability to transmit
that identity themselves.

Parents, then, are supposed to assume two distinctive functions: nurture and filiation. The nurturing function is often perceived as a maternal
role, that is, as an extension of the nourishment provided by the female

body during pregnancy and breastfeeding. As such, it tends to be associated with a state of extreme dependency of the child upon his/her mother that prolongs their original, physically merged state, whose consequences may be seen as potentially hindering the child's advancement toward autonomy. Hence the acknowledgement of the need to introduce another, socially and culturally mediated relationship between mother and child. In traditional settings, such an institutionalized intervention, generally undertaken by adult men, is typically viewed as crucial around the time of puberty, this being especially so when the attainment of manhood is at stake. As Myers (this volume) points out for Pintupi boys in the Australian Western Desert, this transition can be a vulnerable point in the process of identity formation. It is at this moment in an individual's life, when he/she acquires the possibility of becoming a parent, that his/her parents must fully assume their filiative role. In puberty rites, such as those performed in many Aboriginal societies, physical operations aim to alter the novices' bodies so as to allow them to become autonomous beings capable of contributing to the perpetuation of their community and its cultural specificity. They allow for the forging of new intimate relationships – with sexual and ritual partners – in which individuals assume nurturing and filiative responsibilities. This mediates their passage from the status of receivers of care to that of caregivers on different (familial and social) levels.

This institutionalization of the passage from childhood to adulthood ensures the transfer of reproductive capacities from one generation to the next. Requiring the active participation of the parents, such rituals are a reminder that the parental role cannot be reduced to nurturing, but is always subordinated to a filiative function. Adults are expected to contribute to the perpetuation of culture and to the community's identity; they need to assume both nurturing *and* filiative responsibilities if new community members are to embody a viable collective identity. This in turn requires that they themselves enjoy sufficient autonomy as grown-up, responsible beings.

A major flaw, as I see it, in the present-day situation of many Aboriginal people is this: they have inherited the consequences of a hierarchical relationship with non-Aboriginal Australians, initiated during colonization but still pervasive, in which Aboriginal adults have been divested of their parental responsibilities. The forcible removal of children is but one, if particularly flagrant, example of this. Its dramatization acts to mask other ways in which the asymmetry between the two concerned cultural groups continues, in a more insidious but nonetheless effective fashion, to impinge upon the Aboriginal adults' capacity to assume their parental roles.

Nurturing, a Maternal Function versus
Filiation, a Masculine Function

In many cultural representations throughout the world, nurturing, associated with women, is perceived as both necessary and dangerous. Necessary, because it is vital; dangerous because it evokes the encompassing aspect of motherhood which, were it to persist, may prevent the child from becoming autonomous. Conversely, because the male procreative role is a more distanced one, taking place within the body of a sexual alter ego, men are more strongly associated with the filiative function as I have defined it: the transmission of the capacity to perpetuate the cultural specificity of a given population. As adult men are kept at a remove during gestation, and because they are held to have acquired autonomy themselves, they are in a good position to act as mediators between mothers and their offspring, authorizing the latter's transition from a nurturing-based, maternal dependency to one founded upon sociocultural filiation. Creation stories often refer metaphorically to these two functions, a nurturing and predominantly maternal one, and a filiative and eminently masculine one.

Elsewhere (Moisseeff 1995), I have shown this to be the case in an Aranda creation narrative (Strehlow 1964: 727–28; Spencer and Gillen 1927: 307–9) which tells of 'self-existing', spiritual *numbakulla* whose cutting into unfinished, hybrid *inapatua* creatures joined together in a semi-embryonic, undifferentiated mass, leads to the emergence of separate animal and plant species, of male and female sexes and of human individuals. While space prevents me from developing this analysis here, it suggests that traditional Aboriginal conceptions regarding individualization and the acquisition of autonomy fit closely with the model outlined above. Whereas enclosure within the maternal body is portrayed as an original state of sterile, physical hybridity, an outside relationship with the adult masculine collective is represented as the basis of acquiring independent adulthood and the aptitude to participate in the transmission of culture, and the maintenance of its specificity and ongoing creativity. Moreover, an individual's transition from a nurturing-based dependency to a filiation-based one is held to rely upon sexual differentiation, which is seen as the outward sign of an inner transformation whereby a person ceases to be an object of reproduction – as embodied by his/her mother – to become, potentially, one of its active agents. Finally, whereas both men and women are involved in transmitting their reproductive capacities to their children so that the latter may acquire autonomous, adult identities, men have an additional, culturally crucial role to play in this process. They must also be able to transmit from one male generation to the next the ability to uphold the sexual differentiation that lies at the basis of the separation between childhood and adulthood.[8]

Cultural Domination and Nurturing-based Dependency

With these features of traditional Aboriginal culture in mind, one is in a better position to appreciate the repercussions of Aboriginal protection-welfare policies, as these were in place from the 1830s until the 1960s–1970s (Howie-Willis 1994b: 903). Aboriginal adults were attributed the status of minors under state guardianship, subject to bureaucratic regulations affecting most aspects of their lives, including 'place of residence and work, child rearing, social security entitlements, housing and even diet' (Howie-Willis 1994c: 28). This entailed restrictions of their 'freedom to travel, own property and possessions, live and work where they wished, form marital relationships, raise their children as they pleased and use the land' (Howie-Willis 1994d: 22).

Whereas the Dreaming was held to encompass and generate all aspects of traditional Aboriginal life, the welfare era that followed colonization can be seen to have encompassed the Dreaming: Aboriginal men, women and children came to be treated and eventually perceived as a people of children. As such, their needs had to be catered for by non-Aboriginal adults who were thus also entitled to punish them. As we have seen, Peter's childhood memories bear witness to this state of affairs. The ultimate goal of these policies was to assimilate Aboriginal people by substituting European norms, values, know-how, etc. for their own; the latter were deemed to be far too primitive and, therefore, doomed to disappear. European standards were to be inculcated by superintendents and matrons and/or missionaries who acted as 'superparents' over Aboriginal adults and children deported or confined to missions and reserves. The forcible removal of mixed-blood children was initiated for similar reasons: to sever their ties with their Aboriginal families so as to allow them to be assimilated progressively into civilization.

In this postcolonial and intercultural context, the welfare state is held to provide everything, but by the same token it effectively denies Aboriginal people the individual and social differentiation that goes with autonomy, freedom of movement and liveliness. Thus, although Big Mother 'welfare' – like the boards of protection formally – became vital to secure its 'children's' basic needs, it turned out to be lethal as well: its nurturing function acted to enclose Aboriginal adults within the status of minors from which it is difficult to escape. It embodies an encompassing maternal function that prevents an entire population from attaining adulthood.

As a result, Aboriginal people remain highly suspicious of present-day agencies established to help them, such as Family and Community Services; the people I worked with referred to the latter as 'F and C' (f*ck and c*nt). While such agencies are presumed to act as a buffer against stressful situations, their intervention is often felt to have a potentially inverse effect, notably through their role in assessing the quality of parental care.

Undermining the Role of Men

Within the Aboriginal population, nurturing and filiative functions have thus tended to be fused together, both being monopolized by non-Aboriginal institutions (see also Hamilton 1972). The latter act as both mothers and fathers, depriving Aboriginal males of their differentiating responsibilities, which, in the past, ensured the transition from childhood to adulthood. Under these conditions, it has become significantly harder for Aboriginal men to assume what used to be their distinctive filiative role, that of compelling young people to distance themselves from a nurturing relationship so as to acquire sociocultural autonomy. In the mythical story, as in ritual performances, this role relies upon men's ability to encompass the nurturing function by their filiative one. This is difficult to do when they themselves, together with women and children, depend on an all-encompassing 'nurturing' state.

Encapsulated within a dominant, alien society, Aboriginal people can no longer ensure their livelihood in an independent fashion. At the same time, as statistics show (see e.g., Moisseeff 1999a), in comparison with the Australian population as a whole, an overwhelming proportion of Aboriginal adults are unemployed; they occupy often overcrowded houses which they do not own, usually without a car or even a driver's licence. This is indicative of Aboriginal parents' ongoing dependence on welfare that distinguishes their status from that of non-Aboriginal parents in general. In spite of this situation, Aboriginal people, on average, tend to have more children and at an earlier age than the general population of Australia. While parents of teenage parents do not disregard the difficulties this may cause, such babies are usually happily welcomed. As I was told, as long as Aboriginal children continue to be born, the Aboriginal community demonstrates its ability to survive and to fight against its cultural dilution in the White world. Thus, bearing children is still perceived as the means to contribute to the perpetuation of the local community and its cultural specificity. From this point of view, Aboriginal women have maintained the core of what used to be their traditional role and, for a number of them, having children is a way to achieve adulthood. However, according to many women, Aboriginal men, on the whole, tend to be less involved in the upbringing of their offspring. This, I suggest, is to be evaluated in the light of the lowering of Aboriginal men's social status. On the one hand, unemployment makes it harder for them to play the role of breadwinner, leading them to relinquish their nurturing duties to outside agencies (*cf. also* Finlayson 1989). On the other hand, the pervasiveness of Western material culture within Aboriginal communities bears witness to an external orientation and hence to the difficulties men have in carrying out the filiative responsibilities that guarantee their society's cultural specificity.

In appropriating political and economic power, Australians of European origin have diminished both Aboriginal men's ability to uphold their position within the domestic sphere and their ritual authority as initiators, rooted in traditional cosmological values deemed primitive or, at best, exotic. The subsequent loss of Aboriginal men's prestige has deeply altered their social status, inducing transformations in gender and power relations.

Although it is usually not publicly discussed, one of the domains where an Aboriginal man can regain symbolic prestige is that of sexual relationships. The Aboriginal young people with whom I worked explained, for example, that they use the term 'bullockey' to refer to a non-Aboriginal man having sexual affairs with Aboriginal women. Interestingly, this term was first employed by White people to refer to Aboriginal people who had stolen bullocks from them. In borrowing this term and making its meaning theirs, Aboriginal people reveal their own perspective on the situation imposed upon them: the thieves are not they, but White people who have, in the first place, stolen their lands, their wives and their children. In contrast to this, Aboriginal youths call an Aboriginal man having sexual affairs with non-Aboriginal women a 'hero'. Having sex is sharing a highly intimate experience with another person: it allows a crossing of boundaries that, otherwise, on the sociocultural level, are held to be insurmountable, especially in view of the past prohibitions on sexual intercourse and marriage between Whites and Blacks. It is in this sense a highly subversive act that, as such, can be qualified as heroic when undertaken by a member of a dominated group. Significantly, there are no feminine terms equivalent to 'bullockey' and 'hero' used to designate, respectively, an Aboriginal woman having sexual relations with non-Aboriginal men or a non Aboriginal-woman having sexual relations with Aboriginal men. The appropriation of women's bodies has thus become a way of playing out, on another level, the imbalance of power that has developed between men belonging to two opposing groups. Women and their procreative capacity are often at stake in power games played by men (*see also* Haskins and Maynard 2005).

Indeed, the asymmetrical power relations between White Australians and Aborigines would seem to have replaced the traditional hierarchy between men and women: men of European origin hold the position traditionally occupied by men in Aboriginal society, whereas Aboriginal men occupy a position similar to that of women. Symbolically, this new hierarchical order is assimilated to an inversion of the traditional power relations between men and women. This is reinforced by the constant circulation of stories within Aboriginal communities about European settlers eliciting sexual favours of Aboriginal women and the forcible removal of the children – 'tucker babies' (sex for food) – born from these liaisons. From this point of view, the loss of Aboriginal men's former control over women and children implicitly accounts for the disempowerment of the Aboriginal community as a whole.

While the Aboriginal life expectancy is considerably lower than for the rest of the Australian population, that of Aboriginal men is significantly lower than the life expectancy of their female counterparts.[9] This, along with a higher rate of imprisonment and their overrepresentation in criminality and domestic violence, is a concrete indicator of the trouble men have in finding their place in contemporary Australian society. At the same time, Aboriginal men's diminished autonomy has reduced their ability to promote the autonomization of their children, and especially of young men. The latter have an alarming death rate and, compared both to their non-Aboriginal counterparts and to young Aboriginal women, they are much more implicated in delinquency, accidents, murders and other acts of violence; they are also especially prone to suicide and addictive behaviours such as alcoholism and drug addiction. Aboriginal men's loss of power seems to affect sons much more than daughters.

Men's difficulty in assuming their nurturing and filiative roles all too often leads young Aboriginal men to attempt to attain self-sufficiency on their own, becoming fatally entangled in a logic of self-nurturing.

Claiming One's Body as a Source of Independence

Maggie Brady's data on petrol sniffing among Aboriginal young people supports the idea that this practice is a desperate attempt to gain a measure of autonomy in situations, such as those obtaining in remote communities, where the level of independence they are able to achieve seems to be incommensurable with that enjoyed by White Australians. Petrol sniffers vehemently assert their right to manage their own bodies:

when it becomes practically impossible to see themselves in a future filled with self-sufficient, highly valued actions, taking direct control over their own bodies becomes a compelling option. Burning the candle at both ends replaces an obstructed imagination about the future with an exhilarating present; better risk dying than to accept life at a snail's pace and to pass away with a whimper as the adults of their community do. Indeed, as Brady judiciously emphasizes, a refusal to submit to existing norms lies at the heart of petrol sniffing: 'In many communities, the groups of sniffers take on a decidedly "oppositional" style, in which they cultivate the differences between themselves and mainstream Aboriginal society' (1992a: 88). The need for aggressive affirmation is especially evident among male adolescents; it gives rise to claims of hypermasculinity in a context where 'normal' adult masculinity pales before that enjoyed by Whites. In Arnhem Land, such claims take the form of membership in 'hard' gangs with evocative names like 'the Warriors', 'German Rebels', 'Super Huns', 'Bad Brothers' and so forth, whose members wear paramilitary attire, listen to heavy metal or hard rock rather than the widely preferred country-western music, and are fascinated by Kung Fu or Rambo movies. In Central Australia, the need to assert one's masculinity takes a different form: youths engage in petrol sniffing with the avowed intention of losing weight (the inhalation of petrol fumes is well known for its anorexic effects) so as not to resemble women whose fatness and rounded figures they associate with femininity and *being mothered.*

The material concerning male Aboriginal sniffers highlights their fear of remaining under the influence of a maternal-like ascendancy. Thus, by taking on the exterior signs of masculinity, they try to distinguish themselves from women. The violence men exert towards the latter may also be part of their attempt to impose their masculinity, especially as it appears to be easier for women to achieve adult status. Indeed, childbearing remains highly valued and, as a rule, women who become pregnant stop their intake of petrol, alcohol and tobacco, at least temporarily (Brady 1992a, 1995; Moisseeff 1999a).

Brady shows that petrol sniffing has taken root in communities where missions and government settlements were established early on. These are the places where Aborigines most endured the effects of an institutionalization that made them strongly and durably dependent upon Australian social services, and where, as a result, they lost their ability to undertake activities capable of promoting positive masculine models. By contrast, in communities developed on cattle stations, petrol sniffing did not 'take'. In spite of harsh working conditions, Aborigines employed in the pastoral industry, through continuous contact with their land, were able to maintain cultural values and activities considered by them to be essential: ceremonial life, visits to sacred sites, hunting and gathering, etc. At the same time, Aboriginal men's labour and skills were indispensable to pastoralists and as such highly valued. Moreover, camp life and disputes remained largely in Aboriginal hands, Western interference through government officers and schooling being minimal or delayed for a long time. Here, a commitment to the rules of Western society did not entail men's deprivation of their valued masculine identity; on the contrary, they not only preserved it, but also gained the stockman's image of virility.

In these latter cases, the fact that men could maintain their communities' independence, at least partially, by contributing to subsistence and by transmitting their own cultural values, allowed them to personify attractive enough male models for their sons. The prospect of being able to pass from the position of care receiver to that of caregiver makes it easier for young men to envisage the passage from childhood to adulthood. This, in turn, renders them more inclined to accept the male roles present in their own communities rather than assuming the exterior signs of an adult masculinity foreign to their society. In taking on the distinctive, male-centred responsibilities that these roles imply, they are better equipped to become the mediators in the relationship between mothers and their children. Instead of being stuck in the limbo of a never-ending adolescence in which the individual assumes no responsibilities towards others, such young men are better able to leave childhood to become fully grown up persons. In this respect, it is interesting to note that the reasons ex-sniffers give for having stopped are getting married, having a child or becoming 'Christian'. Accepting to change one's identity, on a relational level, in becoming a spouse, a parent or a member of a congregation, allows them to pass from the status of dependent child to that of an adult able to contribute to the perpetuation of a community.

At puberty, individuals undergo in-depth transformations that will allow them to acquire an adult sexual identity. By adopting the dress codes, the look, the hairstyle and the behaviour of the masculine and feminine stereotypes current in their society, adolescents aim to demonstrate their capacity to take on this new identity and their autonomy vis-à-vis their parents. In contexts where it is difficult for youths to see themselves attaining material self-sufficiency, a number of adolescents will tend to confuse physical autonomy with independence itself. They run the risk, then, of becoming substance dependent. Being able to control their body by denying or giving it pleasure or pain becomes, for them, a way of trying to bypass all reliance on others. In this perspective, petrol sniffing, like other types of addiction, is a means whereby individuals attempt to satisfy, by themselves, their most intimate needs. Thus paradoxically, substance dependency can be understood as being the result of a frantic pursuit of independence from others, with the substance in question acting as a substitute whereby individuals attempt to wean themselves on a relational level. Instead of developing other types of relationships so as to gain independence from the familial milieu that provided for their initial needs, they remain entangled in a logic of 'nurturance'. Far from constructing their adult identity in adding other types of relationships – becoming a spouse or a parent for example – to their inherited kinship relations, they end up being identified with the substance they are dependent upon: they are 'alcoholics', 'drug addicts', 'petrol sniffers'. The only remaining positive identity to which they can possibly latch onto is that offered by their brothers in arms who share the same predicament.

In this way, it would appear that Aboriginal young people have replaced the operations formerly undertaken on their bodies by male initiators by another form of treatment which they inflict upon themselves: their bodies have become the only territory they are capable of laying claim to without recourse to an outside, alien authority. Unable to become independent, they try to be self-dependent. This death-dealing logic can lead these young people to suicide as the only liberty which remains open to them. In staging their own death, often in particularly dramatic ways, they appear to take up, on their own account, the first settlers' behaviour towards their ancestors, and with this, self-destructive behaviour becomes a symptom of loyalty towards family and community.

Therefore it is not surprising to find that death has become a major preoccupation of Aboriginal sociality. Indeed, as a result of the high number of untimely deaths in Aboriginal communities, Aboriginal people attend a large number of funerals in the course of their lives. In a survey of the Aboriginal community of Davenport that I undertook in 1993 (Moisseeff 1999a), the average funeral attendance for all ages combined was four funerals a year; there was a clear progression over time such that the number of funerals attended was proportional to age. It is as though funerals had taken the place formerly devoted to ritual activities. They have become one of the most significant social events within Aboriginal communities, and their importance in scale and pervasiveness may be compared to that of former male initiation rites. It is not rare that hundreds of people gather together on such occasions, and they may travel hundreds if not thousands of kilometres, sometimes under very difficult conditions, in order to attend the funeral of a relative, friend or key community figure. However, another thing that became clear to me was that these occasions were also an opportunity for the participants to imagine what would happen at their own funerals. And for young people wondering how they can achieve something in their lives, the prospect

of becoming a deceased 'star' of such a momentous event, with everyone crying over his/her body, was appealing (*see also* Robinson 1990,
1992b). For once, they would be able, literally, to take their life into their
own hands and make it into something memorable. This idea becomes
even more compelling when one or both of parents have passed away.
In this respect, my data on the death of parents (*see also* Gray 1987),
and here again, more particularly of fathers, are telling. At any age, the
death of a parent is a major life event for the children concerned; but it
is even more stressful and disturbing when it happens at an early age,
for the nurturing role of parents is a crucial factor in the construction of
a person's identity and the building up of a sense of self and security. In
such conditions, authorizing oneself to live better and longer than one's
parents is not an obvious choice. Demonstrating loyalty towards family
history can lead to following in one's parents' lethal footsteps, especially
when the latter have died tragically, as is unfortunately often the case.

Substance dependency and self-destructive behaviours are associated with issues of autonomization. As a rule, they arise during adolescence and, in contemporary societies in which individuals' acquisition
of autonomy is increasingly put off until later, they are constantly on
the rise. However, among Indigenous populations having become dependent upon alien agencies for their livelihood as a result of a history
of cultural domination, adolescents are even more affected by this phenomenon. It is as though parents' 'nurturing' dependency on a dominant
culture makes it doubly hard for children to extract themselves from a
nurturing logic, leading to wide-scale addictive and risk behaviour. As
paradoxical as it may seem, in a context of cultural domination, self-destructive behaviours can be interpreted as so many individual attempts to
attain self-sufficiency (*see*, e.g., Robinson 1995a).

Conclusion

The new world order imposed by Westerners has undermined Aboriginal
people's capacity to fulfil a filiative function, which consists in transmitting to others not only the features of a distinctive cultural identity but
also the ability to do so. As a result, what seems to be left to Aboriginal
people to pass on from one generation of children to the next are the
stories relating to the stressful and traumatic experiences they have undergone since colonization.

In rural communities like those in which I worked, where puberty
rites are no longer the norm and where one of the worst insults is to be

called a 'coconut', the explicit demonstration of loyalty towards family, tribal group and the Aboriginal community in general has become one of the major stakes in the passage from childhood to adulthood. Conforming to certain Aboriginal stereotypes by conspicuous and raucous drinking, getting into fights with Whites, defending cousins, becoming involved in political battles and working for Aboriginal organizations are ways in which present-day Aboriginal youths act out this loyalty and acquire a sense of autonomy. From this point of view, becoming an adult consists in a personal reappropriation of a collective identity assigned from without. It means making such Aboriginal stereotypes one's own. Once again, the rules of Aboriginal sociability are forged during childhood, but it is adulthood that requires taking up the responsibilities of sociocultural membership, which, in this case, entails opposing the Australians in power. In principle, the goal of Aboriginal organizations is to hasten the autonomization of Aboriginal people vis-à-vis government bureaucracies administered, for the most part, by Whites. Working in these organizations, sitting on their boards or participating in services that cater to the needs of Aboriginal people in the areas of health, justice, education, housing and welfare, sports and the arts have thus become a realistic way of trying to provide the Aboriginal community with more independence. However, besides the risk they run of being called a 'coconut', those who make this choice know that they will need to endure the criticism and stress inherent in their exceptional status. Whereas members of their own family accuse such persons of not having allowed them to profit sufficiently from the privileges they enjoy (having a decent salary rather than unemployment or supporting parents benefits, for example), rival family members, as well as some non-Aboriginal people, accuse them of nepotism. On the one hand, working in this way for the Aboriginal community, especially since the 1967 referendum, has become a viable alternative to unemployment which increasingly holds sway by reason of the difficulties Aborigines encounter in finding jobs in the private sector; it allows Aboriginal people to become actors within Aboriginal affairs rather than merely to submit to official policies. On the other hand, however, the pressures that this choice brings explain why, for many young people, the option of a successful working life is far less attractive than it should be. They are left trying to actively claim their Aboriginality and their loyalty in other ways, notably by expressing the ongoing dependent status of the community they belong to.

Appendix

AUSTRALIAN APOLOGY TO THE ABORIGINAL POPULATION
We apologise for giving you doctors and free medical care, which allows you to survive and multiply so that you can demand apologies.

We apologise for helping you to read and teaching you the English language, thus opening up to you the entire European civilisation, thought and enterprise.

We feel that we must apologise for building hundreds of homes for you, which you have vandalised and destroyed.

We apologise for giving you law and order which has helped prevent you from slaughtering one another and using the unfortunate for food purposes.

We apologise for developing large farms and properties, which today feed you, where before, you had the benefits of living off the land and starving during droughts.

We apologise for providing you with warm clothing made of fabric to replace the animal skins you used before.

We apologise for building roads and railway tracks between cities and building cars so that you no longer have to walk over harsh terrain.

We apologise for paying off your vehicles when you fail to pay the instalments.

We apologise for giving you free travel anywhere, whenever.

We apologise for giving each and every member of your family $100.00 and free travel to attend an aboriginal funeral.

We apologise for not charging you rent on any lands when white people have to pay.

We apologise for giving you interest-free loans.

We apologise for developing oil wells and minerals, including gold and diamonds which you never used and had no idea of their value.

We apologise for developing Ayers Rock and Kakadu, and handing them over to you so that you get all the money.

We apologise for allowing taxpayers money to be paid towards a daughters' wedding ($8,000.00 each daughter).

We apologise for giving you $1.7 billion per year for your 250,000 people, which is $48,000.00 per aboriginal man, woman and child.

We apologise for working hard to pay taxes that finance your welfare, medical care, education, etc to the tune of $1.2 billion each year.

We apologise for you having to approach the aboriginal affairs department to verify the above figures. For the trouble you will have identifying the 'uncle toms' in your own community who are getting richer and leaving some of you living in squalor and poverty.

We do apologise. We really do.
We are only too happy to take back all the above and return you to
the paradise of the 'outback', whenever you are ready.

Notes

The study on which the present essay is based received funding support from the
Fyssen Foundation (1990–91 Research Grant) and from the Australian Institute of
Aboriginal and Torres Strait Islander Studies (Aboriginal Youth Visiting Research Fel-
lowship 1991–95).

1. An adequate examination of the long-debated subject of male-female relationships in Australian Aboriginal societies is beyond the scope of this paper.
   However, particularly relevant for the systemic stance I have adopted, which
   considers the histories of individuals and families, is Merlan's (1992) overview
   and critical discussion of the topic. She has argued convincingly for an empirical approach that examines actual social practices and action rather than merely
   modelling gender and sexuality as separate domains at the level of social structure. From this perspective, 'gender difference is reproduced in social action
   relationally, that is, always male in relation to female, and vice versa' (Merlan
   1992: 191).
2. I have chosen to keep the word *tribal* because the people with whom I have
   been working used it and did not see it as inappropriate.
3. The recent scandalous assertions of 1962 Nobel Prize–winning geneticist, James
   Watson, in October 2007, is but one illustration of the persistence of such a
   perspective. Milmo (2007) writes that he 'told *The Sunday Times* that he was
   "inherently gloomy about the prospect of Africa" because "all our social policies
   are based on the fact that their intelligence is the same as ours [Whites, Western-
   ers] whereas all the testing says not really." He said there was a natural desire
   that all human beings should be equal but "people who have to deal with black
   employees find this not true."'
4. *See* in the Appendix the email I received from my Aboriginal friends. It was
   released over the internet on 2 February 2008 in reaction to the formal apology
   to be addressed to the Aboriginal people on 13 February 2008 by the newly
   elected Australian government, and illustrates a widespread evolutionist non-
   Aboriginal view of the Aboriginal community. Its circulation through the Aboriginal network is but one example of how Aboriginal people are constantly made
   aware of their sociocultural status as primitives and, as such, forever dependent
   upon the dominant White culture.
5. Aboriginal people referred to these certificates as 'Dog tags' because, as Sally
   Morgan pointed out in her screenprint on paper entitled *Citizenship* (Flinders
   University Art Museum), 'We had to be licensed to be called Australian'.
6. For a focused discussion of the importance of creating domestic-neighbourly
   spaces that can be shared by Black and White families *see* San Roque (this
   volume).
7. In my experience, Aboriginal people tend to be generously inclusive when it
   comes to tracing affiliation in general terms, but, in contrast to this, very de-

manding when specific tribal or places of affiliation are at stake. In the latter case, one must have demonstrated attachment to country in concrete terms. Similarly, in order to legitimately occupy an Aboriginal political position, one is expected to have proven unfailing attachment to one's Aboriginality.

8. John Morton (1993) has provided an important extension of the psychoanalytic interpretation of the Arrernte creation story that Géza Róheim (1945a) had begun. Morton too emphasizes that the myth depicts the link between sexual differentiation, separation from the maternal and the production of culture. However, contrary to my own argument, he concurs with Róheim's view that the myth symbolism (taken as an archetype of Self-Other, Life-Death, Father-Mother, Womb-Phallus) effectively reinstates the mother-child bond; it presents a 'journey *from* the mother *to* the mother, by way of the phallus' (Morton 1993: 335).

9. In 1990, for South Australia, the median age at death for Aboriginal men was forty-two years and for Aboriginal women fifty-seven years, whereas for the total population of South Australia, the median age at death was seventy-two for men and seventy-nine for women (ABSSAO 1993). Note that this represents a significant decrease when compared with statistics dating from five years earlier (whereas the figures for non-Aboriginal Australians remain more or less the same): between 1984 and 1989, the life expectancy at birth of South Australian Aboriginal men was fifty-five years, and for Aboriginal women sixty-seven years, while over the same period, the life expectancy at birth was seventy-three for non-Aboriginal men and seventy-nine for non-Aboriginal women (AIHW 1992).

Notes on Contributors

David Brooks is a PhD candidate in anthropology at the Australian National University. For twenty years he has worked as a consultant anthropologist, primarily in the Ngaanyatjarra region of the Western Desert. From an earlier focus on systems of Aboriginal land tenure, he has moved towards projects and research which addresses issues of social conflict and the viability of life in remote communities.

Dr Ute Eickelkamp is an honorary associate in anthropology at the University of Sydney. From 2004 to 2009 she was ARC Postdoctoral Research Fellow in the School for Social and Policy Research at Charles Darwin University. She is studying Anangu children's imagination and social and emotional dynamics through a traditional form of sand storytelling in the Central Australian community of Ernabella, after therapeutic Sandplay work with Tiwi children in Australia's north. A related ongoing research interest is Anangu art. She studied anthropology and sociology at Marburg, Berlin, and Heidelberg, Germany, and gained a graduate diploma in Infant and Parent Mental Health at Melbourne University.

Sandra Lewis grew up at Ernabella. She was the coordinator of Family Support Ernabella, a government-funded program that supports young mothers who sniff petrol.

Dr Marika Moisseeff, anthropologist and psychiatrist, Research Fellow in anthropology at the French National Centre of Scientific Research (CNRS), is a member of the Laboratoire d'anthropologie sociale in Paris. She has undertaken long-term fieldwork in South Australia as an AIATSIS Research Fellow on Aboriginal youth (1991–1995). Her research is two-fold: monographic, based on ongoing research in South Australia and on a previous document-based study of Arrernte initiation rites; comparative, aiming to uncover the cultural differences between contemporary Western societies and so-called more traditional settings regarding the modalities of achieving an adult identity and status. She is the author of *Un long chemin semé d'objets cultuels* (1995) and of *An Aboriginal Village in South Australia* (1999).

Dr John Morton recently retired from teaching anthropology and Aboriginal studies at La Trobe University's Bundoora Campus in Melbourne but remains an associate of the Anthropology Program in the School of Social Sciences at the University. He has worked with Aboriginal groups in Central Australia (Northern Territory) since 1981 and has also worked in Aboriginal South Australia, New South Wales, Victoria and Queensland. He edited (with Werner Muensterberger) Géza Róheim's *Children of the Desert II: Myths and Dreams of the Aborigines of Central Australia* (1988) and (with Phillip Batty and Lindy Allen) *The Photographs of Baldwin Spencer* (2005).

Dr Yasmine Musharbash (M.A. Freie Universität Berlin 1997, PhD Australian National University 2003) is a lecturer in the Department of Anthropology at the University of Sydney. She has been undertaking research with Warlpiri people since the mid-1990s, focusing on everyday life, social relations and spatio-temporal dimensions. She is the author of *Yuendumu Everyday. Contemporary Life in Remote Aboriginal Australia* (2008) and co-editor (with Katie Glaskin, Victoria Burbank and Myrna Tonkinson) of *Mortality, Mourning and Mortuary Practices in Indigenous Australia* (2008), (with John Carty) *You've got to be joking! Anthropological Perspectives on Humours* (2008), and (with Marcus Barber) *Ethnography & the Production of Anthropological Knowledge* (2011).

Prof Fred R. Myers is Silver Professor of Anthropology at New York University. He has done research with Aboriginal people in Australia since 1973. His first book concentrated on Aboriginal formulations of land tenure, spatial organization and personhood among Western Desert people (*Pintupi Country, Pintupi Self: Sentiment, Place and Politics among Western Desert Aborigines,* 1986). More recently he has studied the development and circulation of Aboriginal acrylic painting (*Painting Culture: The Making of an Aboriginal High Art,* 2002).

Dr Craig San Roque is a psychotherapist living in Alice Springs. He trained in child therapy and analytical psychology in London, helping set up innovative family care facilities, being influenced by Winnicott's notions of play as essential to human health and mental development. Since 1992 he has worked in Aboriginal affairs – especially in petrol sniffing prevention. He writes on the existential paradox in Black/White psychocultural relations.

Dr Carmel O'Shannessy is Assistant Professor of Linguistics in the Department of Linguistics, University of Michigan. She documents the emergence, development and stabilization of a new mixed language, Light Warlpiri, in northern Australia. In doing so she also documents children's acquisition of Light Warlpiri and the Lajamanu variety of Warlpiri. She has spent many years involved in language education programs in the Northern Territory of Australia.

Katrina Tjitayi lives at Ernabella in Central Australia. She currently holds the position of schools improvement coordinator on the Anangu Pitjantjatjara Yankunytjatjara Lands in the northwest corner of South Australia. Prior to this, she was for nine years the director of the Pitjantjatjara Yankunytjatjara Education Committee, which plans education on all levels for the communities on the Lands. Inspired by her mother, Angkuna Akitiya Tjitayi, one of the first Anangu teachers, and by a vision for the future well-being of her community, Katrina trained to fully qualify as a schoolteacher at the Anangu Tertiary Education Program at Ernabella. She worked at Fregon school from 1991 to 1995. In addition to planning and administrative work, she has been developing an emotional support program for young children.

Dr Myrna Tonkinson is an honorary research fellow in anthropology in the School of Social and Cultural Studies at the University of Western Australia. She has done research among Aboriginal people in the Western Desert of Western Australia since 1974. She is currently writing up results of a project, undertaken with two colleagues, examining some of the effects of social trauma on identity, worldview, risk-taking and other aspects of the lives of Indigenous people in two regions of Australia.

References

Ahearn, L.M. 2001. *Invitations to Love: Literacy, Love Letters and Social Change in Nepal.* Ann Arbor: University of Michigan Press.

Alanen, L. 2005. 'Childhood as Generational Condition. Towards a Relational Theory of Childhood', in C. Jenks (ed.), *Childhood: Critical Concepts in Sociology.* London: Routledge, pp. 286–305.

Altman, J. and M. Hinkson (eds). 2007. *Coercive Reconciliation: Stabilise, Normalise, Exit Aboriginal Australia.* North Carlton, VIC: Arena Publications Association.

Andrews, J. 2008. 'Bringing Up Our Yorta Yorta Children', in G. Robinson, U. Eickelkamp, J. Goodnow and I. Katz (eds), *Contexts of Child Development: Culture, Policy and Intervention.* Darwin: CDU Press, pp. 23–35.

Anon. 1929. 'Will Analyse Primitive Man: Expedition to Probe Native History'. *Sunday Pictorial,* 13 January, p. 7.

Aronowitz, T. 2005. 'The Role of "Envisioning the Future" in the Development of Resilience among At-Risk Youth', *Public Health Nursing* 22(3): 200–208.

Attwood, B. 2007. *The 1967 Referendum: Race, Power and the Australian Constitution.* Canberra: Aboriginal Studies Press.

Austin-Broos, D. 1996. '"Two Laws," Ontologies, Histories: Ways of Being Aranda Today', *TAJA* 7(1): 1–20.

Australian Bureau of Statistics (ABS). 2006. 'Census of Population and Housing Cat. No. 2068.0 – 2006 Census Tables'.

Australian Bureau of Statistics South Australian Office (ABSSAO). 1993. *South Australian Year Book No. 27: 1993.* A.J. Secker, Government Printer, South Australia.

Australian Crime: Facts and Figures 2000. Australian Institute of Criminology. ISBN 0 642 24219 4.

Australian Institute of Health and Welfare (AIHW). 1992. *Australia's Health 1992: The Third Biennial Health Report of the Australian Institute of Health and Welfare.* Canberra: Australian Government Publishing Service.

———. 2006. 'Child Protection Australia 2005–6'. Child Welfare Series. Canberra: Australian Government, Australian Institute of Health and Welfare (AIHW).

Barwick, D. 1964. 'The Self-conscious People of Melbourne', in M. Reay (ed.), *Aborigines Now.* Sydney: Angus & Robertson, pp. 20–31.

Bavin, E. 1993. 'Language and Culture: Socialisation in a Warlpiri Community', *Language and Culture in Aboriginal Australia.* Canberra: Aboriginal Studies Press, pp. 85–96.

Behrendt, L. 2007. 'The Emergency We Had to Have', in J. Altman and M. Hinkson (eds), *Coercive Reconciliation: Stabilise, Normalise, Exit Aboriginal Australia.* Melbourne: Arena Publications, pp. 15–20.

Behrendt, P. 1994. 'Assimilation', in D. Horton (ed.), *The Encyclopaedia of Aboriginal Australia. Aboriginal and Torres Strait Islander History, Society and Culture.* Canberra: Aboriginal Studies Press, pp. 68–70.

Benedict, R. 1970. 'Synergy: Some Notes of Ruth Benedict', selected by A. H. Maslow and J. J. Honigmann, *American Anthropologist* 72(2): 320–33.

Berndt, R.M. 1959. 'The Concept of "The Tribe" in the Western Desert of Australia', *Oceania* 30(2): 81–107.

———. 1962. *An Adjustment Movement in Arnhem Land.* Paris: Mouton.

Berndt, R.M. and C.H. Berndt. 1945. 'A Preliminary Report of Field Work in the Ooldea Region, Western South Australia', *Oceania* Reprint. Sydney: Australian Medical Publishing Company, pp. 1–343.

———. 1951. *Sexual Behavior in Western Arnhem Land.* New York: The Viking Fund.

———. 1981. *The World of the First Australians.* Sydney: Landsdowne Press.

Bertalanffy, L. von. 1967. *Robots, Men and Minds. Psychology in the Modern World.* New York: George Braziller.

Bettelheim, B. 1985. *Freud and Man's Soul.* London: Flamingo.

Betz, D. 2007. *Singing the Milky Way: A Journey into the Dreaming.* A Songline Aboriginal Art Productions. DVD Video, 62 mins.

Biddle, J.L. 1996. 'When Not Writing is Writing', *Australian Aboriginal Studies* 1: 21–33.

———. 2003. 'Country, Skin, Canvas: The Intercorporeal Art of Kathleen Petyarre', *Australian and New Zealand Journal of Art* 4(1): 61–76.

———. 2007. *Breasts, Bodies, Canvas: Central Desert Art as Experience.* Sydney: UNSW Press.

Blackett, J. 1997. *Fire in the Outback: The Untold Story of the Aboriginal Revival Movement that Began on Elcho Island in 1979.* Sutherland, NSW: Albatross Books.

Bolt, A. 2006. 'Stolen Generations: My Melbourne Writers' Festival Speech'. Retrieved 2 September 2008 from http://blogs.news.com.au/heraldsun/andrewbolt/index .php/heraldsun/comments/stolen_generations_my_writers_festival_speech/.

Bornstein, M.H., M.O. Haynes, et al. 1999. 'Play in Two Societies: Perspectives of Process, Specificity of Structure', *Child Development* 70(2): 317–31.

Boszormenyi-Nagy, I. and G.M. Spark. 1984. *Invisible Loyalties. Reciprocity in Intergenerational Family Therapy.* New York: Brunner/Mazel.

Boulden, K. and J. Morton. 2007. 'Don't Crash the Ambulance', in J. Altman and M. Hinkson (eds), *Coercive Reconciliation: Stabilise, Normalise, Exit Aboriginal Australia.* Melbourne: Arena Publications, pp. 163–70.

Bourdieu, P. 1980. *Le Sens Pratique.* Paris: Editions de Minuit.

Brady, M. 1992a. *Heavy Metal. The Social Meaning of Petrol Sniffing in Australia.* Canberra: Aboriginal Studies Press.

———. 1992b. 'Ethnography and Understandings of Aboriginal Drinking', *Journal of Drug Issues* 22(3): 699–714.

———. 1995. *Giving Away the Grog. Aboriginal Accounts of Drinking and Not Drinking.* Canberra: Aboriginal Studies Press.

Bretherton, I. (ed.). 1984. *Symbolic Play: The Development of Social Understanding.* Orlando, FL: Academic Press.

Briscoe, G. 2008. 'Assimiliation and Indifference: The Paradoxical Treatment of Indigenous Children in Central Australia, 1914–1951', in G. Robinson, U. Eickelkamp, J. Goodnow and I. Katz (eds), *Contexts of Child Development: Culture, Policy and Intervention.* Darwin: Charles Darwin University Press, pp. 7–22.

Brooks, D. 2002. 'What Impact the Mission?' in *Mission Time in Warburton.* Warburton, WA: Tjulyuru Regional Arts Gallery, Tjulyuru Cultural and Civic Centre.

Brooks, D. and I. Kral. 2007. *Ngaanyatjarra Lands Population Survey, Report One.* Warburton, WA: Shire of Ngaanyatjarra-ku.

Brooks, D. and G. Shaw. 2001. *Cultural Security in the Ngaanyatjarra Lands.* Report to the Ngaanyatjarra Health Service.

———. 2003. *Men, Conflict and Violence in the Ngaanyatjarra Region.* Report to the Ngaanyatjarra Health Service.

Burbank, V.K. 1985. 'The Mirriri as Ritualized Aggression', *Oceania* 56: 47–55.

———. 1988. *Aboriginal Adolescence: Maidenhood in an Australian Community.* New Brunswick, NJ: Rutgers University Press.

———. 1994. *Fighting Women: Anger and Aggression in Aboriginal Australia.* Berkeley: University of California Press.

———. 2006. 'From Bedtime to On Time: Why Many Aboriginal People Don't Especially Like Participating in Western Institutions', *Anthropological Forum* 16(1): 3–20.

Burton, L. 1990. 'Teenage Childbearing as an Alternative Life-course Strategy in Multigenerational Black Families', *Human Nature* 1: 123–43.

Caldwell, J.C. 2002. 'Aboriginal Society and the Global Demographic Transition', in G. Briscoe and L. Smith (eds), *The Aboriginal Population Revisited: 70,000 Years to the Present.* Canberra: Aboriginal History Incorporated, pp. 160–69.

Cane, S. 1990. 'Desert Demography: A Case Study of Pre-contact Aboriginal Densities', in B. Meehan and N. White (eds). *Hunter-gatherer Demography, Past and Present.* Oceania Monograph 39. Sydney: University of Sydney, pp. 149–59.

Central Australian Rural Practitioners Association. 2003. *CARPA Standard Treatment Manual—A Clinical Manual for Primary Health Care Practitioners in Remote and Rural Communities in Central and Northern Australia,* 4th ed. Alice Springs, NT: CARPA.

Chikritzs, T., R. Pascal, D. Gray, A. Stearne, S. Saggers and P. Jones. 2007. 'Trends in Alcohol-attributable Deaths among Indigenous Australians 1998–2004', *National Alcohol Indicators Bulletin* 11. Perth: National Drug Research Institute, Curtin University of Technology. http://www.ndri.curtin.edu.au.

Collmann, J.R. 1988. *Fringe-dwellers and Welfare: The Aboriginal Response to Bureaucracy.* St Lucia: University of Queensland Press.

Coombs, H.C. 1994. *Aboriginal Autonomy: Issues and Strategies.* Cambridge: Cambridge University Press.

Corsaro, W.A. 2004. *The Sociology of Childhood.* Second edition. Thousand Oaks, CA: Pine Forge Press.

Corsaro, W.A. and D. Eder. 1990. 'Children's Peer Cultures', *Annual Review of Sociology* 16: 197–220.

Corsaro, W.A. and T.A. Rizzo. 1988. 'Discussione and Friendship: Socialization Processes in the Peer Culture of Italian Nursery School Children', *American Sociology Review* 53: 879–94.

Cowlishaw, G. 2003a. 'Disappointing Indigenous People: Violence and the Refusal of Help', *Public Culture* 15: 103–25.
———. 2003b. 'Euphemism, Banality, Propaganda: Anthropology, Public Debate and Indigenous Communities', *Australian Aboriginal Studies* 1: 2–18.
deMause, Lloyd. 2002. *The Emotional Life of Nations.* New York: Other Press.
———. n.d. *The Origins of War in Child Abuse.* Retrieved 16 January 2009 from http://www.psychohistory.com/.
Derricotte, T. 1997. *The Black Notebooks. An Interior Journey.* New York: W. W. Norton.
Devisch, R. 2007. 'A Psychoanalytic Revisiting of Fieldwork and Intercultural Borderlinking', in J. Mimica (ed.), *Explorations in Psychoanalytic Ethnography.* New York: Berghahn Books, pp. 121–47.
de Young, M. 2004. *The Day Care Ritual Abuse Moral Panic.* London: McFarland.
Dole, C. and T.S. Csordas. 2003. 'Trials of Navajo Youth: Identity, Healing, and the Struggle for Maturity', *Ethos* 31(3): 357–84.
Dolk, M. 2006. 'Are We Strangers in this Place?', in L. Michael (ed.), *Paddy Bedford.* Museum Contemporary Art, Sydney, 6 December 2006–15 April 2007, exh. cat., pp. 17–49.
Dousset, L. 2003. 'Indigenous Modes or Representing Social Relationships: A Short Critique of the "Genealogical Concept"', *Australian Aboriginal Studies* 1: 19–29.
Dryfoos, J.G. 1998. *Safe Passage: Making It through Adolescence in a Risky Society.* New York: Oxford University Press.
Duelke, B. 2005. 'Über eine Thematisierung des Möglichen', *Zeitschrift für Ethnologie* 130: 99–125.
Dussart, F. 1988a. 'Warlpiri Women's Yawulyu Ceremonies: A Forum for Socialization and Innovation', Ph.D. dissertation. Canberra: Australian National University.
———. 1988b. 'Notes on Warlpiri Women's Personal Names', *Journal de la Société des Océanistes* 86: 53–60.
———. 2000. *The Politics of Ritual in an Aboriginal Settlement: Kinship, Gender, and the Currency of Knowledge.* Washington, DC: Smithsonian Institution Press.
Eickelkamp, U. 2004. 'Egos and Ogres: Aspects of Psychosexual Development and Cannibalistic Demons in Central Australia', *Oceania* 74: 161–89.
———. 2008a. '(Re)presenting Experience: A Comparison of Australian Aboriginal Children's Sand Play in Two Settings', *International Journal of Applied Psychoanalytic Studies* 5(1): 23–50.
———. 2008b. 'Play, Imagination and Early Experience: Sand Storytelling and Continuity of Being among Anangu Pitjantjatjara Girls', in G. Robinson, U. Eickelkamp, J. Goodnow and I. Katz (eds.), *Contexts of Child Development: Culture, Policy and Intervention.* Darwin: Charles Darwin University Press, pp. 138–52.
———. 2008c. '"I don't talk story like that": On the Social Meaning of Children's Sand Stories at Ernabella', in J. Simpson and G. Wigglesworth (eds), *Children's Language and Multilingualism.* New York: Continuum, pp. 79–99.
———. 2010. 'Children and Youth in Aboriginal Australia: An Overview of the Literature', *Anthropological Forum* 20(2): 147–66.
Elkin, A.P. 1934. 'Cult Totemism and Mythology in Northern South Australia', *Oceania* 5(2): 171–92.

Ellingson, T. 2001. *The Myth of the Noble Savage.* Berkeley: University of California Press.

Emde, R.N., D.P. Wolf and D. Oppenheim (eds). 2003. *Revealing the Inner Worlds of Young Children: The MacArthur Story Stem Battery and Parent-child Narratives.* Oxford: Oxford University Press.

Factor, J. 1988. *Captain Cook Chased a Chook: Children's Folklore in Australia.* Melbourne: Penguin.

Fanon, F. 1952. *Peau Noire, Masques Blancs.* Paris: Seuil.

Farver, J.A.M. and Y. Lee Shin. 1997. 'Social Pretend Play in Korean- and Anglo-American Preschoolers', *Child Development* 68(3): 544–56.

Fietz, P. 2005. 'Socialisation and the Shaping of Youth Identity at Docker River', Paper presented at 'Imagining Childhood: Children, Culture and Community'. Charles Darwin University Symposium, Alice Springs, September 2005.

———. 2008. 'Socialisation and the Shaping of Youth Identity at Docker River', in G. Robinson, U. Eickelkamp, J. Goodnow and I. Katz (eds), *Contexts of Child Development: Culture, Policy and Intervention,* Darwin: CDU Press, pp. 49–58.

Finlayson, J.D. 1989. 'Welfare Incomes and Aboriginal Gender Relations', in J.C. Altman (ed.), *Emergent Inequalities in Aboriginal Australia.* Oceania Monograph 38. Sydney: University of Sydney.

Foucault, M. 1979. *Discipline and Punishment: The Birth of the Prison.* Harmondsworth, U.K.: Penguin.

———. 1981. *The History of Sexuality: Volume One: An Introduction.* Harmondsworth, U.K.: Penguin.

———. 1991. 'Governmentality', in G. Burchell, C. Gordon and P. Miller (eds), *The Foucault Effect: Studies in Governmentality.* Chicago: University of Chicago Press, pp. 87–104.

Freud, S. 2001[1913]. 'Totem and Taboo: Some Points of Agreement between the Mental Lives of Savages and Neurotics'. *The Standard Edition of the Complete Psychological Works of Sigmund Freud,* vol. 13. London: Vintage, pp. ix–162.

———. 2001[1919]. '"A Child Is Being Beaten": A Contribution to the Study of the Origin of Sexual Perversions'. *The Standard Edition of the Complete Psychological Works of Sigmund Freud,* vol. 17. London: Vintage, pp. 175–204.

———. 2001[1924]. 'The Dissolution of the Oedipus Complex'. *The Standard Edition of the Complete Psychological Works of Sigmund Freud,* vol. 19. London: Vintage, pp. 171–79.

———. 2001[1925]. 'An Autobiographical Study'. *The Standard Edition of the Complete Psychological Works of Sigmund Freud,* vol. 20. London: Vintage, pp. 1–74.

———. 2001[1930]. 'Civilization and Its Discontents'. *The Standard Edition of the Complete Psychological Works of Sigmund Freud,* vol. 21. London: Vintage, pp. 57–145.

Glaskin, K., M. Tonkinson, Y. Musharbash and V. Burbank (eds). 2008. *Mortality, Mourning and Mortuary Practices in Indigenous Australia.* Surrey, U.K.: Ashgate.

Goddard, C. 1992. *Pitjantjatjara/Yankunytjatjara to English Dictionary.* 2nd edition. Alice Springs, NT: IAD Press.

Goldman, L.R. 1998. *Child's Play: Myth, Mimesis and Make-believe.* Oxford: Berg.

Goodale, J.C. 1971. *Tiwi Wives: A Study of the Women of Melville Island, North Australia.* Seattle: University of Washington Press.

Gould, R. 1969. *Yiwara: Foragers of the Australian Desert.* London: Collins.

Granites, R. J. and M. Laughren. 2001. 'Semantic Contrasts in Warlpiri Verbal Morphology: A Warlpiri's Verbal View', in *Forty Years On: Ken Hale and Australian Languages.* Canberra: Pacific Linguistics, pp. 151–59.

Gray, A. 1987. *The 'Death Bird': Aspects of Adult Aboriginal Mortality.* Working Paper No. 7, Aboriginal Family Demography Study, Department of Demography, Research School of Social Sciences, The Australian National University, Canberra.

Gray, D. and S. Saggers. 2002. *Indigenous Australian Alcohol and Other Drug Issues: Research from the National Drug Research Institute.* Perth, WA: National Drug Research Institute.

Green, J. 1992. *Alyawarr to English Dictionary.* Alice Springs, NT: IAD Press.

Greer, G. 2008. 'Once Upon a Time in a Land, Far, Far Away', *The Guardian* 16 December.

Hale, K. 1973. 'Person Marking in Walbiri', in *A Festschrift for Morris Halle.* New York: Rinehart and Winston.

———. 1992. 'Basic Word Order in Two "Free Word Order" Languages', in *Pragmatics of Word Order Flexibility.* Amsterdam: John Benjamins.

Hale, K., M. Laughren, et al. 1995. 'Warlpiri', *An International Handbook of Contemporary Research.* Berlin: Walter de Gruyter, pp. 1430–49.

Halloran, M.J. 2004. *Cultural Maintenance and Trauma in Indigenous Australia.* Paper presented at the 23rd annual Australia and New Zealand Law and History Society Conference, Perth.

Hamilton, A. 1971. 'The Equivalence of Siblings', *Anthropological Forum* 3(1): 13–20.

———. 1972. 'Blacks and Whites: The Relationships of Change', *Arena* 30: 34–48.

———. 1979a. 'Timeless Transformation: Women, Men and History in the Australian Western Desert', Ph.D. dissertation. Sydney: University of Sydney.

———. 1979b. 'A Comment on Arthur Hippler's Paper "Culture and Personality Perspective of the Yolngu of Northeastern Arnhem Land: Part I" in the *Journal of Psychological Anthropology,* 1978, 1: 221–44'. *Mankind* 12: 164–69.

———. 1981. *Nature and Nurture: Aboriginal Child-rearing in North-central Arnhem Land.* Canberra: Australian Institute of Aboriginal Studies.

———. 1982. 'Child Health and Childcare in a Desert Community', in J. Reid (ed.), *Body, Land and Spirit: Health and Healing in Aboriginal Society.* St Lucia: University of Queensland Press, pp. 49–71.

Hart, J. 2006. 'Saving Children: What Role for Anthropology?' *Anthropology Today* 22(1): 5–8.

Haskins, V. and J. Maynard 2005. 'Sex, Race and Power: Aboriginal Men and White Women in Australian History'. *Australian Historical Studies* 37(126): 191–216. [Paper in Special Issue: Histories of Sexuality. Angelides, Steven and Baird, Barbara (eds.).] [online]. Availability: <http://search.informit.com.au.ezproxy1.library.usyd.edu.au/fullText;dn=200511344;res=APAFT> ISSN: 1031-461X. [cited 26 Aug 08]

Heath, S.B. 2008. 'Foreword', in J. Simpson and G. Wigglesworth (eds), *Children's Language and Multilingualism: Indigenous Language Use at Home and School.* London: Continuum, pp. ix–xiii.

Henderson, J. and V. Dobson. 1994. *Eastern and Central Arrernte to English Dictionary*. Alice Springs, NT: IAD Press.

Herdt, G. and S.C. Leavitt. 1998. *Adolescence in Pacific Island Societies*. Pittsburgh, PA: University of Pittsburgh Press.

Hernández, T. 1941. 'Children among the Drysdale River Tribes', *Oceania* 12(2): 122–33.

Hersey, S. 2004. 'Aranda Games', in M. Cawthorn (ed.), *Traditions in the Midst of Change: Communities, Cultures and the Strehlow Legacy in Central Australia*. Proceedings of the Strehlow Conference, Alice Springs, 18–20 September 2002. Alice Springs, NT: Strehlow Research Centre and Northern Territory Government, pp. 26–29.

Hiatt, L.R. 1975. 'Introduction', in R.L. Hiatt (ed.), *Australian Aboriginal Mythology*. Canberra: Australian Institute of Aboriginal Studies, pp. 1–23.

———. 1987. 'Freud and Anthropology', in D. Austin-Broos (ed.), *Creating Culture: Profiles in the Study of Culture*. Sydney: Allen & Unwin, pp. 89–106.

———. 2007. 'The Moral Lexicon of the Warlpiri People of Central Australia', *Australian Aboriginal Studies* 1: 4–30.

Hill, B. 2002. *Broken Song: T.G.H. Strehlow and Aboriginal Possession*. Sydney: Vintage.

Hilliard, W. 1968. *The People in Between: The Pitjantjatjara People of Ernabella*. London: Hodder and Stoughton.

Hinkson, J. 2007. 'The "Innocence" of the Settler Imagination', in J. Altman and M. Hinkson (eds), *Coercive Reconciliation: Stabilise, Normalise, Exit Aboriginal Australia*. Melbourne: Arena Publications, pp. 287–94.

Hinkson, M. 2007. 'Introduction: In the Name of the Child', in J. Altman and M. Hinkson (eds), *Coercive Reconciliation: Stabilise, Normalise, Exit Aboriginal Australia*. Melbourne: Arena Publications, pp. 1–12.

Hippler, A. 1978. 'Culture and Personality of the Yolngu of Northeastern Arnhem Land: Part I—Early Socialization', *Journal of Psychological Anthropology* 1: 221–44.

———. 1981. 'The Yolngu and Cultural Relativism: a Response to Reser', *American Anthropologist* 83: 393–97.

Hobbes, T. 1968[1651]. *Leviathan*. Harmondsworth, U.K.: Penguin.

Horton, D.R. 1996. *Aboriginal Australia* map. Canberra: Aboriginal Studies Press.

Howard, J. 2007. Address to the Sydney Institute, 25 June 2007. Retrieved 2 September 2008 from http://www.abc.net.au/news/opinion/speeches/files/20070625_howard.pdf.

Howie-Willis, I. 1994a. 'Dog Tags', in D. Horton (ed.), *The Encyclopaedia of Aboriginal Australia. Aboriginal and Torres Strait Islander History, Society and Culture*. Canberra: Aboriginal Studies Press, pp. 298–99.

———. 1994b. 'Protectors of Aborigines', in D. Horton (ed.), *The Encyclopaedia of Aboriginal Australia. Aboriginal and Torres Strait Islander History, Society and Culture*. Canberra: Aboriginal Studies Press, pp. 903–4.

———. 1994c. 'Aborigines Welfare Board (NSW)', in D. Horton (ed.), *The Encyclopaedia of Aboriginal Australia. Aboriginal and Torres Strait Islander History, Society and Culture*. Canberra: Aboriginal Studies Press, pp. 28–29.

———. 1994d. 'Aboriginal Protection Boards', in D. Horton (ed.), *The Encyclopaedia of Aboriginal Australia. Aboriginal and Torres Strait Islander History, Society and Culture*. Canberra: Aboriginal Studies Press, pp. 22–23.

Hughes, D.M. 1987. 'When Cultural Rights Conflict with the "Best Interests of the Child": A View from Inside the Child Welfare System', in N. Sheper-Hughes (ed.), *Child Survival: Anthropological Perspectives on the Treatment and Maltreatment of Children*. Dordrecht, Netherlands: D. Reidel, pp. 377–87.

Hughes, H. 2007. *Lands of Shame: Aboriginal and Torres Strait Islander "Homelands" in Transition*. St Leonards, NSW: The Centre for Independent Studies.

ICHR (Telethon Institute for Child Health Research). 2006. *Western Australian Aboriginal Child Health Survey*. http://www.ichr.uwa.edu.au/files/user17/Volume1_Chapter3.pdf 15/08/06.

James, A., C. Jenks and A. Prout. 1998. *Theorizing Childhood*. Cambridge: Polity Press.

Kearney, S. and A. Wilson. 2006. 'Raping Children Part of "Men's Business"'. *The Australian*, 16 May.

Keen, I. 1994. *Knowledge and Secrecy in an Aboriginal Religion*. Oxford: Clarendon Press.

Kendon, A. 1988. *Sign Languages of Aboriginal Australia: Cultural, Semiotic and Communicative Perspectives*. Cambridge: Cambridge University Press.

Kimm, J. 2004. *A Fatal Conjunction: Two Laws, Two Cultures*. Sydney: Federation Press.

Klapproth, D. 2004. *Narrative as Social Practice: Anglo-Western and Australian Aboriginal Oral Traditions*. Berlin: Mouton de Gruyter.

Klein, M. 1997[1932]. *The Psycho-Analysis of Children*. London: Vintage.

Kowal, E. 2008. 'The Politics of the Gap', *American Anthropologist* 110: 338–48.

Kral, I. 2007. 'Writing Words–Right Way! Literacy and Social Practice in the Ngaanyatjarra World', Ph.D. dissertation. Canberra: Australian National University.

Kral, I. and E.M. Ellis. 2008. 'Children, Language and Literacy in the Ngaanyatjarra Lands', in J. Simpson and G. Wigglesworth (eds), *Children's Language and Multilingualism*. London: Continuum, pp. 154–72.

Kuzawa, C. 2008. 'The Developmental Origins of Adult Health: Intergenerational Inertia in Adaptation and Disease', in W.R. Trevathan, E.O. Smith and J. McKenna (eds), *Evolutionary Medicine and Health: New Perspectives*. New York: Oxford University Press, pp. 325–47.

Laing, R.D. 1965. *The Divided Self: An Existential Study in Sanity and Madness*. Harmondsworth, U.K.: Penguin.

Langlois, A. 2006. 'Wordplay in Teenage Pitjantjatjara', *Australian Journal of Linguistics* 26(2): 181–92.

Langton, M. 2008a. 'Trapped in the Aboriginal Reality Show', *Griffith Review* 19. Retrieved 18 January 2009 from http://www3.griffith.edu.au/01/griffithreview/past_editions.php?id=503.

———. 2008b. 'Faraway Downs Fantasy Resonates Close to Home'. *The Age*, 23 November.

Laplanche, J. and J.-B. Pontalis. 1985. *The Language of Psycho-Analysis*. London: Vintage.

Laughren, M. 1984. 'Warlpiri Baby Talk', *Australian Journal of Linguistics* 4: 73–88.

Laughren, M., R. Hoogenraad, et al. 1996. *A Learner's Guide to Warlpiri*. Alice Springs, NT: Institute for Aboriginal Development Press.

Leach, E. 1968. *The Structural Study of Myth and Totemism*. London: Routledge, Kegan & Paul.

Lévi-Strauss, C. 1963. *Totemism*. Boston: Beacon Press.
———. 1997. *Tristes Tropiques*, trans. J. Weightman and D. Weightman. New York: Random House.
LeVine, R.A. and R.S. New (eds). 2008. *Anthropology and Child Development: A Cross-Cultural Reader*. Maldon, MA: Blackwell Publishing.
MacWhinney, B. 1987. *Mechanisms of Language Acquisition*. Hillsdale, NJ: Lawrence Erlbaum.
MacWhinney, B. and E. Bates. 1978. 'Sentential Devices for Conveying Givenness and Newness: A Cross-cultural Developmental Study', *Journal of Verbal Learning and Verbal Behaviour* 17: 539–58.
Maddock, K. 2001. 'Sceptical Thoughts on Customary Law', in G. Johns (ed.), *Waking Up to Dreamtime: The Illusion of Aboriginal Self-Determination*. Singapore: Media Masters, pp. 152–71.
Mains, D. 2007. 'Neoliberal Times: Progress, Boredom and Shame Among Young Men in Urban Ethiopia', *American Ethnologist* 34(4): 659–73.
Malcolm, I. and S. Kaldor. 1991. 'Aboriginal English: An Overview', in S. Romaine (ed.), *Language in Australia*. Cambridge: Cambridge University Press, pp. 67–83.
Malcolm, J. 1997. *In the Freud Archives*. 2nd edition. London: Papermac.
Manne, R. 2001. *In Denial: The Stolen Generations and the Right*. Melbourne: Schwartz Publishing.
Marcus, G.E. 1998. *Ethnography through Thick and Thin*. Princeton, NJ: Princeton University Press.
Marcus, G.E. and M.J. Fischer. 1986. *Anthropology as Cultural Critique: An Experimental Moment in the Human Sciences*. Chicago: University of Chicago Press.
Marcuse, H. 1955. *Eros and Civilization: A Philosophical Inquiry into Freud*. Boston: Beacon Press.
Martin, D.F. 1993. 'Autonomy and Relatedness: An Ethnography of the Wik People of Aurukun, Western Cape York Peninsula', Ph.D. dissertation. Canberra: Australian National University.
Masson, J.M. 1984. *The Assault on Truth: Freud's Suppression of the Seduction Theory*. London: Faber and Faber.
McCarthy, F.D. 1939. 'Trade in Aboriginal Australia and Trade Relationships with Torres Strait, New Guinea and Malaya', *Oceania* 9(4): 405–38; 10(1): 80–104; 10(2): 171–95.
McKnight, D. 2002. *From Hunting to Drinking: The Devastating Effects of Alcohol on an Australian Aboriginal Community*. London: Routledge.
Meggitt, M. J. 1962. *Desert People*. London: Angus and Robertson.
———. 1987. 'Understanding Australian Aboriginal Society: Kinship Systems or Cultural Categories?', in W.H. Edwards (ed.), *Traditional Aboriginal Society. A Reader*. Melbourne: Macmillan, pp. 113–37.
Merlan, F. 1986. 'Australian Aboriginal Conception Beliefs Revisited', *Man* 21: 474–93.
———. 1992. 'Male-Female Separation and Forms of Society in Aboriginal Australia', *Cultural Anthropology* 7(2): 169–93.
———. 1998. *Caging the Rainbow: Places, Politics, and Aborigines in a North Australian Town*. Honolulu: University of Hawaii Press.

Merleau-Ponty, M. 1964. *Signs.* Evanston, IL: Northwestern University Press.

Milmo, C. 2007. 'Fury at DNA Pioneer's Theory: Africans Are Less Intelligent than Westerners'. http://news.independent.co.uk/sci_tech/article3067222.ece. 17 October.

Moisseeff, M. 1992. 'Les enjeux anthropologiques de la thérapie familiale avec les adolescents', in C. Gammer and M.-C. Cabié (eds), *L'Adolescence, crise familiale. Thérapie familiale par phases.* Toulouse: Editions Erès, pp. 205–27.

———. 1995. *Un long chemin semé d'objets cultuels: Le cycle initiatique Aranda.* Paris: Editions de l'Ecole des Hautes Etudes en Sciences Sociales, Coll. Cahiers de l'Homme.

———. 1998. 'Rêver la différence des sexes: Quelques implications du traitement Aborigène de la sexualité', in A. Durandeau, J.-M. Sztalryd and C. Vasseur-Fauconnet (eds), *Sexe et guérison.* Paris: l'Harmattan, pp. 45–74.

———. 1999a. *An Aboriginal Village in South Australia. A Snapshot of Davenport.* Canberra: Aboriginal Studies Press.

———. 1999b. 'La hiérarchisation des cultures, un autre regard sur les migrations et l'exclusion sociale', *Thérapie Familiale* 20(3): 237–52.

———. 2002. 'Australian Aboriginal Ritual Objects', in M. Jeudy-Ballini and B. Juillerat (eds), *People and Things. Social Mediations in Oceania.* Durham, NC: Carolina Academic Press, pp. 239–63.

———. 2004a. 'Perspective anthropologique sur les rôles parentaux', in P. Angel and P. Mazet (eds), *Guérir les souffrances familiales.* Paris: Presses Universitaires de France, pp. 29–45.

———. 2004b. 'Dépendance nourricière et domination culturelle: Une approche anthropologique des addictions', Special Topic 'Rituels, initiation et thérapie', *Psychotropes. Revue Internationale des Toxicomanies et des Addictions* 10(3–4): 31–50.

———. 2005. 'Penser le métissage: Une interrogation pour les sciences sociales', *L'Autre, Cliniques, Cultures et Sociétés* 6(2): 287–304.

———. 2006. 'La transmission de la parentalité: Un rôle parental secondarisé dans les sociétés occidentales contemporaines', in B. Schneider et al. (eds), *Enfant en développement, famille et handicaps. Interactions et transmissions.* Ramonville, France: Editions Erès, pp. 11–22.

Money, J., J.E. Cawte, G. Bianchi and B. Nurcombe. 1973. 'Sex Training and Traditions', in G.E. Kearney, P.R. de Lacey and G.R. Davidson (eds), *The Psychology of Aboriginal Australians.* Sydney: John Wiley, pp. 395–416.

Moore, K.A. (ed.) 1995. *Report to Congress on Out-of-wedlock Childbearing.* Hyattsville, MD: US Department of Health and Human Services. http://www.cdc.gov/nchs/data/misc/wedlock.pdf.

Morphy, F. 2006. 'Lost in Translation?: Remote Indigenous Households and Definitions of the Family', *Family Matters: Newsletter of the Australian Institute of Family Studies,* no. 73: 23–31. Retrieved 25 May 2007 from http://search.informit.com.au/documentSummary;dn=166689968089022;res=E-LIBRARY ISSN: 1030–2646.

Morton, J. 1987a. 'Singing Subjects and Sacred Objects: More on Munn's "Transformation of Subjects into Objects" in Central Australian Myth', *Oceania* 58: 100–18.

———. 1987b. 'The Effectiveness of Totemism: "Increase Ritual" and Resource Control in Central Australia', *Man* 22: 453–74.

———. 1988. 'Géza Róheim's Contribution to Australian Ethnography'. Introduction to G. Róheim, *Children of the Desert II: Myths and Dreams of the Aborigines of Central Australia*. Sydney: Oceania Publications, pp. vii–xxx.

———. 1989. 'Singing Subjects and Sacred Objects: A Psychological Interpretation of the "Transformation of Subjects into Objects" in Central Australian Myth', *Oceania* 59: 280–98.

———. 1993. 'Sensible Beasts: Psychoanalysis, Structuralism, and the Analysis of Myth', in L.B. Boyer, R.M. Boyers and S. M Sonnenberg (eds), *Essays in Honour of Alan Dundes*. Hillsdale, NJ: Analytic Press, pp. 317–43.

———. 2001. 'Facing the Big Ditch: Is Multiculturalism Really Undermining the Virtues of Civilisation?' Review of Roger Sandall's *The Culture Cult: Designer Tribalism and Other Essays*. *The Age*, 26 May.

Mountford, C.P. 1976. *Nomads of the Australian Desert*. Adelaide: Rigby.

Mullighan, E.P. 2008. 'Children on Anangu Pitjantjatjara Yankunytjatjara (APY) Lands: A Report into Sexual Abuse'. Report of the Commission of Inquiry (Children in State Care and Children on APY Lands). Adelaide: South Australian Government.

Mulvaney, D.J. and J. Kamminga. 1999. *Prehistory of Australia*. Sydney: Allen & Unwin.

Munn, N.D. 1963. 'The Walbiri Sand Story', *Australian Territories* 3(6): 37–44.

———. 1965. 'A Report of Field Research at Areyonga, 1964–1965'. Canberra: Australian Institute of Aboriginal Studies. Unpubl. manuscript.

———. 1966. 'Visual Categories: An Approach to the Study of Representational Systems', *American Anthropologist* 68: 939–50.

———. 1970. 'The Transformation of Subjects into Objects in Walbiri and Pitjantjatjara Myth', in R.M. Berndt (ed.), *Australian Aboriginal Anthropology: Modern Studies in the Social Anthropology of Australian Aborigines*. Nedlands: University of Western Australia Press, pp. 141–63.

———. 1973. *Walbiri Iconography: Graphic Representation and Cultural Symbolism in a Central Australian Society*. Ithaca, NY: Cornell University Press.

Musharbash, Y. 2003. 'Warlpiri Sociality. An Ethnography of the Spatial and Temporal Dimensions of Everyday Life in a Remote Aboriginal Settlement', Ph.D. dissertation. Canberra: Australian National University.

———. 2007. 'Boredom, Time, and Modernity: An Example from Aboriginal Australia', *American Anthropologist* 109(2): 307–17.

———. 2008a. '"Sorry Business is Yapa Way": Warlpiri Mortuary Rituals as Embodied Practice', in M. Tonkinson, Y. Musharbash, K. Glaskin and V. Burbank (eds), *Mortuality, Mourning and Mortuary Practices in Indigenous Australia*. Aldershot, U.K.: Ashgate, pp. 21–36.

———. 2008b. *Yuendumu Everyday. Contemporary Life in Remote Aboriginal Australia*. Canberra: Aboriginal Studies Press.

Myers, F.R. 1976. 'To Have and to Hold: A Study of Persistence and Change in Pintupi Social Life', Ph.D. dissertation. Bryn Mawr, PA: Bryn Mawr College.

———. 1979. 'Emotions and the Self: A Theory of Personhood and Political Order among the Pintupi', *Ethos* 7: 343–70.

———. 1980. 'The Cultural Basis of Politics in Pintupi Life', *Mankind* 12(3): 197–214.

———. 1982. 'Ideology and Experience: The Cultural Basis of Pintupi Politics', in M.C. Howard (ed.), *Aboriginal Power in Australian Society.* Brisbane: University of Queensland Press, pp. 108–52.

———. 1986. *Pintupi Country, Pintupi Self.* Los Angeles: University of California Press.

———. 1988a. 'The Logic and Meaning of Anger Among Pintupi Aborigines', *Man* 23(4): 589–610.

———. 1988b. 'Burning the Truck and Holding the Country: Forms of Property, Time, and the Negotiation of Identity among Pintupi Aborigines', in T. Ingold, D. Riches and J. Woodburn (eds), *Hunter-gatherers, II: Property, Power and Ideology.* London: Berg, pp. 52–74.

———. 1993. 'Place, Identity, and Exchange: The Transformation of Nurturance to Social Reproduction over the Life-cycle in a Kin-based Society', in J. Fajans (ed.), *Exchanging Products: Producing Exchange. Oceania Monograph* 43, pp. 33–57.

———. 2002. *Painting Culture: The Making of an Aboriginal High Art.* Durham, NC: Duke University Press.

———. 2004. 'Unsettled Business: Acrylic Painting, Tradition, and Indigenous Being', special issue, 'Confronting World Art', *Visual Anthropology* 17(3–4): 247–72. Also published in L. Taylor (ed.), *The Power of Knowledge and the Resonance of Tradition.* Canberra: Aboriginal Studies Press (2005), pp. 3–33.

Nash, D. 1986. *Topics in Warlpiri Grammar.* New York: Garland Publishing Inc.

Nash, D. and J. Simpson. 1981. '"No-name" in Central Australia', *Chicago Linguistic Society* 1(2): 165–77.

National Inquiry into the Separation of Aboriginal and Torres Strait Islander Children from their Families. 1997. 'Bringing Them Home: Report of the National Inquiry into the Separation of Aboriginal and Torres Strait Islander Children from their Families'. Sydney: Human Rights and Equal Opportunity Commission, Sterling Press.

Ngaanyatjarra Council (Aboriginal Corporation) Doing Business with Government. July 2003. Alice Springs, NT: Ngaanyatjarra Council.

Nicholls, C. 2000. 'Warlpiri Graffiti', in J. Docker and J. Fischer (eds), *Race, Colour and Identity in Australia and New Zealand.* Sydney: University of New South Wales Press, pp. 79–94.

Nowra, L. 2007. *Bad Dreaming: Aboriginal Men's Violence Against Women and Children.* Melbourne: Pluto Press.

Ochs, E. and B.B. Schieffelin.1984. 'Language Acquisition and Socialization: Three Developmental Stories and their Implications', in R. Shweder and R. Levine (eds), *Culture Theory: Essays on Mind, Self, and Emotion.* New York: Cambridge University Press, pp. 276–319.

Opie, I. and P. Opie. 1974. *The Classic Fairy Tales.* Oxford: Oxford University Press.

O'Shannessy, C. 2005. 'Light Warlpiri: A New Language', *Australian Journal of Linguistics* 25(1): 31–57.

———. 2008. 'Children's Production of Their Heritage Language and a New Mixed Language', in J. Simpson and G. Wigglesworth (eds), *Children's Language and Multilingualism: Indigenous Language Use at Home and School.* London: Continuum, pp. 261–82.

―――. 2009. 'Language Variation and Change in a North Australian Indigenous Community', in D. Preston and J. Stanford (eds), *Variationist Approaches to Indigenous Minority Languages*. Amsterdam: John Benjamins, pp. 419–39.

Pastner, C. 1982. 'Comment on Hippler's Response to Reser', *American Anthropologist* 84: 404–06.

Pearson, N. 2000. *Our Right to Take Responsibility*. Cairns: Noel Pearson and Associates.

―――. 2007. 'White Guilt, Victimhood and the Quest for a Radical Centre', *Griffith Review* 16. Retrieved 18 January 2009 from http://www3.griffith.edu.au/01/griffithreview/past_editions.php?id=382.

Peile, A.R. 1997. *Body and Soul: An Aboriginal View*. Ed. Peter Bindon. Victoria Park, WA: Hesperian Press.

Peterson, N. 1993. 'Demand Sharing: Reciprocity and the Pressure for Generosity among Foragers', *American Anthropologist* 95: 860–74.

Peterson, N. in collaboration with J. Long. 1986. *Australian Territorial Organization: A Band Perspective*. Sydney: University of Sydney.

Piaget, J. 1962[1951]. *Play, Dreams and Imitation in Childhood*. New York: W.W. Norton.

Plant, V. and A. Viegas (eds) 2002. *Mission Time in Warburton: An Exhibition Exploring Aspects of the Warburton Mission History 1933–1973*, Warburton Arts Project Press.

Poirier, S. 2003. 'This is Good Country. We are Good Dreamers: Dreams and Dreaming in the Australian Western Desert', in R.I. Lohmann (ed.), *Dream Travelers: Sleep Experiences and Culture in the Western Pacific*. New York: Palgrave Macmillan, pp. 107–25.

Pupavac, V. 2001. 'Misanthropy without Borders: The International Children's Rights Regime', *Disasters* 25: 95–112.

Radcliffe-Brown, A.R. 1913. 'Three Tribes of Western Australia', *Journal of the Royal Anthropological Institute* 43(1): 143–94.

Reser, J. 1981. 'Australian Aboriginal Man's Inhumanity to Man: A Case of Cultural Distortion', *American Anthropologist* 83: 387–93.

―――. 1982. 'Cultural Relativity or Cultural Bias: A Response to Hippler', *American Anthropologist* 84: 399–404.

Richardson, N. 2005. 'Child Abuse and Neglect in Indigenous Australian Communities'. Child Abuse Protection Resource Sheet No 10. National Child Protection Clearing House and the Australian Institute of Family Studies. Retrieved 31 January 2009 from http://www.aifs.gov.au/nch/pubs/sheets/rs10/rs10.html.

Robinson, G. 1990. 'Separation, Retaliation, and Suicide: Mourning and Conflicts of Young Tiwi Men', *Oceania* 60(3): 161–78.

―――. 1992a. 'Dependence and Conflict: Adolescence and Family in an Aboriginal Community of South Australia', Ph.D. dissertation. Kensington: University of New South Wales.

―――. 1992b. 'W.F.: The Reconstruction of a Suicide'. MS, Kensington: University of New South Wales.

―――. 1995a. 'Violence, Social Differentiation and the Self', *Oceania* 65(4): 323–47.

———. 1995b. 'Informalization, Violence, Uncertainty: Aspects of Family Formation and Family Life in a Contemporary Aboriginal Community', in V.R. Pulla (ed.), *The Family: Asia Pacific Perspectives*. Darwin: Northern Territory University, pp. 258–66.

———. 1997. 'Trouble Lines: Resistance, Externalisation and Individuation', *Social Analysis* 41(2): 122–54. [online]. Retrieved 25 May 2007 from http://search .informit.com.au/fullText;dn=980302296;res=APAFT ISSN: 0155–977X.

Robinson, P. 1972. *The Sexual Radicals: Reich, Roheim, Marcuse*. London: Paladin.

Robinson, G., U. Eickelkamp, J. Goodnow and I. Katz (eds). 2008. *Contexts of Child Development: Culture, Policy and Intervention*. Darwin: CDU Press.

Róheim, G. 1925. *Australian Totemism: A Psycho-Analytic Study in Anthropology*. London: George Allen & Unwin.

———. 1932. 'Psycho-Analysis of Primitive Cultural Types', *International Journal of Psycho-Analysis* 1–2: 1–224.

———. 1933. 'Women and Their Life in Central Australia', *Journal of the Royal Anthropological Institute* 63: 207–65.

———. 1934. *The Riddle of the Sphinx* or *Human Origins*. London: Hogarth Press.

———. 1945a. *The Eternal Ones of the Dream: A Psychoanalytic Interpretation of Australian Myth and Ritual*. New York: International Universities Press.

———. 1945b. *War, Crime and the Covenant*. Monticello, NY: Medical Journal Press.

———. 1950. *Psychoanalysis and Anthropology: Culture, Personality and the Unconscious*. New York: International Universities Press.

———. 1974. *Children of the Desert: The Western Tribes of Central Australia*, vol. 1. New York: Basic Books.

———. 1988. *Children of the Desert II: Myths and Dreams of the Aborigines of Central Australia*. Edited by J. Morton and W. Muensterberger. Sydney: Oceania Publications.

Roth, P. 2000. *The Human Stain*. Boston: Houghton Mifflin.

Rousseau, J.-J. 1973[1755]. *The Social Contract and Discourses*. London: Dent.

Roy, J. 1984. *Hobbes and Freud*. Toronto: University of Toronto Press.

Rubuntja, W. and J. Green. 2002. *The Town Grew Up Dancing*. Alice Springs, NT: Jukurrpa Books, IAD Press.

Sackett, L. 1976. 'Indirect Exchange in a Symmetrical System: Marriage Alliance in the Western Desert of Australia', *Ethnology* 15(2): 135–49.

———. 1978. 'Punishment in Ritual: "Man-making" among Western Desert Aborigines', *Oceania* 49(2): 110–27.

Saggers, S. and D. Gray 1998. *Dealing with Alcohol: Indigenous Usage in Australia, New Zealand and Canada*. Cambridge: Cambridge University Press.

Samson, C. 2004. '"We Live This Experience": Ontological Insecurity and the Colonial Domination of the Innu People of Northern Labrador', in J. Clammer, S. Poirier and E. Schwimmer (eds), *Figured Worlds: Ontological Obstacles in Intercultural Relations*. Toronto: University of Toronto Press, pp. 151–88.

Sandall, R. 2001. *The Culture Cult: Designer Tribalism and Other Essays*. Boulder, CO: Westview Press.

———. n.d. 'About Roger Sandall'. Retrieved 26 October 2008 from http://www .rogersandall.com/About-Roger-Sandall.php.

San Roque, C. 2004. 'A Long Weekend in Alice Springs', in T. Singer and S.L. Kimbles (eds), *The Cultural Complex—Contemporary Jungian Perspectives on Psyche and Society*. London: Brunner-Routledge, pp. 46–61.

Sansom, B. 1980. *The Camp at Wallaby Cross*. Canberra: Aboriginal Studies Press.

———. 2001. 'Irruptions of the Dreamings in Post-colonial Australia', *Oceania* 72(1): 1–32.

———. 2009. 'On Self and Licensed Solitude: "That Very Private Fella, Me"', *Oceania* 79(1): 65–84.

Sansom, B. and P. Baines. 1988. 'Aboriginal Child Placement in the Urban Context', in B. Morse and G. Woodman (eds), *Indigenous Law and the State*. Dordrecht, Netherlands: Forest Publications, pp. 347–64.

Sawyer, R. K. 1997. *Pretend Play as Improvisation: Conversation in the Presschool Classroom*. Norwood, NJ: Lawrence Erlbaum.

Scheper-Hughes, N. and H.F. Stein. 1987. 'Child Abuse and the Unconscious in American Popular Culture', in N. Scheper-Hughes (ed.), *Child Survival: Anthropological Perspectives on the Treatment and Maltreatment of Children*. Dordrecht, Netherlands: D. Reidel, pp. 339–58.

Schieffelin, B. 1990. *The Give and Take of Everyday Life: Language Socialisation of Kaluli Children*. New York: Cambridge University Press.

Schieffelin, B. and E. Ochs (eds) 1986. *Language Socialization Across Cultures*. Cambridge: Cambridge University Press.

Schwartzman, H.B. 1978. *Transformations: The Anthropology of Children's Play*. New York: Plenum Press.

Simpson, J. 2005. 'Expressing Pragmatic Constraints on Word Order in Warlpiri', *Architecture, Rules and Preferences: A Festschrift for Joan Bresnan*. Stanford, CA: CSLI Publications.

Slade, A. and D.P. Wolf (eds). 1994. *Children at Play: Clinical and Developmental Approaches to Meaning and Representation*. New York: Oxford University Press.

Spencer, B. and F.J. Gillen. 1899. *The Native Tribes of Central Australia*. London: Macmillan.

———. 1927. *The Arunta*. London: MacMillan.

Spielberg, S. 1982. *E.T.: The Extra-terrestrial*. Universal Pictures, 115 mins.

Stanner, W.E.H. 1979. *White Man Got No Dreaming: Essays 1938–1973*. Canberra: ANU Press.

Stern, D.N. 1989. 'Developmental Prerequisites for the Sense of a Narrated Self', in A.M. Cooper, O.F. Kernberg and E. Spector Person (eds), *Psycho-analysis: Toward the Second Century*. New Haven, CT: Yale University Press, pp. 168–78.

Strauss, C. and N. Quinn 1994. 'A Cognitive/Cultural Anthropology', in R. Borofsky (ed.), *Assessing Cultural Anthropology*. New York: McGraw-Hill, pp. 284–300.

Strehlow, C. 1913. *Die Aranda- und Luritja-Stämme in Zentral-Australien (IV. Teil): Das Soziale Leben der Aranda- und Loritja-Stämme (1. Abteilung)*. Frankfurt am Main: Joseph Baer.

Strehlow, T.G.H. 1964. 'Personal Monototemism in a Polytotemic Community', in E. Haberland, M. Schuster and H. Straube (eds), *Festschrift für Ad. E. Jensen*. Munich: Klaus Renner Verlag, pp. 723–54.

———. 1971. *Songs of Central Australia*. Sydney: Angus and Robertson.

Sturmer, J. von. 1978. 'The Wik Region: Economy, Territoriality and Totemism in Western Cape York Peninsula, North Queensland'. Ph.D. dissertation, Brisbane: University of Queensland.

———. 2002. 'Click Go the Designs: Presencing the Now in 1000 Easy Pieces', in *Warburton One and Only: Painted Earthenware by Women from the Milyirrt-jarra Ceramics Centre.* Warburton community, Central Australia, 14 May–1 June, 2002, Mori Gallery, Sydney, exh. cat.

———. 2005. 'Prolegomena to a Politics of Announcement', seminar presentation at the School for Social and Policy Research, Charles Darwin University, Darwin.

Sugarman. Videorecording. Written and produced by David Roberts. Antipodes Productions, 1999.

Sutton, P. 2001. 'The Politics of Suffering: Indigenous Policy in Australia Since the 1970s', *Anthropological Forum* 11: 125–73.

———. 2009. *The Politics of Suffering: Indigenous Australia and the End of the Liberal Consensus.* Carlton, VIC: Melbourne University Press.

———. [n.d.] 'Families of Polity: Post-classical Aboriginal Society and Native Title' [pamphlet]. National Native Title Tribunal.

Taylor, J. 2002. 'Population Futures in the Australian Desert, 2001–2016', *Discussion Paper No 231.* Canberra: Centre for Aboriginal Economic Policy Research.

———. 2006. 'Indigenous Peoples and Indicators of Well-being: An Australian Perspective on UNPFII Global Frameworks'. Centre for Aboriginal Economic Policy Research, Working Paper No 33/2006. http://www.anu.edu.au/caepr/.

Thorne, B. 1987. 'Re-visioning Women and Social Change: Where Are the Children?', *Gender and Society* 1(1): 85–109.

Tonkinson, M. 1990. 'Is It in the Blood? Australian Aboriginal Identity', in J. Linnekin and L. Poyer (eds), *Cultural Identity and Ethnicity in the Pacific.* Honolulu: University of Hawai'i Press, pp. 191–218.

Tonkinson, R. 1974. *The Jigalong Mob: Aboriginal Victors of the Desert Crusade.* Menlo Park, CA: Cummings.

———. 1982. 'Outside the Power of the Dreaming: Paternalism and Permissiveness in an Aboriginal Settlement', in M.C. Howard (ed.), *Aboriginal Power in Australian Society.* St Lucia: University of Queensland Press, pp. 115–30.

———. 1990. 'The Changing Status of Women: "Free agents" at Jigalong, Western Australia', in R. Tonkinson and M.C. Howard (eds), *Going It Alone? Prospects for Aboriginal Autonomy: Essays in Honour of Ronald and Catherine Berndt.* Canberra: Aboriginal Studies Press, pp.127–45.

———. 1991a. *The Mardu Aborigines: Living the Dream in Australia's Desert,* 2nd ed. Fort Worth, TX: Holt, Rinehart and Winston.

———. 1991b. '"Ideology and Domination" in Aboriginal Australia: A Western Desert Test Case', in T. Ingold, D. Riches and J. Woodburn (eds), *Hunters and Gatherers,* vol. 2: *Property, Power and Ideology.* New York: Berg, pp. 150–64.

———. 2007a. 'The Mardu Aborigines: On the Road to Somewhere', in G. Spindler and J.E. Stockard (eds), *Globalization and Change in Fifteen Cultures: Born in One World, Living in Another.* Belmont, CA: Thomson Wadsworth, pp. 225–55.

———. 2007b. 'Aboriginal "Difference" and "Autonomy" Then and Now: Four De-cades of Change in a Western Desert Society', *Anthropological Forum* 17(1): 41–60.

Wafer, J. 1982. *A Simple Introduction to Central Australian Kinship Systems*. Alice Springs, NT: IAD Press.

Warlukurlangu Artists. 1987. *Yuendumu Doors, Kuruwarri*. Canberra: Australian In-stitute of Aboriginal Studies Press.

Watson, C. 2003. *Piercing the Ground: Balgo Women's Image Making and Relation-ship to Country*. Fremantle, WA: Fremantle Arts Centre Press.

Wild, R. and P. Anderson. 2007. *Ampe Akelyernemane Meke Mekarle:* 'Little Chil-dren Are Sacred'. Report of the Northern Territory Board of Inquiry into the Pro-tection of Aboriginal Children from Sexual Abuse. Darwin: Northern Territory Government.

Wilkins, D. P. 1997. 'Alternative Representations of Space: Arrernte Narratives in Sand and Sign', in M. Biemans and J.v.d. Weijer (eds) *Proceedings of the CLS Opening Academic Year '97-'98*. Nijmegen, Netherlands: Nijmegen/Tilburg Center for Language Studies, pp. 133–62.

———. 2002. 'The Concept of Place among the Arrernte', in L. Hercus, F. Hodges and J. Simpson (eds), *The Land Is a Map: Placenames of Indigenous Origin in Australia*. Canberra: Pandanus Books, pp. 24–41.

Wilson, R. 1997. 'Bringing Them Home: Report of National Inquiry into the Separa-tion of Aboriginal and Torres Strait Islander Children from Their Families'. Can-berra: Human Rights and Equal Opportunity Commission.

Wilson, M. and M. Daly. 1997. 'Life Expectancy, Economic Inequality, Homicide, and Reproductive Timing in Chicago Neighbourhoods', *British Medical Journal* 314 (26 April 1997): 1271–74.

Winnicott, D.W. 1965a. *The Maturational Processes and the Facilitating Environment: Studies in the Theory of Emotional Development*. London: Hogarth Press.

———. 1965b. 'The Theory of the Parent-Infant Relationship', in *The Maturational Processes and the Facilitating Environment*. London: Hogarth Press, pp. 37–55.

———. 1971. *Playing and Reality*. London: Tavistock Publications. Repr. Harmond-sworth, U.K.: Penguin Books Ltd., 1974.

Yu, P., M.E. Duncan and B. Gray. 2008. 'Northern Territory Emergency Response: Report of the NTER Review Board'. Canberra: Australian Government.

Zinnecker, J. 2003. '"Das Problem der Generationen." Überlegungen zu Karl Mannheims kanonischem Text', in J. Reulecke (ed.), *Generationalität und Le-bensgeschichte im 20. Jahrhundert*. München: R. Oldenburg Verlag, pp. 33–58.

Index

⟨